Taking Liberties

Aryeh Neier

TAKING
LIBERTIES

**FOUR DECADES
IN THE STRUGGLE FOR RIGHTS**

PublicAffairs

NEW YORK

BOOK DESIGN BY JENNY DOSSIN

Library of Congress Cataloging-in-Publication data:

Neier, Aryeh, 1937–

Taking liberties: four decades in the struggle for rights / by Aryeh Neier.—1st ed.

p. cm.

Includes bibliographical references and index.

ISBN 1-891620-82-7

1. Neier, Aryeh, 1937–

2. Civil rights workers—United States—Biography.

3. Human rights workers—United States—Biography.

I. Title.

JC599.U5 N45 2003

323'.092—dc21

[B]

2002031918

FIRST EDITION

10 9 8 7 6 5 4 3 2 1

FOR YVETTE

CONTENTS

III

Introduction

I have been privileged to spend four decades defending rights or, put another way, taking liberties. When I began in the early 1960s, it would have been possible to assemble in a good-sized living room all those professionally engaged in the United States in defending rights. A somewhat smaller room could accommodate their counterparts from the rest of the world. That has changed. Today, thousands of Americans are professional advocates of rights and, worldwide, the number must be in the tens of thousands. Many young people submit essays with their college or graduate school applications saying that they want to embark on careers in human rights. That was unthinkable when I got into the field. Among global civic movements, only the environmental cause is comparable in the scope and sophistication of its organized components.

It is possible to characterize my years of taking liberties as the era of rights. In the 1960s and 1970s, when my work focused on the United States, black Americans and their allies of other races created the civil rights revolution; opponents of the Vietnam War tested the limits of freedom of speech and assembly protected by the First Amendment to bring about a fundamental shift in public policy; and many groups previously marginalized or hidden from view—women, gays, ethnic minorities, the disabled, and inmates of prisons and other asylums, among others—banded together to assert claims for rights never before considered their due.

In the latter part of the 1970s, about the time the focus of my work turned to international concerns, the worldwide human rights movement emerged as an important player. Dissenters in the Soviet Union and Czechoslovakia, families of the "disappeared" in Latin America's military dictatorships, and opponents of apartheid in South Africa were attracting international attention and increasing support in the United States and

Western Europe for their struggle for rights. Today, the international human rights movement is a force to be reckoned with globally. Organized efforts to promote rights have taken root everywhere except in a small number of the most repressive countries on earth, and even these are diminishing. The principal rationale for international military intervention in troubled zones previously considered the affairs of sovereign states, as in Kosovo, Iraqi Kurdistan, and East Timor, is to protect human rights.

Labeling the past few decades as the era of rights is not the same as saying that rights are better protected today than previously. That is the case in much of the world, but the extent of oppression and suffering elsewhere makes me shy away from assertions about global progress. But where headway has been made, whether at home or abroad, it has often come about through assertions of rights and with the participation of rights movements. Even in circumstances where despotic regimes, failed states, and enduring armed conflicts make life miserable, the victims often have a heightened consciousness of rights, and some of their own efforts to improve their circumstances and those by others on their behalf are made in the name of rights.

At times, of course, one suspects that the invocation of rights has an opportunistic quality. An example was President George W. Bush's expressed concern with the Taliban's oppression of women when he was rallying support for the war in Afghanistan, thereby taking a leaf from his father, who cited Amnesty International's reporting on torture by Saddam Hussein's regime when he wanted to ensure public support for the Gulf War. Many rights advocates cringe when their cause is exploited in such a manner. They know that the president's readiness to speak up for women in Afghanistan does not extend to women in Pakistan or Saudi Arabia. Yet even insincere professions of concern for rights are a sign of the place that thinking about rights has come to occupy. Most governments of the world now consider it de rigueur to pretend they respect rights. A public stance of this type by world leaders allows rights advocates to point out the discrepancies between words and practices and, thereby, to press them to live up to their pretenses. That was not possible in an earlier era.

My association with three organizations provided me with most of my opportunities to take part in the rights revolution of the past four decades. The first was the American Civil Liberties Union, founded in 1920, more than four decades before I joined its staff. It had played a central role in many struggles over rights, such as those that accompanied the Red scare following World War I, the free-speech battles of birth-control proponents, book publishers, and movie producers, and labor's struggle to organize America's industrial workers in the 1920s and 1930s. At certain critical moments, the ACLU failed the country, notably when its national office hesitated before championing the cause of the Japanese Americans during World War II, and, more perniciously, in the 1950s, when its response to the loyalty investigations of the era was timorous and some of its officers acted in bad faith. (In both instances, some of its state branches did better.) Despite those important lapses, it carved out a role as an essential institution in American public life. I believe my own service for the ACLU coincided with the period in which, with the possible exception of its founding years, it made its most significant and enduring contributions to the protection and enhancement of American liberties.

Next was Human Rights Watch, of which I was a founder in 1978, when we launched the first of its regional components, Helsinki Watch, in response to the persecution of members of the Moscow Helsinki Group. Human Rights Watch has led the way in transforming the human rights cause into a powerful force in global affairs and, in a relatively short period, has achieved an institutional significance worldwide that equals or exceeds what the ACLU at its high point achieved in the United States. Last is my current post with the Soros Foundations and the Open Society Institute, which I joined a decade after their founder and funder began building the network of foundations that bears his name. With operations in more than sixty countries worldwide where struggles are under way to transform formerly repressive systems into open societies, it is regarded in most of those countries as a force of change.

Though I believe my career could have taken a number of directions, others who know me suggest the path I chose was inevitable. Perhaps they are right. Certainly, I had reason early in life to appreciate the significance of rights or, at least, the deprivation of rights.

I was born in Berlin on April 22, 1937, two days after the parades and festivities marking the annual celebration of Hitler's birthday had taken place. My parents were Jews from what is now Poland who established a comfortable middle-class life for themselves in Berlin before Hitler came to power. As many of their friends left Germany, they remained behind, not wishing to uproot themselves and to begin again and, of course, not knowing what lay in store. We got out at the last possible moment. I have no childhood recollection of Berlin. My earliest memory—if, indeed, it is that and not something I have imagined—was the boat trip from Ostend, Belgium, to England on August 16, 1939, two weeks before Germany's invasion of Poland and the outbreak of war.

I do recall rather clearly some scenes from my first year in England. (I call them "scenes" because I can visualize them fairly clearly but cannot connect them with events that preceded or followed.) For eleven months, I lived in a "hostel" for refugee children, apart from my parents, where, I am told, I stopped speaking for a time. When I misbehaved—which, I think, was rather often—I was required to stand for long periods in a corner of the playroom in the hostel behind a bench angled to confine me. From that spot, I could see out a window and observe my playmates when they went outdoors. Another sharply etched recollection is of the day I left the hostel. My father, a teacher and author in Berlin, found work as a manual laborer as a refugee in London. This job permitted him to reassemble our family—my mother, my older sister, Esther, and I—in a small flat he rented. To celebrate my release from the hostel, where I had stopped speaking, I was dressed in a new, brightly striped shirt. I was so excited by the prospect of leaving the hated hostel that, after drinking a cup of cocoa, I threw up all over the shirt just as my parents were arriving to collect me. I attribute my lifelong preoccupation with prisons and other institutions used for confinement to my loathing for that hostel.

Though I can't sort out just how else I was affected by my eleven months of confinement at a vulnerable age, plainly it was an experience I could not simply shrug off. Others have detected a clue to its impact on my development in my cessation of speech. This, it is suggested, represented a way I could take control in circumstances where I was otherwise helpless, foreshadowing a career in which I always sought control. Perhaps this is right. Since 1965, I have occupied the top staff post in the various institutions with which I have been associated, though for the past decade, in my post as president of the Open Society Institute, the engagement of a living donor, George Soros, who is also a controlling person, has been a significant factor limiting my own ability to take charge. On the couple of occasions when I have been sounded out about taking government appointments, which would have required me to report to superiors, I have declined them. Other factors loomed larger in these instances, however. In government service, I would have had to make more compromises than were required in the positions I held. More important still, I doubt I could have had as much impact on the rights issues that matter to me from a post in government.

Our stay in the flat in London did not last long. The period known as the Battle of Britain began on August 8, 1940, about the time I got out of the hostel. By September, after the Luftwaffe suffered heavy losses during daylight attacks on ports and airbases, German bombers shifted to night-time raids that mainly targeted London. Night after night, along with hundreds of thousands of our fellow Londoners, we made our way to the deep tunnels of the Underground to sleep, or try to sleep, on the station platforms as the bombs fell far overhead.

My mother hated those nights in the Underground and, after a while, refused to keep going there. One night, as we fled fires caused by incendiary bombs that broke out near our house, I was accidentally separated from the rest of the family. A well-meaning stranger took me to a nearby shelter where the grown-ups who sought refuge there fussed over me and fed me while my parents searched for me frantically in the burning streets. This episode, which lasted only a few hours until my parents found me, was far more traumatic for them than for me. In later years, my mother rarely talked of the war without reliving the night she lost me.

Soon after, the house with our flat was largely demolished by a bomb. No longer able to live there, we joined the throngs who headed to the city's great railroad stations for evacuation. We had no idea where we were going but simply got on a train at Euston Station. At each stop, a local official boarded to say how many evacuees that town could take and the designated number of passengers got off. Our turn came when we reached Kettering, a pleasant Midlands town about seventy miles north of London.

At first, we were housed in a school that had been transformed into a makeshift shelter. In the adjoining schoolyard, Esther quickly made friends with a girl her own age who lived nearby. The girl invited Esther to move in to her home, but my sister said she could only do so if her mother and brother could move in as well (my father remained in London for a while, as only women and children were evacuated initially, but he soon joined us in Kettering). The girl went off to consult her parents and returned soon to say they had agreed. Though they lived in a modest home—the father repaired bicycles for a living—on a moment's notice they agreed to share what they had with a family of Jewish refugees. To my great regret, I no longer know the names of our benefactors.

A member of the Kettering Town Council, a Mr. C. E. Goode, took it upon himself to look out for our welfare and helped my father get a job. As the factory where he was initially employed was at the other end of the town and my father did not ride a bicycle, Councillor Goode arranged for us to move to another home that was closer. This time, our hosts were somewhat better off; the family breadwinner was an insurance agent. We moved into their front room, a parlor typically used only on special occasions in middle-class British homes of the period. We stayed with this family, the Howletts, for several months until my father was able to rent a house of our own.

We lived in Kettering for the remainder of the war. I have only fond memories of the town, which had a population of about 30,000, and of Northampton, a nearby town of about 100,000 that we moved to at the end of the war. Both towns were known in England as shoe manufacturing centers, but they did not have a grim industrial aspect. The shoemakers were skilled craftspeople who took pride in their work, and both towns cherished their churches, libraries, parks, schools, social services, and diverse cultural institutions. Though we were Jewish refugees from Germany, and therefore different from almost everyone else in what were nearly homogeneous communities, I have no recollection of ever feeling unwelcome. The war, which for a time threatened England's survival and throughout required significant sacrifices, brought out the best in many people. Though I was too young at the time to think in this way, in retrospect I am astonished by the generosity of the families who invited us into their homes. Many others also took pains to see to our well-being and contributed to my sense of having had a happy childhood in those Midlands towns. Despite my early experience in the hostel, Kettering and Northampton made me into a lifelong Anglophile.

Though I do not recall ever suffering discrimination in England for being Jewish, I did become conscious early on of the significance of racial and religious differences. The schools I attended began each morning with lengthy Anglican prayers. I was excused from these, so I arrived at school later than everyone else. My teachers did not make an issue of the fact that I was Jewish, but I recall an incident when a girl in my class was humiliated because she was Catholic. The teacher had been telling us about the Protestant Reformation and attributed this solely to righteous indignation over the sale of papal indulgences. She managed to make it seem that the only Catholic student in the class was personally responsible for this practice half a millennium earlier. In later years, when I advocated separation of church and state on behalf of the American Civil Liberties Union and opposed prayers and Bible reading in the schools, I often thought about my own childhood discomfort at going to school at a different time than everyone else and about that teacher's probably unintentional cruelty to my Catholic classmate.

When I visited Northampton with my wife Yvette on one of our trips to England in the mid-1980s, the most striking change was its ethnic diversity. Next door to the house where I lived as a child, an Indian restaurant had opened. Forty years earlier there were almost never any dark-skinned people around. The armorial bearings of Kettering show a shield flanked by a loincloth-clad black man with a manacle and a broken chain dangling from his wrist. This celebrates one of Kettering's most distinguished citizens, an early nineteenth-century reformer named William Knibb, who promoted a Charter of Freedom that emancipated 800,000 black slaves. Yet the first time I saw a black man on the street, I was so amazed that several of my friends and I followed him through the streets to make certain he was real.

There were small Jewish communities in both Kettering and Northampton, and they formed an important part of the world in which I grew up. Unlike us, most of the other Jews were not refugees. They were families long settled in Britain. After the war, some 732 young survivors of the Nazi death camps were brought to the country.[1] Their presence helped to reshape our Northampton environment.

Known collectively as "the boys"—although they included some eighty girls—some fifteen of them, all boys, came to Northampton where the town's Jewish community arranged for their care and education. Though they were several years older than me, I made friends and played soccer with them. They told me little about their own experiences, but I learned from them and from the comments of others about them a few things about the Holocaust we had escaped. My other principal source of information in the period just after the war was my parents; I watched and listened as they found out which of their friends and relatives survived and who did not. Few lived.

In Northampton, I also came into contact with Gypsies, a group that became a concern of my work at Human Rights Watch and at the Soros Foundations. Some lived in an encampment at the edge of town. One day, my father took me to visit a caravan there, a large, stationary covered wagon that seemed to be home to a lot of people. To reach it, we had to cross some fields and clamber over several stiles (arrangements of steps that are passageways for people over English fences but keep in the cattle or sheep). I no longer know why we went, but I remember it as an exciting excursion. The Gypsies were acrobats, tightrope walkers, jugglers, and bareback riders in the small circuses that traveled about England. I had seen them perform and was delighted to visit their home.

About this time, the patriarch of the extended family or clan that lived in this encampment died. The Gypsies arranged his burial in a local churchyard and marked his grave with a beautiful marble tombstone adorned with a carving that symbolized his life and work: a cavorting horse. This outraged some parishioners, who demanded the removal of the "undignified" tombstone. The controversy became the talk of the town. I was a strong partisan of the Gypsies and the horse, but, unfortunately, I am hazy about the outcome of this dispute. I think the Gypsies lost and had to replace the tombstone with a monument considered more fitting for its surroundings.

We left England in 1947 to go to the United States. Esther had married a GI stationed in England and went to America in 1946 as a war bride. Having brought their two children through the war while almost all other members of their family were killed by the Nazis, my parents were not about to let an ocean separate them from their only daughter. I attended Stuyvesant High School in New York City during the four years Senator Joseph McCarthy was riding high and opposed McCarthyism to the limited extent possible for a high-school student. That mainly meant becoming active in our school History Club and inviting speakers to the school to debate the burning issues of the day.

The books I read as a high-school student also played an important part in shaping my views. I devoured the works of politically engaged twentieth-century European authors, all of them antifascist and most also anti-Communist—though a few were initially attracted by communism and subsequently wrote about their disillusionment. Among those I read long into the night with great pleasure were Albert Camus, André Malraux, Georges Bernanos, Ignazio Silone, Carlo Levi, Karel Čapek, Arthur Koestler, Thomas Mann, Aldous Huxley, and, especially, George Orwell. Largely missing from my reading, however, was anything to do with the Holocaust—a word that did not come into general usage until much later—because in that period, during the decade after the end of World War II, very little was published on the subject. (By way of contrast, there is already a very large body of literature on the wars of the 1990s in ex-Yugoslavia.) To the extent the Holocaust was even discussed in the period prior to the Eichmann trial in Jerusalem in the early 1960s, it was often by those who expressed fear that it would soon be forgotten. Though the lives of my parents and many of those they knew were dominated by death and survival, their cataclysmic experience was mostly missing from the discourse and the literature of the era.

Today, the bookshelves of my apartment in New York City are laden with books about the Holocaust—diaries, memoirs, biographies, histories, polemics, and a few novels—but they include only a handful of works published in the 1940s and 1950s. Though I was not aware of the absence at the time, in retrospect I find it bizarre and now believe that it contributed to a somewhat distorted political consciousness in which I failed until much later to appreciate the nature and extent of evil in the twentieth century. Though I had a closer brush than most of my peers with the defining events of the era, my knowledge and understanding of what took place remained at best superficial.

In college, I continued paying as much or more attention to world events as to my studies. I began at Cornell University in September 1954. The Army-McCarthy hearings had taken place the previous May and June, and the pall that had descended on college campuses was just beginning to lift. An event that particularly excited me, and created a sense of hope, the Montgomery bus boycott, began a few months into my freshman year. It turned me into a lifelong adherent of the civil rights cause. Another important moment came in November 1956, when Norman Thomas spoke at Cornell. After joining a thousand or more students to listen to his public lecture, I went with a small number to continue a conversation with him into the early morning hours. Most of the talk was about what was going on in Hungary. Imre Nagy had become prime minister in response to demands by students and others for independence from the Soviet Union. Nagy promised the removal of Soviet troops and appointed Anna Kethly, recently released from prison, as foreign minister. She promptly flew to New York to plead the cause of Hungarian independence at the United Nations. From what was then called Idlewild Airport, Kethly went directly to the office of Norman Thomas, her longtime Social Democratic ally, and talked with him through the night. The next evening he spoke at Cornell. Those of us gathered around Thomas shared a vicarious thrill in the historic moment.

One of the more unlikely among those moved by the events in Hungary was John Gates, editor of *The Daily Worker*. He published an article saying it was time to establish an American Communist Party free of Soviet domination. This aroused public interest, and Gates was invited to speak on a number of college campuses. Many colleges had "speaker bans" left over from the McCarthy years, however, prohibiting Communists from appearing on their campuses. I decided to test whether Gates could speak at Cornell and went to New York City to visit *The Daily Worker*'s dingy offices near Union Square—aware, of course, that those offices were under surveillance and my visit would turn up in a dossier somewhere—to issue an invitation. To do this, I first had to establish a campus organization to sponsor his talk. I called it the "Cornell Forum" and enlisted several prominent professors at Cornell to serve as faculty advisers. Gates appeared at Cornell to speak under its auspices, and his talk took place without incident.

In forming the Cornell Forum, I decided to affiliate it with a national student organization so it could join groups on other college campuses in taking stands on questions such as speaker bans. The only appropriate candidate I could identify was the Student League for Industrial Democracy. Its principal attraction, to me, was that Norman Thomas had served as executive director of the parent group, the League for Industrial Democracy (LID), and remained closely associated with it, maintaining his office in the somewhat seedy building it occupied at 112 East 19th Street in New York, close to his home in Gramercy Park. (The building also housed the Citizens Committee for the Children of New York, and it was not uncommon to run into a frequent visitor to its offices, Eleanor Roosevelt, in its rickety elevator.) Another prominent person long associated with LID was the philosopher John Dewey, who was the organization's president until his death in 1952.

The organization was small, but its student division, founded in 1905, had chapters on several college campuses, where they were sometimes known as the John Dewey Society. In the 1950s, one of those who traveled about the country organizing those chapters was James Farmer, who emerged a few years later, when he headed the Congress of Racial Equality, as the leader of the "Freedom Rides" and became known as one of the giants of the nation's struggle for civil rights. The college chapters Jim organized took stands with which I was comfortable, organizing protests against Soviet suppression of the Hungarian revolution, against speaker bans that prohibited Communists from appearing on college campuses, and in support of racial equality. It was a period of little political activity on college campuses—we were known as the "silent generation." I was glad to find a group through which I could engage on issues that mattered to me.

A year later, I was elected president of the student LID and, in that capacity, joined the parent organization's board of directors. The following year, after graduating from college, I went to work for LID for what I thought would be a brief period. It lasted a bit longer than I expected because, soon after I began in 1958, the executive director got into a dispute with the board and resigned. Though I was the youngest and newest member of the small staff, at twenty-one, I was asked to become acting director. A few months later, I was appointed executive director. That was a factor in what may seem an anomaly in my career: that I never attended law school.

Because so much of my career has been concerned with law, and because I regularly speak and write about legal issues, and for more than a dozen years served first as a visiting professor of law and then as an adjunct professor of law at NYU's Law School, many persons naturally assume that I am a lawyer. I am regularly introduced as a lawyer, and though I usually try to correct the error, I do not invariably find it possible to do so, no doubt contributing to the confusion. Many who find out that I never went to law school wonder why not. (I always informed my classes at NYU that I was not a lawyer and invited students who felt cheated to switch to another course; just once, a student took me up on this on the spot and walked out of class.)

From time to time, I have regretted not being a lawyer. Though it is not the province of the director of the ACLU, lawyer or not, to try court cases, there were some matters that arose during my service with that organization in which I would have relished an opportunity to examine or cross-examine witnesses and to take part in oral arguments. Except for that, however, I have felt no disadvantage from the lack of a formal legal education. I have found the areas of law with which I have been particularly concerned—American constitutional law, criminal law, international human rights law, and international humanitarian law—readily accessible. But my reasons for not going to law school had little to do with an assessment of my potential as an autodidact. They were more practical. Yvette and I married immediately on my graduation from college, and our son

David was born a year and a half later. As I had no money, I felt a need to earn a living, albeit a modest one, right away. With my career progressing rapidly, there never seemed an opportune moment thereafter to step back and reenter school.

As director of LID, I decided to try to invigorate its student division. One step in that direction was to rename it. "Student League for Industrial Democracy" sounded like what it was: a leftover from an earlier era. Accordingly, in 1959, I renamed it Students for a Democratic Society (SDS) and hired a University of Michigan dropout, Al Haber, to become the group's principal organizer. I invited two of the political commentators I admired most, Murray Kempton and Dwight MacDonald, to speak at the meeting that launched the group under its new name and, of course, turned to Norman Thomas to give the main address. Unlike the veteran Socialist leader, Kempton and MacDonald were not especially effective public speakers. Their medium was the written word, not the spoken. Yet it was their thinking about politics nationally and internationally with which I identified. I expected SDS to espouse their brand of hostility to all forms of oppression and their skepticism of all orthodoxies.

The newly named group quickly found a cause that served it well in building its membership. In February 1960, black students in Greensboro, North Carolina, staged a sit-in at a luncheonette to demand equal service. Soon, there were sit-ins at many lunch counters in the South, and students at northern campuses organized sympathy demonstrations. I obtained funds to support this effort from the AFL-CIO with the support of Walter Reuther, the president of the United Auto Workers, who had led the CIO in merging with the AFL a few years earlier. Reuther was a longtime member of LID and had been a leader of SLID when he was in college. He had me accompany him to an AFL-CIO Executive Council meeting to make a pitch for support. Before I left the meeting, the labor federation's secretary treasurer, William Schnitzler, handed me a check for $10,000. With the money, I hired two student organizers. One was a University of Michigan friend of Al Haber, Tom Hayden, who was already active in SDS. Soon after hiring Hayden, however, it became clear that he and I had fundamental differences, and I fired him. It was too late. He had established his leadership of SDS and took it in a direction I did not endorse.

I left my post as director of LID in 1960 and became an editor of a short-lived monthly public affairs journal that deserved its early demise. At the same time, I continued as a member of the LID's board and, along with Michael Harrington, who became the organization's chairman, opposed the way its student affiliate, SDS, was developing. I was unenthusiastic about the 1962 "Port Huron statement" drafted by Hayden. I was anti-Soviet and anti-Communist and was appalled by arguments that Soviet repression and the invasion of Hungary were defensive actions in response to Cold War aggression for which the United States bore prime responsibility. Also, the language about "participatory democracy" sounded to me like a justification for demagogy. Like others on the LID board, I exerted little influence. We wanted to hold on to SDS because its work on college campuses was making headway and had become the organization's raison d'être. SDS probably wished to preserve its ties to the parent group mainly because that is where the money came from. After a time, however, it became plain to both sides that the relationship between LID and SDS had to be severed.

Though I disapproved of SDS's leftism, I was also unhappy about LID's rightward drift under the influence of Shachtmanites who had taken over its leadership and espoused a hawkish stand on the developing war in Vietnam. (Max Shachtman was a Trotskyist leader who moved far to the right on Cold War issues. Some of his prominent disciples, including Irving Howe and Michael Harrington, broke with him over the Vietnam War, which Shachtman strongly supported. Others, such as those who became the leaders of the American Federation of Teachers and the International Affairs Department of the AFL-CIO under George Meany and Lane Kirkland, remained loyal Shachtmanites.) There no longer seemed any purpose to the organization, a point driven home by an exchange at a board meeting. Someone said LID reminded him of his old aunt. From the back of the room, Norman Thomas growled in his rasping voice, "Is your aunt dead?" Shortly thereafter, I resigned from the board.

Looking back on my experience with LID after the passage of four decades, I have a sense of lost opportunity. The political views I wanted to promote through its revived student branch were essentially those I have maintained ever since. They were treated dismissively by those who became the leaders of SDS. Todd Gitlin, an early president of SDS and the author of several thoughtful and provocative books on media and popular culture, has written in his own memoir of the era that the groups on the Right and the Left, against which SDS rebelled, were mired in "Talmudic disputations" left over from the 1930s. On "the right," according to Gitlin, "the moribund social democrats of the League for Industrial Democracy sent organizers (including James Farmer, Gabriel Kolko, Aryeh Neier and Andre Schiffrin) to the unfavorable student hinterlands."[2] I am not embarrassed by that company. Far from it. Jim Farmer, who died in 1999, was one of the half dozen or so outstanding civil rights leaders of his century; Kolko is best known as a controversial academic critic of the Vietnam War; and Schiffrin, my immediate predecessor as president of the Student LID, is a leader among American book publishers in the number and quality of the works he has published critically examining America's domestic and international policies. Within a few years, it became clear that it was the thinking of the SDS leaders who rebelled against us, and against Kempton, MacDonald, and Thomas, that was moribund.

One of those I got to know through LID was Roger Baldwin, the founder of the American Civil Liberties Union. When he retired in 1950 after thirty years as executive director of the ACLU, Roger devoted himself to promoting rights internationally. Several years prior to his retirement, he established the International League for Human Rights, and he was also a founder of a group that focused on Latin America, the Inter-American Association for Democracy and Freedom. In 1960, along with Roger and about twenty others from the United States, I attended a conference of the Inter-American Association in Venezuela. It was my first international human rights meeting.

The conference was held under dramatic circumstances. Venezuela had suffered greatly under the cruel and corrupt military dictatorship of General Marcos Pérez Jiménez, who was ousted in 1958 and replaced that December by a democratic president, Rómulo Betancourt. As one of the founders of the Inter-American Association in 1950, Betancourt invited the group to meet in Venezuela. When I joined the other U.S. delegates at Idlewild Airport to board the plane to Caracas, however, we were told our flight was canceled because an armed insurrection was under way in Venezuela. It was put down quickly and the trip was rescheduled for the following evening.

The opening ceremonies for the conference took place in the great hall of the university in Caracas, but they were interrupted by rhythmic chants from thousands of students who crowded in to demand execution of the leaders of the just suppressed right-wing insurrection. On stage, even President Betancourt was unable to quiet the crowd, and the minister of education, humiliated by the disorder, resigned on the spot. The next day, our conference resumed in the quieter environs of Maracay, a nearby resort town. It took place at a luxury hotel constructed by Pérez Jiménez so he and his military friends could stay there when attending the bullfights for which Maracay was known.

The conference in Maracay was sharply split over developments in Cuba, where Fidel Castro had taken power a little more than a year before. Some participants in the meeting, such as Salvador Allende, the future president of Chile, strongly defended Castro, whom they saw as the herald of a social revolution that would sweep the region. Others, such as José Figueres, a once and future president of Costa Rica who led a revolution against his own country's military in 1948, and subsequently abolished its armed forces, denounced Castro for his violations of civil liberties.

I spent much of the time between formal meetings with the English-speaking Caribbean delegates. One of those with whom I formed a friendship was a Guyanan, Forbes Burnham. After the meeting, we stayed in touch for a number of years and, before he became prime minister, he would visit me when he came to New York. If anyone had told me then what a monster he would become after he achieved power, I would not have believed them. Another man I got on with at the conference was a former prime minister of Trinidad, Albert Gomes. I had no inkling his presence there infuriated our Venezuelan hosts.

At the last session of the conference, at what was meant to be a summing up, the organizers suddenly presented a resolution that Gomes should not be invited to any future gatherings. This announcement threw the meeting into an uproar, and Gomes went to a microphone to demand an explanation. As he was speaking, a tall Venezuelan strode down an aisle from the back of the auditorium and punched Gomes in the face, breaking his glasses. I was sitting a few feet away and, without thinking, jumped to my feet and put my arms around the Venezuelan to restrain him from striking Gomes again. Rather than having a calming effect, this generated more excitement, and I found myself at the center of a group yelling at me. The situation would have gotten out of hand if President Figueres—or "Don Pepe," as everyone called him—had not climbed on a chair (he was a small man and needed the elevation) and begun speaking rapidly in my behalf. He said I was only defending Gomes's right to speak, not his actions.

Those actions, I learned, involved his tenure as prime minister of Trinidad. During the Pérez Jiménez dictatorship, many Venezuelans had fled to nearby Trinidad. Gomes had ordered them expelled, endangering their lives. He subsequently claimed he was forced to throw them out by the British colonial office, but the Venezuelans did not believe him. They were outraged when he showed up in their country at a conference on democracy and freedom. As I had mainly associated at the conference with the English-speaking West Indians, I did not pick this up.

That night, at the banquet concluding the conference, Don Pepe introduced me to the Venezuelan who had assaulted Gomes, a prominent Christian Democrat. He walked into the dining room with his arm around my shoulder to show we were friends. Understandably, however, Roger Baldwin formed the impression that I was a hothead. Though I was twenty-three at the time, and though we worked together closely on many matters during my fifteen years at the ACLU and frequently enjoyed wide-ranging conversations over long lunches until he died at the age of ninety-seven some twenty-one years later, I am not sure he ever revised that opinion. In later years, Roger told one of his biographers that I was "much the best of our directors. In fact I think he's better than I was," attributing this in part to the fact that "he's much less impulsive than I am."[3] But I doubt he believed this.

I n 1963, I joined the staff of the American Civil Liberties Union. Shortly before that, I had taken on a temporary assignment to deal with an important civil rights issue of the period: housing segregation in the North.

One way some opponents of segregation tried to confront the issue in that era was through "benign quotas." The theory was that if a neighborhood reached a "tipping point," it would soon become all black. Hence, the way to integrate housing was to provide homes to whites and blacks according to a predetermined formula. Morris Milgram, a builder in Philadelphia who was a proponent of benign quotas, had put up a number of developments along those lines. A company associated with Milgram, Progress Development Corporation, had acquired two tracts of land in what was then an all-white suburb of Chicago—Deerfield, Illinois—on which a purposefully integrated housing development would be constructed. In 1959, when the town discovered Milgram's plan, it took prompt action to preserve segregation. Exercising eminent domain, the town condemned both tracts for park purposes. Litigation was commenced and a number of prominent attorneys, including Willard Wirtz (whom President John F. Kennedy later named secretary of labor) and Joseph L. Rauh argued on behalf of Progress Development Corporation. By the time I was enlisted in 1963, it was evident that an attempt to desegregate Deerfield through the courts would not succeed. Supporters of the development asked me to see whether I could salvage desegregation by organizing a public protest.

I went to Chicago where I obtained an office from a sympathizer, Victor Gotbaum, president of the local affiliate of the American Federation of State, County and Municipal Employees and subsequently of the New York branch of that union. Together with a group of Chicago-area supporters of desegregation, and with the collaboration of a talented organizer fresh from the southern struggle, the Rev. B. Elton Cox from High Point, North Carolina, I planned a march from downtown Chicago to Deerfield. It was a distance of twelve miles. In this period, there were many marches for civil rights in the South. The battle of Birmingham, in which Police Chief Bull Connor used fire hoses and police dogs against demonstrators led by the Rev. Martin Luther King, Jr., was under way. There were also sympathy demonstrations in some northern cities, but a march in the North against northern segregation had few, if any, precedents.

About 200 people, black and white, took part in our march. I walked a good part of the distance carrying another marcher's child piggyback on my shoulders. Deerfield residents who supported desegregation provided spaghetti dinners in their homes for everyone, and the marchers slept overnight in tents we put up on the two properties intended for the integrated housing development. The next morning, a Sunday, the Rev. King was to conduct a religious service on the property.

Events in Birmingham prevented King from getting to Deerfield. Nevertheless, all went well and the march attracted a fair amount of attention, including an article in *Life* magazine with a striking photo of a shopkeeper shuttering his store as the marchers approached. But it did not change anything in Deerfield, which remained segregated for several more years.

Before I went to Chicago to organize the march on Deerfield, I was unsure whether to accept an offer to work for the American Civil Liberties Union. Deerfield resolved my doubts. Though we lost in Deerfield, another town might desegregate before its housing practices entered the spotlight. Also, it was clear Deerfield could not remain lily white indefinitely. Even if we fought a losing battle, I had no regrets about engaging in such a struggle. It was, I thought, what I would like to do for a living.

When I embarked on my professional career as a rights defender, I did not anticipate that I would become involved in the range of issues discussed in these pages. My vision of rights did not encompass many of the causes to which I later devoted myself. Nor did I imagine that I myself would become controversial among some of my fellow advocates of civil liberties, and subsequently among some colleagues in the international human rights struggle, primarily because of the way I would redraw the boundaries of those fields. At the ACLU, I led the effort to extend civil liberties protection to the inmates of prisons, juvenile institutions, mental hospitals, and asylums for the retarded. I took a leading role in challenging criminal sanctions on abortion as a violation of civil liberties and in making the protection of women's rights a priority for the ACLU.

My role was similar at Human Rights Watch. Previously, the focus of the international human rights movement was on protecting particular individuals who were victims of politically motivated violations. I led the way in shifting the focus to the policies of governments directly responsible for abuses and, crucially, those indirectly responsible because of the support they provided to abusive governments. The latter were, in the term I used for them, surrogate villains. Mobilizing against them for their diplomatic, political, financial, or military backing of repression, I discovered, was often much easier and more effective than working against those who actually committed the abuses. It could be a means to shine the spotlight on violations of rights in remote places that otherwise attract little attention. I also took the lead in extending the international human rights agenda to other issues prominent on the domestic civil liberties agenda: nonpolitical police abuses, conditions in prisons and jails for those confined for ordinary crimes, and women's rights.

In what I consider my most important contribution, I initiated the monitoring of abuses committed in armed conflicts by assessing the conduct of combatants in accordance with the laws of war. Human Rights Watch pioneered in this monitoring and, over time, the international human rights movement broadly followed its lead. A consequence is to make the human rights practices of opposing armed forces a focus of public debate over wars in many parts of the world. Embarking on this path also led me to propose such innovations as an international prohibition on landmines, establishment of the international criminal tribunal for ex-Yugoslavia, and, in certain extreme circumstances, advocacy for international military intervention when nothing else will prevent so great a crime as genocide.

Though my critics saw these as radical moves when they were made, I did not regard most of them that way. As far as I am concerned, I was merely invoking the fundamental principles to which the ACLU and Human Rights Watch were committed in different settings or on behalf of different classes of people. A mental patient, I believe, has a right to privacy and should not be coerced to submit to such invasive forms of treatment as electro-convulsive therapy or psychosurgery. Even a convicted prisoner is entitled to due process and may not be severely punished beyond the terms of her or his sentence without a hearing, and may never be treated cruelly. A government's unwillingness to prosecute men who murder their wives or lovers for dishonoring them seems to me, like the failure to prosecute political assassins, a violation of human rights. So, too, is the indiscriminate bombardment of a civilian population center or the use of rape as a weapon of war. It is now so well accepted that such concerns are intrinsic to a rights agenda that it may be difficult to recall that they were once considered radical. It is only my espousal of military measures to protect rights—as in the case of Bosnia—that gives me pause. Though I believe those measures were required to halt a genocidal conflict, I am of course mindful of the potential for abuse.

There were substantial pressures that had to be overcome to take even modest steps. Some who had been longtime leaders of the American Civil Liberties Union when I began work there in 1963 argued that I was doing irreparable harm to their organization by broadening its mandate. Similarly, some who promoted human rights internationally mainly by lobbying for adoption of United Nations resolutions and by campaigning for the release of "prisoners of conscience" (a term associated with Amnesty International) regarded Human Rights Watch as an upstart organization that damaged their cause by its aggressive methods, its broad engagement in public policy debates, and its willingness to deal with issues not then covered by UN-sponsored treaties on human rights such as the laws of war. These were all issues that we made central to our work. These views affected some donors to whom I turned for support. To cite an example, the Ford Foundation, these days a leading supporter of civil liberties in the United States and long a leading funder of human rights internationally, in the 1970s attempted to use its financial clout to limit the work of the ACLU and in the 1980s did the same to Human Rights Watch.

"A large body of money entirely surrounded by people who want some," in the words of Dwight MacDonald, the Ford Foundation never provided support to the ACLU prior to the 1970s. I made a number of attempts to secure support while I was director of the New York Civil Liberties Union (NYCLU) in the second half of the 1960s, but to no avail. When I became national executive director of the ACLU in 1970, I set about trying to change that. I met resistance from Ford Foundation program officers. In an effort to break through, I arranged a meeting with the foundation's president, McGeorge Bundy. It went badly. I hardly spoke a couple of sentences before he launched into a tirade against me and the ACLU that went on for the better part of an hour for our defense of the rights of opponents of the Vietnam War, or "draft dodgers," as he called them.

Nevertheless, a year or so later, we got our first grant from Ford. It was to support our Women's Rights Project. The foundation had newly decided to support women's rights. Though wary of contributing to the ACLU, Ford had to recognize our emerging leadership in the field. I had enlisted Ruth Bader Ginsburg to direct the project and she was pursuing a litigation strategy that was having a transforming impact. Ford insisted, however, that none of its money should be spent on abortion rights. A prime target of some of the limits on foundation activities incorporated in the Tax Reform Act of 1969, Ford was eager to steer clear of so politically controversial an issue as abortion. As I wanted the money to spend on the equal-protection issues that were the focus of Ginsburg's litigation, and did not want to reject Ford's first grant, I reluctantly agreed to the condition. To get around the limitation, I established a separate Reproductive Freedom Project to deal with abortion. Many years later, when Ginsburg was nominated to serve on the U.S. Supreme Court, it occurred to me that her confirmation by the Senate might have encountered more difficulty had she participated in our abortion litigation. Ford's squeamishness spared her that political liability. (In a recent publication celebrating its own history in supporting legal efforts to promote rights, the Ford Foundation misrepresents its role and the way we had to adjust to the Foundation's political timidity, stating: "Another grantee, the American Civil Liberties Union, created the Women's Rights and Reproductive Freedom Project, which were initially directed by Ruth Bader Ginsburg, a current US Supreme Court Justice."[4])

A decade and a half later, the staff at Ford then responsible for funding in the human rights field were adamantly opposed when I established a

Women's Rights Project at Human Rights Watch. They demanded that none of the foundation's substantial support for us should be expended on women's rights. They also cut Ford's general support for our work. They supported women's rights, they said; however, they argued that it was not the business of a human rights organization to espouse that cause. The same staff members—who have since left Ford—criticized our reliance on the laws of war to monitor abuses committed in armed conflicts and pressed us to desist from what I thought was our most vital work. I am glad to say we did not yield to the pressure.

At the same time that I was viewed as a radical by some for going beyond traditional boundaries, I acquired a reputation in other quarters as a conservative, or even as a reactionary, because I strenuously opposed efforts to get the ACLU and Human Rights Watch to deal with economic issues as rights. My critics had scripture on their side. The Universal Declaration of Human Rights, the sacred text of the international human rights movement, consists of thirty articles. The first twenty-one deal with civil and political rights: freedom of speech and assembly; the right to privacy; presumption of innocence; freedom from arbitrary arrest; and so forth. Several of the remaining articles deal with such economic issues as a right to work; to social security; and to an adequate standard of living. Harvard law professor Mary Ann Glendon, who has written a fine account of the adoption of the Universal Declaration, disparaged those who regard it "as a kind of menu of rights from which one can pick and choose according to taste." She preferred to see it as "a geodesic dome of inter-locking principles."[5]

These views are widely shared in the international human rights movement. Even a publication such as *The Economist,* which leans toward a free-market approach to most economic issues, has argued that, "Philosophically ... it is difficult to make clear-cut distinctions between the traditional 'first-generation' rights [civil liberties] and the newer 'second-generation' [economic and social rights] variety."[6] Only practical difficulties are really at issue, the publication has editorialized. Hence, my resistance to involving Human Rights Watch in economic questions, and, more important, my unwillingness to concede it is appropriate even to use the terminology of rights in discussing economic issues, left me open to attack. Though I support political efforts to secure "distributive justice" (Aristotle's term in his *Nicomachean Ethics*), such as an adequate living for all and other economic goals discussed in the Universal Declaration, my rejection of the rights label for these is considered by many as selective commitment to human rights. I have been criticized as insensitive to the rights concerns of the Third World or, in more up-to-date terms, the "global South."

One reason I oppose the concept of economic rights is that the effect is to diminish the protection of political rights. A government should not be permitted to justify censorship, denial of peaceable assembly, torture, or arbitrary arrest because of its stage of development. These practices are defined the same way everywhere and should be condemned according to the same criteria universally. The situation is different in the economic sphere. The understanding of what is meant by an adequate standard of living and of a right to housing varies from place to place and time to time. Governments appropriately argue that their ability to deal with these is a question of resources. They must determine what they can do about such matters in the context of their responsibility to deal with jobs, health care, education—also economic "rights"—and such other concerns as the maintenance of order and national defense. Labeling certain economic interests as rights provides no special basis for telling governments how to determine priorities for their expenditures. Yet it is dangerous, I believe, to accept that a state's compliance with rights may vary in accordance with local or temporal standards or should be subject to resource allocations. The language of universal rights should be reserved for matters where it is possible to insist on adherence to the same criteria everywhere.

Civil and political rights are essential elements of democracy. It is impossible to conceive of democratic government without the rights to speak, assemble, and publish. The same is true of each person's right to count equally regardless of race, gender, or other status. Prohibitions on the mistreatment of citizens by punishing them unfairly or cruelly or by intruding on worship or on the zones of our lives protected by our right to privacy are also crucial if we are to enjoy the autonomy that goes with the status of citizen. By protecting civil and political rights, we uphold the worth and dignity of all and circumscribe all exercise of power. In contrast, the concept of economic and social rights is profoundly undemocratic. It is based on the view that the allocation of resources may not be entrusted to the institutions and processes through which the democratic will is exercised. Moreover, it slights the significance of civil and political rights as it fails to recognize the power of expression and organization, when unfettered, in calling attention to grievances and permitting their redress.

If one assumes, as most of us do, that the major functions of democratic government are to protect public safety and to develop and allocate resources, it is evident that withdrawing the last of these from the political process radically diminishes its role. Rejection of the idea of economic and social rights reflects a commitment to democracy not only for its own sake but also because it is preferable in substance to what we can expect from platonic guardians.

It is sometimes noted that safeguarding certain political rights requires state expenditures, such as those needed to ensure that the poor obtain an adequate legal defense or that the conditions of confinement in prisons are humane. To a limited degree, judges must have the power to direct the allocation of public funds to protect rights in such circumstances. Yet this cannot be equated with the redistribution that would be required to deal with such issues as an adequate standard of living or health care. If redistributive resource allocations are not made democratically in a country that is otherwise democratic, they will lack legitimacy. "Whenever equals receive unequal shares, or unequals equal shares in a distribution," Aristotle observed, "that is the source of quarrels and accusations." The possibility that undemocratic allocations can be enforced in such circumstances seems remote. Authoritarian power is probably a prerequisite for giving meaning to economic and social rights.

Isaiah Berlin's famous distinction between negative freedom and positive freedom is useful to me in thinking about economic rights.[7] Berlin's idea of negative freedom is freedom from coercion to the full extent compatible with social life. Positive freedom, in contrast, encompasses security, status, and prosperity to the extent required for self-realization. It is through what Berlin referred to as "great, disciplined, authoritarian structures" that the proponents of positive freedom have attempted to reach this ideal. Unfortunately, such structures tend to be the enemies of negative freedom. Authoritarian regimes purporting to promote positive freedom—whether the old Soviet Union or contemporary China, Singapore, and Malaysia—contend that negative freedom is an obstacle to achievement of their goals. They claim this as a justification for their violations of political rights.

Amartya Sen has demonstrated that negative freedom, particularly freedom of expression, is important and often critical in assuring the availability to all of the economic essentials of life. In our era, people starve to death not because of food shortages brought on by natural disasters such as droughts, but because famines result from policies adopted by governments that deny their citizens the right to criticize those policies and are accountable only to themselves.[8] The great famines of the post–World War II period have not occurred in states such as India, despite its vast overpopulation and its vulnerability to climatic forces, where there is a measure of respect for democratic liberties. Rather, they result from the exercise of absolute power by tyrants such as Mao in China at the time of the "Great Leap Forward" and Mengistu in Ethiopia in his counterinsurgency campaigns of the first half of the 1980s. In 2002, the threat of famine loomed particularly large in parts of southern Africa, particularly Zimbabwe, suffering from authoritarian rule, but not in democratic Botswana that was affected by the same climatic conditions. Defending negative freedom assists all in speaking out, organizing to secure their own economic well-being, and making their governments responsible to them. I also share Sen's view that freedom is a constitutive part of development. Freedom is not merely a means to an end; it is an end in itself.

During my tenure at the ACLU, I sometimes appeared publicly to take the organization in a radical direction when insiders knew I was a slow and, at times, a skeptical convert to causes championed by others in the organization. Two instances stand out. In the latter days of the Vietnam War, the ACLU engaged in some frantic but ultimately inconsequential litigation challenging the constitutionality of U.S. involvement because there was no congressional declaration of war. Our strenuous efforts never impeded the dispatch of troops to Vietnam or a single aerial bombing run. At most, the litigation had some impact on the adoption by Congress of the War Powers Act, but that legislation has turned out to have little effect. (It has been barely mentioned in the debate over whether America should launch a preemptive war against Iraq.) With misgivings, I went along with the lawyers on our staff, Burt Neuborne and Leon Friedman, who spearheaded the litigation against the Vietnam War. They were among our ablest and most effective advocates, and I found it difficult to counter their well-formulated arguments.[9]

In retrospect, I wish I had held out on the grounds that, however sound their case, it is not the province of the courts to correct every failure by the political branches of government. As Alexander Hamilton wrote in "The Federalist Papers," the courts are "the least dangerous branch" of government because they lack both the power of the purse and the sword.

The war-making power, however misguided its use, is the province of the popularly elected branches of government. Their wrongdoing must be corrected through the democratic process. As it is beyond the courts to deal with claimed economic rights by exercising the power of the purse, so it is inappropriate for judges to tell the democratically elected branches of government when they may exercise their responsibilities to make war.

Another prominent instance where I was a follower rather than a leader because I initially had doubts about whether it was appropriate for us to play a role was the impeachment of Richard Nixon. I was more hesitant than some others in the ACLU to decide we should call for Nixon's impeachment. Once I made up my mind, however, this is not an issue on which I had second thoughts. I devoted myself to the impeachment effort for about ten months in 1973 and 1974 until Nixon resigned. Now as then, I think it was the right thing to do. Nixon's crimes were severe assaults on civil liberties. Holding accountable those who abuse the rights of others has been a focus of my work from my effort to secure effective civilian review of complaints against police in the 1960s to my engagement in the struggle to establish international criminal tribunals to prosecute war crimes in the 1990s and, as I write, in the effort to ensure the success of the new International Criminal Court. Impeaching Nixon, I was persuaded, was the way to hold him accountable for high crimes against the liberties of Americans.

The forced resignation of Nixon in 1974 for violating rights, I believe, was one of a series of unrelated events in different parts of the world that helped give birth to the contemporary international human rights movement. It suggested to many well beyond the borders of the United States that rights are so important that even a president must pay a high price for serious violations. I cannot say I recognized as these things took place that they would contribute to the emergence of the international human rights movement we know today. My own progression from the ACLU to Human Rights Watch seems inevitable only in retrospect. At the time, I perceived only dimly how to have a substantial impact on rights internationally. The ACLU relied first and foremost on litigation to protect rights, and I did not immediately see what could be done internationally in place of going to court. I had to learn on the job how to have an effect on the human rights practices of governments worldwide.

If there is one period in my career that stands out as the most exciting, it is the first half of the 1980s. That is when I was discovering that my colleagues and I in the small organization that we had formed and named

Human Rights Watch could have an impact on rights globally. We did so in the context of struggle with a Reagan administration strenuously hostile to our efforts by turning its hostility to our advantage in bringing pressure to bear on many foreign governments. My shift to the international human rights field and my discovery of the methods that work in that arena were as much fortuitous as planned.

My subsequent move from Human Rights Watch to the Open Society Institute and the Soros Foundations has also worked out in unanticipated ways. I knew I could do many things that mattered to me through a foundation with such large resources. What I did not realize was that George Soros was in the process of becoming, as he has been described, the only private citizen in the United States—or, perhaps, in the world—with his own foreign policy and the capacity to implement it.[10] He is unique in possessing the resources, the institutional mechanisms, the status, and the will to promote his policy on a global scale. Association with him and the foundations he founded and funded has enabled me to help shape that foreign policy and to ensure that a concern for rights is at its forefront both in the United States and internationally. It has permitted me to have a voice in debates about rights at a time when the cause to which I have devoted my career has achieved a significance in world affairs that is far greater than I ever imagined it could. At a time when most of the ideologies that developed and flourished for a period during the twentieth century have been discredited and abandoned, commitment to human rights—at least in theory if not in practice—is among the few beliefs that thrives at the beginning of the twenty-first century, though it has been sorely tested in the period since September 11, 2001. It is, I think, a less dangerous faith than most others because it is not about the exercise of power. Rather, the human rights cause, at least in the definition I favor that confines it to negative liberty, is mainly about limits on power.

In this book, I tell the story of some of the many battles for rights in which I engaged during the past four decades. Some resulted in victories, others in defeats, and in many cases the outcome is ambiguous or remains to be decided. Yet all seem to me battles worth fighting. Some of the most important struggles for rights that I fought were on behalf of lost causes. I do not regret the effort I devoted to those causes. It is, I believe, the struggle for rights itself that matters most. I cannot imagine any other way that I could derive more satisfaction from a career.

I

The ACLU Years: 1963–1978

In 1963, I was hired by John de J. Pemberton, executive director of the American Civil Liberties Union, as the organization's field director. I was twenty-six. My assignment was to assist state affiliates of the ACLU in expanding their work and increasing their membership and income. The "affiliates" have their own boards, staff, and budgets and operate with substantial autonomy. They have primary responsibility for court cases, state legislative campaigns, and public education in their territory but are broadly governed by the policies of the national ACLU. An individual who joins the ACLU simultaneously becomes a member of a state affiliate and of the national organization. In some places where statewide affiliates of the ACLU did not yet exist, such as Oklahoma and Texas, my job was to establish them.

It was a time when the possibilities for expanding protection of civil liberties seemed almost unlimited. The movement for racial equality was in full flower. Though the ACLU had not until then played a leading role in challenging discrimination in the courts or in defending the legal rights of demonstrators against segregation—that role was played by the NAACP Legal Defense Fund—my post gave me an opportunity to make the organization I joined more central to that historic struggle. I took the lead in advocating establishment of a Southern Regional Office for the ACLU based in Atlanta that focused on court challenges to race discrimination in electoral laws and in the composition of juries. To direct that office, I suggested to Jack Pemberton that he hire a flamboyant, charismatic Alabama lawyer, Charles Morgan, Jr., a talented litigator. He joined the ACLU staff in the fall of 1964. Morgan's exploits inside and outside courtrooms, including many in which he represented high-profile clients, played an important part not only in making the ACLU an effective combatant in the fight against segregation but also in building excitement for the civil liberties cause nationwide. In addition, I was able to play a small part in establishing the Lawyers Constitutional Defense Committee, an ACLU-led consortium of the country's civil rights groups, including the NAACP Legal Defense Fund and the NAACP (separate organizations), which established offices in several southern cities and recruited hundreds of volunteer lawyers from across the country to serve as a legal arm for the civil rights movement in the region.

It was also a period when the ACLU was beginning to succeed in the courts in dismantling the legacy of McCarthyism. Loyalty oaths, prohibitions on government employment for members or former members of organizations labeled Communist fronts, speaker bans on college campuses, and other restrictions on First Amendment rights enacted in the late 1940s and 1950s were regularly struck down in ACLU-sponsored lawsuits. And, it was the beginning of the era in which millions of Americans protested U.S. involvement in the war in Vietnam by participating in demonstrations, resisting the draft, or, in the case of a small but significant number of those already in the armed forces, defying orders on grounds of conscience. Almost universally, those opposed to the war turned to the ACLU for legal assistance.

The Supreme Court of the United States, under the leadership of Chief Justice Earl Warren, provided a sympathetic forum. I recall a moment in June 1964 of pure exhilaration at the ACLU's Biennial Conference in Boulder, Colorado, which brought together representatives of ACLU state affiliates from across the country. Our conference coincided with the end of the U.S. Supreme Court's 1963–1964 term, and, as often happened, the Court announced some of its most important decisions on its last day. Each decision was read out in turn by the justices, so it took two or three hours for those gathered in its chambers in Washington, D.C., to learn what the Court did that day. In Boulder, we heard about all the decisions at once at a plenary session of the conference. Several ACLU cases were on the docket raising critical issues ranging from the rights of criminal defendants, to film censorship, to loyalty oaths. The Court decided in our favor in every one of these, and as each in turn was announced, thunderous cheers went up. Several of the lawyers who had litigated those cases were present in the hall. They were mobbed by their colleagues offering congratulations.

Another development during that same conference introduced a more somber note. We heard that three young civil rights workers, James

Chaney, Andrew Goodman, and Michael Schwerner, had disappeared in Mississippi. That news struck home especially hard because one young woman there was a cousin of Andrew Goodman's, and several others at our conference had family members who had gone to Mississippi that "Freedom Summer" or were lawyers going there under the auspices of the Lawyers Constitutional Defense Committee.

In that period of high drama and intense debate over civil liberties, the stands we took enjoyed strong support from a segment of the public, and in this climate it was easy for me to do well in my organizational assignment. Thanks to my apparent success, I assume, a year and a half after going to work for the ACLU, the retiring director of the New York Civil Liberties Union, George Rundquist, asked me to succeed him and arranged my appointment. I was not yet twenty-eight.

My selection by Rundquist astonished me and almost everyone else who knew both of us as it was evident I would not and could not do the job the way he did it. I was four decades his junior, a Jewish refugee from Nazi Germany by way of England, and I had no experience and little aptitude for doing business in the gentlemanly and clubby way that was his style. Rundquist was a businessman who had played a leading role on behalf of the country's Protestant churches opposing the internment of the Japanese Americans during World War II. This role led to his association with the ACLU, which had also taken a prominent part in combating internment after initial hesitation by some in the organization's national leadership. Rundquist defended civil liberties primarily by becoming a voice for their protection within the state and city establishment. Under his leadership, the New York Civil Liberties Union brought a number of court cases, including some that were notable, such as *Engel v. Vitale*,[1] in which the U.S. Supreme Court declared school-prescribed prayers unconstitutional. Rundquist periodically issued public statements on the issues of the day. But most of his work was done in quiet conversations, often over drinks or meals (in his case, the meals consisted mainly of drinks, though I never noticed any ill effects), some in the dining cars of the trains along the Hudson River between New York City and Albany, with city and state officials. He arranged my appointment the way he did everything else. There was no announcement that the post was available and no selection process. Rundquist just talked individually to each of the board members. No one questioned his judgment. Though many hardly knew me, they unanimously endorsed his choice. I was anointed.

I was a witness to an episode that typified Rundquist's style as he was introducing me to the public officials with whom he worked most closely. It involved an incident in which two policemen had been killed in a failed barroom holdup in Lodi, New Jersey, in August 1963. The New York City police tracked Frankie Falco, one of the men wanted for the murders, to a midtown Manhattan hotel room. When they burst in, Falco was lying on the bed asleep. The only item at hand that could be used as a weapon was a Coke bottle. Nevertheless, the police fired several bullets into him. It was an execution. Intent on making the point that this was what cop-killers could expect, the police did little to disguise their actions. Police Commissioner Michael Murphy publicly praised his men. (Nearly forty years later, the case continued to arouse controversy when police groups reacted angrily to a February 2001 decision by the Supreme Court of New Jersey ordering the release on parole of Falco's partner in the murders, Thomas Trantino.[2])

Rundquist telephoned Murphy and told him he would issue a statement denouncing him as a son of a bitch. Though I only heard one side of this conversation, I gathered that Murphy said he would respond in kind. Then the two men made a lunch date, and I accompanied Rundquist to this meeting. At lunch, they sparred about the Falco episode for a bit. Neither gave ground, but there was no unpleasantness. Then they went on to other matters over successive martinis on the rocks. After the second martini, fearful I would do or say something foolish, I gave up trying to keep pace. The conversation had no impact on Murphy's public posture on the Falco case, but Rundquist was able to secure concessions on a couple of minor issues of police practice that he managed to raise.

When he chose me, Rundquist said he expected me to do things differently. In the year and a half I had spent as field director for the national ACLU, I had organized public campaigns on a number of issues. This was not his style, but he told me he thought it was an appropriate direction for the organization to go in at that point in the 1960s. After turning over the post to me, he would move far away—to the west coast of Florida as it turned out—both to stay out of my hair and because he knew he couldn't stand what I would do to *his* organization. He said he admired greatly the way Roger Baldwin, the ACLU's founding director, had managed his retirement. Though Roger had directed the ACLU from 1920 until he stepped down in 1950 at the age of sixty-six, and though his physical and mental health were excellent (as they were right up to his death in 1981 at the age of ninety-seven), Roger refrained from interfering in the affairs of the institution he had created. He had strong views about some things done by his successors, and occasionally let those be known, but he considered it improper to interfere in any more direct way. George Rundquist thought he should model himself on Roger Baldwin, but it would be easier for him if he were far away. He never did interfere with anything I did, though I am sure that if he knew about my actions, some did not sit well with him.

The five and a half years I spent as executive director of the NYCLU, from 1965 to 1970, were years in which I laid the foundation for work I carried out on a broader scale when I subsequently became executive director of the ACLU. I initiated efforts to defend the right of women to obtain abortions, opposed the compulsory commitment of drug addicts and supported their right to obtain methadone maintenance—a novelty at the time—and launched efforts to protect the rights of classes of people who were not previously the objects of civil liberties advocacy, such as primary and secondary school students, soldiers, juveniles in detention, prisoners, and mental patients. At the time, much of this was revolutionary. Though widely accepted in subsequent years, the idea that inmates of what I labeled "closed institutions," or "enclaves" beyond the reach of the Constitution, have rights that should be protected in the courts had not previously occurred to most who came in contact with such places. It was a moment in history when all things were possible. I took full advantage.

Though I lacked George Rundquist's bonhomie, I established friendly relations with some officials and found this occasionally served me well in protecting civil liberties. Often, however, I thought it necessary to engage in confrontational struggles when I sought significant changes in public policy. How much this reflected my personal style and how much it was simply a consequence of objective reality is difficult for me to say.

Ideally, I believe, a rights organization should play an insider and an outsider role simultaneously. Inevitably, however, a time comes when it is impossible to sustain both approaches. It is seductive, at those moments, to preserve an insider approach, both because one is reluctant to give up access to power and simply because it is more comfortable to maintain a collegial relationship with officials one encounters regularly. Infrequently—though more often in the case of George Rundquist than for anyone else with whom I have worked—one can be outspoken in denouncing an official's violations of rights while preserving personal cordiality. For those like me who lack such talents, it becomes necessary to resist the temptation to preserve insider relationships at the expense of doing battle from the outside. At times, it is possible to promote rights by persuading officials that they can achieve their ends without violating civil liberties, or at least by minimizing violations. More often, in my experience, rights are won in public combat.

I n 1970, John Pemberton resigned as national executive director of the ACLU. A Republican lawyer from Minnesota who had previously been a leader of the ACLU affiliate in his home state, Jack was an effective director of the national organization in his first few years at the helm after his appointment in 1962. Under his direction, the national ACLU was far more vigorous in challenging what was left of the country's loyalty and security apparatus than it ever had been in the 1950s. Also, he enlisted the ACLU wholeheartedly in the struggle for racial equality that had taken center stage during the 1960s. Unfortunately, difficulties in his personal life later in the decade when his marriage broke up were reflected in his job performance. A period of drift and demoralization set in at the national office at a moment when several state affiliates were making great strides in broadening the civil liberties agenda to reach classes of people previously excluded from constitutional protection. Unhappy with the lack of leadership from the executive director, I joined with the directors of the Illinois, Michigan, and Southern California affiliates (we were referred to within the ACLU, not flatteringly, as "the Barons") in going to the chairman, Edward J. Ennis, to ask that a change be made. This forced Jack's resignation.

Initially, I was not a candidate to succeed Jack. During the previous two years, I had become a controversial figure in New York City, and even within a portion of the ACLU membership, because of my role in a dispute over what was then called "community control" of the city's school system. The dispute pitted a labor union, the United Federation of Teachers (UFT), against the board of an experimental school district in an impoverished neighborhood of Brooklyn, Ocean Hill–Brownsville. The board transferred ten teachers out of the district claiming they were not teaching children effectively. All the teachers were white, and the majority were Jewish, while the principal officers of the board that summarily transferred them were black. The episode led to a prolonged city-wide strike by teachers and school principals, embittered race relations in the city, and helped make the city's school system unmanageable by decentralizing it without achieving the parental engagement that was the rationale for local control. (In 2002, decentralization was officially abandoned.) NYCLU issued statements on the complex issues in the dispute that were highly critical of the city Board of Education and the United Federation of Teachers and that in part supported and in part were critical of the local Ocean Hill–Brownsville board. These statements pointed out that transfers within the school system were customarily made without due process and aroused no protest by the union. The issue had been raised in an unprecedented way by the UFT. This was part of an ongoing effort by the union to sabotage the experiment in community control, according to "The Burden of Blame," a statement drafted for us by Ira Glasser, whom I had hired at NYCLU the previous year.[3]

Ocean Hill–Brownsville pitted against each other many in the city who were previously allies. I publicly debated the issues with the UFT leader, Albert Shanker. (A Woody Allen film of this era, *Sleeper*, is set in a post–nuclear war world. Asked how the nuclear war got started, the character played by Woody Allen responds that somebody named Shanker got hold of the bomb. When I saw the film, I wondered what audiences elsewhere—say in Des Moines—made of this commentary on the union leader's recklessness in inciting city-wide racial conflict in New York over what could have been a minor episode readily resolved without great strife.) Teachers and school supervisors, including the principal of PS 41 on 11th Street in Greenwich Village, the elementary school attended by my son David, picketed my office. In addition, some members of the NYCLU organized a campaign against me and against the NYCLU board for siding with me. The opposition was led by Shachtmanites with whom I had come into conflict at LID and who were firmly entrenched in the United Federation of Teachers and the AFL-CIO. A meeting of members at which the issues were debated was attended by about 1,000 people. We were required to ask the American Arbitration Association to supervise a contested election for our board in which more than 10,000 of our members in New York voted.

Though my side prevailed by more than a 2 to 1 margin, the consequence was a feeling by many—I among them—that it was an inopportune moment for me to seek the top post in the ACLU. I discussed the matter with Ed Ennis. A successful lawyer in private practice, he had been an official at the Justice Department in the early 1940s and had been the leading opponent within the government of the evacuation of the Japanese Americans from the West Coast and their internment. Franklin D. Roosevelt had overruled him, saying it was a military matter and therefore beyond the jurisdiction of the Justice Department. Yet the president appointed Ed as director of Enemy Alien Control so he would be able to temper the harshness of the internment. It was a typical Roosevelt ploy. In later years when some internees went back to court to reopen their challenge to the evacuation that they had lost during the war, Ed testified for the plaintiffs. He told the court that when the FBI investigated incidents in which Japanese residents of coastal areas had supposedly signaled to offshore boats, it had discovered that many of those living in the area used outhouses. At night they used flashlights. The FBI withheld this information from the courts that considered challenges to the evacuation while the war was under way.

In the years I knew Ed, I often heard him speak of his culpability for a crime against civil liberties, but I did not learn that he had led the opposition within the administration to the measures taken against the Japanese Americans until I read the memoirs of Roosevelt's attorney general, Francis Biddle.[4] Peter Irons, author of the leading study of the evacuation and internment, says that Ed kept up the struggle against the program within the government even as he administered it.[5] With the advantage of hindsight, it seems clear that Ed should have resigned rather than oversee one of the worst violations of civil liberties of the century. Yet it is difficult to say with confidence how one would have advised him in the aftermath of Pearl Harbor when the president, who had rejected his plea against evacuation and internment, and Justice Department colleagues, such as James Rowe, who had joined Ed in opposing the program, asked him to see that the policy was carried out humanely.

Ed told me he would like me to become the ACLU's national executive director, but he wanted me not to be a candidate on this occasion. I was young—thirty-three—and my turn would come. I agreed. Ocean Hill–Brownsville was not the only factor to make me feel the time was not right. I was uncomfortable seeking the post after playing a part in Jack Pemberton's ouster. I didn't want to create the impression that I had sought his removal to further my own ambitions.

In August 1970, as was our practice, I went with Yvette and David to

Nantucket on vacation. While there, I received a call from an attorney I had known for several years who told me he was to be interviewed for the post the following day by the ACLU board's five-member selection committee. He asked my advice to prepare for the interview. Though I considered him wholly unqualified, I was polite and gave him a couple of pointers, imagining the selection committee would quickly determine he was unsuited. To my amazement and horror, I got another call on Nantucket several days later from Ed Ennis to tell me the selection committee had chosen this attorney and asking my opinion of him. I told Ed what I thought and said that, under the circumstances, I had reconsidered. To try to head off the selection committee's choice, I would become a candidate and leave it to the full ACLU board to decide.

Ed told the selection committee what I had said. The members were taken aback and, after further deliberation and another interview, decided not to go forward with their candidate but to reopen their search. By this time, one of the five members, Harriet Pilpel, general counsel of Planned Parenthood and my partner during the previous several years in efforts to legalize abortion, had left for a vacation in Europe and was unreachable. After conducting some additional interviews, the remaining four members split. Robert Carter, general counsel of the NAACP and subsequently a federal judge, and Franklin Haiman, a free-speech scholar and chairman of the Illinois ACLU, announced they would support me; Donald Hackel, a Vermont businessman, and David Isbell, a partner in the Washington law firm of Covington & Burling, would support Lawrence Speiser, an able and principled attorney who directed the ACLU's Washington office. (Though Isbell did not favor me in the selection committee, he absented himself from the board meeting where the choice was made and subsequently became one of my strongest supporters on the ACLU board and a friend.) If Speiser had been nominated previously, I would have stayed out of the contest. Having gotten in, I stayed in.

At the time, the ACLU board of directors had some seventy members. Sixty-seven attended the two-day meeting at which the selection was made. Before the meeting, supporters and opponents of the two candidates engaged in intense lobbying. Everyone liked and respected Larry Speiser. He was not the issue. I was. Some board members strongly espoused my candidacy because they wanted the ACLU to go in the direction in which I had taken the NYCLU. Others were vehemently opposed to me. It seemed that it all came down to a choice between a candidate

who would have a polarizing effect and one who would be broadly acceptable. There were also board members from distant parts of the country—
every state affiliate was represented on the board—who didn't know
much about the broad range of issues in which I had engaged the
NYCLU. They were targets of a lot of the effort to line up votes.

My backers thought it best that I stay out of the lobbying. There was
one exception, however. I would have to talk to Osmond K. Fraenkel, the
ACLU's senior general counsel who was then in his eighties, though remarkably vigorous intellectually and physically. Osmond had been a freshman at Harvard when Roger Baldwin was a senior there. Their paths had
intertwined ever since. Though very different—Osmond was straightforward while Roger was sly and manipulative—they inspired awe in me and
my contemporaries because they were important actors in long past
events that we had studied when we were in school, yet the years did not
seem to take any toll on their energy or acuity. A little later, when we celebrated Osmond's eighty-fifth birthday, I proposed we get him a new bicycle as a gift, but his daughter vetoed the idea as she was trying to get him to
quit biking.

Osmond was the longest-serving member of the board. He participated in such historic cases as the defense of Sacco and Vanzetti and had
probably argued more cases before the U.S. Supreme Court than any other
attorney in private practice up to that point. Universally respected, and a
gentle and kind man, Osmond intimidated some by his terseness and di-
rectness. One of my colleagues on the ACLU staff told of calling him on
the phone and beginning the conversation, "Hello, Osmond," only to
have him respond, "Get to the point." In an appearance before the
Supreme Court, where lawyers normally strive unsuccessfully to complete
their arguments in the brief period allotted and are cut off in mid-syllable
when their time is up, Osmond made all his points with several minutes to
spare and sat down. I was unsure how Osmond felt about NYCLU's assaults on closed institutions and our involvement in issues such as abortion, and I didn't think I would get the opportunity to probe him on those
questions. Knowing how I needed to proceed, I called him and said, "I've
been nominated to be ACLU director and I would like your support." Osmond responded, "You shall have it." The conversation was over. After
that, win or lose, it was all downhill as far as I was concerned.

At the board meeting the qualifications of the two candidates were debated at length, sometimes heatedly. One of my opponents at the meeting

was the civil rights leader Bayard Rustin, a close ally of the United Federation of Teachers who made his office at UFT's New York City headquarters. We had been on bad terms since 1960 when I had invited the Rev. Martin Luther King, Jr., to speak at a conference in Ann Arbor of northern students supporting the southern civil rights movement. Rustin, then serving as an aide to King, accepted the invitation but pointed out that King might not make it if one of his frequent court appearances was required at the same time. On the appointed day, Rustin showed up in King's place and spoke to the gathering. When I encountered King subsequently, I expressed regret that he had been unable to be there. It seemed evident to me that King had never seen my letter of invitation and knew nothing of the event. I confronted Rustin over this. As a result, we generally avoided each other in the decade that elapsed before he spoke against me at the ACLU board meeting. Knowing he was my antagonist, my supporters made sure another well-known civil rights leader, Dr. Kenneth B. Clark (the psychologist whose work the U.S. Supreme Court cited in *Brown v. Board of Education* and my close collaborator in the dispute over the schools in New York), spoke for me immediately after Rustin. When the debate was done, I was elected executive director of the ACLU by a vote of 35 to 32.

I served in the post for eight years, from 1970 to 1978. One of the many satisfactions of that period is that I was able to recruit an extraordinarily talented staff. Three of those whom I picked to direct special projects—Al Bronstein, who directed our Prison Project; Janet Benshoof, who directed our Reproductive Freedom Project; and Morton Halperin, who directed our National Security Project—were selected years later to receive MacArthur Foundation "genius" fellowships. Two others were selected for high government offices involving the protection of rights: John Shattuck, whom I hired as a staff attorney and subsequently appointed as director of the ACLU's Washington office, served for six years as assistant secretary of state for human rights in the Clinton administration before accepting an appointment as U.S. ambassador to the Czech Republic. Ruth Bader Ginsburg, whom I chose to direct the ACLU's Women's Rights Project, was subsequently appointed as a judge of the U.S. Court of Appeals and then as a U.S. Supreme Court justice. In addition, Mort Halperin became director of policy planning for the State Department in the Clinton administration. Today, he directs the Washington office of the Open Society Institute.

Working with such talented colleagues—and several others of comparable ability, among them two outstanding litigators whom I initially hired at NYCLU in the 1960s and who subsequently joined me at the national ACLU and served as successive legal directors, the late Bruce Ennis and Burt Neuborne—made it possible for me to take on a lot of battles and to fare reasonably well in them. An important factor in the successes I enjoyed was my close collaboration with Norman Dorsen, an NYU law professor who served with Osmond Fraenkel as general counsel in my first few years as ACLU director and, subsequently, succeeded Ed Ennis as chairman. Norman played many roles. He was my coeditor and, after I left the ACLU, the sole editor of an extensive series of handbooks on rights. He was a superb strategist from whom everyone on the staff could seek advice. When major matters arose, such as the Pentagon Papers case, we turned to Norman to serve as our lead advocate. And when difficult organizational decisions had to be made, I knew I could count on Norman not only to provide wise counsel but, when necessary, to take on the burdens associated with whatever action we took. Some of what we accomplished is now celebrated. In one of a series of editorials in December 1999 summing up the achievements of the millennium, the *New York Times* wrote that the ACLU in that era "set out to extend the reach of the Bill of Rights to new groups and subject areas. This effort, since joined by other organizations and other lawyers, has helped improve prison conditions, reduce unnecessary government secrecy and achieve significant advances for women's rights, children in foster care and the mentally ill."[6]

Another of the satisfactions of my work at the ACLU was that I was able to undertake many projects that set no legal precedents and made no significant impact on the public conception of rights but made real differences in the lives of a large number of people. One of my favorites was the ACLU's South Texas Project (Yvette suspected I visited it so often because I usually managed to find an evening when I could go across the border to Reynosa or Matamoros, Mexico, to eat at one of the restaurants there specializing in a dish I particularly liked, *cabrito*).

In the early 1970s, I became aware that severe public health problems in the lower Rio Grande Valley of Texas were attributable to a violation of civil liberties. The region was home base for many thousands of Mexican-American farm workers who fanned out across the country during the harvesting season. The rest of the year they lived in *colonias,* farmland divided into small plots on which they built makeshift houses. At the time,

Texas's water district boards were gerrymandered to exclude the *colonias*. As the residents did not vote in elections to these boards, they had no influence on their policies and were not supplied with water. The ground water that could be obtained from wells in the area was not suitable for drinking. As a consequence, many residents of the *colonias* made do with water they obtained from irrigation standpipes in the fields around their homes. As this was untreated water from the Rio Grande that carried many pollutants, the region had disease rates that were the highest in the country.

The main purpose of the South Texas Project that I established in McAllen, Texas, was to bring lawsuits against the water district boards to end the gerrymandering. The court cases made this a public issue that could not be ignored and eventually resulted in state legislation addressing the problem. More than three decades after I launched the South Texas Project, much remains to be done to improve conditions in the *colonias*— which fleetingly attracted notice in the 2000 presidential campaign when compassionate conservative candidate George W. Bush acknowledged that he never visited any of them during his tenure as governor—but they now get the same water as other Texans.

A quarter of a century has passed since I stepped down as executive director of the ACLU. In that period, I have usually agreed with the organization's public stands. The major exception has been its position on campaign finance. I believe the ACLU makes a great mistake in equating money with speech and in claiming, therefore, that the First Amendment bars limits on contributions. This argument seems to me unsustainable in an era when corporate interests, individuals of great wealth, and institutional political action committees deploy large resources to drown out other views during campaign periods and to buy greatly disproportionate influence over public officials. The legalized corruption of the campaign finance system defeats a central purpose of freedom of speech: to make government democratic by providing all an opportunity to be heard and to have their opinions considered.

I remain a supporter of efforts by the ACLU to defend free speech even for those expressing the most despicable views; its progressively less effective efforts to promote the fair administration of criminal justice; its attempts to protect liberties within such public institutions as schools, the armed forces, prisons, and mental hospitals; its defense of privacy; its support for the right of all to count equally; and its attempt to ensure that the state promotes that right, particularly for those who suffer from discrimination.

Unhappily, I have not always been enthusiastic about the manner in which the ACLU has pursued this agenda in recent years. It has relied excessively on the courts in an era when litigation produces diminishing returns and is sometimes counterproductive. As a consequence, the ACLU's public influence has suffered a decline. Living in New York, I was distressed by the unsophisticated and unpersuasive style of the New York Civil Liberties Union under its long-term director, Norman Siegel, who stepped down in 2001 to run a losing campaign for public office. More important, the ACLU has been missing in action from the struggle to deal with the most important violations of civil liberties of the past two decades: the steady deterioration in the quality of legal counsel provided by the states to indigent criminal defendants and the four-fold increase in incarceration. Both are violations that particularly victimize racial minorities and thereby contribute to and exacerbate the country's continuing racial divisions. The low expenditures by the states for defense lawyers for the poor—shamefully, New York ranks near the bottom—and the changes in sentencing laws and practices that are the main cause of the soaring rise in imprisonment rates are not readily susceptible to challenge through litigation, probably a principal reason for the ACLU's absence from these frays.

My distress about the state of the ACLU has been alleviated by what I consider the organization's effective response to the drastic violations of civil liberties by Bush and Ashcroft in the aftermath of the terrorist attacks of September 11, 2001. This challenge to everything for which the ACLU stands took place at an unusually bad moment for the organization. A new executive director, an able and energetic young lawyer named Anthony Romero, for whom I have high expectations, had taken up his duties as national executive director just six days earlier. Romero came to the post after ten years in which he rose through the ranks at the Ford Foundation, a notably cautious institution prone to avoiding controversy and certainly never likely to engage in a public campaign over a sensitive and divisive issue. Prior to taking up his new duties, Romero knew the ACLU as a civil libertarian, as a grant-giver, and as one who had studied it to compete for the post he secured and to prepare himself to lead it, but not from the standpoint of an insider familiar in close detail with its strengths and weak-nesses and its internal political currents or how best to mobilize its re-sources. If he had served as executive director for even six months before confronting the Bush-Ashcroft war on civil liberties in the aftermath of September 11, I think the ACLU's response would have been even better.

Of course, it should not be up to one person to determine how an or-ganization with a long institutional history, an engaged board of directors, state affiliates throughout the country, 300,000 members, and scores of professional staff responds to a crisis. The machinery should be in place to act in any circumstances. It was not. One of the characteristics of Romero's predecessor, Ira Glasser, who served as ACLU executive direc-tor for the twenty-three years between my departure and Romero's arrival, was that he centralized all authority in himself. His longevity in the post was a contributing factor. After a while, no one on the staff could remem-ber a time when it wasn't up to Ira to decide how to deal with a significant matter that required the ACLU to act.

A further difficulty is that the Glasser years at the ACLU were not marked by campaigning. It is difficult to think of any issue on which the organization engaged in an all-out effort during the 1980s and 1990s. Probably most notable were its efforts to combat civil liberties abuses against nonviolent drug users, its work against racial profiling by the po-lice, and—the issue where I part company with the ACLU—its efforts to block campaign finance reform. The organization did not remember how to use simultaneously all the resources available to it: congressional testi-mony; meetings with executive officials; litigation; investigative reports; the formation of coalitions with other organizations; a press strategy deal-ing with radio and television talk-shows, meetings with editorial boards, contacts with columnists, beat journalists, and feature writers, the place-ment of op-ed articles as well as the exploitation of opportunities for spot news; speakers bureaus; special mailings to ACLU members as well as out-siders; and so forth. Despite its diminishing returns, litigation was relied on during the 1980s and 1990s as much as if the judicial climate were the same as in the 1960s and 1970s to deal with every issue of concern to the organization.

These aspects of the ACLU's performance embarrass me because they reflected my own failure to build an institutional culture that would be proof against deterioration. Moreover, because of these failings, my en-thusiasm declined for an organization to which I had devoted fifteen years

Confronting Police Abuse

When I began as director of the New York Civil Liberties Union in 1965, the issue dominating our concerns was police brutality. A stream of complainants came to our offices at 20th Street and Fifth Avenue to report beatings on the street or in station houses. Typically, they were boys or young men, many black or Hispanic, who had engaged in some conduct the police interpreted as defiance of their authority: failing to move along right away when told to do so, answering back, or, worst of all, conspicuously taking note of a badge number. When not using coarser language, the police called them "wise guys" or "troublemakers." Most of the time, there was little we could do. Generally, they could not produce witnesses or evidence other than their bruises to support their complaints. An even greater obstacle was the police practice of bringing "cover charges." Someone abused by the police invariably was charged with an offense; the more severe the abuse, the graver the charges. Bruises were explained by an additional charge of resisting arrest; more serious injuries meant the defendant was also accused of felonious assault. Some defendants were injured when they fell down a flight of stairs at a police station. They claimed they were pushed, but judges tended to believe police officers, who testified that they tripped.

We explained to those who sought our help that if they filed a complaint for brutality, the police would have a heightened incentive to ensure their conviction for the cover charges. That would undercut their complaint. Whatever satisfaction they might derive from pursuing a complaint paled in comparison with their interest in getting those charges dismissed or an acquittal. By the time the criminal charges were settled, months elapsed, marks from beatings disappeared, and many complainants lost interest. If they remained intent, the passage of time before filing a complaint reduced their credibility and increased the difficulty of proving their allegations. Add to these obstacles the practice of most district attorneys—at the insistence of the police—of requiring abused defendants to waive all claims for damages in exchange for the dismissal of charges. Waivers also blocked complaints of abuse in departmental proceedings. Though probably unenforceable as a matter of law, waivers were effective in practice.

Despite all the difficulties, we filed some complaints. The issue was hot in New York in 1965 because of the Harlem and Bedford-Stuyvesant riots the previous summer. Triggered when an off-duty white police officer shot and killed a fifteen-year-old black boy involved in a school dispute, the riots had lasted several days and caused many injuries and much looting and property damage. They also inaugurated an era of urban riots that included far more destructive uprisings over the next few years in Watts in Los Angeles, Newark, Detroit, and other cities. In nearly every case, police violence had sparked the riot. One of our cases in 1965 involved a black youth who had died two days after being hit over the head with a nightstick by a police officer. He had talked back to the officer when told to move on while dancing with his girlfriend to recorded music on the Coney Island boardwalk. A reason that episode did not stir trouble in the city is that the policeman was also black. (The Brooklyn district attorney convened a grand jury to consider the case, but no indictment was issued.)

Another common form of police abuse in that era was coerced confessions. The most notorious was the highly detailed 61-page confession—"with details only the killer could know," according to a police statement—of a young black man, George Whitmore, to the murder in August 1963 of two white women, Janice Wylie and Emily Hoffert, in their Manhattan apartment. Known as the "career girls" murder, it was the most publicized crime of the period excepting only the assassinations of President John F. Kennedy and his killer, Lee Harvey Oswald, three months later. Whitmore also confessed to another murder and an attempted rape. The only difficulty was that the confessions were false, as eventually became clear, thanks in large part to the efforts of Selwyn Raab, a journalist for the *World Telegram and Sun*, a newspaper that expired a few years later.[1]

The police had fed Whitmore all the details of these cases. The NYCLU eventually helped exonerate Whitmore in 1965 when Osmond Fraenkel and a young lawyer new on our staff, Alan Levine, joined in proceedings that secured a new trial for him. About the same time, several other confessions to murders in New York were also demonstrated to be false—in one case, because the young Puerto Rican who had confessed was in jail when the crime was committed. (My private name for one New York police official in that era was "Yagoda," after Stalin's political police chief who specialized in obtaining confessions until he, too, fell victim to the requirement and was forced to confess to a few crimes he did not commit.) These cases had an important influence on the U.S. Supreme Court's famous—or infamous, to some—*Miranda* decision in 1966 requiring that defendants be advised of their right to remain silent and their right to obtain the assistance of an attorney before a statement may be taken from them. The Court cited George Whitmore's false confession in its decision.[2]

Prior to my arrival at the NYCLU, police abuse cases had been handled for us by lawyers in private practice who volunteered their services. I thought this procedure was inadequate. We needed to gain a deeper understanding of how to curb abuses than was possible that way. Accordingly, I raised funds to establish a Police Practices Project. It was the ACLU's first foundation-supported project. To direct it, I hired Paul Chevigny, an attorney I had known since we were both college students. We had met through the Student League for Industrial Democracy. Paul was a member of the chapter at Yale, the John Dewey Society.

After attending Harvard Law School, Paul went to work for a Wall Street law firm, but he left after a few years for a small neighborhood legal services office in Harlem. It was one of the first such offices in the country, preceding creation of the federally funded legal services program under President Lyndon Johnson's Office of Economic Opportunity. The assignment I gave Paul turned into a lifelong focus of his work. He published several books, including a novel, and many articles on police practices both during his tenure at the NYCLU and, thereafter, as a professor of law at New York University, where he has taught for three decades.

Paul combined an ability to investigate cases doggedly in the seediest, most blighted sections of New York City with skill in conducting trials in the city's criminal courts and the capacity to frame affirmative challenges to patterns of police abuse in the federal courts. He had strong sympathies for the outcasts who were often the victims of the worst brutality but maintained a healthy skepticism about the many stories he heard that served him well in taking cases to trial. His investigations led him to some unusual settings, including, on one occasion, a Harlem nightspot where he danced with a transvestite as part of his effort to locate a witness and obtain the testimony he needed. What he learned contributed to a certain impatience with cant. On one occasion, I heard a disturbance outside my office. When I went to see what it was about, I discovered Paul waving his arms and speaking loudly to a journalist whom he was ejecting from his office. It seems the journalist wanted to write a story supporting our efforts and had asked Paul for a case in which a middle-class white who had been doing absolutely nothing was beaten by police. Apparently, Paul got tired of explaining that was not the issue.

Police abuse was such a hot topic in New York in that era that a Republican candidate in the 1965 mayoral election, John V. Lindsay, who represented Manhattan's "silk stocking district" in the U.S. Congress, pledged that, if elected, he would appoint civilians to serve on the Civilian Complaint Review Board (so named because it heard complaints from civilians, not because of its composition). The Review Board lacked the power to discipline police officers. All it could do was send recommendations to the police commissioner. He had authority to impose some penalties on his own and, in serious cases, he could require a departmental trial that might lead to dismissal from the force. Most of the time, however, then as now, the police commissioner simply ignored the Review Board's recommendations. There was no recourse. Despite its relative impotence, the question of the Review Board's composition had become a controversial public issue a few years earlier as a result of the efforts of my NYCLU predecessor, George Rundquist. He was the first to propose that civilians should serve on such bodies.

As George told me the story, he used the occasion of a public-relations embarrassment for the NYPD to make this proposal. The department was feuding over an unrelated matter with the Federal Bureau of Investigation and its director, J. Edgar Hoover. The director, as was his practice, had used the press to discredit his antagonists. He leaked a story to a journalist for one of the city's afternoon newspapers that no disciplinary action had been taken against any of the police officers involved in several notorious cases in which the city had paid large sums to victims of abuse who had filed civil suits. The newspaper made the issue a front-page story for several days running, focusing on the cost to the taxpayers. The resulting uproar provided George Rundquist an opportunity to suggest a change in the way disciplinary actions were initiated. George was gleeful in telling me that J. Edgar Hoover was, therefore, the real father of civilian review. (Many years later, I came across a document in my FBI file that suggested how much Hoover would have disliked this attribution. I had published an article supporting civilian review. An aide to Hoover sent him a copy with a memo asking the director whether the Bureau should call me in and have a talk with me to show me the errors of my ways. Hoover responded with a handwritten note on the memo saying, "Don't bother. He's too rigid.")

With the help of a campaign poster showing the young, handsome John Lindsay in shirtsleeves with his jacket flung over his shoulder and a quote from Murray Kempton ("He is fresh and all the rest are tired"), the Republican Congressman was elected in November 1965 and sworn in as the city's mayor on New Year's Day 1966. He promptly kept his promise by appointing civilians to four of seven places on the Review Board. I was not enthusiastic about the mayor's choices. As chairman, Lindsay designated Algernon Black, the senior leader of the New York Society for Ethical Culture. I knew and liked Black but thought he was an easy target for opponents of the board who pointed out he knew nothing about policing. A retired judge with a background as a prosecutor would be a better choice, I thought. There was no shortage of good candidates in New York.

Predictably, the appointment of Black and the other civilians, who seemed chosen mainly to provide racial balance, was bitterly opposed by the city's police union, the Patrolmen's Benevolent Association. Taking advantage of a provision of the City Charter that allowed certain issues to be decided by referendum, the PBA set about collecting signatures to put the issue on the ballot. A vote was scheduled for November 1966.

As the NYCLU had originated the idea that civilians should serve on such boards and as we were the organization most deeply engaged in efforts to curb police abuses, it fell to me to take the lead in putting together a campaign to defeat the police union proposal to ban civilians from serving on the Review Board. I had no experience in political campaigns and never subsequently took part in an election. But in 1966, at a time when police abuse was the most bitterly divisive issue in the city, I organized a campaign to get the citizens of New York to vote for civilian review.

I began by calling together representatives of scores of other nongovernmental groups in the city to form a coalition, which we called Federated Associations for Independent Review (FAIR). Church groups, labor unions, civic groups, neighborhood associations, and organizations representing the city's many minorities and professional bodies all joined.

I enlisted prominent persons to serve as officers of FAIR, ranging from Herbert Brownell, the austere Republican lawyer who had served as attorney general of the United States in the Eisenhower administration, to A. Philip Randolph, the sonorous-voiced civil rights leader who was president of the Brotherhood of Sleeping Car Porters. I also went to see the two U.S. Senators from New York, Republican/Liberal Jacob K. Javits and Democrat Robert F. Kennedy, and persuaded them to serve as honorary cochairs of FAIR. We established low-cost headquarters in a run-down hotel slated for renovation at the edge of New York's garment district. Our campaign staff was largely made up of volunteers and donated personnel from the constituent organizations of FAIR. In addition, we had a few members of the team who had run Lindsay's successful campaign for mayor the previous year. Lindsay was then a rising star. He was talked about as a future presidential candidate, and participation in the campaign by members of his organization reflected their view that voter rejection of the Civilian Review Board he had appointed would damage his political career. The leader of the Lindsayites was David Garth, who subsequently gained a reputation as a heavyweight political professional and kingmaker in New York politics.

Though we established a large campaign organization, we did not raise much money—less than $200,000, not a lot for a city-wide referendum, even by 1966 standards. In contrast, the Patrolmen's Benevolent Association spent over ten times that much. Our campaign consisted largely of sending speakers all around the city to appear at hundreds of churches, synagogues, parents associations, political clubs, veterans posts, labor unions, and any other place where a score or more people might gather. We also made the case for civilian review in the city's many neighborhood weeklies and its diverse foreign-language press as well as in the major newspapers and on radio and television broadcasts.

The PBA used its treasury to produce spot advertisements for television that played on fears of young hoodlums whose depredations could not be controlled because the police were handcuffed. PBA spots seemed ubiquitous that fall. They were precursors, though less explicit, of the infamous Willie Horton advertisements used by Vice President George Bush against Governor Michael Dukakis in the presidential campaign more than twenty years later. One of them showed a white girl menaced by dark shadows as she walked along a street by herself. The ads had a corrosive effect on race relations in the city. David Garth, with whom I developed an uneasy relationship, was desperate to respond to these, but we only had enough money for him to produce one or two commercials; he bought a handful of showings late at night on a couple of the city's independent television stations with relatively small audiences. I only got to see one commercial just before it aired, but then objected because it attacked our opponents in a way I thought unfair. To Garth, my scruples were symptomatic of amateurishness, for which he had only contempt.

The city was polarized by the campaign. It exacerbated fears and hatreds that had intensified since the Harlem riot in 1964 and the Watts riot of 1965 in which thirty-four people were killed and more than 1,000 were injured. Even so, as a neophyte to electoral politics, caught up in the excitement, I persuaded myself that we had a chance to win. But when returns came in on election night, it was immediately apparent that we had been soundly thrashed. All the big political names, most of the newspaper editorials, the political parties, with the exception of the state's small Conservative Party, and virtually every civic group in the city were on our side. But the voters were on the other side: 63 percent voted to prohibit civilian review and only 37 percent in favor. Two years earlier, when Lyndon Johnson had overwhelmed Barry Goldwater, the death of the Right and the ascendancy of liberalism had been widely proclaimed. Our crushing defeat in New York when racial divisions were exploited made it clear to me that liberal euphoria was not warranted.

By itself, as I knew well, placing civilians on a board that considered complaints against the police did not mean much. What mattered more were the investigators on the Review Board staff. Their careers could only advance by assignment to other duties within the police force, and antagonizing their fellow officers was not the way to get ahead. If the evidence they collected did not support complaints, the makeup of the body that considered their findings mattered little. Moreover, if the police commissioner to whom the board made recommendations was not intent on curbing abuses, there was little that could be done by the Review Board. Yet the public's rejection of civilian participation in reviewing complaints against the police had important consequences, as soon became evident.

The years 1967 and 1968 were turbulent in New York, as in much of the rest of the country and, in 1968, the world. In New York, it was a period of intensifying protest against the draft and the war in Vietnam; of uprisings on college campuses, of which the most notable was the student seizure of several buildings on the Columbia University campus in April 1968; and of counterculture manifestations such as those organized by Abbie Hoffman's Yippies. The New York City police treated these as though each was a deliberate affront against them. They made thousands of arrests, the great majority resulting in court cases for the NYCLU in our "mass defense" project. (One byproduct was Abbie's marriage to Anita Kushner. He got to know her on his frequent visits to our office where she was a shy and conventional-seeming secretary.) The police dealt with a lot of peaceful if irreverent demonstrators with astonishing brutality. More was involved than the defeat of civilian review, but I thought that was a factor in eliminating restraint. Thankfully, no one was killed, but quite a few young people suffered lifelong injuries, such as one youth whose use of his hands was severely impaired. They were cut when police officers threw him through a glass door at a "Yip-In" in Grand Central Station. We referred to these episodes as "police riots."

As we knew we would be asked to provide legal representation to those arrested, we sent observers to demonstrations to see for ourselves whether our prospective clients limited their protests to the exercise of rights protected by the First Amendment. To identify our representatives to demonstrators and police alike, I had large black and white badges made up that said "Civil Liberties Union Observer." We conducted training sessions to teach those who wore the badges the elements of free-speech rights on New York City streets (for example, if demonstrators do not obstruct traffic, as by walking single file on a sidewalk, do not use amplification, and respect traffic signals, they do not require a permit) and how to observe a demonstration (if all hell breaks loose, don't try to take in too much; focus on one scene, try to note as many details as possible, and write them down as soon as you have a chance).

Hand-held video cameras were not available in those days, but movie cameras were used to record demonstrations, preferably from windows of nearby buildings where they were safe from police attempts to smash them. Paul Chevigny had a Moviola permanently attached to his desk so that, frame by frame, he could examine the footage taken at the demonstrations. The film was often valuable because of an observation we made early in this season of mass arrests. The police officers who actually made arrests were often too busy to record the names of those they arrested. Other police were arbitrarily assigned later on to be the arresting officers of record. As they could not truthfully testify they had seen the defendants committing violations of law when they were arrested, the officers simply perjured themselves in court. With the films, we could prove in court that the police who claimed to be arresting officers were often not around when the arrests were made. After a handful of cases in which we produced such evidence, we found prosecutors eager to dismiss the remaining cases from those demonstrations rather than endure continuing embarrassment.

A few years later, as national executive director of the ACLU, I had an opportunity to put this observation to good use in another setting. In May 1971, three days of protests against the war in Vietnam took place in Washington, D.C. Overreacting to statements by organizers that their purpose was to tie up the city, the police made some 13,000 arrests. It was the largest mass arrest in the country's history, justified by a spokesman for President Nixon, William Rehnquist—then an assistant attorney general before his appointment to the Supreme Court—under the novel doctrine of "qualified martial law." (Although responsibility for dealing with demonstrations normally rests with local officials, Nixon had signed an executive order assigning the task on this occasion to Attorney General John Mitchell, who directed local police operations. Mitchell relied on Rehnquist to provide a legal rationale for many of his law-enforcement innovations.)

As news bulletins of the numbers reached me in my office in New York, I called Florence Isbell and Ralph Temple, the director and legal director of the National Capital Area Civil Liberties Union, and suggested that the District police were probably using the same method as the New York police when they made mass arrests. Isbell and Temple quickly enlisted several volunteer lawyers to go to Robert F. Kennedy Memorial Stadium, where the demonstrators were taken to be booked. They found police officers selecting groups of defendants at random to whom they assigned themselves as arresting officers. Like their New York City counterparts, they were prepared to lie under oath when asked in court about the conduct they observed leading to the arrests. This became our basis for getting charges against almost all the antiwar protesters dismissed. In addition, after years of litigation, we ultimately succeeded in obtaining damages for many of those arrested.

In New York, April 27, 1968, confronted us with a major challenge. Large demonstrations against the war were scheduled along both sides of Central Park; a prowar demonstration was to take place in midtown; and a radical group known as Youth Against War and Fascism (YAWF) that had clashed repeatedly with the police was to assemble in Washington Square Park and march up Fifth Avenue. I was sure the last of these would cause the most trouble, decided to observe it myself, and enlisted eight volunteer lawyers for the NYCLU to join me. We assembled at my Greenwich Village apartment a few blocks from Washington Square Park where, over coffee and croissants, I briefed the observers. I told them not to get too close to the action so they would not get caught up in any arrests that might take place.

At Washington Square Park, the scene was not reassuring. The police had brought a lot of paddy wagons to transport arrested demonstrators. In addition to many uniformed officers, a lot of beefy men were standing around in scruffy civilian clothes wearing color-coded plastic buttons to identify themselves to each other as police. There seemed about as many of them as of the would-be demonstrators, most of whom were very young.

At the appointed hour, 150–200 antiwar demonstrators lined up on the sidewalk next to the park to begin their march. A few carried placards saying, "The Streets Belong to the People." A uniformed officer with a bullhorn stepped up in front to announce that the march was illegal. (It was not.) He ordered the demonstrators to disperse. They listened to him and then started to move forward. Within seconds, the men with the plastic buttons charged the marchers, kicking, punching, and wrestling them to the ground. As the marchers were subdued, they were led off to the waiting police wagons, often with additional kicks and punches along the way.

Our observers, wearing lawyerly suits and ties and thus looking very different from both the demonstrators and the police, stood a little distance away, watching the tumultuous scene. Two other observers were Jay Kriegel, a young lawyer who served as an aide to Mayor Lindsay, with responsibility for relations with the Police Department, and William Booth, a former judge who served as chairman of the city's Human Rights Commission. I chatted with both men before the demonstration began, speculating about what was about to happen but not anticipating that it would get so nasty. As we watched the beatings and the arrests, I saw a boy who had been thrown into a paddy wagon moments earlier jump out and try to run away. He was caught by one of the men with plastic buttons and surrounded by several of them, who seemed to be beating him as he lay on the ground. At that point, I violated the rules I had set for the other observers and went to peer over the shoulders of the men surrounding the boy to see exactly what was happening. I was promptly arrested myself and—more gently than the others—put into a paddy wagon. It turned out that one of my fellow occupants was Walter Teague, the leader of YAWF and a frequent client of the NYCLU. Sitting handcuffed on the bench inside the wagon, he looked up at me and said, "I thought you were supposed to be a conservative."

We were taken to a police station to be booked. As we arrived, so did one of the observers who had assembled at my apartment, Jeremiah Gutman. He had parked his Mercedes near the site of the demonstration and used it to follow the paddy wagon. "I am this man's lawyer," Gutman, who had a flamboyant manner, announced loudly to everyone in the station house as I was led in to have my name and address recorded. After a few minutes at the station house, I was put back in the wagon and driven to 100 Center Street, the city's main criminal court building, where I was put in a holding pen with about twenty other prisoners to await my turn for arraignment. After a few minutes, the presiding judge of the criminal courts appeared at the bars at the front of the cell to see me and to ask, in what I guessed was an unknowing echo of Emerson, "What are you doing in there?" I felt I could only respond in the manner of Thoreau, "What are you doing out there?" The judge didn't get it but went on to tell me that Kriegel, the mayor's aide, had called his office to let him know I had been arrested. He wanted to be sure I was treated properly. I assured him I was all right, but the same was not true of my fellow arrestees who had been beaten by the police and, in some cases, had sustained injuries.

Arraignment was embarrassing. Two lawyers from the Northern California ACLU happened to be in town. As we expected a lot of arrests, we invited them to see how the NYCLU coped with such matters. Many demonstrations were also taking place in San Francisco, and our colleagues might benefit from our experience. They were in the courtroom as I was arraigned, much amused that the show we put on for them included my arrest. I knew I would not soon live that down.

An hour later, I was back in my apartment in Greenwich Village telling Yvette about the events of the day. She knew I had been arrested because one of the other observers had called to tell her, and she was angry that Kriegel had not intervened to stop the police. Though not fond of Kriegel or the other Lindsayites with whom I had worked on civilian review, I defended him on the grounds that the mayor would come under fire if one of his civilian aides interfered with an arrest, no matter how un-justified. At that moment, the phone rang and it was Kriegel on the phone. He chatted with me for a few moments about Washington Square Park, but then urged me to focus on what was happening at Columbia Univer-sity. The student occupation of University President Grayson Kirk's office and several academic buildings had been under way for a few days. Ac-cording to Kriegel, the mayor's office was trying to hold back the police but could not do so much longer. They were intent on going in to beat up the students. He expected violence at Columbia far worse than in Wash-ington Square Park or at the Yip-In at Grand Central Station a few weeks earlier.

The takeover of the buildings on the Columbia University campus by some 800 students began on April 23, 1968, with a rally organized by SDS to protest the university's involvement in classified, war-related govern-ment research. At the rally, other grievances were also aired, including the university's plan to build a gymnasium on public park land separating the Columbia campus on Morningside Heights from the streets of Harlem below. Students marched to the construction site, where some tore down part of the fence around the site, leading to a confrontation with the po-lice and the arrest of one of the students. The occupiers of Hamilton Hall on the campus demanded that student's release.

In the next few days, the confrontation between students on one side and the university administration and the police on the other escalated until, starting about 2:00 A.M. on the night of April 29–30, buses brought more than 1,000 police to the campus to clear the occupied halls. I went to Columbia earlier in the day but, not anticipating what was in store that night, returned home by evening. The following morning, I found out what happened. More than 700 arrests had been made and more than 150 of those arrested required medical treatment for injuries of varying de-grees of seriousness. Though they met no resistance, the police were even more violent than they'd been in Washington Square Park. They had dragged students by the hair down flights of stone steps and beat them over the head with blackjacks and nightsticks, causing many severe lacera-tions and fractures. Bystanders not arrested were also injured. They in-cluded faculty members and other spectators. Some were hurt when mounted police charged them on a nearby street.

Led by Paul Chevigny, we set about collecting testimony from wit-nesses. Collaborating with Columbia's Sociology Department, we obtained detailed statements from 372 of the students, faculty, and journalists at the scene, and we published these in a 159-page report, *Police on Campus: The Mass Police Action at Columbia University, Spring 1968.* With the exception of a report published by a national commission that investigated the events in the parks and streets of Chicago a few months later during the Democratic Convention,[3] it was probably the best documented account of an episode of police violence published in the United States.

Three weeks after the demonstration in Washington Square Park at which I was arrested, on May 18, 1968, Youth Against War and Fascism assembled at the same spot to try again to hold their march. Once again, large numbers of uniformed and plainclothes police showed up at the site. The circumstances had changed, however. Police conduct at the earlier demonstration, and especially at Columbia, had been widely condemned. The police knew they were losing the public support expressed in the 1966 referendum on civilian review. Violence against black and Hispanic teenagers on the streets was one thing, but when it was directed against the middle-class students at Columbia University—even though their occupation of buildings was also condemned—it was quite another matter.

My own arrest at the previous Washington Square Park demonstration had attracted a lot of attention, including a front-page story in the *New York Times* on April 28. As a consequence, I was no longer just an observer. What might happen to me at the second try to hold the march was itself an issue, so the *Village Voice* hired a film crew to follow me about. This time, the police did not break up the march before it took place. They allowed the demonstrators to walk out of the park even though they had provided no route for their march.

The YAWF marchers set off at a fast pace, proceeding seemingly at random along the streets east of the park, chanting, "The streets belong to the people" and slogans denouncing police brutality. The police had a hard time keeping up, and I felt I should stay in range of the film crew. At a corner in the East Village an hour or so after the march began, with the marchers far ahead of us, I encountered a red-faced Sanford Garelik, chief inspector of the New York police and its highest-ranking uniformed officer. Or, rather, he encountered me. Garelik, who had taken personal command of a number of police mass actions, including the Yip-In at Grand Central Station in March and the raid on the buildings at Columbia, began screaming at me: "You're responsible for this. This is all because of you." His rage apparently reflected frustration that he could do nothing to stop the march, which continued for about another hour up and down East Village streets and then petered out with no harm done.

Later that same evening, Chief Inspector Garelik returned to Columbia and led a group of police in removing and arresting a group of students demanding that repairs be made to a university-owned tenement building on West 114th Street. This time, the police action was carried out with scrupulous restraint. All the police who took part were uniformed, and they did not carry nightsticks. A total of 117 arrests were made and several hundred people were cleared from the area without any reported injuries.

Three days later, on May 21, some 400 students reoccupied Hamilton Hall in protest against the way the university was handling disciplinary proceedings against those involved in the earlier occupations. I went to the campus that evening and stood outside the building chatting with Dwight MacDonald, speculating on what might take place. Because of the restraint at the second Washington Square Park demonstration and in the evacuation of the tenement building, I guessed the police would avoid violence. Unsure whether anything would happen that night, I returned home about 11:00 P.M., thus managing to miss the second battle of Columbia as well as the first.

Hamilton Hall was cleared without violence at about 2:30 A.M. by police who entered the building through underground tunnels. When word got out that the police were in the building, a crowd gathered outside to yell at them. To prevent more students from coming onto the campus, all the gates were locked and barricaded. At about 4:00 A.M., University President Grayson Kirk announced over the college radio station that the police had been ordered to clear the campus. This information did not get to many of those milling about, and, as the gates were locked, those who did hear of it had no place to go. Police charged those on the campus and, if anything, were even more violent than they had been three weeks earlier. Though they made fewer arrests, they caused almost as many injuries.

After the second battle of Columbia, mass police actions in New York became less violent. There was no letup, however, in "routine" brutality in individual encounters on the street until a couple of years later when Mayor Lindsay appointed a new police commissioner. The outgoing commissioner, Howard Leary, had been appointed because, in his previous post as commissioner in Philadelphia, he had worked with a review board with civilians on it, and he had expressed his readiness to cooperate with such a board in New York. This turned out to be no indication of how he would control police abuse. To succeed Leary, whose reputation was also tarnished by an investigation of rampant corruption in the department by a body known as the Knapp Commission (for its chairman, Whitman Knapp, subsequently a federal judge), Lindsay appointed Patrick Murphy. I had been introduced to Murphy several years earlier by George Rundquist when I became director of the NYCLU. Murphy was then commander of the New York City Police Academy, and he enlisted me to take part in some of the academy's training programs. (He also offered to let me use the academy's swimming pool on East 20th Street, a few minutes' walk from my office at 20th Street and Fifth Avenue. Momentarily tempted, I declined the offer, as it occurred to me that it might not be prudent to share a pool with a lot of police officers who were the targets of NYCLU lawsuits.)

In the years that intervened before he was appointed to lead the NYPD, Murphy served as commissioner of a number of other big city police departments where he compiled a distinguished record. He was commissioner in Washington, D.C., when Martin Luther King, Jr., was assassinated in 1968 and helped prevent the capital from going up in flames. A member of a family of police officers, he had risen through the ranks of the NYPD and knew the department well. As commissioner, he set about curbing abuses and demonstrated that this could be done. An example involved the use of firearms. Murphy required that a departmental hearing should be held every time an officer fired his gun, whether or not anyone had been injured. The result was a dramatic reduction in police shootings.

During the 1990s, police abuse again became a matter of intense debate in New York City and once again civilian review was an issue. The public pronouncements of former Mayor Rudolph Giuliani, and his contention that the decline in the New York crime rate was a direct consequence of aggressive policing—though a similar decline took place in other cities, such as Boston, where there was no comparable pattern of police abuse—were the moral equivalent of the 1966 referendum. If there is a lesson to be derived from the 1960s, it is that the composition of any board reviewing civilian complaints is not of great importance. What matters more is the expression of public opinion on police abuses.

The role of the mayor can be crucial. John Lindsay had little impact on police practices, despite his good intentions, because his support for civilian review and his appointments to the board antagonized the police. He compounded these political difficulties by appointing an ineffectual commissioner who served for several years. Rudolph Giuliani, in contrast, was in a position to control police abuses because he portrayed himself as the friend of the police. He enjoyed the political credibility to make it clear that abusive conduct would not be tolerated without seeming to betray the force he so resolutely defended. Also, he could have appointed a commissioner intent on stopping abuses. Instead, the commissioner who served longest under Giuliani, Howard Safir, seemed resolute on matching the mayor in refusing to acknowledge police misconduct. The quality of police leadership is the most important factor of all. Organized along military lines, a police department responds to the will of an effective commander. Civil liberties advocacy plays a part in limiting abuses, but there is no substitute, I discovered, for a mayor and a commissioner with both the determination and the ability to see to it that the guardians of the law are law abiding.

CHAPTER TWO

Defending Draft Opponents

I n August 1965, Representative Mendel L. Rivers of South Carolina proposed an amendment to the Universal Military Training and Service Act to make it a crime to "knowingly destroy" or "knowingly mutilate" a draft card. The amendment was prompted by an episode earlier in the year when some students at Berkeley had burned their draft cards to protest American intervention in the Dominican Republic, and by rising opposition to the war in Vietnam. It was adopted quickly by Congress. Previously, the main use of draft cards was by young men showing their age to buy a beer. Though widely regarded as proof of registration, the cards had no role in administering the draft.

It was not long before the new law was tested. That October, David Miller, a member of the pacifist Catholic Workers movement, got in touch with the NYCLU to let us know he would be burning his draft card at a rally against the war in front of New York City's draft headquarters on Whitehall Street in lower Manhattan. Miller was the first indicted for the newly minted crime. He faced a five-year prison sentence.

The following month, at another antiwar gathering in Union Square, five more young men burned their draft cards. I went to observe. The occasion was punctuated, at first startlingly, and then as I realized what was happening, somewhat comically, by a well-aimed spray from a fire extinguisher carried by one of those in attendance that put out the cigarette lighter flame used to burn the cards. Though this may have prevented the crime from taking place, four of those who had tried to burn their cards— Tom Cornell, Marc Edelman, Roy Lisker, and David Wilson—were indicted. The fifth, veteran antiwar activist David McReynolds, was not prosecuted, apparently because he was too old to be called up, though the law applied equally to him.

The NYCLU provided legal representation to each of these defendants, as we did in subsequent cases where indictments were brought. We argued, as in several cases that occurred about the same time involving flag burning, that this action was "symbolic speech" and as such deserved protection under the First Amendment. Those who did not hold public office and could not afford to purchase access to the mass media, I contended in essays I wrote at the time—sometimes citing A. J. Liebling's famous line that "freedom of the press is guaranteed only to those who own one"[1]— had to use visually dramatic ways to express their views. If they could not convey their ideas in a striking image that would appear in a newspaper or magazine, or in a few seconds on television, they could not compete in the marketplace of ideas. So long as they did not injure or interfere with others or damage the property of others, they should be free to express themselves by symbolic means. In the words of my ACLU colleague Franklin Haiman, the sit-ins, pray-ins, and other protest forms from that era were "body rhetoric." The U.S. Supreme Court was extending First Amendment protection to such conduct in civil rights demonstrations. I hoped it would do the same for antiwar protest activities such as draft-card burning.

Before such questions could be decided, however, I found myself embroiled in peripheral disputes with the U.S. Attorney's office prosecuting the Miller and Union Square draft card–burning cases. One involved a memorandum prepared by a law student intern in our office for the three attorneys we assigned to represent Miller: Henry di Suvero, a staff attorney; Marvin Karpatkin, a lawyer who played a leading role in the ACLU and was emerging as one of the country's foremost civil liberties advocates until his premature death of a heart attack at forty-eight; and Osmond Fraenkel. In passing, the memo stated that it was noisy at the rally where Miller burned his card. Those present could not hear what he said.

To our horror, the U.S. Attorney's office introduced this memorandum into evidence as part of the prosecution's case. The purpose was to show that the inability of those present to hear what Miller said contradicted our assertion that the burning of the card was part of his effort to communicate his views. It wasn't much of a point, but that was not our concern. The working papers of lawyers are confidential. We demanded to know how the U.S. Attorney's office had obtained our memo. Required to answer this question by the judge presiding over the case, the prosecutors eventually said the memo was found by a prisoner in the federal house of detention who turned it over to the government. We were unable to get more information, such as the identity of the prisoner who allegedly found the memo.

Although our attorneys had visited the house of detention a number of times while the trial was pending because, in those days, so many young men were held there in draft cases, this explanation was far-fetched. Copies of the memo were only distributed to the three attorneys handling the case. They did not make additional copies and did not carry the memo around with them. Moreover, the copy presented to the court by the prosecutors was unmistakably made from the copy belonging to Henry di Suvero, our staff attorney, as it showed the two-hole punch mark he used for his files. Yet the machine on which the prosecutors' copy was made was not the one in our office (in those days, photocopiers often left distinctive markings). We believed this was an FBI "black bag" job—not uncommon when J. Edgar Hoover directed the Bureau—but we did not know whether the U.S. Attorney's office knew how it had been obtained or whether the story that a prisoner found the memo was simply told to the prosecutors, who chose to believe it.

Though we were never able to resolve the provenance of the copy, it embittered our relations with the office of the U.S. Attorney for the Southern District of New York, Robert Morgenthau. He remains, as of this writing, district attorney of New York County (seemingly for life). He is a highly respected prosecutor, but we clashed with him repeatedly on civil liberties. Many of our disputes with Morgenthau involved draft cases. We objected to the practice by his office of seeking high bail in cases in which young men with solid claims for conscientious objector status were prosecuted for evading the draft. There was little likelihood those defendants would flee to avoid trial; if they wanted to go to Canada or Sweden, they could have done so before they were indicted, thereby evading the risk of arrest and improving their prospects for eventual return to the United States. Setting bail high simply ensured they were held in jail in advance of trial where the FBI would visit them and try to intimidate them to give up their conscientious claim and accept conscription.

The U.S. Attorney's zeal in draft cases was exemplified by the case of Vincent McGee, a divinity student at Union Theological Seminary. Though he could have readily obtained an exemption from the draft as a seminarian, McGee chose to express his opposition to the war by declining to cooperate with the draft. For this, Morgenthau prosecuted him on two counts of violating the Selective Service law, each carrying a five-year sentence.[2] At his trial, he testified that he had torn up a number of draft cards that had been sent to him, and for this he was indicted on four additional counts. After he was sentenced to prison for two years on each count to be served concurrently, we continued to press appeals on his behalf. As an appellate court prepared to consider his release on the grounds that his sentence was too harsh, a parole commission convened. McGee was released after serving more than ten months in prison. (While in prison, he was "adopted" by Amnesty International as a "prisoner of conscience." Years later, he became Chairman of Amnesty USA, and today he is a well-known foundation executive.)

Our most acrimonious dispute with Morgenthau was over the Union Square Park protests. Morgenthau's office convened a federal grand jury in the case. Those summoned to testify were the organizers of the rally where the draft cards were burned, including the grand old man of the American antiwar movement, A. J. Muste. (Muste was not new to the destruction of draft cards as a form of protest. He was a speaker at a rally in New York on February 12, 1947, at which, according to Dwight MacDonald, "63 persons destroyed their draft cards in the presence of reporters, cops, FBI agents and an audience of about 250" in a protest against conscription and preparations for war. MacDonald wrote that 400–500 persons destroyed their draft cards or mailed them to President Truman on that date. The participants in the 1947 protests were not prosecuted because no law then made it a crime to destroy a draft card.[3]) Concerned when early witnesses told us they had been interrogated about their views on the Vietnam War, we arranged to have stenographers (this was the 1960s) go to the courthouse. As witnesses emerged from the grand jury room, we had them immediately dictate all the questions they recalled.

The statements we obtained were consistent with what we had heard from earlier witnesses. The U.S. Attorney questioned them at length on their views of the Vietnam War. As this was highly improper, I organized a press conference to denounce use of the grand jury to investigate matters clearly protected by the First Amendment. A photo the *New York Times* published to accompany its account of this press conference brought my relationship with Morgenthau—such as it was—to its lowest point. It showed me standing with my arm extended, pointing *J'Accuse* style. When I saw it in the paper the next day, I recalled the moment when I was pointing in that way. It was before the press conference actually began: I was motioning to an associate in the back of the room to close the door. A press photographer had captured the moment. Published in connection with my accusation that Morgenthau's office violated First Amendment rights, it suggested I had embarked on a crusade.

Morgenthau denied that his office was investigating such matters. At the next meeting of the NYCLU board, one member reported that Morgenthau had called him to complain about me and to express outrage over the press conference. Morgenthau had said that he had called that person because he was the only board member he knew. Two other board members, however, reported getting similar calls from Morgenthau. Each said Morgenthau professed not to know anyone else on the board. Another member, Helen Lehman Buttenwieser—a famously feisty lawyer whose father had served as governor of New York and as a U.S. senator and who was among my strongest supporters—interjected to point out that she did not get such a call even though she was Morgenthau's cousin. This provoked laughter as we all knew she would give him a hard time if he called. It helped create an atmosphere in which the board gave me its solid backing in a dispute with a figure who was already an icon in New York City. It took years until a transcript of the sealed grand jury proceedings was made available, and only then could we prove that the questions asked were just as the witnesses recounted to our stenographers. By then, of course, public interest in the matter had long evaporated.

On April 15, 1967, a large antiwar rally, the Spring Mobilization for Peace, was held in New York City. It was a notable occasion. Public sentiment against the Vietnam War was rising sharply. Hundreds of thousands of New Yorkers marched to the United Nations Plaza for a rally addressed by prominent speakers including the Rev. Martin Luther King, Jr., who was denounced in newspaper editorials across the country for mixing the issues of race with opposition to the war. Dwight MacDonald noted that "*Time* even got in a few sneers at some American Indians who headed the march. (If they don't like it here why don't they go back where they came from?)"[4] As was common in that era, more radical groups used the occasion to stage their own protests against the war. One of the events planned for the day was a mass draft-card burning in Central Park.

The evening prior to the Spring Mobilization, the would-be draft-card burners assembled in a dingy lower Manhattan hall to discuss their plans. The organizers asked me to speak to the group about the legal consequences they would face. In my talk, I took care not to endorse what they were planning to do and limited myself to explaining the law and telling them what had happened in the prosecutions brought up to that point. I mentioned that in all the cases I knew about, the FBI had recovered fragments of the burned cards and prosecutors had used these as evidence against the draft-card burners.

The next day, about 150 young men purportedly burned their draft cards in Central Park, taking care that the cards were completely consumed by the flames; "purportedly" as there could be no way for an observer to tell what they had burned. For all anyone knew, they could have set fire to photocopies of the cards or other bits of paper of the same shape and size. None of the Central Park 150 were prosecuted.

More than a decade later, I obtained part of my FBI file and discovered that one prosecution had been considered. An agent or informer was present at my talk to the prospective card burners. Noting my remarks, the Bureau referred the matter to U.S. Attorney Morgenthau's office for possible prosecution of *me* for obstructing justice. The U.S. Attorney's office declined to prosecute "in the interests of the United States." I am confident that I would have prevailed on First Amendment grounds, but it would have been very unpleasant to be indicted. It was sobering to discover that I owed the decision not to prosecute to an office with which I so frequently did battle.

The failure to prosecute those who said they burned their draft cards in Central Park illustrated what was wrong with the law making this a crime. There was no circumstance in which any agency of government required someone to produce a draft card to facilitate its performance of its duties. Even if production were required, it was no crime to lose or misplace or accidentally destroy a card. Only protest was criminalized. Federal officials could ascertain that someone actually burned his card, and prove it in court, only by recovering an identifiable fragment. Lacking such evidence, and unable to coerce defendants to testify against themselves, prosecutions would founder. Nevertheless, in 1968, the U.S. Supreme Court upheld the constitutionality of the law against draft-card burning in *United States v. O'Brien*[5] as a valid exercise of the congressional war power. Only Justice William O. Douglas dissented in this case in which the First Circuit U.S. Court of Appeals had previously sustained the ACLU's symbolic speech argument. As a consequence, most of those prosecuted for burning their cards served three years in prison, the standard sentence federal judges imposed for this crime.

D raft cards figured prominently in the most celebrated prosecu-
tion of opponents of the Vietnam War: the indictment in Boston on January 5, 1968, of Dr. Benjamin Spock, the Rev. William Sloane Coffin, Jr., Mitchell Goodman, Marcus Raskin, and Michael Ferber for conspiring to obstruct the draft. I played two bit parts in the case: as a protagonist in an internal battle within the American Civil Liberties Union over whether we should provide direct representation to the defendants, and as a trial witness for Dr. Spock.

The case was peculiar. Though the charge was conspiracy, the defendants barely knew each other. Most of the overt acts cited in the indictment were clearly protected by the First Amendment: signing and distributing a public statement, making speeches, and participating in demonstrations. The only overt act charged that had more substance was the one involving draft cards. Four of the defendants (all but Ferber) were accused of entering the Justice Department building in Washington on October 20, 1967, along with other unindicted coconspirators, where they "abandoned a fabricoid briefcase containing approximately one hundred eighty-five (185) registration certificates and one hundred seventy-two (172) notices of classification together with other materials."

The prosecution arose out of a dispute within the Johnson administration. Frustrated by the failure of the Justice Department to prosecute war opponents who were publicly advocating resistance to the draft, Selective Service System director General Lewis Hershey sent a letter on October 26, 1967, to the nation's more than 4,000 local draft boards, calling on them to reclassify young men of draft age who participated in "illegal demonstrations" and induct them immediately. This created a public storm over the use of the draft to punish conduct that in many cases was protected by the First Amendment. It quickly produced a slew of court cases for the American Civil Liberties Union and its affiliates. President Johnson reacted by ordering his disputing subordinates to settle their differences. Six weeks later, General Hershey and Attorney General Ramsey Clark issued a joint statement announcing the formation of a special unit in the Justice Department to investigate and prosecute violations of the Selective Service law.

The indictment the following month of "The Boston Five"—the defendants chosen for their high public profile and because they represented different sectors of the antiwar movement—was the consequence. It was the closest thing to a political show trial in the United States in the period following World War II. Other possible contenders for that distinction are the prosecution of the twelve (then eleven) top Communists in 1948–1949 and of the Chicago Eight (then Seven) after the confrontations between antiwar demonstrators and the Chicago police at the 1968 Democratic Convention. I think the case of the "Boston Five" takes pride of place for the selection of individuals as well known as Spock and Coffin from among many others who did as much or more to oppose the draft. (Ramsey Clark's part in this prosecution comes to mind whenever I see one of the insufferably sanctimonious statements that have become his hallmark when he takes up the cause of some particularly reprehensible defendant. His practice seems to be not only to defend the rights of his clients—an honorable role—but also to become the champion of their causes, however obnoxious or bizarre.)

The national legal director of the ACLU, Melvin Wulf, immediately issued a public statement denouncing the indictments of Spock and the others, saying the ACLU was ready to represent all the defendants. At the time, the New York Civil Liberties Union customarily provided direct representation to defendants at the trial stage and was doing so in scores of draft cases. In contrast, the national ACLU largely restricted itself to participating in cases at the appellate level, where the focus was on discrete legal questions raising civil liberties issues, and often dealt with these through submissions of amicus curiae (friend of the court) briefs rather than by direct representation of clients. This practice permitted the ACLU to maintain a certain distance from the litigants on whose behalf it intervened, many of whom held views that were anathema to the ACLU. Public statements by the ACLU in those days frequently included lines such as, "Our only client is the Constitution." Mel Wulf, who had joined the ACLU staff a decade earlier and was appointed legal director by Jack Pemberton, was attempting to play a more activist role with some success, but he was often constrained by the national body's deeply ingrained resistance to close identification with clients such as the Boston Five.

In accordance with this tradition, the ACLU board of directors held a meeting the following week and, by a vote of 11 to 4, repudiated Wulf's statement and declined to provide direct representation. In their own reactions to the indictment, the defendants spoke about putting the draft and the Vietnam War itself on trial. The ACLU had no stand on those matters. Hence, the only appropriate way to participate, a majority of board members argued, was as amicus curiae on First Amendment issues arising in the case.

The ACLU board's decision was disingenuous. Whatever the defendants said about putting the draft and the war on trial, it was apparent that the judge presiding over the case would not allow this. All overt acts spelled out in the indictment involved activities the ACLU considered well within the First Amendment rights of the defendants. From first to last, the trial was about civil liberties. It was a crucial opportunity to uphold rights we were committed to defend. I found it unthinkable for the ACLU to shun direct representation.

As director of what was then the largest and most influential ACLU affiliate—the NYCLU declined greatly in relative size and significance subsequently—I presented the matter to our board, which called on the ACLU board to reverse its stand. In addition, I contacted other state affiliates. Several joined in our call to the ACLU board. One of my phone calls was to Gerald Berlin, chairman of the Civil Liberties Union of Massachusetts (CLUM). Berlin invited me to attend a meeting of the CLUM board in Boston, and there, the affiliate on the scene voted to provide representation to defendants who sought its help. (This was permissible, as the ACLU Constitution provided that relations between the national organization and its state affiliates should reflect "general unity without uniformity.") Two did, so William Homans became CLUM's lawyer for Michael Ferber, the youngest of the defendants, a Ph.D. candidate in the English Department at Harvard when he was indicted; and Edward Barshak represented Mitchell Goodman, a novelist and the husband of poet Denise Levertov. (About this time, Rev. Coffin, the chaplain of Yale University, and I appeared together as speakers at a public forum. Afterward, Coffin asked if I would serve as his counsel. I told him I would be delighted to do so, but there was one small impediment: I am not a lawyer.)

The actions by the state affiliates forced the ACLU board to consider the matter again. At the time, the national board was in the middle of a process that would transform it. When Roger Baldwin was director, almost all board members lived in the New York area and met for lunch every Monday.[6] After Roger retired in 1950, the frequency was reduced and meetings were held every other Monday over lunch. Governance by this tight-knit, clubby group was no longer sustainable as the network of state affiliates, a few of them comparable in the scale of their operations to the parent body, expanded to cover the country. An awkward system developed in which the state affiliates were represented on the board but met as a national body only infrequently to deal with long-range issues. The New York area board members continued to meet biweekly.

Reconsideration took place at an emergency meeting of the expanded board, which voted 26 to 20 to back CLUM in providing direct representation. That vote made no difference to the Boston Five, as CLUM's attorneys were already representing Ferber and Goodman and the other defendants had by then arranged their own representation. But it meant a lot for the ACLU, steering it in the direction of the NYCLU and several other state affiliates in placing primary emphasis on entering cases at trial in direct representation of clients. It also spelled the end of the bifurcated board of directors. Thereafter, representatives of the state affiliates participated in all board meetings, which became two-day affairs every other month.

I was called as a witness for Dr. Spock in the Boston Five's trial because I observed a demonstration in front of the Whitehall Street draft headquarters in New York on December 5, 1967. The demonstration was scheduled to start at 6:00 A.M., the hour some draftees were required to report. Plans were carefully worked out in advance with the New York Police Department. They called for participants to sit down on the sidewalk in front of the building momentarily and then submit peaceably to arrest. Concerned nevertheless that there might be trouble, I arrived at the scene an hour early with Ira Glasser, whom I had hired earlier that year, and found a large pen constructed in the street out of police barricades. The pen was entirely surrounded by police officers standing shoulder to shoulder. As the first to arrive on the scene other than the police, we were let into the pen to wait for the demonstrators to arrive. The wait was unpleasant, both because it was dark and bitterly cold at that early hour and because the police officers signaled their readiness for trouble by rapping their nightsticks on the barricades, producing a menacing sound.

When the demonstrators showed up at 6:00 A.M., however, everything proceeded according to plan. They lined up to be let into the pen, walked around inside in a circle, and were let out at the steps immediately in front of the draft headquarters. Each in turn sat down on the sidewalk in front of the building and, after a few seconds, was gently led away by police officers and put into a paddy wagon. This routine continued for two or three hours, and hundreds of arrests were made. Dr. Spock was at the head of the line of those arrested. Another of the Boston Five, Mitchell Goodman, was also there, but when the time came for him to be let through the barricades, they were closed. Perhaps no more paddy wagons were available. Goodman called out, "Inspector Garelik, Inspector Garelik." After getting the attention of the NYPD chief inspector, who, as usual, was on the scene, Goodman asked to be let through "to commit civil disobedience." He was granted permission, sat on the sidewalk for a few seconds, and was taken off.

My testimony in defense of Dr. Spock, and that of Mayor John V. Lindsay, who testified about the painstaking planning for the demonstration and the arrests, in which he had directly participated, showed that the entire event had been carefully choreographed. (When the demonstration was being planned, David McReynolds—one of the organizers—had expressed the hope that he would be arrested very quickly because it was cold in New York in December and he didn't want to sit on the pavement too long.) In subjecting themselves to arrest, the demonstrators had engaged in a classic form of civil disobedience. They had harmed no one and had caused no interference with a government function but succeeded in calling attention to their public protest against the draft and the war in Vietnam. As John Rawls has argued, when civil disobedience is conducted in this manner, "It expresses disobedience to law within the limits of fidelity to law, although it is at the outer edge thereof."[7]

At trial, four of the five defendants were convicted. The exception was Raskin, a White House disarmament specialist under President John F. Kennedy, and subsequently a founder of the Institute for Policy Studies. He was represented by Telford Taylor, the former chief U.S. prosecutor at Nuremberg and a great defender of civil liberties as well as a Pulitzer Prize–winning historian and a scholar of the laws of war. The strong bias against the defendants by Judge Francis J.W. Ford, eighty-five at the time, who conducted the trial before a jury, was undoubtedly a factor in the convictions. Typically, at a bench conference with counsel that was supposed to be out of earshot of the jury, he derided two defense witnesses in a tone loud enough to be audible throughout the courtroom as "your two so-called priests." His rulings almost invariably sided with the prosecution. I thought one of the defendants, Rev. Coffin, and his counsel, James St. Clair, also contributed to the outcome. Testifying in his own defense,

Coffin answered questions from St. Clair about the most important episode at issue, the delivery of draft cards in the "fabricoid briefcase" to the Justice Department:

> QUESTION: Now, sir, did you at that time believe that the delivery of the draft cards to the Attorney General would hinder or impede the function of the draft?
> ANSWER: Certainly not.
> QUESTION: Why not?
> ANSWER: Because turning in a draft card speeded up a man's induction and in no way impeded induction. [Coffin was referring to General Hershey's scheme of punitive reclassification.]
> QUESTION: How did you believe it speeded induction?
> ANSWER: I knew a man lost his 2-S deferment [that is, deferment while a student] and became a 1-A delinquent [subject to immediate induction] if the government chose to use this occasion to change his classification.

As Jessica Mitford observed in her book about the case, this statement was "too clever by half."[8] It seemed to me that the argument was legalistic in the worst sense, undercutting an essential element of the defense: These were men of principle who opposed the war and the draft as a matter of conscience. Their protests were reasonable ways to express strongly held views. The pretense by Coffin that he was actually engaged in an effort to speed up inductions fooled no one. It not only lacked credibility, but worse, made the defendants seem unprincipled. I have no way of knowing how Coffin's testimony affected the jury, but I recall the groans among those who sympathized with the defendants when they heard of it. (A few years later, when President Richard Nixon hired the same lawyer, James St. Clair, to defend him against impeachment, I told friends that Nixon was doomed.)

On July 11, 1969, the verdict was overturned on appeal on the grounds that Judge Ford's instructions to the jury had deprived the defendants of a fair trial.[9] Though the appellate decision left open the possibility that two defendants, Coffin and Goodman, could be retried, the Justice Department did not pursue the matter. By then, the tide had turned in the courts. In one ACLU Selective Service case, the U.S. Supreme Court ruled in December 1968 that removal of a divinity student's statutory exemption from the draft for turning in his draft card was "basically lawless";[10] and in another of our cases a year later, the High Court invalidated General Hershey's entire scheme of designating as delinquent and subject to immediate induction those who took part in protests against the war.[11] The Nixon administration, which took office in January 1969, and its attorney general, John Mitchell, felt no responsibility to honor Ramsey Clark's commitment to General Hershey and let the matter drop.

Though I was the same age as many of the draft opponents we represented, I never had to decide what to do if I were called up. I was spared from making that choice by the unintended consequences of actions by military and Selective Service officials who wanted to punish me for a minor rebellion of my own.

When I attended Cornell in the 1950s, enrollment in the Reserve Officers Training Corps (ROTC), as at other land grant colleges, was compulsory. But I got into a dispute with Lieutenant Colonel Hugh Osborne, who commanded ROTC at Cornell, over a form we were asked to sign. Colonel Osborne sent a letter to my draft board saying I had "a negative attitude toward military training and lack of motivation essential in an officer." As a consequence my local draft board denied me a student deferment. That meant I could be called up at any time. But I turned eighteen in 1955, after the end of the Korean War, and reached twenty-six in 1963, just before the United States began sending large numbers of soldiers to Vietnam. When President Kennedy was assassinated on November 22, 1963, America had 15,500 troops in Vietnam. As there was little need for conscripts in that era between our Asian wars, I never got a draft notice. A student deferment would have extended the years I was eligible. I could have been drafted up to the age of thirty-five if Osborne had not given me that negative report. Three years after Lyndon Johnson became president, the number of American troops in Vietnam had soared to 400,000, and this number would rise to 525,000 by 1968.

I don't know how I would have responded to "Greetings," the government salutation used on all induction notices. Colonel Osborne was right about my negative attitude toward military training and I certainly was not eager to go to Vietnam. However, I was physically fit. In common with almost all whose worldview was shaped by World War II, I was no conscientious objector. Nor, as an immigrant with a background as a refugee, could I imagine leaving the country. Probably, my only choice would have been to go. Colonel Osborne and my draft board inadvertently spared me.

T imes of war are bad for freedom of speech, in the United States as elsewhere. Probably the lowest moment for the First Amendment in American history was during World War I and its immediate aftermath. Discussing the Espionage Act adopted by Congress on June 15, 1917, after the United States entered the war, the scholar known in his time as the country's leading authority on freedom of speech, Zechariah Chafee, Jr., wrote:

> It is unnecessary to review the two thousand Espionage Act prosecutions in detail, but a few general results may be presented here. The courts treated opinions as statements of fact and then condemned them as false because they differed from the President's speech or the resolution of Congress declaring war. . . . Under the second and third clauses against causing insubordination or obstructing recruiting, only a few persons were convicted for actually urging men to evade the draft or not to enlist. Almost all the convictions were for expressions of opinion about the merits and conduct of the war.
>
> It became criminal to advocate heavier taxation instead of bond issues, to state that conscription was unconstitutional though the Supreme Court had not yet held it valid, to say that the sinking of merchant vessels was legal, to urge that a referendum should have preceded our declaration of war, to say that the war was contrary to the teachings of Christ. Men have been punished for criticizing the Red Cross and the YMCA, while under the Minnesota Espionage Act it has been a crime to discourage women from knitting by the remark, "No soldier ever sees these socks. . . ." All genuine discussion among civilians of the justice and wisdom of continuing a war thus becomes perilous.[12]

The war in Vietnam was far more deeply divisive in the United States than World War I was. It also took a heavy toll on civil liberties. Scores of thousands of Americans were arrested for exercising their First Amendment rights to take part in peaceable protests against the war. Thousands more were imprisoned because the Selective Service System did not accept their claims of conscientious objection to the draft or for crimes such as turning in or burning their draft cards. Others fled the country for Canada, Sweden, or some other country to escape the choice of conscription or prison.

Yet it cannot be said that the prosecutions during the Vietnam War had anything like the impact of those that accompanied World War I. There was never a moment when everything to do with the war was not robustly—even fiercely—debated. The difference, I believe, is that by the time of the Vietnam War, the courts had established many protections for freedom of speech that did not exist in an earlier era. Judges were not ready to abandon those precedents because of the passions generated by the war. Any tendencies in that direction were strenuously resisted by a civil liberties bar ready to litigate all threats to freedom of expression. In the 1960s and 1970s, thanks to the spirit of the era and the special way it affected the legal profession because of the Warren Supreme Court, thousands of American lawyers stepped forward to handle such cases without a fee. Most did so under the auspices of the ACLU. At any earlier period, only a handful of lawyers would have been available to play such a role.

The American Civil Liberties Union was born in 1920 out of an attempt to make permanent the systematic defense of civil liberties that began during World War I. Though the national ACLU waffled initially when the Boston Five were indicted, it soon righted itself—just as it had done a quarter century earlier when Franklin Roosevelt began relocating and interning Japanese Americans, thanks to the leadership of Arthur Garfield Hays, Osmond Fraenkel, and Norman Thomas. Overall I believe its defense of war opponents and draft resisters during the Vietnam War was one of the ACLU's finest hours. It is in difficult times, such as in the period since September 11, 2001, that the organization's mettle is tested. The ACLU has risen to the current challenge, and I believe it also did so the last time that its efforts were reviled by many Americans as unpatriotic. Our unstinting defense of freedom of expression then, not only on behalf of antiwar activists and conscientious objectors but also in such matters as the Pentagon Papers case in 1971, has helped to ensure that this is not one of the areas in which our civil liberties are likely to be threatened during today's war against terrorism. The opportunity to take part in organizing the defense of objectors to the Vietnam War is one of the high points of my career.

CHAPTER THREE

Opening Asylums

Not long after I began work at the New York Civil Liberties Union, I took a phone call from a woman at New York's Bellevue Hospital, an institution well known for its psychiatric division. She had been on the Staten Island Ferry with her husband, a blind man. Somehow, in a crush of people getting off the boat, she was separated from him and became distraught. A policeman was summoned. Apparently deciding she was crazy, he took her to Bellevue. She was admitted for observation for a thirty-day period. My caller told me she had been unable to contact her husband and was worried about him. He did not know where she was and so could not contact her. Up to that moment, she said, she had not been able to use the phone. She called the Civil Liberties Union only because a helpful attendant took a chance.

At the time, I knew little about mental commitment. The issue was not on the civil liberties agenda. I had not then read the works of Thomas Szasz, the psychiatrist who had long crusaded against the deprivation of liberty on grounds of mental illness. It came as something of a shock to me to discover that New York State law permitted the involuntary hospitalization of someone for thirty days on the basis of an allegation—by a policeman, a family member, a neighbor, or anyone else—that the person needed "immediate observation, care or treatment for mental illness." (In Tennessee Williams's *A Streetcar Named Desire* of a slightly earlier era, Blanche is taken away to a mental hospital at the instigation of her brother-in-law, Stanley, after he rapes her. His complaint suffices to end her liberty.) There was no requirement for a hearing before a judge where the allegation had to be proven or the person could rebut it. The law did not even require that a doctor endorse confinement. Someone held for thirty days could be confined for another sixty days if two physicians agreed the person was mentally ill. The inmate could ask for a hearing at that point. Under the influence of the drugs routinely administered in Bellevue and other such institutions, however, many did not exercise that right. Some began a lifetime of confinement without ever appearing before a judge for a hearing to determine whether they should be deprived of liberty.

We got the woman out of Bellevue in fairly short order. She quickly located her husband, and they were reunited. But the case left me wondering what role the ACLU and its affiliates could play in dealing with confinement of those accused of mental illness. We got involved in a few more cases that helped me to learn more about the subject. When I thought I had some grasp of the issues in the field, I drafted a proposal for funding and persuaded three small family foundations to provide grants to support the establishment in 1968 of a Civil Liberties and Mental Illness Litigation Project. It was our second special project; one of the donors, the Norman Foundation, had also supported the first, our Police Practices Project. I recruited a lawyer, Bruce Ennis, from a Wall Street law firm to direct the project. He had volunteered his services to the NYCLU after he saw me take part in a televised debate with William F. Buckley and was one of the lawyers who watched me get arrested at the demonstration in Washington Square Park earlier that year. Though he had no background in dealing with mental illness, I guessed Bruce would be a quick study.

It turned out to be one of my best hiring decisions. A man of contrasts who carried himself with great dignity in a courtroom and by thirty had a gravitas when he appeared before a judge or a jury matched by few lawyers twice his age, he projected a rather different image to those who saw him riding his motorcycle. Bruce, who died of leukemia as I was writing this book, ended up having a transforming impact on the lives of mental patients and the mentally retarded in the United States. He became a coolly passionate advocate of their rights and—through a combination of arduous preparation, strategic calculation, incisive intelligence, commanding courtroom presence, and excellent rapport with his clients—as effective a litigator as any with whom I had the opportunity to work.

At roughly the same time we began suing mental hospitals, we also started to deal with prisons and juvenile institutions. Up to the 1960s, the general rule with respect to prisons was that what happened inside was not the business of the legal system. The courts adopted a "hands off" policy. "We think it is well settled," a U.S. Court of Appeals said in 1951, "that it is not the function of the courts to superintend the treatment and discipline of persons in penitentiaries, but only to deliver from imprisonment those who are illegally confined."[1] The decision, rejecting the effort of Robert Stroud, the "Birdman of Alcatraz," to obtain the right to correspond with a publisher, reflected the law's prevailing attitude that prisoners had only those rights their jailers permitted. One judge's concurring opinion was blunter: "A judge . . . should not be compelled to listen to such nonsense." Prisoners were, as some court decisions put it, "slaves of the state."

As in so many other fields, this all changed in the 1960s. Several factors were at work. First was the confinement of two new categories of prisoners: black Muslims and opponents of the Vietnam War. The Muslims sought the same right to worship as other prisoners, pork-free meals, and the ability to get their movement's newspaper. The war opponents also wanted publications not ordinarily circulated in the prisons. I recall one prisoner in a draft case who wrote to us to complain that the warden barred him from receiving *The New York Review of Books*. These were First Amendment issues, an area where the courts were comfortable. They could rely on well-established doctrines to uphold the rights of prisoners. Also, those prisoners belonged to organized movements. They had access to lawyers prepared to pursue constitutional questions.

Another factor was a decision by the U.S. Supreme Court in a 1961 case brought by the Illinois ACLU involving police abuse, *Monroe v. Pape*,[2] that made it possible to bring cases for violations of constitutional rights by state authorities directly to federal courts. This landmark decision, second in importance only to *Brown v. Board of Education* seven years earlier in making possible the rights revolution of the 1960s and 1970s, proved particularly important in cases involving state prisons and other asylums. State judges are elected with the support of the political parties in their state or appointed by the governors of their state. They were not inclined in those days—nor are they much more inclined today—to question the administration of state institutions. Federal judges appointed for life, in the era before judicial selection was as politicized as it is now, were not comparably beholden. It was in the federal courts that the "hands off" doctrine began to disintegrate.

Probably the most important factor of all was the spirit of the era. The rights revolution, inspired by the U.S. Supreme Court in *Brown, Monroe,* and other decisions, and by civil rights demonstrators in the South, had consequences everywhere in the 1960s. It even reached into the prisons.

One of the attorneys who began representing prisoners in the 1960s was Herman Schwartz, then a professor of law at the State University of New York at Buffalo, an active volunteer lawyer for the NYCLU, and someone with whom I have collaborated in efforts to protect rights at every stage of my career up to the present moment. In 1969, Herman told me he thought he could open an office in Attica Prison—about thirty miles away from Buffalo—where prisoners would have access to him to discuss cases. Would the NYCLU sponsor the project? I readily agreed. Ultimately, he was denied permission to establish the office, but he commuted regularly to Attica and filed a number of lawsuits for the NYCLU in federal courts dealing with conditions of confinement. In 1971, when the Attica uprising took place, the rebellious prisoners asked that Herman mediate between them and the state authorities. He was the first outsider to enter the section of the prison taken over by the inmates during the riot. He attempted to negotiate a peaceful settlement, but any chance of success ended when Governor Nelson Rockefeller ordered the state police to retake the prison. They did, slaughtering thirty-nine inmates and hostages.[3]

O ur entry into juvenile institutions, as in the case of mental hospitals, began with a phone call I got at the NYCLU. This time it was not an inmate but a judge of one of the state's family courts who got in touch with me. Judge Beatrice Burstein told me she made it a practice to visit all institutions to which she sent those who appeared in her court. In one such institution where children were confined, she had obtained a list of the inmates, but noticed that a fourteen-year-old girl, Nettie Lollis, was missing. After some probing, she found the girl in solitary confinement in a stripped room with no access to recreation where she had been held for two weeks for a disciplinary infraction. Nettie had talked back to a matron who had scolded her for wearing cosmetics. Lacking authority to do anything about the matter on her own, Judge Burstein asked us to start legal proceedings to get the girl out of solitary.

We filed a lawsuit in federal court that resulted in a landmark decision holding this treatment to be cruel and unusual punishment in violation of the Constitution.[4] In addition, we looked into the reasons Nettie Lollis was in that institution. She was what New York law referred to as a PINS: a "person in need of supervision." (In other states, this might be CINS, JINS, or MINS, for a child, juvenile, or minor, respectively, in need of supervision.) New York law defined a PINS as a child under sixteen who does not attend school as required or "who is incorrigible, ungovernable or habitually disobedient and beyond the lawful control of parents or other lawful authority." It was not necessary for anyone to show she had committed a specific violation of the law. New York has delinquency laws to punish such acts. It was the status of being "incorrigible" or "ungovernable" that led to her confinement.

S oon after becoming executive director of the American Civil Liberties Union in 1970, I launched a National Prison Project, a Juvenile Rights Project, and, in collaboration with two other organizations, the Center for Law and Social Policy and the American Orthopsychiatric Association, established an independent group known as the Mental Health Law Project, later named the Judge David L. Bazelon Center on Mental Health Law. The last of these was an outgrowth of a court case that played an important role not only in efforts to protect the rights of the mentally ill but also of the mentally retarded.

Our involvement in the case began soon after I assumed my new post as ACLU director when a prominent Alabama lawyer, George Dean, got in touch with me. He told me he had been retained by members of the staff at a mental hospital, Bryce State. Previously, according to Dean, Alabama was last among the fifty states in its per capita spending on patients in state hospitals. Then, Governor George Wallace cut spending further in an effort to reduce the state budget. As a result, Dean's clients had been fired. In his attempt to help them regain their jobs, Dean had filed papers with a federal court saying the state's action denied inmates of Bryce a right to treatment. The case had come before a renowned federal judge, Frank Johnson, Jr., an Eisenhower appointee. Judge Johnson was known for his role in cases against racial segregation, such as the Montgomery bus boycott case, the Freedom Rider cases, and many other civil rights struggles of the era. His role in these matters had inspired the enmity of

Wallace, who denounced him during his 1962 gubernatorial campaign as an "integrating, scalawagging, carpetbagging, bald-faced liar." Wallace's rhetoric, in turn, had probably inspired some of the efforts by others to intimidate Johnson—none successful—such as the arson of his mother's home. Judge Johnson was interested in the claimed right to treatment and had ordered a hearing on what constituted such a right. At that point, Dean, an experienced and able lawyer, decided he needed help.

I put Dean in touch with Bruce Ennis. At the time, Bruce was already involved in a Florida case on the right to treatment that would eventually result in a landmark U.S. Supreme Court decision, *O'Connor v. Donaldson*[5] (discussed below). Bruce went to Alabama to help Dean. So did another lawyer who had experience with the right to treatment, Charles Halpern, director of the Center on Law and Social Policy, who became the attorney in the case for the American Orthopsychiatric Association, a professional group committed to civil liberties for patients.

The conditions at Bryce State Hospital, with a population of about 5,000, were terrible. Aside from administrative staff, only two full-time psychiatrists and one psychologist with a Ph.D. cared for the patients. Most of the time, patients sat around a bare dayroom with nothing to keep them occupied except a television set that worked intermittently. In short order, Judge Johnson ruled that the inmates of Bryce were denied their constitutional rights because "to deprive any citizen of his or her liberty upon the altruistic theory that the confinement is for humane therapeutic reasons and then fail to provide adequate treatment violates the very fundamentals of due process."[6]

Yet even Bryce turned out to be less bad than another institution brought into the lawsuit, Partlow State School, where Alabama confined some 2,400 mentally retarded men, women, and children. As Bruce Ennis described what he saw on a first visit:

> There were eighty to ninety [residents] to a ward, often staffed by only one attendant. Partlow was so crowded that many residents had to sleep on floor mats. The conditions were barbaric. We saw a man who had been locked in solitary confinement for seven years. A little girl was tied to her bed—otherwise she would try to stand—because there was no one there to catch her if she fell. Agitated residents stuffed dirt and rocks down their throat or lapped garbage water like dogs; we saw one woman in a strait jacket trying to spit the flies out of her mouth. Helpless children lay

for hours in pools of urine. Everywhere was hopelessness, neglect, and despair.[7]

Bruce's choice of words echoing Dante's *Inferno* was deliberate.

In launching programs to deal with mental hospitals, prisons, and juvenile institutions, I had until then neglected institutions for the mentally retarded that I should have put in the same category. I was ignorant of the plight of the retarded, my only excuse being that none ever got in touch with us. Almost by definition, the retarded themselves were in no position to seek our assistance. Even their families generally knew little about conditions at institutions like Partlow. Some had little or no contact with their institutionalized relatives. When they saw them, it was in visiting areas where the retarded were often unable to convey what conditions were like in the living quarters.

There were even then well-developed and politically influential associations of parents of retarded children. These were mostly parents who cared for their children at home. The organizations represented and served the interests of those families. An attitude I encountered three decades ago from some members of those groups was that parents who put their children in institutions deserved what they got. This was understandable as parents who kept their retarded children at home often made them the center of their lives. They had difficulty sympathizing with parents whom they considered uncaring. In general—though there were many exceptions—inmates of institutions for the retarded came from poorer families and were more severely retarded than those cared for at home. If they were not severely retarded when placed in institutions, the children deteriorated in confinement. Many families of inmates had difficulty identifying with their retarded relatives or felt guilty about putting them away, and so abandoned them.

In 1972, while Bruce was in Alabama litigating conditions at Partlow before Judge Johnson, a young lawyer turned investigative journalist for ABC-TV, Geraldo Rivera (*that* Geraldo Rivera), broadcast some film he had shot without the management's permission showing conditions in a New York institution for the retarded, Willowbrook. Occupying a pleasant-looking campus-like facility of about 300 acres on Staten Island with many squat brick buildings, Willowbrook's wards, which held about 6,000 inmates, were every bit as dreadful as those at Partlow. Conditions there had been a public issue several years earlier for a brief time when Senator

Robert F. Kennedy had made a surprise visit. Nothing had changed as a result. The television images Rivera broadcast provoked a renewed public outcry, however. They also inspired Bruce to turn his attention to Willowbrook as soon as he returned to New York from Alabama. Contacting a few parents who wanted to do something about the care of their children there, he filed a lawsuit for the NYCLU over treatment, or its absence, at Willowbrook.

The Willowbrook case was heard by Federal District Judge Orrin Judd. He was troubled by the claim of a right to treatment because, unlike mental patients, the retarded were not confined against their will. So far as mentally ill patients are concerned, Bruce's argument in the Alabama case and in the Florida case then on its way to the U.S. Supreme Court, *O'Connor v. Donaldson,* was that non-dangerous mentally ill patients stripped of their liberty must be accorded treatment designed to help them regain their freedom. If not, their confinement is incarceration without due process of law. This became known as the quid pro quo argument. As the retarded at Willowbrook were admitted with the consent of their parents, who were their legal guardians, however, and as their parents could remove them at will, arguments about deprivation of liberty without due process seemed out of place to Judge Judd. But he visited Willowbrook during the course of the litigation, was appalled by what he saw, and came away persuaded he had to do something for the inmates.

Relying on precedents such as old cases asserting that southern sheriffs had a duty to protect their prisoners from lynchings, Judge Judd ruled that the State of New York was obliged to protect the inmates of Willowbrook from harm. Once the state takes custody, he said, it incurs obligations to the retarded even if their admission is voluntary. New York had failed in that duty because confinement in Willowbrook exacerbated the retardation of the retarded. Deterioration, Judge Judd recognized, was inevitable if the retarded were not provided with a full range of education and training programs. He ruled that the state's obligation to protect those in its custody from harm requires it to provide adequate programs.[8]

A new governor, Hugh Carey, expressed a willingness to enter into a settlement to remedy the conditions at Willowbrook and commit the state to providing programs. During his electoral campaign, in an interview conducted by Geraldo Rivera, Carey pledged that, if elected, his first order of business would be to visit Willowbrook. Bruce Ennis took Carey up on this and took him on a tour. Carey was shocked by what he saw. The incident that upset him most was his discovery of a man tied spread-eagled to a bed exactly where Bruce predicted he would be because the man had been kept in that position for years. Seeing flies crawling over the man's face, the governor, exasperated, demanded to know from officials of Willowbrook accompanying the tour whether the state could afford a fly swatter. Carey then directed aides to negotiate a settlement.

Over the next couple of months, Bruce and Peter Goldmark, Carey's budget director, negotiated line by line a twenty-nine-page, single-spaced document that comprehensively set forth the programs the state would provide to comply with Judge Judd's decision. The settlement required the population of Willowbrook to be reduced over six years to no more than 250, the number of inmates estimated to come from Staten Island. The remainder were to be prepared for placement in community facilities housing no more than fifteen persons each (in the case of the mildly retarded) and no more than ten persons each for all others. In addition, the settlement—which was approved by Judge Judd and then became known as the consent decree—established a seven-member review board to oversee its implementation. Those provisions revolutionized care for the retarded.

Transferring the retarded from Willowbrook to community residences of no more than ten or fifteen persons each was no easy task. In Willowbrook, many of the retarded people had grown up and become adults or even middle-aged without learning to feed themselves, clothe themselves, or take care of their bodily functions. When they soiled themselves, they were hosed down by attendants. Before they could live in small supervised residences, they had to acquire social skills. An anecdote in a book about the Willowbrook case by David and Sheila Rothman, who, like Herman Schwartz, have been my collaborators at every phase of my career, suggested the difficulty: "A month after a number of blind and deaf clients from Willowbrook moved into their group homes, they and their staff went out for a walk. A few minutes later, it started to rain and the clients, to the staff's bewilderment and horror, started to take off their clothes. As the counselors frantically tried to keep them covered, it dawned on them that the clients assumed it was shower time at the facility. They had never before felt the rain."[9]

To prepare the Willowbrook 6,000 for community residence, intermediate institutions were required. They included the Bronx Developmental Center (BDC), which was housed in a building that was one of the masterworks of noted architect Richard Meier. The BDC, which began operation in the mid-1970s, was described rapturously in an architectural guide of that period:

> Dramatically located on a spacious and serene site along the edge of the Hutchinson River Parkway, its long prismatic forms evoke the majesty of a rectilinear dirigible. Clad in a tightly stretched skin of natural anodized aluminum panels, it looks as if it were fabricated by an aircraft manufacturer, not by earth-bound building contractors. Windows, resembling enormous elongated portholes, add to the machine-age look, as does the proud expression of the intricate and colorful central mechanical system which controls the building's inner environment. It is a consummate work of architecture and is sure to be ranked among the great buildings of its time.[10]

The BDC's architectural splendor was not matched by its suitability in preparing former residents of Willowbrook to live in an ordinary community setting. At a forum I organized with historian Thomas Bender at New York University on the architecture of confinement, Richard Meier was asked why he put those elongated porthole windows at floor level. He responded that when visiting institutions for the retarded while preparing to design the building, he saw that the inmates spent a lot of time sitting or lying on the floor. Meier said he wanted them to be able to look out the windows. To another question, he answered that his inspiration for the building was the Monastery of Saint Gall, a great work of early medieval architecture noted for its serenity. Yet the purpose of the consent decree was to assist the retarded in living like others. They should not spend their time sitting or lying on the floor, and their environment should not be as self-enclosed, inward looking, and peaceful as a monastery. The retarded needed to acquire the ability to live in the noisy, bustling, fast-paced environs of a city.

Despite the architecture, BDC operated in a way that assisted former residents of Willowbrook in making the transition. Apartment-like settings were created in the building. Staff knocked on apartment doors and sought permission from residents before entering. Residents left their apartments in the morning for field trips, shopping, educational programs, and workshops outside the building. They returned in the late afternoon to eat dinner in their own apartments rather than in the BDC's communal dining hall. After dinner they often went out again for bowling or a movie. Dr. Herbert Cohen, the young psychiatrist who became director of the center when it opened, told me with some pride that residents even attended performances of the New York City Ballet without embarrassing themselves or the BDC.

From the BDC—which, in disregard of its architectural virtues, is being gutted and transformed into commercial office space at this writing—former inmates of Willowbrook, including the severely retarded (IQ of 20–40) and the profoundly retarded (IQ of 0–20), categories covering about 5 percent of the retarded population, or about 300,000 people nationwide, went to live in supervised apartments. They were assisted by "homemakers" and neighborhood teams serving many apartments that included team leaders, psychologists, social workers, mental retardation nurses, teachers, occupational therapists, physical therapists, and job counselors. Bus services were provided to educational programs and to jobs in such occupations as wrapping packages. The BDC continued to provide outpatient medical and psychiatric care and speech therapy to former Willowbrook inmates after they made the transition to apartment residences. Though the cost of such services is high, it is not as great as the costs the state would incur if it confined the retarded in Willowbrook in more or less decent conditions.

A crucial factor in the shift to community care was the support of associations of families of the retarded. Though such groups previously distanced themselves from the institutionalized, they enthusiastically embraced the Willowbrook consent decree because it provided the retarded with a semblance of the normal living conditions to which the families were devoutly committed. Without their political clout, the community care approach could never have gotten so far.

Notoriously, many of the homeless who appeared on the streets of American cities in the 1970s and 1980s were former inmates of mental hospitals. Their deinstitutionalization resulted from three factors that coalesced and reinforced each other. The first, and by far the most important, was eagerness by some state officials, led by Governor Ronald Reagan in California and Governor Nelson Rockefeller in New York, to reduce state budgets by cutting expenditures on mental hospitals. Before deinstitutionalization, some states spent more on their mental-health departments than on any other state agency. Second was the widespread introduction of long-lasting psychoactive drugs. These permitted administration of such drugs once every two or three weeks instead of three or four times a day. Often, the only outpatient care available to former mental patients is the drug treatment they receive to control their behavior and make them docile or even zombie-like. Third, and probably least significant, was civil liberties litigation challenging denials of reasonable standards and due process in the civil commitment process, seeking better conditions of confinement, and attempting to end long-term custodial confinement— that is, incarceration—of the non-dangerous mentally ill without treatment. Though outweighed by the other factors, civil liberties litigation was not negligible. Because a focus of our court cases was improving conditions of confinement and ensuring adequate treatment, we drove up the cost of confining those accused of mental illness. This added urgency to efforts by state officials to cut costs by cutting the number of inmates held in mental hospitals. In addition, we gave them a principled rationale— though this did not seem important to most officials—for emptying the vast institutions that warehoused the mentally ill.

What is generally overlooked, however, is that the mentally retarded, deinstitutionalized during the same period, rarely ended up on the streets among the homeless. The legal theories that freed the mentally ill did not require judges and state officials to provide them alternative care such as supervised apartments or outpatient treatment. Where such care is provided to the mentally ill, it is not because of litigation. In contrast, the Willowbrook approach, which recognized that confinement exacerbates the retardation of the retarded and requires that they be protected from harm, compels the state to provide care outside institutional settings to assist them in leading lives as near normal as possible. As some other states followed the Willowbrook approach, deinstitutionalization of the retarded was both a civil liberties and a social policy success. Unhappily, I concede that deinstitutionalization of the mentally ill was a civil liberties success but, for many of those released and for their urban neighbors, a social policy failure.

An important factor in that failure was the absence of a lobby comparable to the associations of the families of the retarded to take up the cause of community care for the mentally ill. That no effective group entered the fray reflects the differences between the two forms of handicap. Mental retardation is evident at birth or soon thereafter. Dealing with it is often the foremost concern of parents. If anything, parents of the retarded I have known seem to me even more devoted to the well-being of their children than other parents. Mental illness, in contrast, is more often manifested in adolescence or during adult life when families are no longer preoccupied with care for their children or when bizarre behavior may estrange them. Some associations of former inmates of mental hospitals have formed, but they are a far less formidable lobby than the organized families of the retarded.

Conceding a social policy failure in dealing with the mentally ill does not imply that I regret the civil liberties success. Many of those deinstitutionalized or freed, like Kenneth Donaldson, for whom we won a landmark victory in the U.S. Supreme Court in 1975, are simply entitled to liberty. When Donaldson was forty-eight, his elderly father filed a petition with a court in Florida for a sanity hearing for his son. The younger Donaldson, a divorced carpenter, had expressed suspicions that someone was tampering with his food. His father alleged that Kenneth was paranoid and suffered from a persecution complex. Police arrested him and brought him before a judge, who ordered an examination that took place the same day before two physicians (not psychiatrists) and a deputy sheriff. It was, at best, cursory. The three signed a form saying Donaldson suffered from paranoid schizophrenia. At a subsequent hearing before the judge, Donaldson demanded that the doctors come forward to say why he was crazy. No doctor appeared in court. This hearing lasted a few minutes, after which the judge signed another form remanding him to the Florida State Hospital. He was held there for fifteen years, one among some 5,000 inmates, in degrading and at times brutal circumstances. Donaldson never again appeared before a judge and rarely saw a doctor. A typical medical visit, according to Donaldson, consisted of the doctor asking three questions:

"What ward are you on?"
"Are you taking medication?"
"Are you working any place?"
"That will be all."

A literate man, Donaldson repeatedly sent petitions to courts, including the U.S. Supreme Court, asking for a hearing. Eventually, in denying one of those petitions, the Supreme Court said it did so without prejudice to his right to seek relief from a U.S. district court. This backhanded way of saying there might be an issue in his petition worth considering finally led to a hearing before a federal judge. Just before the hearing was to take place, Florida State Hospital decided Donaldson had suddenly become sane, released him, and asked the judge to dismiss Donaldson's complaint on the grounds that the case was moot.

By then, Donaldson had the assistance of Morton Birnbaum, who was both a medical doctor and a lawyer and pioneered in promoting the concept of a right to treatment, and Bruce Ennis. They persuaded the federal judge that Donaldson's case was not moot because he sought damages for his confinement without treatment for fifteen years. The judge held a jury trial on the claim for damages that resulted in an award of $38,500 to Donaldson. Florida appealed. Ultimately, that led to a unanimous decision by the U.S. Supreme Court that "a state cannot constitutionally confine without more a non-dangerous individual who is capable of surviving safely in freedom by himself or with the help of willing and responsible family members or friends. Since the jury found, upon ample evidence, that O'Connor [superintendent of Florida State Hospital], as an agent of the State, knowingly did so confine Donaldson, it properly concluded that O'Connor violated Donaldson's constitutional right to freedom." The opinion vacated the portion of the jury's decision awarding Donaldson $38,500, probably because a brief from the American Psychiatric Association objected to holding psychiatrists individually liable. Donaldson had to settle for $20,000 for the fifteen years he was wrongfully confined in Florida State Hospital.

I first met Kenneth Donaldson after his release when Bruce Ennis brought him to my office. A pleasant and intelligent man, he did not seem embittered by his fifteen years of custodial confinement. Although he was sixty-three at the time and of course had not held a job for many years, his genial manner and evident acuteness helped him to find work as a clerk and an auditor at a hotel and to hold on to that job without encountering difficulties.

It is impossible to say how many among the hundreds of thousands accused of mental illness freed from mental hospitals in the deinstitutionalization of the 1970s were, like Kenneth Donaldson, capable of caring for themselves, and how many required substantial outpatient services or care in noninstitutional settings where they could retain their civil liberties. In any case, the state was not willing to provide the resources that were needed to assist the mentally ill outside of institutional settings. In spearheading their cost-cutting measures, the Reagans and the Rockefellers released the inmates of mental hospitals without assuming the costs—even though they were substantially lower—of outpatient treatment. (In Reagan's California, the reduction in the population of state-funded mental hospitals was accompanied by a sharp rise in the number of inmates of nursing homes eligible for federally funded Medicaid reimbursement. The actual savings were illusory. In fact, some of the state's nursing-home operators became leading donors to the California governor's electoral campaigns.) My part in that failure is that my focus was on wrongful confinement and wrongful treatment in confinement. It was not also on providing services to those we helped to free. This was, I regret to say, a shortcoming of my civil liberties perspective. The legal theories on which we based our efforts on behalf of the mentally ill, unlike the protection from harm theory that Judge Judd relied upon in Willowbrook, did not compel the state to provide community care.

If we had focused on providing services to the mentally ill outside of institutions, however, it is not evident we would have made a difference. We would have had to persuade judges and legislatures, and even then we might not have succeeded in the absence of a lobby on behalf of community care for the mentally ill comparable to the associations of families of the mentally retarded, who made it possible for the elements of the Willowbrook consent judgment to be replicated across the country. Whatever the chances of success, however, they do not excuse my own failure to anticipate the unintended consequences of deinstitutionalizing the mentally ill.

I n the case of prisons, our focus in that era, when the incarcerated population was only a fraction of what it is today, was on conditions of confinement. The uprising and slaughter at Attica, which made conditions in prisons an important public issue in the early 1970s, persuaded the courts to extend greatly the range of complaints they were willing to consider. The ACLU's National Prison Project took the lead in bringing cases challenging cruel conditions and asserting a prisoner's rights to a hearing before punishment within prison, to due process in probation and parole matters, and to adequate medical care. We also challenged censorship of prison mail to eliminate unflattering opinions about prison officials and other matters unrelated to security. We filed lawsuits that were comprehensive challenges to conditions in state prison systems. The courts responded with decisions ordering sweeping changes and, in several instances, appointed special masters to take control of prisons away from state corrections agencies to ensure the judge's orders were carried out. Between 1974 and 1977, we persuaded federal courts to require major changes in the operations of entire prison systems in eight states: Alabama, Florida, Louisiana, Mississippi, Nevada, Oklahoma, Rhode Island, and Wyoming.

The Alabama case[11] was the most publicized, both because of the wretched conditions in the prisons and because the case was decided by the same judge, Frank Johnson, who had led the way in upholding a right to treatment for mental patients at Bryce and for the retarded at Partlow. His decision became the focus of renewed attacks against him by Governor George Wallace. Wallace accused Johnson of wanting to confine prisoners in hotel-like comfort and added—in a comment that was vintage Wallace—that he would like to see Johnson get a "barbed wire enema."

In his decision, Johnson wrote, "The indescribable conditions in the isolation cells required immediate action to protect inmates from any further torture by confinement in those cells. . . . As many as six inmates were placed in four foot by eight foot cells with no beds, no lights, no running water, and a hole in the floor for a toilet which could only be flushed from the outside." Johnson's decision that this was unacceptable apparently inspired Wallace's reference to "hotel-like comfort."[12]

The case we brought against Rhode Island for the way it treated prisoners demonstrated that atrocious conditions were prevalent in prisons in all parts of the country, not only in the South. One aspect of prison conditions in Rhode Island was unique: As a very small state, it had a single prison in those days, the Adult Correctional Institute, with maximum-, medium-, and minimum-security buildings. About 125 pretrial detainees were held in the maximum-security building along with some 300 sentenced prisoners. Prisoners were frequently shifted between buildings, often after suffering sexual assaults by other prisoners.

In 1977, the year after Judge Johnson decided the Alabama case, Federal District Judge Raymond Pettine ruled that conditions at the Adult Correctional Institute "were a total environment where debilitation is inevitable, and which is unfit for human habitation and shocking to the conscience of a reasonably civilized person." (The judge's use of the word "debilitation" reflected the discrediting of the idea of "rehabilitation" in that era. Advocates of the rights of prisoners tried to turn this around by pointing out the debilitating effects of prison conditions.) Judge Pettine cited filth, fire and safety hazards, lack of sanitation, inadequate lighting, deafening noise, midday cell temperatures of fifty degrees in January, unbearable heat and dampness in the summer, enforced idleness, a "dangerously low standard of medical care," and rampant violence.

Worst was the treatment of the pretrial detainees. Some were ultimately acquitted of the crimes for which they were held, while others were sentenced to no more time than they had spent awaiting trial. They got the harshest conditions, as they were held in the maximum-security building, but were denied any opportunities for prison jobs because they did not spend extended periods of time there. "It is truly shocking," Judge Pettine wrote, "that convicted felons are routinely warehoused for years in the less than human atmosphere of ACI, but it is absolutely intolerable that the same treatment is accorded to pre-trial detainees who have not yet been found guilty of the offense with which they are charged and yet are kept for months in Maximum in the midst of convicted inmates and denied even the meager access to constructive programs that the latter enjoy."[13]

Though the National Prison Project accomplished much, I had difficulty raising funds for it. The very first contribution came from the Playboy Foundation. When I was chosen director of the ACLU, one of the congratulatory calls I received was from a Chicago lawyer, Burt Joseph, a friend who had been involved in the failed effort to desegregate Deerfield, Illinois, several years earlier. When he called, Burt said he also had a new job. What was it? In his private practice, as a well-known lawyer in free-speech cases, Burt was serving as counsel to *Playboy* and would also be devoting part of his time to chairing the Playboy Foundation. He thought the foundation could help me implement the new agenda I planned for the ACLU. It was not difficult to persuade Burt to support our work on prisoners' rights, both because he was himself active in the Illinois ACLU, where he had become familiar with such issues, and because *Playboy* had its own interests at stake. Many prisoners wanted to subscribe to the magazine. Our insistence that they retained rights under the First Amendment could enable them to do so.

The next contribution also involved an element of self-interest. I was approached by a young woman who was the daughter of a well-known and wealthy toy manufacturer. Her father headed the firm that made Lionel Trains. She told me she was close to someone who was going to prison and therefore wanted to contribute to the ACLU's efforts to protect prisoners' rights. I did not ask about the prospective prisoner, and she did not volunteer any details, but I guessed that a friend or a relative was probably a draft resister. Many were then being sent to prison. Several weeks later, when the *New York Times* began publishing the Pentagon Papers, her contribution helped me to guess the source. About the time she contributed, I read an unusually well-informed article in *The New York Review of Books* about Laos and Vietnam by Daniel Ellsberg,[14] someone whose name I had not known previously, and wondered whether he was connected to my visitor, Patricia Marx Ellsberg. Given the immense importance of the First Amendment issues at stake, the ACLU immediately intervened in the court cases brought by the government against the *New York Times* and the *Washington Post* to suppress publication of the Pentagon Papers and, like many others at the time, I speculated privately about who had leaked them to the press. But I had the advantage of knowing that Ms. Ellsberg was close to someone who faced prison and that this might be another Ellsberg who knew a lot about the Vietnam War. Putting two and two together was not difficult.

I learned a more surprising twist to the story somewhat later. Daniel and Patricia Ellsberg subsequently told me that I had been responsible for delaying his disclosure of the Pentagon Papers. How so? I had been speaking at a conference at Columbia Law School on civil liberties issues related to the Vietnam War. During a break in the proceedings, the couple had approached me to pose a question. This was before Patricia Ellsberg visited me in my office to offer a contribution, and I did not know who they were. Apparently, however, Dan Ellsberg was already engaged in photocopying the papers with the idea of making them public. In hypothetical terms, he described what he was doing and asked my opinion on the possible consequences. I turned to one of my ACLU colleagues who was with me at the time and asked his view. "About twenty or thirty years," he said. Thoughtlessly, I responded, "That sounds about right to me." This was more than the Ellsbergs had imagined. When they told me later how this affected them, I had forgotten the exchange, but I remembered well the conference where it took place and had no doubt their recollection was accurate. It made me resolve to take greater care in the future not to dispense off-the-cuff advice, even for supposedly hypothetical situations.

By far the largest and most steadfast supporter of the National Prison Project and, during my tenure at the ACLU, our biggest donor overall was the Edna McConnell Clark Foundation. A Florida lawyer who was vice president of the foundation, Rod Petrie, played a crucial role in helping us launch both the National Prison Project and the Mental Health Law Project. Later in the decade, a labor economist who had previously served as president of Haverford College, Jack Coleman, was appointed president of the Clark Foundation. Coleman was known for studying work in America by getting himself hired as a dishwasher at a luncheonette and other jobs requiring manual labor. Jack followed the same path at Clark, getting himself committed to a prison and also serving for a period as a prison guard in Texas. Building on Rod Petrie's efforts, he made the Edna McConnell Clark Foundation into a leading force for prison reform.

Despite Clark's support, I ran into trouble sustaining the National Prison Project and, at a moment when it was enjoying great success in the courts, found it necessary to tell the director, Al Bronstein, that we would have to make substantial cutbacks. We had to let go of some of the lawyers on the project staff. This was a disaster, as they were handling complex court cases we could not abandon. We reached a critical point one December. I called all the potential donors I could think of, without success. Then, I had a lucky break. Struck by a description in *The Foundation Directory* of the W. T. Grant Foundation, with which I had no previous contact, I called its president, Philip Sapir. After a few minutes of conversation on the phone, he suggested I come over that afternoon. The foundation's chairman, a psychiatrist from Cleveland, was coming into New York. I could meet with both of them.

I did so, and we spoke for three hours. They had never dealt with prisons previously, but that seemed no barrier to their readiness to consider support. By the time I got to the office the next morning there was a message from Sapir. When I called him back, he told me that he and the chairman of the foundation were making an immediate grant to the National Prison Project in accordance with their discretionary authority between board meetings and would recommend a grant for the balance of what we needed at the next meeting. I called Al Bronstein and told him to revoke the notices of dismissal and to wish everyone on his staff a Merry Christmas. It was one of the best experiences I ever had with a foundation.*

---

*Many years later, when I myself became president of a foundation, I thought often of Rod Petrie, Jack Coleman, and Philip Sapir and of another person who held such a post, Leslie Dunbar of the Field Foundation. Leslie actually initiated some of the efforts in which the ACLU became involved, such as the establishment of the Center for National Security Studies. Their approaches were very different, but what united them was a readiness to act boldly. Although foundations are institutions that are almost unique in their autonomy, I regret to say that boldness is not a common characteristic of the fraternity I have joined.

Afer I left the ACLU in 1978, the National Prison Project continued to challenge conditions in prison systems across the country. Its court victories had a dramatic impact in eliminating many gruesome and degrading aspects of incarceration and in reducing the prevalent lawlessness. Prisons remain nasty, brutish places; sexual violence between prisoners continues to be commonplace; and new abuses emerged, such as those associated with private profit-making and "supermaximum" prisons. Even so, conditions such as those in Alabama, Rhode Island, and many other states in the 1970s improved dramatically for a decade or more as a consequence of litigation in which the ACLU's National Prison Project led the way.

Unfortunately, the impact of some of our efforts proved temporary. They were defeated by the rapid increase in imprisonment that took place in the quarter of a century since my departure from the ACLU. A recent Associated Press account of Alabama prisons described conditions reminiscent of those that prevailed when we went before Judge Johnson in the 1970s. "Alabama's troubled corrections system was thrown into crisis today when two sheriffs sent more than 200 inmates from their overcrowded jails to state prisons where cellblocks were already packed," the A.P. reported. "Armed with a court ruling, sheriffs in Jefferson and Houston counties delivered inmates who were supposed to be in state lockups, not in crowded county jails where prisoners have little choice but to sleep on floors and tables. ... A federal judge, U. W. Clemon, last month described jail conditions in Morgan County as 'medieval,' with inmates squeezed into quarters so cramped they resembled a 'slave ship.'"[15]

Looking back, whatever satisfaction I derive from our effectiveness in ameliorating the conditions of confinement in the 1970s is tempered by awareness that I did not anticipate the explosive growth of incarceration during the 1980s and 1990s and did not set in motion programs to check that growth. Indeed, I am sorry to say that some of my efforts may have inadvertently contributed to that growth.

An increase in incarceration was already evident during my tenure at the ACLU. When I started dealing with prisons and jails in the mid-1960s, their population was about 400,000; when I left the ACLU in 1978, that figure had risen to close to 500,000, or a 25 percent growth in about a dozen years. The increase accelerated dramatically in the 1980s and the 1990s, so that by 2000, about 2 million people at a time were incarcerated in the United States. The number imprisoned today for nonviolent drug offenses by itself exceeds the total of all prisoners held for every variety of crime in the mid-1960s. It also exceeds the combined total of all prisoners held for all offenses in all fifteen countries of the European Union. Worldwide, only Russia, Kazakhstan, and one or two other countries of the former Soviet Union now match the United States in the proportion of their nationals incarcerated. Our rate of incarceration is six to ten times higher than in the countries of Western Europe.

There are many reasons for the growth in imprisonment: the war on drugs; racial profiling by the police; the U.S. Supreme Court's vitiation of Fourth Amendment protections against search and seizure; mandatory minimum sentences; "three strikes" laws; the elimination of parole in many states; efforts by state legislators from rural areas to get prisons built in their districts; the powerful lobbies that have emerged of prison construction firms and prison guards; and a broad public acceptance of the unproven assumption that the growth in imprisonment is a major factor in the decline in crime rates over the past decade. (One example of why this is unproven: Imprisonment has gone up most dramatically in the South, least in the Northeast. But crime—especially violent crime—has declined most in cities such as New York and Boston, but least in the South.)

In the early part of the nineteenth century, when Quaker reformers invented the precursors of contemporary prisons, the purpose of confinement was rehabilitation. Over time, the primary purpose became deterrence. Briefly, in the 1970s, a reform rationale for confinement that reflected an earlier Kantian approach to justice, retribution, or "just deserts," became popular. Today, though the language of retribution is still used, the main purpose is incapacitation. A retributive approach—to which, in essence, I subscribe—does not require the extended prolongation of sentences of the past two decades and it is at odds with the incarceration of hundreds of thousands of drug users and small-time distributors. They are locked up because many Americans feel safer with a lot of other Americans, especially young black males, behind bars for long periods. No more crimes are committed than twenty years ago, most violent crimes have declined, and no more arrests are made, but sentences are very much longer.

My own unwitting contribution to the growth of incarceration was to advocate elimination of parole on the grounds that the criteria for granting or denying conditional release from prison are unrelated to the severity of the crime committed, and because the procedures employed by parole boards are completely lacking in due process.[16] This was a widely held position by civil libertarians in that era, as exemplified by the work of an organization called the Citizens' Inquiry on Parole and Criminal Justice, which published a comprehensive report on parole in New York State.[17] We wanted judges to control the length of sentences. Our objection was not to the possibility that sentences could include a period of restricted liberty, but to the arbitrary decision-making process. Unfortunately, in a period when many state legislators and governors were intent on demonstrating their toughness on crime, when black youths were being portrayed as "super-predators" who had to be locked away forever, and when significant lobbies with economic interests at stake emerged for more prisons, the elimination of parole simply became one of the ways to lengthen prison sentences, thereby quadrupling incarceration rates. With the advantage of hindsight, there is much I would do differently. Yet, I am glad of the opportunity to play a part in introducing the rule of law into closed institutions and trust that others who share my beliefs will yet find ways to learn from my mistakes and achieve better results.

CHAPTER FOUR

Legalizing Abortion

J ust weeks after I became director of the New York Civil Liberties Union in 1965, we adopted a policy that laws criminalizing abortion were unconstitutional and should be repealed. No other branch of the ACLU had yet taken such a stand. From time to time, Dorothy Kenyon,[1] an outspoken and sharp-tongued former New York City judge appointed to the bench by Mayor Fiorello La Guardia in the 1930s, a strong feminist, and one of the few women on the ACLU board of directors, tried to raise the issue in the national organization. She pressed the abortion issue in the ACLU board with her customary verve. To no avail.

Although hardly anyone else was speaking out for repeal of criminal sanctions at that time, reform of the abortion laws was being discussed. A taboo was smashed in 1962 when an Arizona television personality, Sherri Finkbine, host of a popular children's show and a married mother of four, pregnant again, discovered that a drug she was taking contained thalidomide, which was by then known to cause severe birth defects. Finkbine's attempt to obtain an abortion in Arizona became a cause célèbre. Failing in her bid, she went to Sweden for the procedure. The doctors who performed the abortion reported that the fetus was badly deformed.

The Finkbine case stirred wide debate but did not directly lead the NYCLU to take a stand. More prosaic factors led us to adopt what was then a revolutionary position. A commission created by the New York legislature had proposed comprehensive revision of the state penal law. We established a committee chaired by a prominent attorney on our board, Ephraim London, to review the revision line by line so we could offer comments. A teacher and a scholar as well as a litigator, Ephraim was noted for representing literary and theatrical figures called before the House Un-American Activities Committee such as New York Shakespeare Festival founder Joseph Papp and criminal defendants such as Lenny Bruce when the comedian was prosecuted for obscenity. When we got to the passage in the penal law on abortion, Ephraim asked whether any member of the committee thought the state could properly make it a crime. None did. Ephraim then presented the matter to the NYCLU board, which readily agreed.

At the time, our main grounds were that the abortion laws impermissibly established religion as they were based on a religious theory of when life begins, and they violated "substantive due process." The latter is a doctrine of dubious constitutional standing invoked by the courts in the latter part of the nineteenth century and the early years of the twentieth century to strike down social welfare legislation such as laws regulating wages, hours, and other labor conditions. We embraced it in considering abortion because it had been rehabilitated a few years earlier in a notable dissent by Supreme Court justice John Marshall Harlan.

There was scant constitutional authority for a right of bodily privacy or of privacy in personal relationships. Privacy is never mentioned explicitly in the Constitution. The issue arose, however, in a Connecticut case in which the ACLU was involved that challenged a state law prohibiting possession and use of contraceptives. A majority of the Court declined to rule on the law's constitutionality because no prosecution had been brought against the two married couples and the physician who sued. In his dissent, Justice Harlan wrote that due process "is not merely a procedural safeguard"; it also protects rights that are "fundamental . . . which belong to the citizens of all free governments." Those rights, he said, include protection against "an intolerable and unjustifiable invasion of privacy in the most intimate concerns of an individual's personal life."[2]

An element not considered in the NYCLU board's discussion of abortion was women's rights. In those days we took on few cases on behalf of equality for women. One involved a group of airline stewardesses—in the days before they were known as flight attendants and included both sexes. The stewardesses had complained that they would be forced to retire at age thirty-two or thirty-five (depending on the airline) or even earlier if they married. Our lawsuit became moot when they won elimination of those rules in labor negotiations. The principal lawyer for a major airline in these negotiations tried to persuade me that the union leaders, most of whom were reaching this early retirement age, had sold out their younger colleagues by accepting a lower wage package than they otherwise could have obtained as part of the deal. He didn't get it when I told him I thought they felt demeaned by being treated as flying sex symbols, and that this wouldn't change so long as only young girls could hold these jobs.

The NYCLU's concept of women's rights in 1965 embraced such blatant employment discrimination but did not yet include a right of a woman to control her own reproduction. That was a few years off.

In June 1965, soon after the NYCLU took its stand, the Supreme Court again ruled on the Connecticut law on contraceptives, this time striking it down because arrests actually had been made for possession. The Court's opinion in *Griswold v. Connecticut,* in which the ACLU also participated, was written by Justice William O. Douglas. It did not rely on substantive due process as the basis for a right to privacy. Douglas said this right emanates from several provisions of the Bill of Rights that "create zones of privacy." He cited the right of association protected by the First Amendment; the prohibition on quartering soldiers in anyone's home in times of peace in the Third Amendment; the right of people to be secure in their persons, papers, and homes against unreasonable searches and seizures in the Fourth Amendment; and the Ninth Amendment's open-ended assertion that the enumeration of certain rights does not deny or disparage others retained by the people.[3]

This argument provided far broader and more robust constitutional protection for privacy than had existed a little while earlier when we had taken our stand. In addition, though barely recognized at the time, it provided the crucial underpinnings for the Supreme Court's resolution of the abortion issue several years later.

One of those who took a strong interest in our stand on abortion was Albert Blumenthal, a member of the NYCLU board until he entered the state legislature at the beginning of 1965. As the Democrats took control of the Assembly by riding Lyndon Johnson's coattails when he soundly defeated Barry Goldwater the previous November, the freshman Blumenthal had been appointed chairman of the Health Committee. In March 1966, Blumenthal organized what may have been the first legislative hearing on abortion law reform anywhere in the country in the twentieth century. About a dozen witnesses testified for reform, including, planned parenthood, including medical, religious, and civic groups. They supported measures that allowed abortion in cases of rape or incest, when there was a likelihood of birth defects, or when a number of physicians agreed that a woman's health was endangered. The only firm voice for repeal of all criminal sanctions was the NYCLU. No one appeared to argue for maintenance of the old law that permitted abortion only to save the mother's life. The Catholic Church, which we all saw as the great obstacle to any change in the law, declined to testify lest it dignify the proceedings, and Assembly Speaker Anthony Travia refused to allow the customary use of state funds to pay for a transcript. Al Blumenthal had to seek my assistance to obtain private financing to publish the proceedings.

Our witness at the hearing was Harriet Pilpel, a lawyer recently elected to the ACLU board, where she joined Dorothy Kenyon in pressing for a stand on abortion. Harriet was also general counsel of Planned Parenthood Federation of America. She and Ephraim London became my collaborators in our campaign to end criminal sanctions on abortion. At the outset, much of our effort focused on the state legislature, where Al Blumenthal and Harlem Assemblyman Percy Sutton led the way in obtaining progressively wider support for efforts to change the abortion laws. A call I got from the Rev. Howard Moody[4] of New York City's Judson Memorial Church in early 1967 opened an important new front for our campaign. Howard told me he and a number of fellow clergy were organizing to provide referrals to physicians who would perform the procedure for women seeking abortions. Would I meet with them to advise them on the risks they would run?

I asked Ephraim London to join me in meeting with Howard and his associate, Arlene Carmen. They told us they had enlisted a score or so clergy of different denominations to counsel women about abortion. They would tell the women what to expect from the procedure. If the women wished to go forward, the clergy would refer them to licensed physicians prepared to perform abortions. At the time, many women obtained "therapeutic abortions" in hospitals purportedly to save their lives. Others had the procedure performed in the privacy of their own doctors' offices. Many more, however, were unable to obtain abortions, tried to perform the abortions themselves, or obtained what were referred to as "back street" abortions from unlicensed practitioners in degrading, unsanitary, and unsafe circumstances. A lot of women suffered injuries or even died from botched abortions. The service Howard and his colleagues were prepared to provide was sorely needed.

Ephraim and I told them the NYCLU was ready to defend their right to provide this service. They were taking a risk, but Ephraim thought if they proceeded with care they might avoid prosecution. He advised them not to do anything clandestinely. Everything should be out in the open and above board. The clergy should take the position that they were acting within the law, ministering to women who sought their pastoral guidance.

He also pointed out that the risk of prosecution would diminish if they only referred women to licensed physicians outside New York State. Diversity of jurisdiction would complicate the task of prosecuting the clergy under state law.

Acting as a volunteer for the NYCLU, Ephraim London became counsel to the Clergy Consultation Service on Abortion. Its existence was made public in a highly sympathetic front-page story in the *New York Times* in May 1967 by the newspaper's religion editor, Edward Fiske.[5] The story stirred great interest. By then, legislative proposals to change abortion laws were under serious discussion in a number of states, but this was the first time since the Sherri Finkbine case five years earlier that the actual performance of abortions was so openly discussed. One immediate consequence was formation of similar clergy consultation services in other parts of the country. By the following year, there was a national federation of these groups.

Abortion remained illegal, however, and Howard and his associates continued to worry about criminal indictment. As time passed, I thought the chances of prosecution were receding. With change in the air, it seemed unlikely that a district attorney would try to persuade a jury to convict a minister or a rabbi for counseling a pregnant woman. Eventually, in 1969, I was able to provide some reassurance. I was guest speaker at a meeting of the New York State Association of Chiefs of Police. In their book about the Clergy Consultation Service, Howard Moody and Arlene Carmen reported, "In response to a question about what he would do differently if he were the Police Commissioner of New York City, Neier stated that he would begin by eliminating all arrests then being made for 'victimless crimes' such as prostitution, homosexuality and abortion." In those days, I always pointed out that the police had already decided not to enforce the law on adultery, which remained a crime in New York, and could do the same with similar consensual acts. "When he finished," they continued, "one police chief volunteered that they were doing just that with the Clergy Consultation Service on Abortion. From then on we knew we were home free."[6]

By then, things were moving in a rush. The national ACLU adopted the same position on abortion as the NYCLU. State affiliates of the ACLU all across the country were at work in their legislatures promoting change. A new group, NARAL, the National Association for the Reform of Abortion Laws (now the National Abortion Rights Action League), was formed at a meeting of more than 300 persons, which I attended, in Chicago. Lawrence Lader, a writer who had promoted repeal of criminal sanctions even before the NYCLU took its stand, and who had helped persuade Howard Moody to form the Clergy Consultation Service, played a central role in creating NARAL, and in many of the other efforts of that period. In New York, the focus of state legislative efforts shifted to a bill introduced by a Republican assemblywoman from upstate New York, Constance Cook, that would repeal all criminal sanctions. With her bill, the effort took on a women's rights character.

About the time Constance Cook's bill was introduced, the NYCLU joined in opening yet another front in the campaign by filing the first lawsuit challenging the constitutionality of abortion laws. The litigation was primarily the work of Roy Lucas, a recent law graduate. I had heard of him even while he was a student from a member of the NYCLU board, Robert McKay, professor and subsequently dean of NYU Law School. Bob told me one of his pupils had written a brilliant paper on abortion. Lucas's theories, building on the Supreme Court's decision in *Griswold*, the case that struck down the Connecticut law on contraceptives, laid the groundwork for *Roe v. Wade* a few years later.[7]

In 1970, while our lawsuit was pending, the New York legislature took up Assemblywoman Cook's bill to repeal the abortion laws. At the time, polls showed widespread public support for repeal and more and more voices were calling for an end to criminal sanctions. Among these were a number of feminist groups. Newly formed, they provided repeal with a grassroots constituency it previously lacked. Along with many others, I engaged in intense lobbying. In March, the Senate voted for repeal and, a few days later, the bill was taken up in the Assembly. When the votes were tallied, we had a majority but fell just short of the absolute majority needed to pass the measure. Another vote was scheduled a few days later. It would be the crucial test, as we knew Governor Nelson Rockefeller would sign the bill if it passed the legislature.

We needed two additional votes. In caucusing with other lobbyists, we agreed I would focus on Arthur Eve, a black assemblyman from Buffalo who had missed the first vote. Eve was ordinarily a proponent of civil liberties, so it seemed an easy assignment. It turned out to be more complicated than I imagined. Eve told us he favored repeal but he owed his seat in the Assembly to a group of black women in Buffalo who had campaigned for him. They thought repeal was a racist attempt to suppress black population growth. Eve had pledged to these women that he would not vote for repeal; his absence from the earlier vote was intentional. He would only cast his vote for the right to an abortion if the women who had campaigned for him would release him from his pledge.

I consulted Eleanor Holmes Norton, then ACLU assistant legal director, and in recent years, the District of Columbia's nonvoting member of Congress, and with her guidance conducted a brief but intense effort to persuade Assemblyman Eve's constituents. I never found out what part this played, but when the roll was called on a second vote, Eve was present and with us. We also picked up the other vote we needed, but, to our dismay, one of those who had supported repeal on the first vote, Hulan Jack, another black assemblyman, switched to the other side. We were short one vote.

As Hulan Jack's vote came fairly early in the slow alphabetical roll call still in effect, those of us who had lobbied for repeal sat crestfallen for what seemed an eternity in the Assembly chamber as our defeat was confirmed. But when the voting was completed and the Speaker was preparing to announce the result, an assemblyman from Auburn, New York, on whom none of us had focused, George Michaels, rose to ask leave to change his vote. In a hushed chamber, Michaels said his children were coming home for Passover the following week. He had to have peace around the Passover table. That was not possible if his vote made the difference in preventing repeal. He also said he knew that switching his vote would end his political career—as it did. Michaels was defeated for reelection.

David Garrow wrote in his history of *Roe v. Wade* that Constance Cook, whose district bordered Michaels's, knew he would change his vote if it made a difference.[8] But I did not know, and I doubt the others who lobbied for repeal had any idea what he was prepared to do. In a short space of time, we went from victory to defeat to victory. It was one of the most emotionally draining moments of my career.

New York was not the first state to repeal criminal sanctions. That distinction belonged to Hawaii, which had acted the previous month—though its legislature, probably unconstitutionally, had said the measure only applied to state residents and the procedure could only take place in hospitals. New York's action, we knew, was the beginning of the end of criminal sanctions against abortion in the United States. The "right to life" movement had materialized in 1967, but it did not seem to have an organizational structure and had little clout. The only important opposition to changes in the abortion laws came from the Catholic Church and, as polls showed, many lay Catholics did not support the Church's stand.

The Church's influence on the abortion debate was impaired because it had another issue that mattered more to it in New York State politics in that era: aid to parochial schools. Two years earlier, the Church had been badly defeated in a statewide referendum on a change in the state's constitution to make it easier to secure public funding for its schools. In the aftermath of that defeat, the Church urgently needed help from the legislature to keep its schools going. Some legislators realized their votes on abortion would not make them targets of denunciations from the pulpit if they voted for textbooks, school buses, and other services for children attending Catholic schools. Fundamentalist Protestant organizations—what became known much later as "the Christian Right"—did not play a part in the New York lobbying. I expected not only that criminal sanctions would be abolished but also that the battle over abortion would soon end.

Repeal mooted our New York lawsuit. Roy Lucas turned his attention to suits challenging other state laws, including *Roe v. Wade* in Texas. In New York, Judge Henry Friendly of the U.S. Court of Appeals let it be known that he had breathed a sigh of relief, telling a law school audience:

I can speak with feeling because I was to have presided over a three-judge court before which the constitutionality of the old law was being challenged. Although we had not yet heard argument, I could perceive not merely how soul wrenching but how politically disturbing—and I use politically in the highest sense—[the] decision either way would be. If we upheld the old law, we would be disappointing the expectations of many high-minded citizens, deeply concerned over the misery it was creating, its discriminatory effects, its consequences for the population explosion, and the hopes of the least privileged elements in the community. . . . If we were to decide the other way, many adherents of a deeply respected religion would consider we had taken unto ourselves a role that belonged to their elected representatives. . . . How much better that the issue was settled by the legislature! I do not mean that everyone is happy: presumably those who opposed the reform have not changed their views. But the result is acceptable in the sense that it was reached by the democratic process.[9]

Half a year after our victory in New York, I was appointed executive director of the ACLU. Of the many legislative battles and court cases over abortion in which we were engaged nationally, the most significant was a lawsuit filed by the Georgia ACLU, *Doe v. Bolton*. Unlike the law challenged in Roy Lucas's lawsuit in New York and the one at issue in *Roe v. Wade* in Texas, Georgia's statute was a 1968 reform measure that permitted therapeutic abortions along the lines of the bills introduced in New York by Al Blumenthal and Percy Sutton. Margie Pitts Hames, the attorney who brought *Doe v. Bolton*, represented Georgia on the ACLU board. Her suit was accepted for review by the Supreme Court along with *Roe v. Wade*, which heard argument in the two cases in December 1971 and then required reargument in both cases in October 1972. Three months later, the Court decided *Roe* and *Doe*, invalidating both the highly restrictive Texas law and the more permissive Georgia law.[10] For a moment, it seemed, as I had anticipated when the New York law was repealed, that the battle for a woman's right to an abortion was over.

Unfortunately, there were elements of the Court's opinion itself and political forces at work that soon made it apparent the issue would become more contentious in the wake of *Roe* and *Doe* than it had been before. The Supreme Court held that a woman's decision to terminate a pregnancy is a fundamental right. The fetus is not a person with rights to protect and the state does not acquire a compelling interest in protecting potential life until "viability" occurs during the final trimester of pregnancy. Before that, the state has a compelling interest in the health of the mother during the second trimester when abortion becomes dangerous. During that trimester, the state may regulate abortion to the extent reasonably required to protect maternal health but may not prohibit or otherwise impede abortion. In the first trimester, no state interference is warranted.

The opinion adopted a line of reasoning familiar to those who follow Supreme Court decisions: Fundamental rights may only be circumscribed to the extent necessary to protect a compelling state interest. Yet holding that state authority to intervene varies according to the trimester in which a woman seeks an abortion made the Court an easy target for the criticism that it had usurped legislative authority. Many reputable legal scholars were scathing. Professor John Hart Ely of Harvard Law School derided this "super-protected right" that "is not inferable from the language of the Constitution, the framers' thinking respecting the specific problem in issue, any general value derivable from the provisions they included, or the nation's governmental structure. Nor is it explainable in terms of the unusual political impotence of the group judicially protected vis-à-vis the interest that legislatively prevailed over it. And that, I believe is a charge that can be responsibly leveled at no other decision of the past twenty years."[11] Ely's Harvard colleague Archibald Cox added that the Court's holding on trimesters "reads like a set of hospital rules and regulations."[12]

Politically, "right-to-life" proponents grew stronger in the wake of *Roe* and took the lead in persuading state governments to hamper exercise of the right in myriad ways: requiring fetal death certificates; spousal and parental consent; public identification of doctors collecting Medicaid reimbursements for performing abortions; denial of Medicaid reimbursements; limitations on where abortions could be performed, such as only in hospitals; enforced delays for women to undergo counseling; orders that doctors inform their patients of the human characteristics of the fetus; and more.

Meanwhile, the constituency opposing the right to abortion was undergoing a transformation. Largely Catholic before *Roe,* from the mid-1970s, leadership shifted to Protestant fundamentalists. Their opposition had a different character that made the struggle ever nastier. Catholic opposition was rooted in religious beliefs about when life begins. It had a moral quality. I believe that many Protestant fundamentalists, and some Catholics who adopted their ways, were motivated by hatred—of the Supreme Court, feminists, civil libertarians, and the permissiveness embodied by the easy availability of abortions. They fought a cultural war against everything represented by *Roe.* There was also an opportunistic element to the focus on abortions by some of their leaders. In joining and taking over the right-to-life movement, they saw a chance to defeat forces in American public life that they identified as their arch-enemies.

A few years after the Protestant takeover began, in a televised debate on William Buckley's program, *Firing Line,* I pressed Rev. Jerry Falwell, head of the Moral Majority, about his lateness in taking up the fight against abortion. Falwell, then at the height of his political influence, acknowledged that he and those associated with him had been silent about abortion prior to *Roe.* It was only after the Supreme Court decision, he said, that they recognized the issue's potential.

The political assault on abortion rights had consequences. The Supreme Court retreated under fire. Three 1977 decisions particularly hampered exercise of the right: In *Beal v. Doe* the Court upheld Pennsylvania's denial of Medicaid reimbursement for nontherapeutic abortions for poor women;[13] in *Maher v. Doe* the Court upheld Connecticut's policy of reimbursing only medically necessary abortions in the first trimester;[14] and in *Poelker v. Doe* the Court sustained the refusal by two municipal hospitals in St. Louis to perform abortions except when there was a threat of death or grave physical injury to the mother.[15]

Judicial backtracking under the onslaught of a segment of the scholarly community and the invigorated right-to-life movement required me to strengthen the ACLU's capacity to defend the right of women to obtain abortions. I established a Reproductive Freedom Project—for which we obtained financial support from a number of donors unaccustomed to contributing to the ACLU. The largest donor was John D. Rockefeller III. His aide, Joan Dunlop, hired to assist him in promoting population control internationally, persuaded him that the way to advance that cause was to promote women's rights and that his efforts should encompass support in the United States for a woman's right to choose. Though I repeatedly clashed with his brother Nelson over such issues as his draconian drug laws when he was governor of New York, in my limited contact with John, the eldest of the five Rockefeller brothers, I found him a much different person with strong sympathy for civil liberties. I also liked his unpretentious manner. On one occasion, when Joan Dunlop had brought us together for lunch, he leaned forward and fingered my tie. It was a moment when very wide ties were briefly in fashion and I had worn one. Rockefeller said he had owned some ties like that before he was married, but that, just the previous year, his wife Blanchette had made him throw them away. Now they were back in style, and he regretted not having them. At the time, he and Blanchette had been married for close to half a century.

A far more unusual donor was Richard Mellon Scaife, more than twenty years later the financier of a campaign to collect dirt on President Bill Clinton and, already then, a leading backer of right-wing causes. Scaife took care not to leave any trace of his contribution to the ACLU. The director of his foundation came to New York for lunch with me to discuss what we were doing about abortion. Money was never mentioned. As we were about to part, my guest said that if I called Al Moran, director of New York Planned Parenthood, he would have something for me. I waited a day and then called Moran. He told me his organization would make a grant in support of our Reproductive Freedom Project. It was the only time I can recall that a foundation laundered a grant to us through another organization. I suspect the women's rights and privacy concerns of the ACLU were not Scaife's reasons for supporting our efforts. Yet as no conditions were placed on the grant, I had no hesitation about taking it.

To direct the project, I hired Janet Benshoof, a recent Harvard Law School graduate, launching her on a career defending women's reproductive rights to which she has now devoted more than a quarter of a century. A passionate—and also mirthful—advocate who conducted one of her early trials for the right of women to obtain abortions while she herself was in her ninth month of pregnancy with twins, Benshoof soon established herself as the foremost litigator in the field. Some years after I left the ACLU, she got into a dispute with my successor, leading her to sever her project and establish it as the independent Center for Reproductive Law and Policy, which she directed for a decade. Today we continue to collaborate on efforts such as an attempt to overturn President George W. Bush's "global gag rule" prohibiting organizations around the world that receive U.S. family planning support from using their own funds to provide abortions, counsel clients about abortion, or advocate abortion. The rule was initially imposed by President Reagan, continued by President George H.W. Bush, dropped by President Clinton, and reimposed immediately upon taking office by the younger Bush. I submitted an affidavit on its impact on free speech in a lawsuit Janet filed against the rule and, at her request, testified on the issue before the Senate Foreign Relations Committee.

I n the quarter century since my departure from the American Civil Liberties Union, abortion has been second only to race as the country's most divisive issue. Proposals for a constitutional amendment to override *Roe* are a ritual of American politics. Litigation over all manner of restrictions continues. Legislative appropriations for foreign assistance or payments due to the United Nations are held hostage over the abortion issue, as are appointments of diplomats and judges. It can be a decisive factor in campaigns for public office. Opposition to abortion rights has been a litmus test for many appointments by the Bush administration. Although abortion remains legal, it is available to many women only at specialized clinics that patients reach by crossing picket lines where they are denounced as baby killers. Doctors who work at such clinics wear bullet-proof vests, and a few have been assassinated.

Supreme Court Judge Ruth Bader Ginsburg, who did not take part in ACLU litigation on abortion because the Ford Foundation restricted its grant for our Women's Rights Project, has argued that the divisiveness of *Roe*'s legacy might have been avoided if the Court had dealt with the issue differently. Noting that the Texas law made abortion criminal except as a procedure to save the life of the woman, Ginsburg asked: "Suppose the Court had stopped there, rightly declaring unconstitutional the most extreme brand of law in the nation, and had not gone on, as the Court did in *Roe* to fashion a regime blanketing the subject, a set of rules that displaced virtually every state law in force. Would there have been the twenty-year controversy we have witnessed?" Ginsburg is particularly critical of the companion *Doe v. Bolton* ruling because the Georgia law it struck down was less extreme than the Texas statute as it permitted therapeutic abortions on a number of grounds. The thrust of Ruth Ginsburg's argument is that the proper basis for resolving *Roe* was in accordance with the cases decided at the same time dealing with the rights of women to obtain the equal protection of the laws. Those were cases Ruth Ginsburg herself was then bringing to the Court from another office at the ACLU. In this view, a woman's right to control her reproduction is an essential component of her ability to participate equally in economic activity. This would have avoided the Court's attempt to read into the Constitution the regulation of state action on the basis of the trimesters of pregnancy.[16]

Ruth Ginsburg may be right in suggesting that a woman's equality approach to abortion might have escaped some of the scholarly criticism directed against *Roe* and *Doe*. If so, the fault goes back to the virtual absence of judicial protection for women's rights when the NYCLU took its stand on abortion in 1965 and when Roy Lucas began his seminal work defining abortion as a fundamental right of privacy in accordance with the Supreme Court's decision in *Griswold*. Even if we had had the consciousness of women's rights that emerged a few years later, I doubt we would have gotten anywhere. The ground had shifted by the time *Roe* was decided in 1973, but not when the effort that culminated in the Supreme Court's holding got under way. Perhaps we should have tried to change course.

However, I believe Ruth Ginsburg was mistaken in arguing that this road not taken could have staved off political divisiveness. From the standpoint of the Christian Right and its cultural war allies, it is precisely because *Roe* symbolized a triumph for feminism that it was a favorite target. That the case was decided on privacy grounds is immaterial to its most militant antagonists.

Ruth Ginsburg was on surer ground, I believe, in suggesting the issue would have been less contentious if it had been resolved in the state legislatures, as in New York. Noting that such a movement was under way when *Roe* was decided, she contrasted the situation with that when the Supreme Court struck down racial segregation in 1954. Then, she said, the prospect for reform through state legislatures was bleak, or nonexistent. Indeed, she might have added that in southern states, where segregation was required by law, discriminatory practices prevented most blacks from voting. This made it impossible for the victims to participate in the state legislative process. A federal legislative remedy was also precluded by the control of crucial committees by southerners who had gained seniority through the one-party system of that era. As they were elected by constituencies that excluded almost all blacks, it was unthinkable for them to support desegregation. The Supreme Court was the only institution capable of taking on segregation. Its intervention did not thwart the democratic process; rather, it made it work. In contrast, there were no limits on participation by women in the electoral process in the 1970s; women are not a minority requiring special protection by the courts because of their weakness in the legislative process; and it was a time of great advances for women's rights through legislation as well as litigation.

Of course, the same argument could be applied to the women's equality cases that Ruth Ginsburg was winning in the Supreme Court in that period. Yet if the abortion issue had been resolved by the popularly elected branches of government, as it was in New York, I believe that much of the strife of the post-*Roe* era could have been avoided. By itself, that is not a sufficient basis for the Supreme Court to duck the issue. Where fundamental constitutional rights are at stake—as I believe is the case in the abortion issue because the abortion laws violated both the right to privacy and the right of women to compete equally by controlling their own reproduction—the courts have a responsibility to act even if the issue *might* be resolved over time through the legislative process. Still, proponents of abortion rights might have achieved more if we had focused on an arduous state-by-state campaign to repeal criminal sanctions. Between 1965 and 1973, thirteen states liberalized their laws on abortion and criminal

sanctions were repealed in Alaska, Washington, and the District of Columbia as well as in New York and Hawaii. The trend was in our direction
when *Roe* was decided. The right-to-life movement had not yet achieved
significant momentum; certainly there was nothing like the backlash later
generated by the Supreme Court's 1973 decision. The women's movement
was gaining in strength and the right to obtain abortions could have been a
more effective mobilizing cause than the ill-fated Equal Rights Amendment of the same era.

Thanks to a 1992 decision by the Supreme Court, the likelihood that
Roe will be reversed outright has receded, though it has not been eliminated. An opinion by Justice David Souter that commanded the support
of a majority of the Court makes it clear that whatever a new generation
of justices think about the rationale on which *Roe* rested and its trimester
approach, there is no turning back now. Souter pointed out, "An entire
generation of women has come of age free to assume *Roe*'s concept of
liberty in defining the capacity of women to act in society." Thereby, his
opinion retroactively endows the decision with the women's rights dimension advocated by Ginsburg. Adding a crucial statement on the importance of adhering to the 1973 precedent, Souter wrote:

> [When] the Court decides a case in such a way as to resolve the sort of in-
> tensely divisive controversy reflected in *Roe* and those rare, comparable
> cases, its decision has a dimension that the resolution of the normal case
> does not carry. . . . The Court is not asked to do this very often, having
> thus addressed the Nation only twice in our lifetime, in the decisions in
> *Brown* and *Roe*. But when the Court does act this way, its decision acquires
> an equally rare precedential force to counter the inevitable efforts to over-
> turn it and thwart its implementation. Some of those efforts may be mere
> unprincipled reactions; others may proceed from principles worthy of
> profound respect. But whatever the premises of opposition may be, only
> the most convincing justification under accepted standards of precedent
> could suffice to demonstrate that a later decision overruling the first was
> anything but surrender to political pressure. . . . So to overrule under fire
> in the absence of the most compelling reason to reexamine a watershed
> decision would subvert the Court's legitimacy beyond serious question.[17]

The justices signing on to Souter's opinion included supporters of the
reasoning behind *Roe v. Wade* as well as others who probably had doubts

about it. In essence, that majority refused to abandon *Roe* on grounds of judicial integrity as well as on grounds of the rightful place of women in society. They put the constitutional right to an abortion on a different and more secure footing than it enjoyed previously. True judicial conservatives now support maintenance of *Roe*. Seeking its reversal is jurisprudentially radical. At this writing, it is unclear whether President Bush will nominate to the Supreme Court radicals intent on overturning *Roe* or even if such nominees could survive Senate confirmation. What is certain is that their public utterances will be scrutinized closely for clues to their stand and that if a position can be ascribed to them this will figure prominently in the consideration they receive. Very likely, it will be the decisive factor.

Constitutional jurisprudence aside, it is difficult to imagine that abortion could ever again become criminal. If states adopt laws punishing abortion, the consequence would be wholesale civil disobedience. If prosecutors indicted women or doctors for abortions, they would be hard pressed to find juries to convict. The right-to-life movement retains the capacity to harass those exercising their rights for the foreseeable future. It can deny many women, especially the poor, access to the health care they require. Also, it maintains substantial political clout and will continue to do much mischief. But even in the era of a president with close links to the Christian Right, it probably lacks the capacity to turn back the clock.

CHAPTER FIVE

Forging Restraints on Stigma

Shortly before I became director of the New York Civil Liberties Union, one of our volunteer attorneys won dismissal of all charges against a group of students arrested for a peaceful protest at the opening of the 1964–1965 New York World's Fair. The students worried that the records of their arrests would still cause them difficulties, so we sued to expunge their arrest records. The arrests violated their First Amendment rights, and it seemed unfair that they might have trouble getting jobs or entering the professions as a consequence of illegal police conduct.

I had my own reason for wanting to deal with arrest records. When I had married Yvette a few years earlier, she was working for Bloomingdale's Department Store, where for a time her job was hiring sales personnel. After they started work, they had a thirty-day probationary period before they became union members. During probation, they could be discharged without cause or explanation. In that period, the store detectives—most of them retired police—checked with their contacts in the New York Police Department and with credit bureaus to get information on arrests or other information that might reflect badly on the new employees. If they turned up anything, they would ask Yvette to fire the people she had hired. Frequently, the records did not indicate the outcome of cases. The police department had no systematic way to record decisions by prosecutors to drop charges or acquittals. Nor was such information of interest to credit bureaus. I heard many stories from Yvette about her indignant battles with the store detectives over those records. Hiring was heaviest as Christmas approached, and Yvette hated being asked to fire someone without explanation during the holiday season. I was glad of an opportunity to deal with the issue.

To learn more about the subject, I asked a student intern to interview the managers of employment agencies. She went through the alphabetical list in the phone book and asked those willing to answer her questions on the phone whether they would knowingly refer an applicant for a job who had been arrested but not convicted. Of the first twenty firms from which she got answers, fifteen said no.

I mentioned this result in a brief article I wrote for our newsletter on the lawsuit to expunge the arrest records of the World's Fair demonstrators. To my surprise, that quick survey—which probably took the student no more than a day's work—was subsequently cited in the 1967 report of the President's Commission on Law Enforcement and in a 1974 decision by the U.S. Court of Appeals for the District of Columbia.[1] The survey was hardly scientific, but there was a dearth of information on the subject.

Arrest records became a focus—some would say an obsession—of my work for the ACLU. As I became known for my interest in the issue, many people told me about the problems they had encountered from such records. The effect was to intensify my concern. Millions of Americans are stigmatized by arrest records. The impact is severe. Minorities are especially victimized, both because police are quicker to arrest them—racial profiling was routine long before that term was coined—and because employers are less willing to take chances on them. They are presumed guilty. I organized lawsuits to expunge arrest records; promoted litigation to limit their dissemination and to bar employer inquiries about such records; and published numerous articles on the subject.[2] Not to much effect. A few states enacted restrictions on inquiries by employers about arrests not followed by convictions. Federal regulations were adopted on the circulation of records, but with many loopholes. Ultimately, most controls proved of little value because federal, state, and local law-enforcement agencies promiscuously share such data with each other. Restrictions that apply to one agency often do not prevent dissemination of arrest records by the recipients. The casual availability of such records was shown by the testimony of an FBI official in one of the ACLU's leading cases dealing with them, *Menard v. Saxbe,* which we litigated for six years. It was finally decided in a way that gave us a technical victory without a material result.[3]

Our client, Dale Menard, an ex-Marine, was arrested and detained for two days by Los Angeles police for "suspicion of burglary." He was never actually charged, and it was not clear any crime had been committed. Menard was arrested because he was sitting on a park bench when someone called the police—so the police said—to complain of a prowler in the

arrest was not really an arrest, as he was never charged. The FBI notified Menard's ACLU attorney that the Bureau had complied by returning his record to the Los Angeles Police Department—which, no doubt, had kept a copy—and also notified the Defense Department and the Marine Corps to which it had disseminated the record. If Menard wanted to be sure his record of an arrest that was not an arrest caused him no trouble, he would also have to take on the LAPD, the Defense Department, the Marine Corps, and anyone else who had received the record from them. It seemed a page out of Kafka. At one point, Joseph K. in *The Trial* is informed of the distinction between definite acquittal and ostensible acquittal. "In definite acquittal," the painter Titorelli tells him, "the documents relating to the case are said to be completely annulled, they simply vanish from sight, not only the charge but also the records of the case and even the acquittal are destroyed. That's not the case with ostensible acquittal. The documents remain as they were. . . . The whole dossier continues to circulate as the regular official routine demands."

A couple of years later, in 1976, the U.S. Supreme Court decided a case we had brought in Kentucky for a photographer for the *Louisville Courier-Journal.* Edward Charles Davis III had been arrested for shoplifting in 1971. The arrest was apparently a mistake and charges against Davis were dismissed. A year and a half later, however, the police distributed a five-page flyer to merchants in Louisville with photos of known "active shoplifters" carrying his name and photo. Davis's newspaper found out and told him he could no longer cover the city's downtown area. If he got into further difficulty, he would be fired, the *Courier-Journal* told him. We sought an injunction against additional dissemination of Davis's arrest record and damages for the harm he had suffered. Writing for the Supreme Court's majority, however, Justice William Rehnquist said stigma does not deprive a citizen of either liberty or property to an extent that suffices "to invoke the procedural protection of the Due Process Clause" of the Fourteenth Amendment. Davis's only remedy, Rehnquist wrote, was to file a suit for defamation in state court. This was disingenuous—or outright dishonest—as Kentucky law, in common with the laws of most states, provides government officials with immunity against lawsuits for defamation for actions they take in their official capacity. Rehnquist suggested an alternative form of redress that was foreclosed. No doubt he knew this. Justice William Brennan wrote in his dissent that the Supreme Court's decision in Davis's case meant that police officials, acting in their official capacities as law enforcers, may on their own initiative and without trial constitutionally condemn innocent individuals as criminals and thereby brand them with one of the most stigmatizing and debilitating labels in our society. If there are no constitutional restraints on such oppressive behavior, the safeguards constitutionally accorded an accused in a criminal trial are rendered a sham, and no individual can feel secure that he will not be arbitrarily singled out for similar *ex parte* punishment by those primarily charged with fair enforcement of the law.[4]

The Supreme Court's decision in Davis's case was as bad as any in my fifteen-year tenure at the American Civil Liberties Union. It confirmed a deep antipathy I had developed against Justice Rehnquist.

My failure to make significant headway on arrest records was a leading frustration of my work for the ACLU. It was not an issue on which I was publicly persuasive. Whatever lip service Americans give to the presumption of innocence, all of us know cases where someone has gotten away with murder, or another serious crime. Call it the O. J. Simpson syndrome. If we are hiring, why take chances? Yet the consequence of many decisions that, by themselves, seem prudent is that vast numbers of Americans who are innocent of the crimes for which they were arrested—as DNA evidence is demonstrating even in cases of murder convictions—suffer lifelong harm. Another probable result is damage to public safety. Young black males are particularly prone to arrest. Many are marginalized by their records. Unable to obtain stable jobs with public and private enterprises that screen employees, they may see few alternatives to activities that endanger others. In this way, racial profiling and the arrests that are the result become self-fulfilling prophecies.

Though I was unsuccessful in dealing with arrest records, we made progress in dealing with another category of records that also stigmatized people unfairly. At the New York Civil Liberties Union, I established a Project on Students Rights. It was an issue I assigned Ira Glasser to work on when I hired him in 1967, and when the volume of administrative battles and court cases got to be heavy, I sought funding to add staff just to document abuses and to handle litigation in that field. One of our priorities was the practice in schools of compiling "confidential" anecdotal records on children. These were records kept by teachers and school psychologists for their own use and to guide other school personnel in dealing with children. Unfortunately, they were also widely available to many outside agencies. If a teacher said a second grader had "exhibitionist tendencies" because one time he rushed out of a lavatory unzipped, or another said a sixth grader had "Marxist tendencies"—actual cases—those labels stuck.

In 1970, we persuaded the New York City Board of Education temporarily to stop circulating such records outside the schools. Within a fifteen-day period, twenty-eight outside agencies complained—the FBI, the U.S. Army, the Selective Service System, the New York City Police, the Welfare Department, and the Civil Service Commission among them. Under this pressure, the board of education quickly rescinded its prohibition. We did better in the courts, winning a number of court cases providing parents with access to records about their children. The publicity persuaded several states to enact laws restricting the dissemination of records. Then, in 1974, Congress adopted the Family Educational Rights and Privacy Act (FERPA), which provides parental access to such records nationwide, allows challenges to inaccurate or misleading information, and bars disclosure of the records to outsiders without consent of the student or parent. As a consequence, such school records have not been a significant concern for more than a quarter of a century. The problems they caused have long been forgotten. FERPA was a huge victory for privacy, though it may be somewhat less effective in the future because of a recent decision by the U.S. Supreme Court holding that it does not provide a private cause of action. That is, lawsuits for damages by individuals victimized by improper disclosures are now prohibited; the law may only be enforced by governmental authorities.

Other categories of records on which we focused with varying degrees of success were less-than-honorable discharge records—in most cases without hearings—that stigmatized some 400,000 Vietnam-era veterans; gossipy credit bureau reports (another area where we achieved victory through federal legislation, the Fair Credit Reporting Act of 1971); juvenile court records; and medical records, including records of treatment for mental illness or drug addiction, an area where we failed to make headway and where no progress took place until the final days of the Clinton administration, when the outgoing president signed an executive order on patient privacy. (Unfortunately, because the matter was dealt with by Clinton as an executive order and the protection of privacy was not incorporated in legislation, it was subsequently easily overturned by his successor,

President George W. Bush.) The issue that evoked much the greatest public interest, however, was our struggle against the compilation and dissemination of political dossiers by a host of government agencies.

The FBI was the prime offender. Two among the scores of cases we took on against the Bureau typify its practices. One concerned a demonstration on November 15, 1969. Several hundred thousand people from all across the country went to Washington, D.C., that day for the largest protest against the Vietnam War and one of the largest ever to take place in the nation's capital. Many traveled by chartered bus. FBI agents went to the bank where the organization that had chartered the buses kept its account to record the names of those who had paid by check for their transportation. We found out when a bank clerk called to alert us, which allowed us to rush into federal court to halt the practice.

The other arose a few years later. Lori Paton of Chester, New Jersey, sixteen at the time, wrote a letter for a high-school social studies assignment to the minuscule Socialist Labor Party. By mistake, she sent it to the equally tiny Socialist Workers Party. The ideological differences between the two groups mattered greatly to them, but a high-school student confused them easily. Noting the return address, the FBI conducted an investigation of Paton and her family, interviewing her principal and other school officials and checking on her parents with the local credit bureau. When the Patons found out about the investigation from the school and sought our help, the FBI tried to deceive us by saying, "The FBI has no knowledge of any letter Ms. Paton may have sent to the Socialist Labor Party." Strictly speaking, that was true, as we did not yet know the letter had mistakenly been sent to the Socialist Workers Party. (This was known as "Bureauspeak" or "Hooverspeak," a form of communication in which deception was the primary goal.) Though no discreditable information turned up about Lori Paton or her parents, on the witness stand the FBI special agent in charge of security matters in the Newark office acknowledged that the Bureau had classified her file as a "subversive matter."

If anything, the "Red squads" of many city police departments were even more abusive than the FBI. In city after city, we filed lawsuits to put these busybodies out of business. In New York City, the police department destroyed dossiers on about a million persons while our lawsuit was under way. In Memphis, our case took on a burlesque flavor. While our lawyers were in federal court seeking an order against destruction of the files so the people spied on could see them, police in the city hall basement were shoveling them into a furnace. When the judge issued an order barring their destruction, one of our attorneys raced across the street and burst past the guards in the city hall (the guards followed him with drawn guns) to serve an order on the mayor. Some files had not yet been burned and were preserved. In Chicago, the police were required to turn over to the court about 400,000 dossiers, including many providing information on the activities and associations of prominent citizens. This made the police department look absurd. Mockery, we discovered, was a potent weapon against political surveillance.

After the revolutions of 1989 in Eastern Europe, dealing with the files compiled by such notorious police agencies as the Stasi in East Germany and the StB in Czechoslovakia has been central to decommunization. In unified Germany, an agency known as the Gauck Commission (for its chairman, a Lutheran minister named Joachim Gauck) has employed some 3,000 persons for a decade to sort through the files and make them available to those who were spied upon. What is generally overlooked in discussions of such matters is that the practices of American police agencies that we brought to an end in the late 1970s were as extensive and, at times, as abusive as those of the Communist governments. Their methods were similar. What made them less effective is that Americans, aided by the First Amendment and a small army of advocates of their rights—most acting under the auspices of the ACLU—were not comparably cowed by the surveillance practices of their government and the dossiers stigmatizing them as subversives.

The most important court case we took on against political surveillance was one we lost in the U.S. Supreme Court. Even so, *Laird v. Tatum,*[5] decided in 1972, played an important part both in ending the practice that was its target and in dismantling the apparatus of political surveillance in the United States. The case began when we read an article in *The Washington Monthly* by a former U.S. Army intelligence officer, Christopher Pyle, revealing that the military had compiled extensive political dossiers on civilians.[6] Though there were earlier examples of domestic political surveillance by the military—during both World Wars, including an episode during World War II when a unit in Chicago bugged a hotel room occupied by Eleanor Roosevelt, and at times such as the veterans' Bonus March in Washington in 1932—the most extensive program originated during the Johnson administration. In that era, National Guard units were occasionally called out to cope with urban riots, and military leaders were deeply offended when some in the New Left carried Vietcong flags in demonstrations. Not content with the data gathering of local police departments and the FBI, the U.S. Army decided to supplement these with its own domestic political surveillance.

Some 1,500 plainclothes agents were deployed on domestic espionage assignment by the army. They went far beyond the collection of information about potential civil disorders. They made antiwar groups their targets on the theory that they might promote disaffection with military service. In addition, the army collected information on groups it suspected were subversive because they might engage in such practices as sabotage. With those vague criteria, its surveillance program had few limits. Some military agents used phony press credentials to pose as journalists. Others infiltrated the groups on which they spied.

Our lead plaintiff, Arlo Tatum, was a well-known pacifist leader. Although individuals like Tatum had nothing to do with riots, we learned from Chris Pyle that they had been targets of the army's spying. We sought an injunction against continuing political surveillance by the army and demanded destruction of all the dossiers it had compiled on civilians.

Christopher Pyle's revelations also persuaded Senator Sam Ervin, chairman of the upper house's Subcommittee on Constitutional Rights, to hold hearings in 1971 on political surveillance by the army and other federal agencies. Inspired by Pyle's example, about 125 military intelligence agents and former agents came forward and provided statements to Ervin's committee. The witness for the Nixon administration at the hearings was Assistant Attorney General William Rehnquist, often its spokesman in upholding political surveillance. He testified that the president had "inherent power" to conduct domestic political surveillance under the authority of the constitutional requirement that he should "take care that the laws be faithfully executed." Ever one to uphold violations of civil liberties, Rehnquist said judicial review of abuses was not appropriate because "self-restraint" by the president sufficed. Moreover, he argued, the targets of surveillance were not harmed and enjoyed no constitutional rights protecting them against the collection of data on their political associations and beliefs.

When our suit was scheduled for argument in the U.S. Supreme Court, Senator Ervin asked to share in oral argument. Ordinarily, we would not agree to this, but Ervin—who looked and sounded like a caricature of a southern senator of a certain era and was our antagonist on issues such as racial equality and women's rights—had emerged as the country's foremost champion of constitutional liberty against the political surveillance that was the hallmark of the Nixon administration. He eloquently denounced the army's surveillance program at the hearings he conducted. My colleagues and I welcomed his appearance before the High Court.

Ervin's performance was not enough. The Supreme Court ruled against us 5–4. Unfortunately, as a result of some bad judgments by our lawyers, the case had gone to the Court on an expedited basis without a trial where we could have demonstrated the uses the army made of its surveillance data. The Court had no record before it except our claim that political surveillance by the army was having a chilling effect on the exercise of First Amendment rights. This was not enough for the five-member majority, which said "allegations of a subjective 'chill' are not an adequate substitute for a claim of specific present objective harm or a threat of specific future harm." Instead of remanding the case to a lower court to give us an opportunity to demonstrate specific harm, Chief Justice Warren Burger's opinion for the five-member majority said our plaintiffs lacked standing to bring the matter before the judiciary. As Justice William O. Douglas pointed out in dissent, "To withhold standing to sue until that time arrives [when the 'harm' referred to by Burger has taken place] would in practical effect immunize from judicial scrutiny all surveillance activities, regardless of their misuse and their deterrent effect."

When news of the decision reached me, I was stunned. Revelations about the army's role in political surveillance had drawn widespread condemnation, and hardly anyone outside the Nixon administration defended the practice. One of the shocking elements was participation in the majority by William Rehnquist. In the period between his testimony before Senator Ervin's subcommittee and the Court's decision less than two years later, he had been appointed to the Supreme Court by President Nixon. (Two or three weeks before Nixon nominated him, I took part in a panel discussion with Rehnquist at the New School in New York. Regarding him as a lightweight, I didn't bother to take him on, concentrating instead on a disagreement I had with another panelist who seemed a worthier adversary, Nicholas Katzenbach.) Ordinarily, if a Supreme Court justice participates in a controversy before his appointment to the Court, he does not take part in the Court's decision on the matter. The same rule applies to lower courts. Yet Rehnquist cast the decisive vote against us and in favor of the very army surveillance program that he had defended as the

Nixon administration's spokesman. As Chief Justice Burger's opinion adopted the same reasoning as Rehnquist's testimony before Ervin, it seemed likely the new justice had been influential. If Rehnquist had not taken part in the decision, a 4–4 split would have affirmed the lower court's decision, which we had won.

The morning I got this news, before I had a chance to absorb it fully, I had a call from Lawrence Baskir, Senator Ervin's chief counsel. Baskir told me he had been talking to the senator about the decision. Ervin had asked him to call me to suggest we go back to the Supreme Court and retroactively move to recuse Rehnquist. As far as I know, nothing of the sort had ever been done before. The ACLU appeared frequently before the Supreme Court, and I was apprehensive about doing anything so confrontational. Yet we were incensed by the Court's judgment and by Rehnquist's participation. With trepidation, we decided to file a motion as Ervin suggested.

We had little hope of succeeding. I thought the Court as a whole would summarily reject our motion. Instead, Rehnquist himself responded with a lengthy defense of his participation in the decision. It seemed his brethren (no women had yet joined the Court) were requiring him to deal with the matter on his own instead of rising collectively to his defense. Though he conceded that reasonable persons could differ on whether it was appropriate, he wrote that he believed he should take part in the judgment to break the tie. Although the effect of a tie vote is to affirm the decision of the lower court in the particular case, it does not set a precedent. The "principle of law presented by the case is left unsettled," he noted. Rehnquist thought it important that the Court should deal with the broader issue we raised and, therefore, had cast his vote. That explanation hardly mollified us, of course. If anything, it helped form my view of Rehnquist, subsequently reinforced by decisions such as the one in which he denied Edward Charles Davis III relief from being branded as a known active shoplifter: that his claim to be a judicial conservative is a fraud. He is an activist for a particular political philosophy ready even to cast aside the rule against sitting in judgment on a matter in which he was an advocate to promote his own political views.

It is through William Rehnquist that Richard Nixon has placed a lasting imprint on American liberties. Nixon knew what he was doing. As the *Washington Post* reported recently when the National Archives released additional tapes made in the Oval Office, Nixon considered the appointment a "masterstroke" following the Senate rejection of his two previous nominees, Clement Haynsworth and Harold Carswell. The tape was made on October 27, 1971, six days after Rehnquist was nominated. The *Post* reported: "'You've got one guy, Rehnquist, who wouldn't have a snowball's chance of getting on that court if you had just walked up and nominated him earlier,' Haldeman told Nixon. By now, all sides were somewhat exhausted from the bruising battles that had already taken place. 'He [Rehnquist] is pretty far right isn't he?' said national security adviser Henry A. Kissinger, the third man in the room. 'Oh, Christ,' Haldeman exclaimed, 'he's way to the right of [then White House aide Patrick] Buchanan.'"[7] Rehnquist, who demonstrated his frivolous side by adorning his judicial robe with comic opera gold stripes to preside over the Senate trial of President Clinton, seems to me to dishonor the Court over which he presides as chief justice of the United States.

Our loss in *Laird v. Tatum* turned out not to do the damage I feared. Lower federal courts found ways to distinguish cases we brought against other surveillance practices. An example was the lawsuit we brought for Lori Paton, the sixteen-year-old who corresponded with the Socialist Workers Party for a school assignment. The Third Circuit U.S. Court of Appeals decided in 1975 that in stigmatizing Paton and her family as subversive, the FBI had caused her specific harm. Therefore, the Court reasoned, more was at stake than a chilling effect on First Amendment rights.[8] This was a paper-thin distinction from the surveillance at issue in *Laird v. Tatum,* which, the Supreme Court said, provided no basis for a lawsuit. I believe there were two reasons the Court of Appeals nevertheless decided in our favor in *Paton.* First was the widespread view in judicial circles that the Supreme Court's decision in the army surveillance case was bad law. Rehnquist's participation and our attempt to recuse him retroactively, highlighting his impropriety, may have contributed to that view. Second, and more important, was that the period between the Supreme Court's decision in *Laird v. Tatum* in 1972 and the Third Circuit Court of Appeals decision in Lori Paton's case in 1975 was dominated by Watergate. While the Court of Appeals purported to follow Supreme Court precedent, its decision was handed down in the post-Watergate atmosphere of heightened national consciousness of the danger of government political espionage.

We benefited from the climate created by Watergate in much of our litigation against political surveillance in the second half of the 1970s. Watergate was also crucial in securing passage of the 1974 Privacy Act and the 1974 amendments to the Freedom of Information Act. Along with our court cases, these bills dismantled the surveillance apparatus of the federal government. The Privacy Act limits the collection of information protected by the First Amendment, and both laws require disclosure to citizens of much of the data the federal government collects on them. Disclosure is crucial. Our lawsuits exposed practices that thrive in dark corners. Government spying on citizens cannot withstand sunlight, which Justice Louis Brandeis called "the best disinfectant."

Through litigation, we revealed not only activities by government that many Americans abhor but also the identities of informers: neighborhood gossips; switchboard operators who listened in on telephone conversations at colleges to pass on what they had heard to police; school principals who betrayed the confidences of their pupils; banks that furnished information to the FBI about those who wrote checks to their depositors; and so forth. No one wants to snitch if they will be found out. Our lawsuits against police department Red squads and against federal agencies, and the access to records required under the Privacy Act and the Freedom of Information Act, ended most of the surveillance and collection of political dossiers that government agencies had engaged in since the Red scare of the post–World War I era.

A mong the privacy issues that create alarm these days are those associated with the Internet. Americans worry about the information about us that is easily accessible in cyberspace. This is the focus, for example, of a popular recent book on privacy, Jeffrey Rosen's *The Unwanted Gaze: The Destruction of Privacy in America*.[9] Rosen, the legal affairs editor of *The New Republic*, covered the Clinton impeachment saga for that magazine and became interested in privacy, he has said, because of Kenneth Starr's investigation. The testing of Monica Lewinsky's dress for traces of Clinton's DNA, the retrieval of e-mails between Lewinsky and a friend, and Starr's subpoena of a Washington, D.C., bookstore's receipts of purchases by Lewinsky aroused Rosen's concern. Calling these records "electronic footprints," he argued that "the protection of privacy has emerged as one of the most salient political, cultural, and technological issues around the globe. As our lives are increasingly lived in cyberspace, citizens are beginning to experience the misunderstandings and indignities that occur when personal information is taken out of context."[10]

Astonishingly, however, the author never mentioned any of the federal privacy laws enacted in the 1970s or the promiscuous circulation of often misleading or false data before they were enacted. A reader of Rosen's widely praised book gets no inkling that privacy was violated far more frequently and with much more profound consequences before the advent of the personal computer or the invention of the concept of cyberspace. Rosen's approach to the issue is characteristic of many contemporary commentators on privacy. They seem unaware that daunting challenges were met and largely overcome in the not-too-distant past. Worse, most recent recruits to the privacy cause pay no attention to a form of data collection and dissemination that we failed to control a generation ago: arrest records. It is an issue primarily of concern to an underclass and, perhaps for that reason, they seem oblivious to it. Yet because of the technological revolution that inspires their fears for privacy, it seems likely that the stigmatizing impact of such records will be all the greater in the future. Though forging restraints is no less urgent than when I was dealing with those records in the 1960s and 1970s, I regret to say that the issue does not even seem to be on the agenda for many of today's privacy proponents.

At this writing, it is still too early to estimate the collateral damage to privacy that will take place as a consequence of our preoccupation with terrorism resulting from the events of September 11, 2001. Obviously, there is a legitimate law-enforcement role in keeping track of those who prepare to commit such crimes. Differentiating conspiracy to engage in violence from activities protected by the First Amendment undoubtedly will continue to cause difficulties. Some intrusions on privacy are already taking place post–September 11, such as the Bush administration's claimed right to eavesdrop electronically on conversations between attorneys and their clients in cases of alleged terrorism; new incursions on health privacy resulting from the concern about bio-terrorism; and increased surveillance of Internet communications. More damaging than all these would be the adoption of a proposal for a national identity card championed by such self-proclaimed civil libertarians as Harvard Law Professor Alan Dershowitz. The main difficulty with this proposal is that it would be easy to encode an identity card with a large amount of information that could be scanned electronically, including, of course, health data and arrest records. The consequence would be to exacerbate greatly discrimination

CHAPTER SIX

Impeaching Nixon

On September 30, 1973, the American Civil Liberties Union board of directors adopted a resolution calling for the impeachment of President Richard M. Nixon. By then, the Watergate scandal had been unfolding for the better part of a year. The Senate Watergate Committee had been formed and had taken extensive testimony. And, two months earlier, Representative Robert Drinan of Massachusetts had introduced a resolution in Congress calling for Nixon's impeachment. Yet the ACLU's decision, which we announced publicly on October 4, was a noteworthy development. We were the first national organization to take this stand. The timing was significant, as many Americans were just beginning to recognize that radical measures were required. Our announcement gave shape to the national outrage against the abuses that were revealed. The campaign we launched helped get the ball rolling.

We annotated our resolution with detailed descriptions of Nixon's high crimes and misdemeanors, citing his approval of the "Huston Plan," named for one of his aides who had proposed it, which had authorized political surveillance by burglary, electronic eavesdropping, mail covers, and the use of the military to spy on civilians; Nixon's use of these methods against political opponents, journalists, and government employees suspected of disloyalty to the president; his deployment of the Internal Revenue Service and other agencies of government to harass political enemies; his establishment within the White House of a personal secret police, the "Plumbers," to operate outside the constraints of the law; his attempt to influence the trial of Daniel Ellsberg, who had been charged with espionage for disclosing the Pentagon Papers, by offering the judge the post of FBI director while the trial was pending and by keeping from the Court his knowledge of the burglary by his agents of the office of Ellsberg's psychiatrist; his interference with the FBI investigation of the

Watergate break-in; and his misuse of various federal agencies, including the Departments of Justice, Defense, and State, the National Security Council, and the Central Intelligence Agency for purposes of political surveillance and the falsification of information.

Within the ACLU, the Washington office and a few of the state affiliates, particularly those in Southern California and New York, had taken the lead in calling for the impeachment resolution. I was a latecomer to the effort, concerned about deviation from the ACLU's historic refusal to take stands for or against candidates for public office. Ultimately, however, as evidence of Nixon's violations of civil liberties piled up, I supported the proposal and spoke for it at the board meeting where it was adopted. An analogy that helped persuade me came from our work on police abuses. Just as we sought remedies against police officers who violated civil liberties, so we should support redress against the nation's chief law-enforcement officer for severe violations of citizens' rights. Impeachment is the constitutionally prescribed remedy.

Our Washington office director at the time was Charles Morgan, Jr., the Alabama attorney I helped recruit for the ACLU in 1964. He was then one of the country's best-known civil liberties and civil rights lawyers. For him, impeaching Nixon was a personal crusade. He lobbied hard for adoption of the ACLU board's resolution. Morgan first came to national attention in 1963 when the bombing of the Sixteenth Street Baptist Church in his hometown of Birmingham, Alabama—the scene of some of the most dramatic civil rights protests of the era—killed four black girls attending Bible classes. A rising political star in the state, Morgan made a speech the following day at the Young Men's Business Club luncheon in Birmingham indicting the city's political and business leadership for creating the climate of racial hatred in which the murders had taken place. Harrison Salisbury of the *New York Times* was in Birmingham to cover the killings, and he reported Morgan's speech on the paper's front page.[1]

The speech ended Morgan's political career in the state, ruined his legal practice, and forced him to install floodlights around his home because of the many death threats he received. At about this time, I was promoting establishment of a southern regional office to strengthen our work on racial equality; once we decided to go ahead with it, I urged Jack Pemberton, then ACLU executive director, to hire Morgan to direct the office, which we based in Atlanta. When he started work there in 1964, he focused on bringing lawsuits to desegregate juries and to challenge discriminatory state electoral laws and practices. A talented litigator, Morgan also took on cases on behalf of a number of high-profile clients: Captain Howard Levy, a young dermatologist who was court-martialed in South Carolina for refusing to train Green Berets in medical skills lest he become complicit in what he alleged were their war crimes in Vietnam; Julian Bond, when he was expelled from the Georgia legislature; Muhammad Ali, in his prosecution for refusing military service for religious reasons; and Colonel Anthony Herbert, America's most decorated soldier during the Korean War, when the Pentagon gave him punitive assignments for alleging that fellow officers committed war crimes in Vietnam. Colorful, highly quotable, and a drinking buddy of many of the journalists who covered the civil rights struggle in the South—before he became a teetotaler—Morgan was rarely out of the news for long.

I was a strong supporter of Morgan's during his tenure as director of the regional office. In turn, when I was a candidate to become ACLU executive director in 1970, no one lobbied for my election more vigorously than Morgan. He only told me about one of his efforts after I was chosen, for fear I would have objected if I had known in advance (he was right). A sure voice and vote against me was a nationally known law professor at a leading southern university. He was also a very vain man. Morgan persuaded a reporter for the *New York Times* to schedule an interview in the law professor's office at the university on the day of the vote by the ACLU board. Given the closeness of the vote—35–32 in my favor—the law professor's absence made a difference. No story appeared in the *Times* as a result of the interview.

In 1972, I appointed Morgan to direct our Washington office. It did not take long until he became involved in the events surrounding Watergate. When the trial of those arrested for the burglary took place, the prosecutors failed to connect the defendants with the White House. Their theory of the case was that the burglars were "on a frolic of their own." That left open the question of motive. As it happened, the bug installed on the phone of Democratic National Committee Chairman Lawrence O'Brien had not worked, but that on the phone of one of his aides had produced a number of tapes. The prosecutors had these tapes and planned to introduce them into evidence to demonstrate a possible motive for the burglary: blackmail. Spencer Oliver, the aide whose phone was tapped, objected. This strategy would compound the invasion of his privacy.

To block use of the tapes, Oliver sought Morgan's assistance. As Judge

John Sirica, who presided over the trial of the Watergate burglars, refused to exclude the evidence, Morgan obtained an interlocutory ruling from the U.S. Court of Appeals barring use of the tapes. In Morgan's view, this small intervention played a crucial role in the trial as it left the prosecutors without evidence to support their theory about a motive. The episode assumed the importance in his mind of the horseshoe nail in George Herbert's famous poem. He thought it opened the way for Judge Sirica to take over the questioning of witnesses, leading to the exposure of White House involvement. I thought Morgan inflated greatly the significance of his walk-on part in the great drama that was being played out. Judge Sirica was plainly dissatisfied with the prosecution's case, especially the failure to explain the large amounts of money provided to the Watergate burglars. The availability of that money made it evident the break-in did not have a financial motive. Yet I did not attach much importance at the time to what I thought was Chuck Morgan's harmless self-aggrandizement.

Believing all along that the president was connected to the Watergate burglars and, over time, seeing his theory confirmed, Morgan became an ardent supporter of impeachment. I also favored impeachment but continued to be skeptical about the propriety of an ACLU stand on the issue until shortly before the board meeting where we were to debate the issue. Once I made up my mind, however, I, too, became a dedicated advocate. Though our role was not central, we made three contributions to the impeachment effort. The first was to get involved early. Second was our publication of a series of full-page newspaper advertisements calling for impeachment. And third was our role in helping to develop information that went into one of the three counts of impeachment that was endorsed by the House of Representatives Judiciary Committee.

I worked on the newspaper advertisements with Ira Glasser, then executive director of the NYCLU. Shortly after he had begun work there in 1967 as associate director, I had sent him to South Carolina to assist Morgan in his defense of Captain Howard Levy. Ever since, they had been close allies. Ira was another committed proponent of impeachment, and he played a prime part both in the intense lobbying that preceded the ACLU board's resolution and in the campaign we organized. His part in the campaign was a factor, I believe, in his selection a few years later to succeed me. It seemed to demonstrate his capacity to provide leadership on an issue of national significance.

The first of our visually striking advertisements appeared in the *New York Times* on October 14, 1973, with a bold headline that read: "Why it is necessary to impeach President Nixon. And how it can be done." The text that followed tracked the ACLU board resolution's litany of complaints of civil liberties abuses and provided information on the impeachment process. It was accompanied by a coupon asking for contributions "to help the impeachment campaign" and was signed by Ed Ennis, the ACLU chairman, and by me.

Contributions poured in. We recycled receipts to place the same advertisement in other newspapers and to publish additional ones. Each advertisement attracted more contributions and each paid for still more advertisements. The largest number of contributions came in response to advertisements that, by chance, appeared in some newspapers the Sunday morning after "The Saturday Night Massacre"—that is, the night Nixon fired Watergate Special Prosecutor Archibald Cox—and after Attorney General Eliot Richardson and Deputy Attorney General William Ruckelshaus resigned rather than carry out Nixon's order, leaving the assignment to Solicitor General Robert Bork, the highest-level Justice Department official ready to do the dirty deed. In the course of about two months, we published more than 150 full-page advertisements in major newspapers across the country calling for impeachment. A nice irony was that we won an advertising award that required the U.S. Information Service to include our impeachment advertisements in an exhibit it took around the world. Another consequence was a sharp increase in the ACLU membership rolls as thousands joined because of our campaign for impeachment.

Our contribution to the Judiciary Committee's charges against Nixon was on wiretapping. We brought a lawsuit on behalf of Morton Halperin, a former aide to Henry Kissinger in the National Security Council (where some called him "Kissinger's Kissinger"), against Nixon and Kissinger for an illegal wiretap on Halperin's home phone. The president and his National Security Adviser ordered the tap on Halperin and others in an apparent attempt to discover who had leaked to the press the information that the administration had launched the secret bombing of Cambodia. Nixon testified in the lawsuit we brought for Halperin that he told Kissinger "it was essential that he try to get to the bottom of it. I said if this can leak, anything can leak. I said that I felt that this was one of those cases where he should directly call Mr. Hoover [FBI Director J. Edgar Hoover] and provide for Mr. Hoover, in his assessment, individuals who might have had access to this information."

Mort Halperin was a suspect because he had resigned his White House post to protest the bombing. The tap on his phone was left in place for twenty-one months. It did not turn up anything that showed his disclosure of secrets, but it did collect a lot of personal information on Mort and his family. In addition, as he became an adviser to a Democratic presidential candidate, Senator Edmund Muskie of Maine, it gathered political information on a potential opponent of Nixon's. It also picked up information on the former Defense Department official charged with disclosure of the Pentagon Papers, Daniel Ellsberg. Mort had worked for the Department of Defense before joining Kissinger's staff. One of his assignments there had been to help compile the documents on the history of the Vietnam War that became known as the Pentagon Papers. Ellsberg, a friend of Mort's, had made phone calls from Mort's home phone that were overheard. The government was obliged to disclose this information to Ellsberg's defense attorneys, but initially denied it listened to his conversations. When the information was finally revealed long after the trial began, the charges against Ellsberg were dismissed because, Judge Matthew Byrne said, government misconduct had "incurably infected the prosecution."

President Nixon defended himself against the charge of illegal wiretapping by claiming that the taps, which began in mid-1969, were "legal at the time" that he authorized them because the U.S. Supreme Court did not rule specifically on such wiretaps until June 1972, when it held unanimously (Justice Rehnquist not participating this time) that they were illegal.[2] The Judiciary Committee did not buy Nixon's "legal at the time" argument. An illegal act is illegal when it takes place, not only when it comes before a court that confirms it is unlawful. The House Judiciary Committee made Nixon's illegal wiretapping of Mort Halperin and other officials, former officials, and journalists one of the counts for impeachment.[3]

As long as the impeachment campaign was under way, Charles Morgan and I worked together on it harmoniously. After Nixon resigned in August 1974 in the face of certain impeachment by the House of Representatives and near-certain conviction by the Senate, tensions emerged between us. Morgan believed that the prosecutors who had tried to prove the Watergate burglars were off on a frolic of their own had engaged in a deliberate cover-up. When the chief prosecutor, Earl Silbert, was nominated by President Gerald Ford as U.S. Attorney for the District of Columbia, Morgan saw the appointment as a payoff for Silbert's attempt to protect Nixon. It was, he thought, of a piece with Ford's pardon of his predecessor.

Silbert's nomination required Senate confirmation, which Morgan was determined to block. In light of Silbert's dismal performance in the prosecution of the Watergate burglars, I agreed he was a poor choice for promotion. I objected to Morgan's effort to block his appointment, however, both because I was not persuaded that Silbert was part of a cover-up and because of the ACLU's policy of not taking stands on candidates for public office. In addition, I objected to Morgan's diversion of staff in our Washington office from other responsibilities to spend their time gathering information he could use to discredit Silbert. Underlying our dispute was Morgan's view—as he repeatedly made clear to me—that he deserved credit for his role in exposing the Watergate cover-up by blocking use of the tapes the prosecutors wanted to play in court to support their blackmail theory. Journalists Bob Woodward and Carl Bernstein were being lionized for their role in unraveling Watergate. By making the alleged cover-up an issue in Silbert's confirmation, Morgan expected at long last to obtain his share of the glory. In obstructing his efforts, he argued, I was denying him his due.

An unrelated episode brought matters to the breaking point between us. A *New York Times* story appeared on Governor Jimmy Carter's quest for the Democratic Party's nomination for president. It quoted Morgan as Washington director of the ACLU, saying that though he preferred Senator Fred Harris, a populist candidate from Oklahoma, he thought opposition to Carter was based on bias against southerners. Furious over a further transgression of our policy, I fired off a note to Morgan asking what steps he was taking to dissociate the ACLU from his remarks. I probably should have picked up the phone to talk to him about it, but at the time I was so exasperated by our ongoing dispute over the Silbert matter that I did it by letter. Morgan responded with a letter of his own, saying the step he was taking was to resign. He immediately informed his friends in the press. Several of them published stories recounting his heroic actions in Birmingham and his long list of stellar court cases. The impression created by these articles, such as the one that columnist Tom Wicker published in the *New York Times,* was that the heroic Morgan was an independent spirit forced out of his post by the bureaucrats in the ACLU's head office.

Publicly, I did not get into the Silbert matter. In a letter published in the *New York Times*, I dealt with Morgan's resignation on his chosen grounds. I wrote:

> Articles in The Times have described Charles Morgan's resignation as director of the ACLU's Washington office as rooted in disagreement with an aspect of ACLU policy. I write to describe that policy.
>
> The ACLU constitution requires us to act "wholly without political partisanship." To comply with that constitution we ask our staff to take special care that personal political views they express are clearly distinguished from those of the ACLU.
>
> The importance of this is illustrated by the struggle over amending the Federal Election Campaign Act, in which the ACLU is deeply involved. If a method is found to release subsidy payments to candidates, it will aid Jimmy Carter. If payments are blocked, it will aid Hubert Humphrey. The ACLU's interest is rooted in civil liberties principles, and our lobbying position should advance them publicly. That is difficult if our chief lobbyist simultaneously identifies himself publicly with particular candidates and much more difficult if our lobbyist does not go to some pains to distinguish his personal partisan political views from those of the ACLU.
>
> Similarly, the ACLU played a leading role in the effort to impeach Richard Nixon. When Gerald Ford pardoned Nixon, we denounced the pardon. We insisted that our actions were rooted in civil liberties principles and not in political partisanship. Republicans, Democrats and others in the ACLU joined in these actions. It is difficult to advance the civil liberties principles underlying these actions when our chief lobbyist, who was given responsibility for much of this effort, identifies himself publicly with Democratic candidates for President. It is made more difficult if our chief lobbyist does not go to some pains to distinguish his personal partisan political views from those of the ACLU.
>
> When I asked Mr. Morgan what he was doing to distinguish his personal partisan political views from those of the ACLU, he resigned publicly. He chose this course rather than even discussing the matter with the ACLU executive committee or board. . . .
>
> One final comment: Mr. Morgan resigned. He was not fired. His contributions to civil liberties have been too significant for the ACLU to act against him over this matter, whatever unhappiness it caused us in compromising our efforts to obey the ACLU's own constitution.

Though Morgan resigned, he attended the ACLU board of directors meeting soon thereafter where his supporters attempted to persuade the board not to accept his resignation. On this occasion, his normally astute political instincts failed him. He thought he had a chance to get a majority of the board to reject his resignation. The effect would have been an expression of no confidence in me that would have forced me out. I was not apprehensive about the outcome. Morgan had many admirers, and I was once one of them, but I knew many board members considered him a loose cannon. They were happy to have him working for the ACLU as long as they could count on me to point him in the right direction. When I lost control over him, they were ready to see him leave. Also, adherence to the organization's policies on political nonpartisanship mattered to most board members. When the vote was tallied, ten called for rejection of Morgan's resignation and sixty-one for acceptance.

Following his departure from the ACLU, Morgan established a successful private practice in Washington, D.C. For a number of years, he continued to attract press attention, usually when he took on matters that put him into collision with his erstwhile civil liberties and civil rights colleagues. He represented southern states resisting college desegregation in opposition to the NAACP Legal Defense Fund; championed "free speech" for the American Tobacco Council in objecting to Surgeon General warnings in cigarette advertising; filed a lawsuit for Sears, Roebuck, attacking the federal Equal Employment Opportunities Commission, then headed by his former ACLU colleague Eleanor Holmes Norton; and represented the Atlanta law firm of former Attorney General Griffin Bell, King & Spalding, in the U.S. Supreme Court, arguing that federal laws prohibiting employment discrimination did not apply to rejection of a woman's bid to become a partner in the firm (the Court ruled against him unanimously). Whether Morgan took on such clients out of conviction, because they were remunerative, in spite against an institution he thought treated him badly, or out of some combination of those reasons, I do not know.

Though the aftermath of the impeachment effort was at times trying for me within the ACLU because of the conflict with Morgan, it was also a very satisfying period because of great advances for civil liberties through federal legislation. In the few months that remained in 1974 after Nixon's resignation that August, Congress adopted the Privacy Act, the Family Educational Rights and Privacy Act, and a series of important amendments to the Freedom of Information Act (passed over President Ford's veto) greatly enhancing that law's value in obtaining access to government information. Invasions of privacy and government secrecy were hallmarks of Nixon's abuses of civil liberties. The adoption of federal laws expanding the rights of Americans in these crucial areas was largely attributable to national distaste for the violations of constitutional rights symbolized by Watergate.

Another set of laws adopted by Congress in late 1974 and in 1975 provided the foundations for the promotion of human rights internationally as a goal of American foreign policy. Among their provisions were a prohibition on U.S. military aid to countries practicing gross violations of internationally recognized human rights; a requirement that the State Department publish annual country reports on human rights practices worldwide; and establishment of the Bureau of Human Rights within the State Department to be headed by an assistant secretary of state for human rights (some of these were also adopted over Ford's veto). What made those innovations in the legal regulation of foreign policy most remarkable is that they were enacted *before* the emergence of a significant international human rights movement. Heightened consciousness of rights, a byproduct of Watergate and Nixon's ouster, was one factor in the passage of this legislation.

I did not realize it at the time, but it was the legacy of the impeachment campaign in shaping American laws dealing with international human rights that was to have the most profound impact on my own future career. Of far greater consequence, of course, has been its lasting influence on the role of the United States in world affairs. Looking back on that period nearly three decades later, it seems the high point in the country's rights consciousness. There was never a moment that I can recall comparable to the hearings of the House Judiciary Committee on the impeachment resolutions when Americans took greater pride in the protections for liberties set forth in the U.S. Constitution. We continue to reap the benefits at the present moment of national testing despite the continuing leadership of the U.S. Supreme Court by a Nixon designee and the Bush administration's appointment of an attorney general who seems a clone of Nixon where civil liberties are concerned.

CHAPTER SEVEN

Defending Free Speech in Skokie, Illinois

W hen I started work for the American Civil Liberties Union in 1963, I was familiar with the organization's defense of free speech for racist bigots, including self-styled American Nazis. Some ACLU court cases on behalf of Nazis, such as one challenging denial of a permit for a demonstration in New York City's Union Square park on July 4, 1960—a case the ACLU eventually won[1]—had attracted a lot of attention, and I had no doubts about the ACLU's stand. Rights, I believe, are only meaningful if they apply to all, regardless of the views they espouse. At the time, my parents were still alive, and I was more or less able to persuade my father, intellectually if not emotionally, that the Nazis had a right to speak. My mother thought I was out of my mind.

In those days, the Nazi cases were very visible because the reemergence in the late 1950s of groups in the United States identifying themselves with the World War II enemy was still a novelty, and also because the "führer" of one of these minuscule groups, George Lincoln Rockwell, had a flair for publicity. A typical Rockwell stunt was to picket showings of the movie of Leon Uris's novel *Exodus* wearing full Nazi regalia. On occasions when the police refrained from intervening and allowed him and a handful of associates two or three hours to walk back and forth on the sidewalk carrying placards, the attention they received was minimal. But Rockwell counted on the authorities to respond promptly to a few complaints from irate passers-by or from those who heard he was engaged in one of his provocations. Law-enforcement officials often met his expectations. An arrest, or a court order prohibiting his demonstrations, produced the media coverage he craved. In that era, pictures of Rockwell adorned with swastikas, and with the hateful messages on the placards he carried clearly visible, appeared often in newspapers and on local television evening newscasts. His success in disseminating his views depended, as he understood well, on efforts to silence him.

On the many occasions the police did intervene, Rockwell turned to the local branch of the ACLU for assistance. We knew this was Rockwell's game. From his standpoint, civil liberties attorneys were easy to manipulate. He could deride us and our principles and, simultaneously, get the Civil Liberties Union to put those principles into practice for him. That the organization was a leading voice of American liberalism and well known for defending labor strikers, antiwar activists, civil rights demonstrators, and assorted leftists, or reputed leftists, in their battles with congressional investigating committees, loyalty-security boards, and other public bodies engaged in the anti-Red crusades of the times, and that some of the lawyers who represented him for the ACLU were Jews, was a bonus for the publicity-seeking Rockwell. A picture of a Jewish lawyer accompanying Rockwell as he walked up the steps of a courthouse had a man-bites-dog quality he eagerly exploited.

Some lawyers who defended the Nazis suffered consequences. A well-known New York lawyer who lived in my Greenwich Village neighborhood appeared with Rockwell on a late-night radio talk show and was asked on the air by the host whether he would defend Rockwell's rights. He said he would. Rockwell soon took him up on the offer. The lawyer arranged with me that he would appear in court for the Civil Liberties Union. As a result, a shopper in our neighborhood supermarket spat in his face, and his Democratic Party political club made him abandon a plan to run for public office.

As ACLU field director, I usually did not deal with clients directly and had no contact with Rockwell. That changed in January 1965 when I was appointed director of the New York Civil Liberties Union. I spoke with him on several occasions before his assassination by one of his followers in August 1967. Most of our contacts were limited to phone conversations, but one time I dealt with him more directly.

Rockwell phoned me in early 1967 to tell me he had been subpoenaed to appear at a hearing of a committee of the State Assembly investigating the activities of far right organizations in the New York Police Department. The subpoena was preposterous. While some New York police officers joined groups such as the John Birch Society, as was their right, there was no evidence any of them were associated with Rockwell's American

Nazi Party. I handled the matter myself because I had led the campaign in New York a few months earlier for civilian review of complaints of police abuse and was identified publicly as a strong critic of police misconduct. In addition to objecting on First Amendment grounds to the inquiry in which the committee was engaged, I welcomed the opportunity to appear at the hearing to defend the police against an unwarranted slur. It would help make the point that we were not anti-police; we upheld the rights of all.

The hearing to which I accompanied Rockwell and James Madole, the leader of a rival Nazi group who was also subpoenaed (the two führers said not a word to each other, at least in my presence), was a publicity stunt by the state legislators on about the same level as one of the Nazi demonstrations. It provided television footage showing the assemblymen on the committee hectoring the Nazis, but had nothing to do with racist behavior by the New York police, which was and is a serious issue. To get attention for themselves, the legislators maligned the police unfairly and, in the process, gave the Nazis the publicity they sought and made them appear more important than they deserved. By going to the hearing with the two Nazis, I knew I was contributing to the circus atmosphere. Yet by insisting on answering the questions directed by the legislators to the two führers, and by emphasizing in my responses both my First Amendment concerns and my objections to the calumny against the police, I succeeded in shifting the focus of media attention to the propriety of the hearing, embarrassing the legislators who had organized it. The Assembly committee never again pursued this line of inquiry.

In the years following Rockwell's assassination, the Nazi movement in the United States did not disappear but, lacking a charismatic leader and no longer a novelty, declined as a focus of attention. Still, with some frequency, little groups of men who dressed up in Nazi uniform—I don't recall the involvement of any women—got into various forms of legal difficulty. Whenever this happened, it seemed, they called the local ACLU. We took these cases for granted. They were part of our job.

When I was appointed national executive director of the ACLU in 1970, I stopped having any direct contact with the Nazis. Their cases were routine matters involving settled principles of law and were handled by our local affiliates without participation by the national office. In previous years, a handful of ACLU cases on behalf of groups espousing Nazi-like doctrines had set landmark national legal precedents. In *Terminiello v. City of*

Chicago,[2] the Supreme Court decided in 1949 that the threat of a disturbance by a hostile crowd does not justify suppression of a speech, in that
instance by a white racist defrocked priest. Then, in 1969, the Supreme
Court decided in *Brandenburg v. Ohio,*[3] a case involving a Ku Klux Klan
group, that advocacy of violence may only be suppressed where there is
incitement to imminent lawless action and a likelihood, as a result, that
such action will take place. Between them, *Terminiello* and *Brandenburg*
strike at principal justifications that law-enforcement authorities customarily invoke to suppress speech by groups they find repugnant. With such
precedents firmly in place, most Nazi cases that arose during my tenure as
director of the ACLU in the 1970s were too mundane to bring to the attention of the national office. I often learned that ACLU affiliates took on
such cases only when I saw items about them in the press or read about
them in the affiliate's newsletter.

Today, a quarter century later, the Nazi attempt to march in Skokie, Illinois, is still remembered. Yet when it began in 1977, it did not stand out as
special. For the Illinois ACLU, which had handled a number of cases involving the same small Nazi group, with one still under way when Skokie
began, so far as the legal issues that were involved went, the case was routine. Skokie was not a special target of the Nazis. When they first announced their intent to hold a demonstration there, they probably did not
even know the suburban town was home to a large number of Holocaust
survivors, the distinguishing characteristic that turned this Nazi case into a
cause célèbre.

The Nazis stumbled onto Skokie when the Chicago authorities temporarily blocked them from holding demonstrations in a city neighborhood, Marquette Park, where they were attempting to exploit racial
tensions. Seeking a way to sustain attention to themselves while the ACLU
litigated the Marquette Park exclusion, the Chicago Nazis wrote letters to
about a dozen suburban communities seeking permits to demonstrate in
their parks. The other communities all ignored these letters. Only Skokie
took the bait and responded to the Nazis, writing back that they would
have to post a bond of $350,000 to pay for any damage to park property if
they wished to demonstrate. Recognizing that Skokie had played into their
hands, the Nazis sent another letter announcing a demonstration in front
of the Village Hall on May 1, 1977 (though calling itself a "village,"
Skokie's population was more than 70,000).

The town's Synagogue Council attempted to ensure that Skokie would respond with restraint and permit the demonstration to go forward with as little fuss as possible and initially won cooperation by the mayor and other local officials in pursuing this course. This sensible strategy failed. Popular sentiment was aroused and town officials felt obliged to try to prevent the demonstration. Four days before it was scheduled, the town sued to prohibit it. In its legal papers, Skokie argued the demonstration would be a "symbolic assault" against residents who were Holocaust survivors. Though the papers did not allege the Nazis would engage in violence, the town invoked the possibility that violence would occur because announcement of the demonstration "has aroused the passions of the survivors of the Nazi concentration camps who are taking measures unknown to the plaintiffs [i.e., town officials] to thwart the threatened march."

There is no legal precedent for forbidding the exercise of First Amendment rights as a "symbolic assault." As to "measures unknown" by survivors of the concentration camps, this is precisely the issue the Supreme Court had settled in *Terminiello*. A hostile reaction—or what has been called a "heckler's veto"—may not be the basis for suppressing freedom of speech or assembly. If the authorities believe a hostile crowd might engage in violence, they have a duty to provide police protection so that demonstrators may exercise their First Amendment rights. By filing a lawsuit before the demonstration, Skokie indicated it knew the potential for violence in time to take the measures needed to assure public safety. If such a rule were not in place, any group could suppress anybody else's freedom of speech simply by threatening to respond violently.

The lawsuit was only the first of Skokie's legal maneuvers to block the march. Next, the town adopted three new ordinances. The first extended the requirement for a $350,000 bond to pay for possible property damage so it also applied to demonstrations on Skokie's town streets. This ordinance authorized town officials to provide a permit only if "the conduct of the parade, public assembly, or similar activity will not portray criminality, depravity or lack of virtue in, or incite violence, hatred, abuse or hostility toward a person or group of persons by reason of reference to religious, racial, ethnic, national or regional affiliation." A second ordinance made it a crime to disseminate in Skokie any material "which promotes and incites hatred against persons by reason of their race, national origin or religion." It forbade "markings and clothing of symbolic significance" in promoting hatred. Nazi clothing was also the target of the third ordinance, which provided that, "No person shall engage in any march, walk or public demonstration as a member or on behalf of any political party while wearing a military style uniform."

Not content with the town's efforts, the Chicago Anti-Defamation League (ADL) got into the act, filing a lawsuit on behalf of Holocaust survivors residing in Skokie for "menticide." It was a word I had not encountered previously that the ADL defined as emotional harm. The remedies sought included a permanent prohibition on Nazi marches in Skokie. Legally absurd, this frivolous lawsuit was designed to be as insulting as possible to the ACLU as the papers filed with the Illinois courts repeatedly characterized the (Jewish) lawyer representing the Nazis as "Neo-Nazi Counsel." (The author of a book critical of our stand says the ADL lawyer who brought this suit "execrated the ACLU in interviews with me and during the controversy."[4]) I had to have strong words with national officers of the ADL to get their Chicago branch to back off and inform the court this was their way of saying "Counsel for the Neo-Nazis."

When Skokie filed its lawsuit, the director of the Illinois ACLU, David Hamlin, and the staff attorney representing the Nazis, David Goldberger, called me to inform me the matter could prove troublesome. It was attracting a lot of attention from the Chicago press. Despite that call, I was not initially alarmed. After all, a lot more Jews and a great many more Holocaust survivors lived in cities such as New York and Los Angeles, where there had been many Nazi demonstrations over the years. These no longer got much notice. It did not take long, however, until I realized my mistake.

Within a few days, the national ACLU office was besieged by calls from the news media asking for statements on Skokie. I got requests from all over the country to take part in radio call-in broadcasts and television interviews about the case, and some from foreign media. More disturbingly, we started getting phone calls and letters from hundreds of people who said they were resigning as ACLU members because they were outraged by our representation of the Nazis. When we checked, it turned out that many were in no position to resign as they had never been members. That still left a sufficiently large number of actual members who did resign, however, so it was apparent there would be significant financial consequences for the ACLU. I could not respond individually to all who wrote to me criticizing our stand, so I devised a form letter that addressed the arguments that appeared most frequently. It said, in part:

One comment that often appears in letters I receive is that, if the Nazis come to power, the ACLU and its leaders would not be allowed to survive. Of course, that is true. Civil liberties is the antithesis of Nazism.

Perhaps that explains best why we defend free speech for Nazis. We don't share their values. We don't take guidance from them. We defend free speech for Nazis—or anyone else—because we say that government may not put any person or group beyond the pale of constitutional protection.

The Constitution is absolute in its language. It allows "no law . . . abridging the freedom of speech, or of the press; or the right of the people peaceably to assemble and to petition the Government for a redress of grievances." No law means no law. It does not mean giving government officials some leeway to pick out groups that are so despicable that they should be denied freedom of speech. Does anyone really believe that the exercise of such discretion by government will defeat the values represented by the Nazis?

Some of the people who write to us about Skokie point out that free speech does not protect the right of a person falsely to shout fire in a crowded theater. Quite right. When a person shouts fire in a theater, no one else has an opportunity to express a contrary view before a panic ensues. Free speech can't operate. This is what the courts call a "clear and present danger."

Suppose a Nazi speaker, in front of a mob of sympathizers, said: "There's a Jew. Let's get him." If the Nazi refrained from participating directly in any resulting violence, he still would not have any valid defense of free speech. As in the example of shouting fire in a crowded theater, the violence would follow before anyone could present an opposing view. Free speech could not operate.

Skokie is altogether different. It has a large Jewish community and is very hostile to the Nazis. If a Nazi marching in Skokie should call for violence against Jews, it won't take place. The only likelihood of violence in Skokie is on the part of listeners to the Nazis who become so enraged at the message of the Nazis that they attack the Nazis.

But listener rage against a speaker can never be the basis for banning speech. If that were allowed, Martin Luther King, Jr. could never have marched in Selma, anti-war demonstrators could never have marched on or near a military base, the ambassador from South Vietnam could not have spoken on a college campus, the Jewish Defense League could never have picketed the Russian embassy and anti-Nixon demonstrators could never have picketed the White House. A prohibition of speech based on listener antagonism is sometimes called a "heckler's veto." It is a veto the ACLU has always opposed and we oppose it in Skokie. If the people of Skokie want, they have every opportunity to make free speech operate. They are free to denounce the Nazis as vigorously and often as they choose. I hope they do so.

Some letter writers say that group defamation should not be permitted. The late Edmond Cahn dealt with this subject in a notable address delivered at the Hebrew University in Jerusalem in 1962. If there were a prohibition against group defamation, said Cahn:

"The officials could begin by prosecuting anyone who distributed the Christian Gospels, because they contain many defamatory statements not only about Jews but also about Christians; they show Christians failing Jesus in his hour of deepest tragedy. Then the officials could ban Greek literature for calling the rest of the world 'barbarians.' Roman authors would be suppressed because when they were not defaming the Gallic and Teutonic tribes they were disparaging the Italians. For obvious reasons, all Christian writers of the Middle Ages and quite a few modern ones could meet a similar fate. Even if an exceptional Catholic should fail to mention the Jews, the officials would have to proceed against his works for what he said about the Protestants and, of course, the same would apply to Protestant views on the subject of Catholics. Then there is Shakespeare who openly affronted the French, the Welsh, the Danes, and sundry important residents of the fairy kingdom. Dozens of British writers from Sheridan and Dickens to Shaw and Joyce insulted the Irish. Finally, almost every worthwhile item of prose and poetry published by an American Negro would fall under the ban because it either whispered, spoke, or shouted unkind statements about the group called 'white.' Literally applied, a group-libel law would leave our bookshelves empty and us without desire to fill them."

Some letter writers complain that the ACLU should use its limited resources elsewhere. If we wanted to duck the issue, we could have said something along those lines. But it would have been false. The ACLU takes all cases in which we believe free speech is at stake. We have always viewed free speech as our prime responsibility. Other kinds of cases—prison, mental commitment, juvenile rights, political surveillance, abortion, race and sex discrimination, privacy—involve major commitments of resources. Not so with most free speech cases. They don't require the construction of complex evidentiary records. They are generally simple and straightforward and it would be untrue to say we don't have the resources to handle them.

The Nazis may despise us—and we certainly despise them—but we intend to continue to be governed by our rules and the rules of the United States Constitution. That means defending free speech for those we despise and those who despise us. It means not being governed by the rules of the Nazis. Their rules and the values they represent have already come to power if governments are allowed to pick and choose who is entitled to freedom of speech.

It was not a good moment for the ACLU to suffer losses. Ironically, we were not doing well financially in 1977 because Jimmy Carter had become president earlier in the year. Especially during the first two years or so of Carter's term, it appeared to many of our supporters that the need for the ACLU to defend civil liberties had declined dramatically. As a result, there was a fall-off in contributions. Like many other cause organizations, the ACLU thrives institutionally on adversity, or the appearance of adversity.

In the ACLU's case, the advent of Carter was especially important because our membership and contributions had grown rapidly during Richard Nixon's presidency. Our challenges to political surveillance by the U.S. Army, the abusive use of grand juries for political investigations, the punitive treatment of opponents of the Vietnam War, the wiretapping of critics of Nixon administration policies, the harassment and prosecution of journalists and newspapers, and the many other intrusions on freedom of speech, press, and assembly that culminated in Watergate had won us many new adherents. Our early espousal of impeachment had rallied thousands of new supporters to the organization.

During the year and a half of Gerald Ford's presidency, the ACLU had held on to the members we recruited during the Nixon era. Ford was generally respectful of civil liberties, and his attorney general, former University of Chicago president Edward Levi, restored dignity to that office and engaged in none of the assaults on rights that were pervasive when John Mitchell and Edward Kleindienst had headed the Justice Department. Yet ACLU members remained mistrustful. Ford's pardon of his predecessor had cast a shadow over his presidency. Newcomers to the ACLU made up by far the largest number of members who quit over Skokie. Longer-term members were familiar with our representation of groups such as the Nazis and most agreed with our defense of free speech for all. Because such cases had not attracted much attention since the 1960s, however, many who had joined more recently were not aware, or were only dimly aware, that the ACLU also defended freedom of speech for those professing hateful views. It came as a shock when they heard about Skokie.

In the six years of Nixon's presidency, ACLU membership had roughly doubled, to about 275,000, and we had rapidly expanded our activities. Skokie caused or contributed to a fall from that peak of about 15 percent, or about 40,000 members. We remained a much larger organization than before Nixon, but we were forced to make substantial cuts in our programs.

The resignations of ACLU members over Skokie was part of the story in the press and in public debates over our defense of the Nazis. For a period, it seemed no day passed without new stories about Skokie. Every editorial writer and columnist in the country seemed to have a say. The majority supported our stand, but some commentators who could ordinarily be counted on to defend civil liberties disappointed us. An example was Garry Wills. He wrote, "The woman tortured by obscene phone calls is afflicted by another person's speech. Is that speech protected by the Constitution? . . . The Nazis . . . are, in effect, broadcasting an obscene phone call to a whole neighborhood instead of a single house. I see no problem with police 'suppressing' a march through Skokie."[5] With lawsuits challenging the initial exclusion of the Nazis from Skokie as well as the three ordinances enacted by the town, and with the ADL lawsuit, there was a rich harvest of legal developments to report. Also, other public bodies, such as the Illinois state legislature—before which I testified on the matter—got into the act. When nothing happened, the media found human interest stories to publish, such as accounts of the family background and upbringing of the Nazis—it turned out the father of their leader was a converted Jew who had changed his name from Cohn to Collin—or the personal sagas of Holocaust survivors living in Skokie.

Though I thought the attention disproportionate, the media coverage had a salutary impact. It made the question of whether the Nazis had a right to march not only an issue for the courts but also a topic for discussion and debate everywhere. I made many public speeches about Skokie during the fifteen months the court cases dragged on, and after a while, began regularly posing a question to my audiences: How many of those present had gotten into arguments with friends or family over Skokie? Toward the end, it seemed almost everyone raised a hand. I guessed no other question involving First Amendment rights—not even far more important matters such as the Pentagon Papers case several years earlier—provoked so many arguments.

As time went by, I thought my audiences were increasingly sympathetic to my stand. Of the many invitations I received to speak or debate, I always tried to accept those from synagogues. I thought I had an obligation to explain the ACLU's position to their congregations. At the outset, those were tough crowds, but I enjoyed an uphill battle in persuading my audiences. Some in any group to which I spoke always remained harshly critical of the ACLU, and bitterly criticized me as a Jew for my stand. Yet I think that growing sympathy for our position was a product of the many arguments people got into over Skokie. The more people debated the issue, it seemed, the more they were persuaded by the argument for free speech.

After the litigation over Skokie had been under way for more than a year, sensing that public opinion was turning in our favor, I thought we might reverse the loss of membership support we had suffered. I decided to send a fund-raising appeal to the entire remaining membership of the ACLU asking for extra contributions to compensate for the losses we had suffered because of defections. The letter, a product of extended discussion that involved several outside advisers as well as others in the ACLU, went out over the signature of David Goldberger, the attorney with the unmistakably Jewish name who had represented the Nazis in the Skokie cases and had endured the most extreme vilification while the case was under way, and for a long time thereafter. Sent in August 1978, shortly after the Skokie case had ended and a couple of months before I ended my service with the ACLU, it turned out to be the most successful fund-raising appeal we had ever sent. We struck the same theme in mailings that summer to outside lists seeking new members—with similar results. These efforts, and the advent of the Reagan administration a couple of years later, made the ACLU's financial losses short-term. But while the media played up our difficulties due to the resignations of members, I could not get much attention to our reversal of fortune. To this day, many who remember Skokie believe erroneously that it did long-term financial damage to the ACLU.

One group attempted to exploit Skokie for its own ends. The Jewish Defense League (JDL) was known for its violent protests, including one in which a woman in the office of impresario Sol Hurok had been killed by a bomb. I had encountered Rabbi Meir Kahane, the group's founder, a number of times previously and found him as racist and as loathsome as the Nazis. On one occasion, at the State University of New York at Binghamton, I had made the mistake of debating Kahane, giving him a dignity he did not deserve and feeling myself dirtied by the experience. While the Nazis were under a court order excluding them from Skokie under the ordinances requiring a bond, prohibiting uniforms, and barring groups promoting hatred, Kahane and a group of helmeted followers carrying clubs staged their own demonstration in the town with no interference. Arriving in Skokie, Kahane announced, "We intend to bloody the Nazis. . . . I am not predicting violence—I am promising violence." The JDL also conducted a number of noisy demonstrations *inside* the ACLU offices, blocking the entrance, preventing access, and harassing our staff. On one such occasion, they arrived carrying baseball bats. Kahane taunted me to call the police, and I was sorely tempted to do so, but I decided the tabloids would have a field day with the story. This would give the JDL the publicity they sought and probably provoke them to escalate their harassment. I decided to ignore Kahane and put up with the disruption.

Then, on April 20, 1978, as I returned from Brooklyn Law School, where I had debated a leftist lawyer representing the National Lawyers Guild on the propriety of defending free speech for Nazis, I found the JDL conducting a demonstration in front of the building. Several of the JDL leaders visited our offices on the building's eleventh floor to leave a "gift" for me: a wooden board covered with a photograph of a crematorium, shards of glass, and half a lampshade, and spattered with red paint. To this object, they had affixed a small brass plaque inscribed to indicate that it was presented to me on Hitler's birthday. While I did not appreciate this, I liked even less the fact that they located my home in Greenwich Village and staged demonstrations there, requiring Yvette to use a garage entrance to the building on another street to avoid them.[6]

Though many ACLU members resigned over Skokie, there was no disagreement about our defense of free speech for the Nazis within the organization's leadership. Not one of some eighty members of the ACLU's national board expressed doubts about Skokie at any of our meetings. Nor were there questions about the organization's stand from any of our state affiliates. Two cases at the same time involving the Ku Klux Klan, raising analogous issues, did cause division, however.

The Mississippi ACLU had played a significant role in the struggles in the state over racial desegregation, and some of its board members had paid substantial personal costs for their efforts. The face of one board member, the Rev. Ed King, a white clergyman who then represented Mississippi on the national board of the ACLU, was permanently scarred by the beatings he had suffered in the civil rights struggle. Yet in Mississippi, as elsewhere, defending free speech for all was what the ACLU did as a matter of course. When the Klan was denied permission to hold a rally in a school ballpark regularly used for gatherings by many groups, its leaders appealed to the Civil Liberties Union for assistance. Our affiliate executive director, following routine procedures, assigned an attorney to appear before the school board to challenge this violation of First Amendment rights. Members of the Mississippi Civil Liberties Union board of directors heard about the matter from press accounts, and several objected. A special meeting of the board was hastily called. I asked Clinton Deveaux, a young black attorney who served on the national board of directors of the ACLU and also chaired the Georgia affiliate, to attend. Deveaux was an articulate and effective advocate of free speech and I assumed he would readily persuade our Mississippi colleagues that representing the Klan was the right thing to do. The matter proved more troublesome than I expected. The board vote to go forward with representation of the Klan was only 8–7, with the chairman casting the tie-breaking vote. Six members had missed that mid-August meeting.

The matter continued to cause dissension, so two weeks later, I went to Mississippi to attend another board meeting. Though that meeting was difficult, it seemed to go well. I discovered soon after that I had misread the board, however, as all seven of its black members joined in issuing a statement objecting to pressure from the national office to represent the Klan and announcing their resignations. They were joined by three of the whites on the board. New members were elected in their place by the eleven remaining members of the board, but they were no more favorably disposed to representation of the Klan. When procedural difficulties required the lawsuit to be refiled, the board treated the matter as though it were a new case and declined to authorize it.

I decided to bring the matter before the national ACLU board, which considered it in March 1978. At the time, Skokie had been under way for about ten months. To my dismay, a number of national board members attempted to distinguish representation of the Klan in Mississippi from representation of the Nazis in Skokie. One board member, a well-known professor of constitutional law, said that the Klan rally could be "an overt act in a conspiracy" to deny blacks their rights. It was an argument we were used to hearing from law-enforcement officials attempting to suppress freedom of speech by unpopular groups. The national ACLU board's vote to override the Mississippi affiliate and go forward with representation of the Klan was 47–15. Though not close, I was dismayed that a quarter of the board was ready to duck a case that went to the marrow of what the ACLU was about.

Another case involving the Klan arose at about this time at Camp Pendleton, California. It exposed a similar fault line in another branch of the ACLU. A group of black Marines at the large military base had raided a room where they thought a Klan group was gathering and assaulted the occupants with screwdrivers, injuring several. As it happened, the black Marines had made a mistake and attacked a nonpolitical group of fellow Marines holding a beer party. A Klan meeting was taking place at the time, but in a different room down the hall. The authorities at Camp Pendleton arrested the black Marines and charged them with various crimes and also took action against the Klan members. To disrupt their association with each other, they transferred the Klan members to other Marine installations in various parts of the country.

Klan members contacted the San Diego chapter of the ACLU, which agreed to represent them. They did not engage in violence, and therefore should not have been transferred for exercising their First Amendment rights to associate with each other peacefully, according to the attorney assigned to them by the San Diego ACLU. This decision did not sit well with the chapter's parent body, the ACLU affiliate in Southern California. Its board voted 26–25 to ask the San Diego chapter to drop its representation of the Klan. The chapter refused.

At this point, officials of the Southern California ACLU asked me to get involved. To find out more, I went to Camp Pendleton. The base commander acknowledged to me that he had taken action against the Klan members solely because of their membership. That seemed to justify the San Diego chapter in defending their rights. In talking to the black Marines in the jail on the base, however, I discovered there had also been serious violations of their rights. Wide-ranging conspiracy charges had been brought that implicated Marines who had taken part in conversations about Klan activity at Camp Pendleton but had not participated in the assault. Those arrested for the assault had been interrogated day and night for seventy-two hours before they were allowed to see attorneys.

I recommended to the Southern California ACLU that they provide counsel to the black Marines while simultaneously permitting the San Diego chapter to go forward with their representation of the Klan members. I thought there was no direct conflict in defending the civil liberties of both groups, as different offices and different lawyers would be involved; there was no clash between upholding the First Amendment rights of the Klan and the due-process rights of the black Marines. This Solomonic solution seemed to satisfy—or, at least, mollify—all concerned. An organizational rift was averted. (The Southern California ACLU succeeded in narrowing the charges against the black Marines while the San Diego chapter failed to persuade the courts that the First Amendment rights of Klan members had been violated. In subsequent years, the San Diego chapter continued to chafe under the authority of the Southern California ACLU; it eventually separated and was recognized by the national ACLU as a separate affiliate.)

Although the outcome was satisfactory, as in Mississippi I had to confront the fact that some in the ACLU—a quarter of the national board as well as roughly half of the boards of the Mississippi and Southern California affiliates—were not ready to apply the organization's free-speech principles to representation of Ku Klux Klan groups. The contrast with the lack of controversy on ACLU boards over representing the Nazis was striking. Reluctantly, I concluded that this attitude reflected a noxious form of political correctness that made some members of the national ACLU board and of various affiliate boards more sympathetic to black victims of racist violence than to Jewish survivors of the Holocaust.

A dismaying aspect of the disputes over these Klan cases is that there was a tradition in the ACLU of black attorneys representing white racists comparable to the involvement of Jewish lawyers in defending free speech for American Nazis. One such case arose in 1968. George Wallace was running for president. A highlight of his campaign was to be a rally at New York City's Shea Stadium that would demonstrate his appeal in the heart of liberal America. But Wallace was denied a permit for use of the stadium by the Lindsay administration (ironically, the official who turned him down was the parks commissioner, August Heckscher, a former ACLU board member) on grounds of potential disorder and damage to the facilities. Wallace's campaign manager got in touch with me at the New York Civil Liberties Union and I agreed we would be in Queens County Supreme Court the following morning to uphold Wallace's right to speak. Time was of the essence, as the date for the rally was close and the campaign workers needed time to promote it if they wanted to fill the stadium.

Having said we would be in court the following morning, I walked around the office to look for an attorney to handle the matter. Not finding Alan Levine, the lawyer I wanted, I was told he was upstairs in the national ACLU office meeting with Eleanor Holmes Norton, the ACLU's assistant legal director. I went to Eleanor's office, found Alan, and told him what I had in mind. He couldn't do it, as he had a court appearance in another matter in Manhattan the next morning. Half jokingly, I said to Eleanor, "What about you?" "Sure," she replied, not joking.

Eleanor, who served as chair of the New York City Human Rights Commission and then chair of the federal Equal Employment Opportunities Commission after leaving the ACLU and before her election to Congress, won the case for Wallace. Even so, he did not hold his rally at Shea Stadium, claiming the victory came too late for it to receive adequate publicity. Instead, it was held at Madison Square Garden, which holds about a third of the crowd, without serious incident. The same year, Eleanor argued her first and only case in the U.S. Supreme Court. Her client was the National States Rights Party, a white supremacist group that had held a hate-filled rally in Maryland. A local prosecutor had then secured a restraining order against further rallies. Eleanor persuaded the high Court to rule unanimously overturning the restraining order.[7]

Several years later, Eleanor told an interviewer:

> The most gratifying thing about my racist cases—defending the rights of the Klan or of George Wallace and the like—was the way they were received by the black community. Blacks felt proud that the principled person turned out to be in black America. They were proud that I had the skills to represent George Wallace, that old dog George came to a black woman at the ACLU to defend his constitutional rights. . . . Whenever I spoke before black groups at that time and today too—I used this experience to make the point that Rap and Stokely's right to speak anywhere, especially in the South, would depend on whether George Wallace would be allowed to speak in New York City. Telling about this case and my other racist cases in order to make the civil liberties point has been among the most satisfying experiences of my professional life.[8]

I associated the political correctness that damned the principles that Eleanor Holmes Norton put into practice with leftists such as those in the National Lawyers Guild (NLG), a group founded in 1937 that had a membership in the 1970s of about 5,000 lawyers, law students, and others.

Some volunteer attorneys for the ACLU, and some members of ACLU boards, were also members of the National Lawyers Guild. Though the organization had a political agenda that the ACLU did not share, it had previously avoided public criticism of the ACLU. In 1977, however, it broke with this tradition and issued a statement entitled "Sterile Civil Libertarianism Builds Racism." Camp Pendleton was a principal target. The NLG argued, "When the ACLU fights for Klan members against being transferred for their Klan activities, it must argue that the Klan has a right to organize, speak out, grow and develop at a military base like Camp Pendleton." The statement went on to justify the assault, asserting that, "When their lives and freedom are threatened in this way, black people can be expected to fight back. . . . They should be vigorously supported in that fight." Summing up, the National Lawyers Guild said the ACLU suffered from "poisonous evenhandedness." It was an accusation with an Orwellian flavor I cherished as a vintage example of the genre.

I did not realize it at the time, but this denunciation of the ACLU was an early manifestation of a movement that gained considerable strength not long thereafter. Leftist groups that considered themselves to be victims, or the defenders of victims, of racism and sexism became zealous opponents of freedom of speech for those whom they considered the victimizers. An example was the segment of the feminist movement, led by Andrea Dworkin and Catherine MacKinnon—who called pornography "our Skokie"—that campaigned for the use of police power to suppress words and pictures portraying women as sexual objects. (I was a target of one of the first demonstrations organized by a group with which they were associated, Women Against Pornography.) That movement even won support from some professed civil libertarians. Its impact has endured. Prior to the late 1970s, the main opposition to free speech in the United States came from the political Right. In the past quarter century, those advocating the positions espoused by the National Lawyers Guild and by Dworkin and MacKinnon achieved comparable significance as opponents of First Amendment rights.

The litigation by the ACLU challenging Skokie's attempt to ban the Nazis included one case that went to the U.S. Supreme Court. In June 1978, the High Court refused to review a lower court decision striking down the three ordinances Skokie had enacted to keep the Nazis from marching.[9] The following day, the Illinois Assembly defeated two new laws to prevent the Nazi march. In combination, the judicial and legislative decisions swept away the remaining obstacles to the march. After being put off many times, it was scheduled for June 25, 1978. But the march never happened. Nor did the Nazis appear the previous day in Chicago, where an ACLU lawsuit had also cleared away all legal restraints on their exercise of their rights. Rabbi Kahane and his followers who showed up in Chicago spoiling for a fight were no doubt disappointed, but the Nazis were nowhere to be seen.

What happened? Once their rights were vindicated, I believe the Nazis were afraid to exercise them. It was probably not physical fear. Given the tremendous attention for more than a year, the Skokie, Chicago, and Illinois authorities were sure to be out in force to prevent violence. The Nazis knew they would be well protected. More likely, they feared ridicule. Their numbers were pathetically small. The Nazi organization in Chicago never attracted more than about two dozen members. Despite all the attention, they could not enlist additional adherents. Perhaps the number they could muster to march in Skokie was even smaller. Yet a march there by the Nazis after all the litigation and all the press attention was sure to attract thousands of spectators. Hundreds of state and local police officers would be on hand to maintain order. All the Nazis could expect was derision.

Two weeks later, on July 9, 1978, the leader of the Nazis, Frank Collin —who had acquired his fifteen minutes of fame as a result of Skokie— did show up for a demonstration in Marquette Park in Chicago, the neighborhood from which he had been excluded the previous year. He was accompanied by about twenty-five followers. In that setting, where racial hostility remained high, and any appearance by the Nazis was bound to be anticlimactic after their failure to march in Skokie, Collin probably felt less vulnerable to ridicule. After strutting about Marquette Park in their uniforms, however, the small Nazi group disintegrated. Having succeeded in their effort to exercise their First Amendment rights, they were no longer news. They had no further incentive to exist, and seemed simply to disappear.

That the Nazis did not profit from all the publicity the ACLU helped obtain for them in furnishing legal representation was gratifying to me. I believe today, as then, that it is essential to defend First Amendment rights for all. Skokie's effort to declare itself off limits for those rights had to be defeated. The differences between a street demonstration for a repugnant point of view and shouting fire falsely in a crowded theater, or Garry Wills's facile analogy to an obscene phone call, had to be explained. Yet I did not want to assist the Nazis in building their organization. I did not anticipate they would fade away as soon as the litigation was successfully concluded, but I was very glad that happened.

While Skokie was under way, I was the target of many bitter denunciations. "My only hope," a man from Boston wrote to me, "is that if we are both forced into a march some day to some crematorium, *you* will be at the head of the parade at which time you will in your rapture have an opportunity to sing hosannas in praise of freedom of speech for your tormentors." Another letter proposed a new motto for the ACLU: "The First Amendment *über alles.*"

I still encounter people whose first response when they hear my name is to recall Skokie and tell me that that was when they parted company with the ACLU. Yet the comments I get these days lack the hostility I experienced then. Perhaps the passage of time has been accompanied by a cooling of passions. I sense another factor as well. Even those who still insist on disagreeing with our defense of free speech for the Nazis manifest a measure of respect for our adherence to principle. Skokie, I think, has acquired a symbolic significance that makes it as important as if it actually set a legal precedent. For many Americans, it symbolizes the breadth of the protection provided by the First Amendment. On a number of occasions, I have heard people say about some form of expression they find reprehensible that it should not be suppressed "if the Nazis could march at Skokie." Such comments make me feel that the toll Skokie took on all of us involved in it over a fifteen-month period was more than worthwhile.

Though I have not wavered in my view that even groups propounding Nazi doctrines must be free to speak, I was forced to refine my thinking on the subject when my focus shifted from the United States to defending rights internationally. At home, I uphold freedom of speech for all in circumstances in which a wide range of views is expressed. Everyone picks and chooses the ideas, insights, and information to which they wish to give credence. The diversity of views, including many that are mutually contradictory, promotes a healthy skepticism and encourages critical thought. Where government exercises tight controls on expression, however, the situation is different. In a setting where the principal media are directly owned by the government or by cronies of officials who publish or broadcast in conformance with state policy, the wide dissemination of hateful messages directed against a particular racial, ethnic, or religious group is government policy. As when Dr. Joseph Goebbels dictated the messages of the media in Nazi Germany, the effect may be calamitous. There is little or no possibility in such circumstances for contrary views to be expressed.

In the 1990s, ethnic cleansing was promoted in ex-Yugoslavia and genocide was incited in Rwanda by government-controlled or -connected media. I did not defend those media on free-speech grounds. They were instruments of state policy. The government prohibited or narrowly circumscribed speech by those expressing different views. In Skokie, I fought against government control over expression to ensure that every point of view could be heard, even a message of hate. But in ex-Yugoslavia and Rwanda, those expressing hate enjoyed exclusive or virtually exclusive power to communicate. In those circumstances, I advocate prosecuting media officials who directly incite and organize ethnic cleansing and genocide before UN-sponsored criminal tribunals.[10]

Is there a contradiction between the stand I took in Skokie and those I took two decades later in Yugoslavia and Rwanda? I don't think so. Yugoslavia and Rwanda added a dimension to my understanding of the principles at stake in Skokie. I had not previously appreciated how a government could use its monopolistic control over expression to enlist its peaceful citizens in the most despicable acts of cruelty against their neighbors. The lesson I derived from Yugoslavia and Rwanda is that ensuring that all may speak, and that every point of view may be heard, is yet more crucial than I previously recognized.

CHAPTER EIGHT

Exposing Betrayal: The ACLU and the FBI

I n July 1977, a staff attorney who specialized in cases involving freedom of information and the right to privacy, Jack Novik, stopped by my office to report a small triumph: That morning, the Post Office had delivered to him a large number of cartons containing a copy of the files the FBI had maintained on the ACLU since its founding in 1920. Jack, whose life was cut short by cancer a few years later, had been seeking the files for a long time and, after threatening to sue under the Freedom of Information Act, had pried them loose. Curious to see them, I walked back to Jack's office with him and found the room half full with cartons piled about six feet high. At random, I slit one open and pulled out a document. What I found was shocking. It was a copy of a letter from Irving Ferman, Washington director of the ACLU in the 1950s, to a contact at the Bureau reporting suspicions of Communist activity in one of the ACLU's state affiliates.

Long before I saw that letter, I knew the ACLU record in the 1950s was, at best, mixed. At a time of national hysteria about Communist subversion in such sectors of American public life as the universities and the motion picture industry, the organization did not provide forceful leadership in defending First Amendment rights. Several state affiliates had far better records, but the assault on civil liberties was nationwide and the parent ACLU was often missing in action. It participated in most of the important court cases of the era, but generally only as amicus curiae, often limiting itself to such questions as the procedural rights of witnesses before congressional investigative committees or the loyalty boards of the era. One ACLU legal brief from the period attacked the constitutionality of the House Un-American Activities Committee (HUAC), but that was because it was written by Osmond Fraenkel. Along with noted Columbia law professor Walter Gellhorn, Osmond led the wing of the ACLU board that espoused the most robust defense of freedom of speech.

Another wing of the board was led by Morris Ernst, an attorney who had acquired prominence from the 1920s on for his efforts in anticensorship cases, such as his successful challenge in 1933 of the ban on James Joyce's *Ulysses,* and his defense of the rights of Margaret Sanger and other birth-control advocates to distribute materials on contraception. I knew that Ernst, who considered communism in the United States a criminal conspiracy, and therefore a proper subject for congressional investigations even when the issue was its penetration of institutions with no relationship to national security, had been accused by Gellhorn and others of nefarious negotiations with Martin Dies, the first chairman of HUAC. Though the story is murky, it appears that in 1939, in the period after the Hitler-Stalin Pact, when even many who harbored illusions about communism turned sharply hostile, Ernst had met with Dies and struck a deal. One part of the bargain became manifest on October 23, 1939, when Dies issued a statement purporting to clear the ACLU of any accusations of Communist connections. The apparent quid pro quo was that the ACLU soft-pedaled any criticism of HUAC. Author John Dos Passos, not satisfied, resigned from the ACLU national committee on November 20, 1939, alleging that the board included members "still able to compromise with communist-directed organizations."

Not long thereafter, in February 1940, the ACLU board adopted a resolution barring Communists and those supporting any other form of totalitarianism from leadership positions in the organization. This was followed by an effort within the board to expel one of its members, the legendary labor organizer famed in song and story as "the rebel girl," Elizabeth Gurley Flynn. An avowed Communist and a member of the party's National Committee, Flynn resisted her expulsion, pointing out that her membership was known when she was reelected to the ACLU board in 1939. The board scheduled a "trial" on the question in which Osmond Fraenkel acted as Flynn's counsel. When the board divided 9–9, the deciding vote to expel Flynn was cast by the chairman, Unitarian clergyman John Haynes Holmes.[1]

Eventually, in 1968, the ACLU board repealed the 1940 Resolution and, in 1976, the year before we obtained the FBI files, voted to reinstate Flynn to board membership posthumously. I was not enthusiastic about the latter development. On the one hand, I thought it wrong to expel Flynn from the board after she had been duly elected. On the other hand, I thought it inappropriate that an apologist for gross repression of civil liberties in the Soviet Union was ever elected to the board to begin with. I sympathized both with those like Osmond Fraenkel, who argued that the ACLU should uphold civil liberties in the conduct of its own affairs by respecting the results of an election, and with vehement anti-Communists such as Norman Thomas, who were outraged by Flynn's membership on the ACLU board. Norman argued that the stands she took did not encompass civil liberties defense for those for whom the party lacked sympathy. Her opponents should have organized a campaign to defeat her in the board election, I thought. My preference was a resolution expressing the board's objection to the *manner* in which Flynn had been removed. Posthumous reinstatement implied she had been a fitting member.

My discovery of Irving Ferman's letter to the FBI made me realize there were more skeletons in the ACLU closet than I had known. Also, I understood right away that we would have to make public what we found in the ACLU files. Though the ACLU in 1977 was a very different organization than it had been in the 1950s, the revelations would give us a black eye. This was an inopportune moment to face such embarrassment. We were embroiled in public controversy over our defense of free speech for Nazis in Skokie and, at that moment, were suffering financial losses as a consequence. Our best defense, I believed then and now, was to insist on our adherence to principle. Disclosure that ACLU staff had behaved in an unprincipled way, even if a quarter of a century earlier, undermined our public presentation of our stand.

A n ironic aspect of the embarrassment we faced is that we were much engaged in that period in criticizing others whose long past misdeeds had been revealed by the disclosure of FBI files under the Freedom of Information Act (FOIA). One such case in which I was particularly engaged in 1977 involved Irving Kaufman, the federal judge who had presided over the trial of Julius and Ethel Rosenberg in 1951 and had sentenced the couple to death for stealing atomic secrets for the Soviet Union. The Rosenbergs, who were executed at Sing Sing Prison in 1953, were the only civilians ever executed for espionage in American history. Documents obtained from the FBI under the FOIA by the children of the Rosenbergs revealed that Kaufman had secretly instructed the prosecutor to ask for the death penalty. This was a gross violation of judicial ethics, which forbid a judge from communications with one party to a case that are not disclosed to the opposing party.

I knew Kaufman well, as I had served for several years as a commissioner of a Juvenile Justice Standards Project that he chaired under the auspices of the American Bar Association and the Institute of Judicial Administration. Our commission met about three times a year at whichever resort hotel Kaufman favored in that season. Eventually, we produced twenty-four volumes of model legislation and commentary dealing with such topics as abuse and neglect, juvenile delinquency, and juvenile records.[2] At the time, Kaufman was a much-honored judge of the U.S. Court of Appeals for the Second Circuit who frequently wrote opinions upholding civil liberties, particularly in First Amendment cases. As he was well aware, however, he would be remembered mainly for sentencing the Rosenbergs to death.

The case obsessed him. One time, I attended a meeting of the Juvenile Justice Standards Project in Tucson. I was late, arriving at the lunch break of the first day of the meeting. After checking in, I had to pass the hotel's swimming pool in the courtyard to get to my room. Kaufman was at the pool. He stopped me and, without greeting me, thrust a letter into my hands saying, "Here, this will interest you." As I was coming direct from wintry New York, I put down my coat and suitcase to read the letter. It was from a lawyer in Missouri whose name I did not recognize saying that Harry Truman thought highly of Kaufman's conduct of the Rosenberg case. Kaufman told me the author was "Truman's personal lawyer."

When I saw copies of the documents obtained by the Rosenberg children, I circulated them to the ACLU Executive Committee suggesting we issue a statement and also wrote to Kaufman asking if he wanted to comment on them before we acted. I did not hear from Kaufman but got a call from Simon Rifkind, a former federal judge who was Kaufman's lawyer and the senior partner at a major New York law firm. Judge Rifkind also chaired a committee of the American Bar Association established for the express purpose of defending Judge Kaufman. Rifkind attempted to persuade me not to issue a statement on the documents, reminding me that he served on the board of a foundation that supported the ACLU. I did not need the reminder, but I suggested he might not wish to read in the press that he attempted to influence our decision in that way.[3]

After we issued our statement, a journalist got in touch with me to say she was writing an article on Kaufman for *The New York Times Magazine.* I knew Kaufman enjoyed a close relationship with the *Times.* He wrote for the magazine and other sections frequently. Though taking care not to identify itself as a Jewish newspaper—to the extent of playing down reports on the Nazi death camps during World War II, so as not to convey the impression that the war was about the Jews—the publishers of the *Times* were thought to be grateful to Kaufman for being the Jewish judge to sentence the Jewish atomic spies. He had helped to prevent the case from inspiring American anti-Semitism, some believed.

The journalist who got in touch with me was Dorothy Rabinowitz, a fine writer and subsequently a Pulitzer Prize–winning columnist for the *Wall Street Journal.* We met in my office. At the outset, she made it plain she considered the matter of the documents released under the Freedom of Information Act merely the latest installment in a long-running campaign against Kaufman by leftist partisans of the Rosenbergs. I showed her the documents, and we talked about them at length. It was plain she was shaken. Rabinowitz called me a couple of times to follow up on her interview. In her last call, referring to the documents, she told me: "As we used to say, just because the Communists say two and two are four doesn't make it wrong." I did not hear from her again, and the article she said she was writing never appeared.

When the ACLU's own files from the FBI arrived, the first step was to review what we had obtained. Much was of public record. Some items of great interest, such as documents that might have identified FBI informants who had infiltrated the ACLU, had been excluded or partially blanked out. The material we found in the files that concerned me mainly involved three key officials of the ACLU who had maintained long-term relationships with the FBI: Irving Ferman, who served as Washington director from 1952 to 1959; Morris Ernst, general counsel from 1930 to 1954; and Herbert Monte Levy, staff counsel from 1949 to 1955. In addition, the files contained one troubling document dealing with Patrick Murphy Malin, the executive director from 1950 to 1962; and one involving John de J. Pemberton, executive director from 1962 to 1970. Jack was, of course, my immediate predecessor and the man who had hired me in 1963 to work for the ACLU.

By far the most serious breaches of the ACLU's principles and of the position of trust held in the organization involved Ferman, whose letter, by chance, I pulled from the first carton I opened. A typical item was a letter he wrote on November 5, 1956, to his regular contact at the FBI, Assistant Director Louis B. Nichols. "I am attaching herewith," said Ferman, "a copy of the Executive Committee minutes of the Massachusetts Civil Liberties Union, and call your attention to Item 4 which reflects what appears to be a real movement to involve the Union in attacking the Smith Act over and above the filing of *Amicus* briefs."[4] This memo from Ferman was followed in the files by a letter from FBI Director J. Edgar Hoover to the special agent in charge of the Bureau's Boston office:

> There are enclosed two photostats of the minutes of an Executive Committee meeting of the Civil Liberties Union of Massachusetts on October 1, 1956. You are instructed to review the enclosed and furnish the Bureau with a biographical sketch concerning the individuals referred to therein together with any information in the files of your office regarding subversive affiliations on the part of these individuals. You should furnish the Bureau with all information contained in the files of your office reflecting that the Civil Liberties Union of Massachusetts has been infiltrated or is being controlled by the Communist Party (CP) and CP members.

There were many similar items in the FBI files. At times, Ferman added comments to internal documents that he sent along, such as: "the intemperateness to me is a dead giveaway"; "another indication of how much this gang really believes in free speech. I will enjoy knocking heads together one of these days"; "there is no question in my mind but this is a product of Communist coercion"; and so on. His targets were principally ACLU state affiliates that were doing the work for which the national ACLU should have been providing leadership in resisting the loyalty investigations, prosecutions, oaths, and purges of the era. In one instance, he sent along material on an affiliate that said something critical of Ferman's own role in the ACLU. Routinely, the FBI used the material that Ferman sent to compile dossiers on the people he identified.

Herbert Monte Levy, whose tenure on the ACLU staff overlapped Ferman's for about three years, enjoyed cordial relations with the FBI and corresponded with Louis B. Nichols, who was also Ferman's regular contact. He discussed ACLU policies and programs with his Bureau contacts, and the files show that he was receptive to their suggestions. He appears to have accepted a view that had some currency in that era: Congressional investigations such as those conducted by Senator Joseph McCarthy and the House Un-American Activities Committee were a threat to civil liberties because witnesses were denied procedural protections. The best way to counter this threat was to leave the job of protecting the country against subversion to the FBI. In fact, many more people were harmed by dossiers compiled by the Bureau. No count is available, but it is likely that scores of thousands of Americans were adversely affected, generally without their knowledge, by the circulation of dossiers containing material that branded them, often unfairly, as disloyal or as security risks.

Although much more is known today than in the 1950s about the FBI's practices—thanks in large part to the Freedom of Information Act—a lot was known then. Certainly, the ACLU knew about the FBI. The two institutions were born in the same era and grew up together. As far back as 1918, the Bureau of Investigation (predecessor of the FBI) raided the offices of the Civil Liberties Bureau, one of the two predecessor groups of the ACLU that operated during World War I—the other was known as the American Union Against Militarism, an organization that assisted conscientious objectors—and seized all its files. The ACLU's first court case after its establishment in 1920, *Colyer v. Skeffington,*[5] in which its attorneys were Felix Frankfurter and Zechariah Chafee, Jr., helped stop the "Palmer raids" of 1919–1920 in which Attorney General A. Mitchell Palmer and his young aide, J. Edgar Hoover, had rounded up thousands of suspected radicals and summarily deported hundreds, including famed radical Emma Goldman, to the Soviet Union. In 1924, the ACLU published a pamphlet on the FBI entitled, "The Nation-Wide Spy System Centering in the Department of Justice."

Thereafter, President Calvin Coolidge and Attorney General Harlan Fiske Stone reined in the political surveillance activities of the FBI, but a decade and a half later, President Franklin D. Roosevelt removed those restrictions to meet the emergency created by the onset of war in Europe. In the post–World War II period, the compilation of dossiers on those it considered Reds was seen by the Bureau and its director as its foremost mission. An indication of how much was known at the time about the Bureau can be found in Max Lowenthal's well-researched 1950 book, *The Federal Bureau of Investigation.*[6] The collaborative relationship between the Bureau and the congressional investigating committees of the period was manifest when HUAC summoned Lowenthal to testify when his book was published while the FBI leaked derogatory information about him to the press.[7]

Though Herbert Monte Levy, unlike Ferman, did not make a practice of pointing the finger at those in the ACLU whose views he disliked, the FBI files contain a memo of July 14, 1954, describing an episode of similar character. It was written by Assistant Director Nichols and summarized a conversation with Levy in which the latter sought "guidance" in determining the accuracy of a report that nine of fifteen members of the board of an ACLU affiliate were Communists. Nichols's memo says that FBI files did not substantiate the report about Communists among board members. "I, accordingly," Nichols added, "told Levy while we could not be of assistance to him, he might want to check back on this to ascertain where they got the figure nine out of 15, as I was quite certain that the Bureau had not covered this in its investigation."

When press accounts of the ACLU files appeared, much of the focus was on Morris Ernst, as he had been the best known among those who had maintained ties to the FBI. Ernst was an attorney in private practice whose role as general counsel was unpaid. It was a title he shared with two other prominent lawyers in private practice, Osmond Fraenkel—Ernst's ideological opposite on the board—and Arthur Garfield Hays, who more often sided with Fraenkel than with Ernst. Their role was to oversee ACLU litigation and to take the lead in many of the organization's most important cases.

One newspaper labeled Ernst "the FBI spy in the ACLU." Nothing in the files warranted that accusation, which applies to Ferman more than to anyone else. Yet the files do show how it was possible for the press to go astray in characterizing Ernst. A typical FBI memo starts with the words: "Morris Ernst confidentially advised . . . "; Ernst willingly inspired such references, introducing a letter to Hoover: "My dear Edgar: For your eyes alone." Despite the promise, nothing Ernst provided was confidential information. The documents he did send to the Bureau did not focus on individuals, and so his letters did not result in the compilation of dossiers.

Ernst's motive apparently was to ingratiate himself with the Bureau and with Hoover. He also did this by publishing an article in the December 1950 *Reader's Digest* entitled, "Why I No Longer Fear the FBI," which one historian of the ACLU has characterized as "practically written by the Bureau."[8] The timing suggests it was intended to offset Max Lowenthal's harsh critique. Ernst even liked to boast that he was J. Edgar Hoover's lawyer. The basis for this was that Ernst, much of whose private practice involved the publishing industry, once represented Hoover in connection with a book contract. The FBI files themselves show Hoover somewhat disdainful of Ernst. An internal FBI memo dealing with a matter that Ernst had informed the Bureau about "confidentially" has a handwritten note by Hoover appended saying: "This seems to conclusively prove that ACLU & Ernst just out played FBI and when they got what they wanted broke all confidences."

Though Ernst was not a spy, he used his post as ACLU general counsel in the early 1950s to try to sanitize the image of the FBI, and he cultivated cordial relationships that probably helped prevent the ACLU from tackling FBI abuses of civil liberties head-on. His role was similar to the one he had played with respect to HUAC a decade earlier. As much as anyone, he was to blame for the ACLU's poor performance in that era. That Ernst valued his relationship to J. Edgar Hoover, who, in his half century as the FBI's director did as much harm to American liberties as anyone in the twentieth century—his only rival is Justice Rehnquist—and freely used his access to confidential files in his struggles against his antagonists in and out of government, suggests that the ACLU general counsel lacked both good judgment and good taste. His *Reader's Digest* encomium was published just a few months after a speech by J. Edgar Hoover in which the director characteristically attempted to blur the distinction between opinion and espionage. Hoover said: "Behind this force of traitorous Communists, constantly gnawing away like termites at the very foundations of American society, stand a half million fellow travelers and sympathizers ready to do the Communist bidding. These individuals, though not identified as Communists, are extremely dangerous to the internal security of this Nation, because as hypocrites and moral swindlers they seek the protections of the freedoms which they constantly seek to destroy."[9]

Irving Ferman and Herbert Monte Levy both worked for the ACLU during the period beginning in 1950 that Patrick Murphy Malin served as executive director, which also covered the final four years of Morris Ernst's service as general counsel. The files show that Malin knew Ferman and Levy maintained regular contacts with FBI officials. Occasionally, Malin accompanied Ferman on a visit to the FBI, and, at other times, Levy or Ferman arranged for Malin or for an ACLU delegation to visit Hoover to protest some FBI activity or to enlist FBI cooperation in opposing some program of another government agency. There is no indication in the files, however, that Malin knew Ferman was regularly informing the FBI about those within the ACLU whom he considered left-wing or anti-FBI.

All the material in the files dealing with Malin's contacts with the FBI shows him engaged in appropriate matters, except for one Bureau memo dated August 20, 1956. Again, the author was Louis B. Nichols. Patrick Malin "called at my office on 8–15–56," Nichols reported. "He is having problems with his 23 affiliates. He is particularly concerned about the affiliates in Detroit, Los Angeles, Denver and Seattle, Washington. He is trying to keep Communists off the Board of Directors and asked that we keep in mind alerting him if anything came up."

The files also show that Irving Ferman periodically advised the Bureau on how to deal with letters from Malin protesting its activities. One FBI memo says Ferman "expressed the thought that we should be very firm with Malin and set him down." This suggests that Malin did not know what Ferman was doing and would have disapproved. At the same time, it is difficult to understand how Ferman could have held a top post under Malin for seven years without the executive director's awareness that something was seriously amiss. Given the fact that Malin himself asked the Bureau for help in screening affiliate board members, and identified four affiliates he considered troublesome, the FBI files cloud his reputation. Also, of course, it was during his tenure that the ACLU failure was greatest. It appears he tried to steer a course between the two wings of the board represented by Morris Ernst and Osmond Fraenkel, getting the ACLU peripherally involved in the great issues of the era.

Jack Pemberton succeeded Malin as executive director in 1962. During his tenure, the ACLU at long last took the lead in dismantling the Red-hunting apparatus of the late 1940s and 1950s, winning cases before the U.S. Supreme Court that made it impossible for the congressional investigating committees to function, sharply limiting security checks, and invalidating loyalty oaths. Many of these cases were brought by the state affiliates of the ACLU, but, under Pemberton, they had the support of the national office's legal department and its director, Mel Wulf. All Pemberton's dealings with the FBI that are revealed in the files—with one exception—were at arm's length. He regularly criticized the FBI, and the FBI regularly and angrily rebutted that criticism.

Knowing Jack's record well, as I joined the ACLU staff only a year into his tenure, and worked with him closely, I was startled and upset to discover the single document that was sharply at odds with his overall record. It was a memo dated February 13, 1964—about eight months after I joined the ACLU staff—from William Sullivan, assistant director of the FBI. The memo described a conversation between Sullivan and Jack several weeks earlier in which the ACLU director had asked for "public source" information on a man suspected of being a Communist who was becoming active in the Georgia ACLU. In his memo, Sullivan said he had referred Jack to some old clippings from left-wing newspapers and some San Diego newspapers containing references to the man in Georgia that showed "his affinity to Communism."

The only explanation I have for this action by Jack Pemberton was that he suffered a lapse in judgment. As indicated, I had serious questions about Pemberton's leadership during his final years at the ACLU helm, but I never had any doubts about his devotion to civil liberties principles. It is possible that a contributing factor in his misstep was that the official with whom he spoke was William Sullivan, who had a reputation as a relatively enlightened Bureau official. An FBI veteran once touted as a possible successor to Hoover, Sullivan raised eyebrows by declaring publicly in the early 1960s that the Ku Klux Klan was a greater threat to the country than the Communist Party. Several years after his conversation with Jack Pemberton, in 1970, Sullivan gave a speech in which he said the Communist Party was "not in any way causing or directing or controlling the unrest we suffer today in the racial field or in the academic community." This statement led to a final break with Hoover, who forced Sullivan's retirement from the FBI a year later.[10]

After ascertaining what was in the FBI files, I consulted the ACLU chairman, Norman Dorsen, on how to proceed. Norman had succeeded Ed Ennis the previous year and was playing a far more assertive role than his predecessor had. I was very fond of Ed and respected him greatly but welcomed Norman's much more hands-on approach to his duties as chairman. We had worked together closely on projects such as our series of handbooks on rights even before he became chairman, but once he assumed that post, I found we spoke two or three times a day about the issues we confronted. To make clear we were holding nothing back, we decided to invite a journalist to go through all the files. As it would take an extended period to examine the more than 40,000 pages, we thought it best to work with a single journalist who enjoyed a reputation for thoroughness and integrity. That way, the entire story would come out at one time. We thought it unwise to allow journalists to compete with each other by publishing piecemeal information. The journalist I chose was Anthony Marro, then of the *New York Times* (subsequently editor of Long Island *Newsday*) because he had published a number of perceptive stories on political surveillance. I called to tell him we had obtained the FBI files on the ACLU and there was a big story in them, but I did not tell him what it was. He would have to read through the files himself and could not publish until he went through all of them. Marro accepted and spent about two weeks reading the files.

At the same time, Norman and I sent copies of the relevant documents to the three former ACLU officials who were still alive—Ferman, Levy, and Pemberton—and informed them that the files were being made public. We offered them the opportunity to prepare statements, which the ACLU would give to journalists covering the story. Each provided a statement. Ferman defended his conduct, asserting that it reflected "the wisdom that any struggle for human liberty requires manning many battle stations." He also talked about the Communist conspiracy and claimed that his contacts had protected the ACLU and were instrumental in preventing HUAC from issuing a report attacking the organization. Levy said, "The documentation should be considered in the context of the years to which it relates—years when McCarthyism was running rampant, years when J. Edgar Hoover was one of the relatively few government officials issuing a clear call to the defense of civil liberties." Pemberton said he had contacted Sullivan when an officer of the Georgia ACLU said he had information that one of his colleagues on the affiliate board should be disqualified because of the 1940 Resolution (still in effect in 1964) and asked for Jack's assistance. According to Jack, the information he got from Sullivan allowed him to tell the Georgia affiliate that the evidence he found did not support disqualification.

Anthony Marro's story was front-page news in the *New York Times* and remained a prominent news item in that paper, and in the press generally, which besieged us with calls after his story appeared for weeks. (As luck would have it, I had jury duty the day Marro's story appeared. I annoyed several of my fellow jurors by tying up the pay phone in the room where we were waiting our turn to be assigned to a case—this was long before cell phones—as I tried to field press calls.) Much to my relief, the revelations did not damage the ACLU. Some on the Left treated the disclosures merely as confirmation of what they had always suspected. Yet the affair had no discernible impact on support for the organization. At the time, we were being deluged with letters from members resigning over Skokie, but I don't recall a single resignation over the contacts with the FBI. Perhaps it was because the conduct revealed had taken place a long time ago; because we ourselves had washed our dirty laundry in public; or because members recognized that the ACLU in 1977 was a far different organization than in the 1950s. Earlier in the decade, Murray Kempton had published an article in *The New York Review of Books* criticizing the performance of the ACLU in the 1950s but said it had "rebounded magnificently."[11] I hoped that perception was widely shared.

Though these were comforting thoughts, I could not help wondering about the contrast with the response to Skokie. Most of those who had written letters explaining their resignation argued that the way to defend liberty was by denying the Nazis the freedom to express their views or by permitting Skokie to deny them that freedom. Similarly, in the 1950s, many argued that denying Communists the opportunity to express their views was the way to defend liberty. Restricting the civil liberties of those who would deny others civil liberties makes sense to many people. Irving Ferman probably believed he was defending liberty when he raised suspicions about ACLU colleagues. What Ferman and others did was betrayal, but Skokie helped me to grasp the pressures of an earlier era and to recognize that it could happen again.

II

The Human Rights Watch Years: 1978–1993

In 1978, I got a telephone call from Robert L. Bernstein, chairman and CEO of Random House, asking if I would join him in forming a US Helsinki Watch Committee. I readily agreed. Bob told me he was also thinking of asking a prominent lawyer, Orville Schell, Jr., to join us in putting together such a group. I knew Orville, thought highly of him, and enthusiastically supported the suggestion. We three became the organization's founders.

Bob's purpose in establishing Helsinki Watch was to protest repression against dissenters in the Soviet Union. A Moscow Helsinki Group had been established in 1976 to monitor the Soviet Union's compliance with the human rights provisions of the Helsinki Accords signed six months earlier by the leaders of thirty-five governments of Europe and North America, including President Gerald Ford for the United States and Leonid Brezhnev, secretary general of the Communist Party, for the Soviet Union. Within a year, several of the organizers of the Moscow Helsinki Group, including its chairman, physicist Yuri Orlov, were imprisoned for their efforts. I had previously been involved in campaigns against Soviet abuses only sporadically and superficially. From time to time, I had signed statements criticizing the persecution of dissidents, and, on a few occasions, I had spoken at gatherings held to call attention to their plight. The ACLU limited itself to civil liberties in the United States, and, therefore, dealing with human rights internationally was not part of my professional duties. Yet as one who had followed closely accounts of resistance to Soviet repression since the Hungarian Revolution of 1956, and as an admirer from afar of the handful of brave men and women, mainly in Moscow, who had taken great risks, and paid a great price, for daring to speak out for the rights of their fellow citizens, I welcomed Bob Bernstein's call.

I had known Bob for several years and worked with him previously. The first time was in 1972 when the ACLU was approached by a former CIA agent, Victor Marchetti, who had signed a contract with a division of Random House to publish a book about the agency. The CIA had learned about the book and, citing a secrecy agreement required of Marchetti and all other agents, had attempted to prevent its publication. Random House and the ACLU joined in a court battle that eventually resulted in publication of Marchetti's book, *The CIA and the Cult of Intelligence,* with blank spaces marking passages deleted by court order and with passages the CIA had sought to remove, but which we persuaded the courts to allow, in boldface type. It was Bob's idea to publish in this form. In certain respects, the format made the book more interesting than if it had appeared intact. As Random House was then owned by RCA, a major defense contractor, I admired his readiness to take on the CIA. Though Random House paid far more in legal costs than it earned from publishing Marchetti's book, Bob did not hesitate to take on the CIA again, and a few years later we collaborated in a court battle on behalf of another agent, Frank Snepp. His 1977 book, *Decent Interval,* was published without deletions, but the agency succeeded in collecting all the author's earnings from it.

Because of our battles against the CIA, I knew that with Bob's involvement Helsinki Watch would not be merely a Cold War exercise in denunciations of the Soviet Union. Robert Bernstein was committed to freedom of expression across the board. I had similar confidence in Orville Schell, with whom I had joined in doing battle against some of the Nixon administration's assaults on civil liberties.

Bob's call came at a moment when a number of people were thinking seriously about how to promote human rights internationally. Several of the American organizations that are prominent today in the field—among them the Lawyers Committee for Human Rights, the International Human Rights Law Group, and, a little later, the Committee to Protect Journalists—were born about the same time. So were a lot of the human rights organizations in other countries. Developments in the mid-1970s in widely scattered parts of the world came together to provide the inspiration for the formation of an international human rights movement. These included worldwide outrage over the crimes committed by Augusto Pinochet at the time of his 1973 coup in Chile—which, as it happens, took place on September 11—and its aftermath; the 1974 fall of Richard Nixon, occupant of the world's most powerful office, as a direct consequence of his violations of rights; the 1976 student uprising in Soweto and the murder of Steve Biko the following year, which galvanized international attention to South Africa and apartheid; the formation of the Moscow Helsinki Group in 1976, signaling that a spark of dedication to rights, and a willingness to take enormous risks for these beliefs, was alive at the heart of the Soviet totalitarian system; the arrest and imprisonment in early 1977 of the Moscow group's leaders; the formation of Charter 77 in Prague at about the same moment the arrests took place in Moscow; the election of Jimmy Carter in November 1976 and his espousal of human rights as a new moral basis for U.S. foreign policy after the humiliating end to the Vietnam War; and the award of the 1977 Nobel Peace Prize to Amnesty International, the first time the human rights cause had obtained such recognition.

Pinochet's coup in Chile, and the role played by Richard Nixon, Henry Kissinger, and the CIA in bringing it about, were crucial in the emergence of the human rights movement in the United States. The U.S. contribution to the coup had outraged some members of Congress led by Representative Don Fraser of Minnesota and Senator Edward Kennedy of Massachusetts. They were soon joined by another Democrat, Representative (now Senator) Tom Harkin of Iowa, as the sponsors of a number of measures in Congress to limit U.S. economic assistance to Chile (which under Nixon, Ford, and Kissinger went from $3.3 million in FY 1973, Allende's last, to $93.7 million in FY 1975, Pinochet's first full year in power) and to require that the promotion of human rights internationally become a goal of U.S. foreign policy. Fraser and Kennedy succeeded in persuading Congress to adopt what remains the most important law on human rights, Section 502B of the Foreign Assistance Act requiring establishment of a Bureau of Human Rights in the State Department headed by an assistant secretary of state; mandating the publication of country reports on human rights worldwide; and barring U.S. military assistance to governments practicing gross abuses of human rights. It was adopted over the veto of President Gerald Ford acting on the advice of his secretary of state, Henry Kissinger. 502B was soon supplemented by the Harkin Amendment, which bars U.S. economic assistance to such governments.

Fraser, Kennedy, and Harkin acted before the emergence of a U.S. human rights movement. The only significant organization then operating in the United States, Amnesty International, founded in 1961, did not open a Washington office until after the main human rights laws were adopted, and when it did open in the capital, refrained from lobbying. By 1978, when Helsinki Watch and other human rights groups were formed, the ground had been well prepared by members of Congress acting largely on their own initiative and in response to church groups, which were early backers of the human rights cause, and a commitment to the promotion of rights internationally was already embedded in U.S. law. Jimmy Carter had complied with Section 502B in appointing my longtime ACLU colleague Patricia Derian as the first assistant secretary of state for human rights and, in the year we formed Helsinki Watch, marked the thirtieth anniversary of the UN's adoption of the Universal Declaration of Human Rights by announcing that "Human rights is the soul of our foreign policy."

When Bob Bernstein called me about Helsinki Watch, I had already decided to leave the ACLU, and not long thereafter, I announced this publicly. He called again and asked if I would serve as the new group's director. After fifteen years at the ACLU, I was not ready to direct another organization. I was eager to get away from the day-to-day responsibilities of dealing with a board of directors, managing a staff, and especially, the wearying grind of raising funds. As we lacked an endowment or substantial reserves, our operations had depended entirely on funds raised as we went along. It was work I did not successfully delegate to anyone else. As executive director, much like a college president, I was the organization's principal fundraiser. I wanted to read, write, teach, and travel to parts of the world I had never visited.

I left the ACLU in the fall of 1978 and became a visiting professor of law at New York University and a fellow (and subsequently director) of its newly established New York Institute for the Humanities. In addition, I undertook a study on behalf of the Twentieth Century Fund of the uses and limits of litigation in promoting causes. That led to my fourth book, *Only Judgment*.[1] None of those duties proved onerous. I was able to take my first trips to Africa and Asia and devoted substantial time to establishing Helsinki Watch, which I served as vice chairman.

Though I was very comfortable at NYU, the election of Ronald Reagan as president in November 1980 convinced me it was time to go back to work more directly in public policy. I thought Helsinki Watch would provide a good platform to oppose the new administration's appalling policies on international human rights. I did not want to be restricted to a focus on the thirty-five countries of Europe and North America that had signed the Helsinki Accords, but I was concerned that our resources were not adequate to promote human rights globally. I discussed the matter with Bob Bernstein and Orville Schell, and we agreed to begin by establishing an Americas Watch Committee to operate alongside Helsinki Watch. Orville would chair Americas Watch, while Bob would continue as chair of Helsinki Watch, and I would oversee the work of both groups.

Adding a focus on Latin America seemed obvious to us at the time. It was the region where the new administration seemed intent on demonstrating that its stand on human rights would differ sharply from the outgoing Carter administration's policies. If we wanted to have an impact on human rights policy, we had to establish a capacity to work on Latin America. Also, I felt comfortable dealing with the region. My background in the 1960s serving on the board of a pioneer human rights group, the Inter-American Association for Democracy and Freedom, had allowed me to establish connections to a number of Latin American political leaders of that era, such as former President José Figueres of Costa Rica, who were defenders of human rights in their own countries and in the region. Though I knew I had a lot to learn about current developments, I thought my previous engagement with the region would provide me with useful background.

When I proposed that Orville should serve as chairman of Americas Watch, he understood very well that I wanted to trade on his establishment credentials. As senior partner at a leading Wall Street law firm, counsel to major corporations, and a past president of the Association of the Bar of the City of New York, those credentials were impeccable. He had no hesitation in using them on behalf of the controversial stands Americas Watch took opposing Reagan administration policies on countries such as El Salvador, Guatemala, and Argentina. A decade earlier, Orville had led a large delegation of New York lawyers on a visit to Washington to lobby against the Vietnam War. His prestige in the legal profession encouraged many other lawyers to take part. He was ready to be similarly outspoken about the new administration's human rights policies in Latin America.

An important factor in Orville's readiness to speak out forcefully on such matters, I believe, was his pride in his sons Jonathan and Orville, both writers. Jonathan had written essays about Vietnam in *The New Yorker* that had shaped public opposition to the war, and Orville was writing perceptive essays and books about China. The senior Orville Schell wanted to be worthy of his sons. I recall an occasion when Bob, Orville, and I had lunch with Henry Kissinger. At the time, he was chairing President Reagan's Kissinger Commission on Central America. Kissinger had brought along another member of the commission, Boston University President John Silber ("I brought him so he'd make me look like a liberal," Kissinger told us). Introducing Orville to Silber, Kissinger said, "He's the father of the writing Schells." Orville fairly glowed with pride. A man of accomplishments in his own right, there was no introduction that pleased him more.

I thought that Bob, Orville, and I complemented each other well. Bob contributed not only his prestigious position and wide-ranging contacts but also a flair for showmanship and, above all, visible passion for the human rights cause. He identified with the victims of abuses, suffering along with them. Not surprisingly, his identification was strongest with men his own age, such as the Russian scientist Andrei Sakharov, who was just a year or two older than Bob, and the Argentine newspaper publisher Jacobo Timerman, who was Bob's exact contemporary. Sakharov and Timerman became his friends, and when Sakharov was force-fed to break a hunger strike, and when Timerman was tortured, it was as if Bob was also force-fed and tortured. The strength of Bob's commitment was sur-prising—even shocking—to many who were unused to such manifest dedication to a cause unrelated to making money by the CEO of a sub-stantial corporation. Orville brought patrician respectability to our efforts and a quality of natural authority. I liked visiting government officials with him because, if we got into a dispute, Orville would assume a judicial role. The officials and I would set forth our arguments, and eventually Orville would hand down his ruling—invariably, on my side.

I brought my years of experience in promoting rights in the United States, and my grasp, based on that experience, of how to endow the new field of international human rights with a quality of professionalism that it previously lacked. Where Bob Bernstein's emotional engagement was al-ways apparent, my style was reserved. In part, this was a matter of person-ality, but to some extent, it also reflected strategy. I persuaded myself that our cause would be best served if I followed my natural tendencies. Also, I thought Bob supplied more than enough intensity to go around.

For a time, Americas Watch meetings were held every other Wednesday morning at 8:30 A.M. (alternating with Helsinki Watch meetings). Presid-ing at these meetings, Orville always began on time. I used to joke that he would start punctually if he was the only person in the room. That never had to happen; with Orville in the chair, everyone took care not to arrive late. At first, we spent those meetings puzzling over how a handful of people sitting in a room in New York could have an impact on decisions by powerful governments thousands of miles away. But over time, the meetings acquired an institutional significance for us that none of us had foreseen. They became a forum at which important issues were debated and where those who were fresh from conducting investigations, often in difficult or even dangerous circumstances, would present their preliminary findings. This gave the meetings a quality of freshness and immediacy. When we wanted to enlist a new donor in support of our work, we would invite the person to attend a Wednesday morning meeting. Many attended repeatedly, sometimes bringing along friends who also became contributors.

Initially, the meetings were held in the board room at Random House, which helped convey a sense that we were important even when we were only a fledgling organization. It was also convenient because the room had a very large, well-worn, boat-shaped wooden table that could seat a lot of people. (On one occasion, a visitor expressed admiration for that table and asked Bob Bernstein where he got it. He told her he had acquired it when he heard that the Rockettes were getting a new practice stage. Apparently, she believed him, because he subsequently had the story repeated back to him.) Subsequently, when Random House refurbished, Bob donated the table to what had by then grown from Helsinki Watch and Americas Watch to become Human Rights Watch. We accommodated it in a very large conference room in offices I leased in a building at 41st Street and 5th Avenue.

At the time, I had the possibility of getting a much better deal on office space elsewhere because the Ford Foundation had made a program-related investment in a building in lower Manhattan, not far from the World Trade Center. The NAACP Legal Defense Fund was moving in, and I liked the idea of sharing their building. But it was an inconvenient site for the Wednesday morning meetings. The location I chose was the most centrally located in the city. Though the building we moved into was not particularly attractive, it did have one outstanding feature. Our offices had a wall of windows framing a beautiful view of the gleaming white marble New York Public Library and the stately lions guarding the entrance directly across the street. At the time, with Vartan Gregorian as its president, the library was the liveliest cultural institution in the city. Because those Wednesday morning meetings were so important, I chose an interior office for myself and devoted that wall of windows to the conference room. (After my departure, Human Rights Watch expanded further and, in need of larger quarters, moved seven blocks away to the Empire State Building, an only slightly less central location for meetings.)

The alliance of Helsinki Watch and Americas Watch in the early 1980s proved propitious. Though often on the same side as the Reagan administration in Helsinki Watch in denouncing Soviet abuses, our work with Americas Watch demonstrated that our goal was not the opportunistic use of human rights rhetoric for Cold War purposes. When the Reaganites attacked Americas Watch for criticizing governments aligned with the United States, our engagement in Helsinki Watch made it difficult for them to portray us as Soviet dupes. The two Watch Committees established each other's credibility, helping us to emerge as a potent force for the protection of human rights.

Because the Americas Watch side of our work put us into conflict with the Reagan administration, it consumed the lion's share of my time. The day-to-day activities of Helsinki Watch were managed by Jeri Laber. Though she lacked a significant background in defending rights, and never acquired a grasp of international human rights law, she proved an effective advocate by writing frequently for newspapers and magazines about the Russians, Poles, Czechs, and others she encountered on her frequent travels to the region who stood up to persecution. Her impressionistic articles humanized men and women with unfamiliar-sounding names struggling against apparently all-powerful regimes with what seemed then little or no prospect of making headway. Thereby, Jeri helped many in the West care what happened to individuals who otherwise had only a blurred collective identity as dissidents.

Jeri's anecdotal efforts were backed up and given substance by a dogged and intrepid young researcher for Helsinki Watch, Catherine Fitzpatrick. On one occasion, Cathy talked her way into a mental hospital in Moscow to see a peace activist held there and took photos inside the institution. When I asked how she did this, she told me she had gone on a Sunday when the supervisory staff would not be present and told a guard she was the activist's cousin from Riga in Moscow visiting just for the day. Why Riga? Cathy told me that some Muscovites have difficulty distinguishing a Latvian accent in Russian from an American one. Despite such exploits,

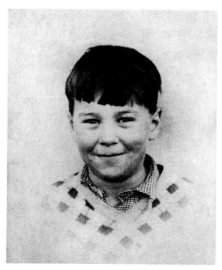

Aryeh Neier in Kettering, England in 1944 at age seven. (Courtesy of the author)

With sister Esther in Northampton, England in 1946. (Courtesy of the author)

Yvette and Aryeh Neier on the beach at Nantucket with David and their dalmatian, Max, in 1968. (Courtesy of the author)

CIERRE CON PEGA   Por YEPES

—¿Y ese ojo negro?
—Nada, mija; que vengo del Congreso Pro Democracia y Libertad...

A Venezuelan newspaper's cartoon based on an incident at Neier's first international human rights meeting in April 1960. A man responds to his wife's inquiry about his black eye saying: "It's nothing dear; I just went to the Congress for Democracy and Liberty." (Courtesy of the author)

From left, Edward J. Ennis, Alan Reitman, Norman Dorsen, Roger Baldwin and Neier. Taken at Baldwin's Greenwich Village home in 1976 to mark Dorsen's replacement of Ennis as ACLU Chairman. Baldwin was then ninety-two. Reitman was the longtime Associate Director of the ACLU. (Benedict J. Fernandez)

Chatting with Judge William Booth, Chairman of the New York City Human Rights Commission in Washington Square Park, New York City, in April 1968 while observing an anti-war demonstration. Moments later, Neier was arrested when he tried to get a closer look at a youth being beaten by plainclothes police. (Courtesy of the author)

Speaking at a press conference during the 1966 campaign for civilian participation in reviewing complaints against the police with U.S. Senator Robert F. Kennedy and New York City Mayor John V. Lindsay. (Courtesy of the author)

A press conference with Rev. A.J. Muste, grand old man of the anti-war movement and Professor Gordon Christiansen. The press conference was called to protest questions at a grand jury hearing about attitudes toward the Vietnam War. U.S. Attorney Robert Morgenthau convened the grand jury after five men burned their draft cards at a demonstration. When the *New York Times* published this photo it appeared that Neier was making accusations against Morgenthau. Neier recalls that he was motioning to a colleague to close a door. (The New York Times Photo Archives)

A nationally syndicated cartoon published in 1976. (© Tribune Media Services, Inc. Reprinted with permission. All rights reserved.)

One of a series of advertisements published by the ACLU in newspapers across the country in the fall of 1973 in its campaign to impeach Richard Nixon. (ACLU)

In 1987, with plans underway to extend its work globally, Neier began using the name Human Rights Watch. Previously, the organization only used the names of its regional components (Helsinki Watch, Americas Watch, Asia Watch) leading some to believe erroneously that they were separate organizations. (HRW)

Robert L. Bernstein, Human Rights Watch's founding Chairman, with Kenneth Roth who Neier hired as his Deputy in 1987 and who became his successor as Executive Director in 1993. (Fitzroy Hepkins/HRW)

Orville Schell, a prominent New York lawyer, joined with Robert L. Bernstein and Neier to found Human Rights Watch. (HRW)

Juan E. Méndez, then the director of the Americas division of Human Rights Watch, takes testimony from a Nicaraguan wounded in a Contra attack. Today Méndez, himself a torture victim of his native Argentina in the 1970s, is Professor of Law at Notre Dame and President of the Inter-American Commission of Human Rights of the Organization of American States. (HRW)

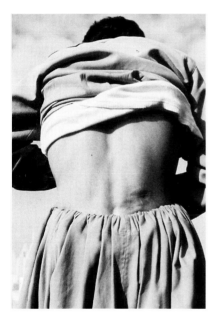

Taymour, a Kurdish youth shot in the back by Iraqi troops in 1988 when he was twelve. He nevertheless managed to climb out of a trench in the desert before a bulldozer covered him and others from his village with sand. Human Rights Watch found him three years later after he made his way back to Kurdistan. His story, and those of a few other survivors, helped HRW piece together information about the murder of about 100,000 Kurds by Saddam Hussein's forces. (© Susan Meiselas/Magnum Photos)

A mass grave is unearthed in Iraqi Kurdistan. The man with the hat on the right is famed forensic anthropologist Clyde Snow. Human Rights Watch asked Snow to go to Kurdistan as part of its investigation of the killing of about 100,000 Kurds in the period immediately following the Iran-Iraq war. (© Susan Meiselas/Magnum Photos)

A press conference in besieged—and freezing—Sarajevo in January 1993. From left, the participants are Lionel Rosenblatt, then President of Refugees International; Senada Kreso, a Bosnian who served as translator; Neier; Mark Malloch Brown, now Administrator of the United Nations Development Program; Morton Abramowitz, then President of the Carnegie Endowment for International Peace; and Zdravko Grebo, then Chairman of the Soros Foundation in Bosnia-Herzegovina. Abramowitz, Malloch Brown and Neier served on a committee guiding the expenditure of $50 million George Soros donated for humanitarian assistance in Bosnia. (OSI)

Abramowitz, Grebo, Malloch Brown, Neier and Rosenblatt at lunch in the office of Hakija Turajlç (at the head of the table), deputy Prime Minister of Bosnia, during the January 1993 visit to Sarajevo. Four days later, Turajlç was murdered. En route to the airport in an armored personnel carrier, he was stopped at a Serb checkpoint. A French officer directed that the APC should be opened and a Serb soldier shot Turajlç point blank. (OSI)

With George Soros and Sonja Licht, President of the Soros Foundation Yugoslavia, in 1997 at a children's center in Kosovo supported by the foundation. (Fotografija/Vesna Pavlové)

Fred Cuny, a relief specialist sometimes called the "master of disaster" in Somalia in 1992. Neier collaborated with Cuny on relief projects in Sarajevo and subsequently enlisted him to go to Chechnya in 1995 to advise the Soros Foundations on projects there. Cuny and three Russians accompanying him disappeared there that April. Though their purpose was to assist the victims of the conflict, almost certainly they were murdered by Chechens. (© Judy Walgren/Dallas Morning News/ Intertect)

Soon after Neier's arrival in 1993, the Open Society Institute established a Burma Project to support the country's democracy movement. In 1996, Neier paid a visit to the leader of that movement, Aung San Suu Kyi, whose political party had won national elections in 1990 but was prevented from taking office by the armed forces. Subsequently, the Nobel Peace Prize winner was put under house arrest and barred from receiving visitors. In 2002, when she was released, Neier returned to Rangoon to see her again. (OSI)

Chatting with students on a 1997 visit to Serbia. (Fotografija/Vesna Pavlović)

she never got into serious trouble on her travels for us to the Soviet Union. Collaborating with Ludmilla Alexeyeva, an historian and one of the founders of the Moscow Helsinki Group who had migrated to the United States, Cathy made it possible for us to produce the most comprehensive and reliable reports on Soviet human rights abuses published anywhere. (Now in her mid-seventies, Ludmilla Alexeyeva is back in Russia directing the work of the Moscow Helsinki Group; Cathy Fitzpatrick moved on to direct the International League for Human Rights.)

One of my main contributions to the Helsinki Watch side of our work was to establish an international organization that could sponsor national Helsinki committees throughout the regions of Europe and North America covered by the 1975 Accords. In 1978, Andrei Sakharov had appealed for the establishment of such a body to defend all Helsinki monitors in countries where they were subject to persecution. National Helsinki groups were formed about that time in a few Western countries: Norway and the Netherlands as well as the United States—though only the U.S. group carried substantial weight—but these had no contact with each other. When we took the initiative in 1982 to form an international organization, Sakharov had already been in internal exile in Gorky (now Nizhny Novgorod) for more than two years. He had been sent to the provincial city, from which westerners were barred, for denouncing the Soviet invasion of Afghanistan in December 1979. By 1982, arrests had virtually wiped out the Moscow Helsinki Group as well as Helsinki organizations formed in other parts of the Soviet Union that monitored human rights in their regions.

The disastrous human rights situation in the Soviet Union was not the only factor in making me propose that we form an international organization. I was also concerned about our effectiveness in the US Helsinki Watch in opposing Soviet abuses. At that point, it had been a little more than a year since Ronald Reagan had become the fortieth president of the United States, and relations between Washington and Moscow had hit an all-time low. Some Reaganites, and allies in the media such as *New York Times* columnist William Safire, even wanted to withdraw from the Helsinki process.[2] The two superpowers were barely talking to each other and were engaged in proxy wars all over the world. Within the United States, the creation of Americas Watch ensured we were not perceived as an adjunct of the Reagan administration. Yet I was concerned that this would mean little or nothing to the Soviet Union. Helsinki Watch could have scant impact on Moscow's human rights abuses, I feared, at a moment when our denunciations seemed simply to echo the rhetoric emanating from the Cold War antagonist.

And yet, the hostility between Washington and Moscow made the Soviet Union eager to cultivate public opinion in Western Europe. It was a period of frequent protest demonstrations in countries such as Britain, France, and Germany against the deployment in Europe of U.S. missiles armed with nuclear warheads. Moscow sought to exploit divisions between Europe and the United States. In such circumstances, denunciations of Soviet human rights abuses by European Helsinki groups and by an international group with a strong European base had a chance to be effective. It seemed urgent to demonstrate that concern about Moscow's treatment of the Helsinki monitors and other dissenters was not confined to the United States.

We established the International Helsinki Federation for Human Rights (IHF) at Bellagio, Italy, in September 1992 at a meeting attended by twenty-two participants from eighteen countries. In advance of the meeting, Jeri Laber and I had traveled about Western Europe to enlist participants. My part included stops in the four Scandinavian countries. The visit I made to Sweden was fortuitous. Before going to Sweden, I had called a writer I knew in Stockholm, Per Wästberg, president of International PEN, and told him I wanted to visit to establish a group to promote compliance with the human rights provisions of the Helsinki Accords. Would he help me? Wästberg agreed to invite several people to his home for a luncheon at which I would talk about what such a group might do. One of those at lunch was Gerald Nagler, a well-to-do businessman. At the end of lunch, Gerald told me we had met several years previously. I didn't recall. Where and when? Gerald said that Ruth Ginsburg had spent a sabbatical year in Sweden where they had become friends. His daughter subsequently did an unpaid internship with Ruth at the ACLU. When he visited his daughter at our offices, Ruth had brought him around to introduce him to me.

In the course of this conversation, Gerald told me he was at the point of selling his business. That meant he would have time on his hands. I wondered whether he would take the lead in forming a Swedish Helsinki Committee. He was amenable, so I invited him to Bellagio. Subsequently, when the IHF established its headquarters in Vienna, Gerald moved there—while keeping his apartment in Stockholm—to become its executive director. Vienna was a comfortable place for Gerald as it was home to his wife Monica's family, the Wittgensteins.[3]

An episode soon after we established the IHF exemplified our bizarre relationship with the Reagan administration. It was a moment when we were engaged in running combat with the administration over Central America. As if oblivious to this, a prominent Democrat who had undertaken a number of top diplomatic assignments for the Republican president called to invite Jeri Laber and me to lunch at the White House Mess to talk about the IHF. When we got there, we found that a number of senior officials from the State Department and the National Security Council were there, and they were eager to hear about our plans for the new body we were launching. Most of the questioning was directed by a National Security Council (NSC) official, the only person present whom I had not known previously. I told them we expected the IHF to generate Western European pressure against Soviet human rights abuses.

The NSC man asked if we had funding for the new entity. I said we had just started raising money and had obtained an initial grant of $45,000 from the Ford Foundation. He said he had in mind giving us ten times that amount at the outset—roughly equivalent to the US Helsinki Watch's own budget at that moment, and therefore a substantial sum for us—though he did not say where the money would come from. As this was prior to establishment of the National Endowment for Democracy, which was created by legislation to provide funding for such causes openly, and as I could think of no overt legal way the government could provide us with such support, I was eager to discuss the source of these funds—though I doubted he would reveal their real provenance. As it was, I limited myself to saying that we had a firm policy of not taking government funds. I thought it inappropriate for human rights monitoring groups that exist to criticize governments to accept government support. With that, it was clear the business part of the lunch was over. Though the International Helsinki Federation was always short of funds, it fulfilled the role I envisioned for it.

Former CIA director Robert Gates wrote in his memoir: "The Soviets desperately wanted the CSCE [the Conference on Security and Cooperation in Europe, the official name of the meeting in 1975 that produced the Helsinki Accords], they got it and it laid the foundations for the end of their empire. We resisted it for years, went grudgingly, Ford paid a terrible price for going—perhaps reelection itself—only to discover years later

that CSCE had yielded benefits beyond our wildest imagination. Go figure."[4] What confounded both Moscow and Washington was the little
group of brave men and women who had organized in Moscow in 1976,
the inspiration they provided to kindred souls elsewhere in the Soviet
bloc, the determination by Bob Bernstein and those of us he enlisted in
the US Helsinki Watch to call attention to their struggle, and our success
in launching an international movement to take up the cause. Today, the
IHF is the umbrella organization for a network of human rights organizations operating throughout Western and Eastern Europe and the former
Soviet Union. Its most important contribution in the post-Soviet era has
been to assist in the formation of its national affiliates and to legitimize
them by their association with the IHF.

We established Asia Watch in 1985, Africa Watch in 1988, and the last
of the regional Watch Committees, Middle East Watch, in 1989. With
that, there were no longer any geographical limits on our capacity, so we
started using the name Human Rights Watch to establish our identity as an
organization with global reach. The availability of funding was essential in
allowing us to expand. A grant of $3.5 million from the MacArthur Foun-
dation, our largest to that point, made it possible to launch Africa Watch
and Middle East Watch. Other factors also played a part in the sequence in
which we established the regional Watch Committees.

A stimulus for the formation of Asia Watch was that I was approached
by an aide to the Dalai Lama. At the time, unpublicized discussions were
under way for a visit to Tibet by the exiled spiritual leader. The Chinese
government then saw a visit as confirmation of the legitimacy of their
rule. One condition set by negotiators for the Dalai Lama was that a three-
member team should go in advance to assess the human rights situation in
his homeland. Would I be a member of that team? I readily agreed and
began informing myself about Tibet. Also, I spent time with the Dalai
Lama on his periodic visits to the United States and, on one memorable
occasion, organized a luncheon at his request for him to meet "the New
York intellectuals." I recall that as we were entering the room where the
luncheon was held, Susan Sontag said to Joseph Brodsky, "It's like meeting
the Pope." Joseph replied, "Much more. He's a living god."

Relations between the Dalai Lama and the Chinese government soured,
and neither his visit nor mine took place. When I visited China in 1988,
the authorities turned down my request to go to Tibet. After the Dalai
Lama was awarded the Nobel Peace Prize in 1989, which enhanced his

celebrity and his symbolic representation of resistance to Chinese oppression, relations were further embittered so it now seems difficult to imagine they once negotiated about his visit. Though those plans came to naught, a consequence was that some of Asia Watch's earliest investigations focused on Tibet. I was fortunate in enlisting as our principal investigator an academic specialist who speaks fluent Tibetan and Chinese and had access to the territory for scholarly work. This was unusual, as many scholars are fearful that their identity will be discovered and they will be denied future entry, cutting off their ability to pursue their research. We took care never to disclose his or her identity. The specialist made it possible for us to produce well-informed and reliable reports on human rights developments in one of the most difficult places on earth to monitor.

A factor in the development of Africa Watch was that I got to know a brilliant Oxford- and Cambridge-educated Somali lawyer, Rakiya Omaar. Though she had a reputation as a difficult person, I was so impressed by her abilities as a researcher and a public advocate that I asked her to become the founding director of Africa Watch. For a few years, I found her work outstanding. Largely through her efforts, Africa Watch quickly made its mark. For a time, I was pleased that I had disregarded the advice of colleagues in the human rights field who had told me she was trouble.

The year 1992 was difficult for Rakiya, however, and it produced my most serious conflict with an employee since my rift at the ACLU sixteen years earlier with another exceptionally talented lawyer, Charles Morgan, Jr. As in the Morgan case, my insistence on adherence to organizational policy led to a blowup. Rakiya was distraught over the clan warfare in her homeland that was causing starvation. Though the numbers may have been somewhat inflated, it was widely reported at the time that as many as 1.5 million people were at risk, or about 20 percent of the population. Rakiya and I visited senior U.S. and UN officials to urge explicit condemnation of the clan leaders responsible for the violence and to call for effective measures to relieve the famine. She was outspokenly critical during this period of UN Secretary General Boutros Boutros-Ghali, both for firing an effective mediator, Algerian diplomat Mohamed Sahnoun, who had denounced the sluggishness and timidity of UN relief agencies, and for Boutros-Ghali's failure to implement a Security Council resolution to deploy 3,500 troops to protect the delivery of relief assistance.

Rakiya published many articles about events in Somalia and appeared frequently on radio and television to discuss the situation there. As a highly articulate Somali with a prestigious position as director of Africa Watch, she was ready to speak forcefully and passionately about the situation in her own country. As one who minced no words in denouncing her fellow Somalis for indiscriminate warfare to further their own ambitions, and as a strong critic of other African political leaders for their passivity during the crisis, Rakiya was much in demand. For a brief period, she became a minor media celebrity.

At the end of September, for personal reasons, Rakiya left her post as director of Africa Watch. As she had some projects that had not been completed, I arranged that she should stay on as a consultant, based in our London office, for another six months. In November, on the eve of Thanksgiving, President George H.W. Bush—by then a lame duck as he had lost his bid for reelection to Bill Clinton earlier in the month—announced that the United States was ready to provide up to 20,000 ground troops to the United Nations as part of a multilateral force to safeguard delivery of humanitarian assistance to starving Somalis.

Yvette and I went away that Thanksgiving weekend. Though I was deeply concerned with developments in Somalia, I only followed them during the four days I was away by reading the newspaper. As hardly anyone knew where we were going, no one called to tell me what was happening. So I was unaware that in London, where there was no holiday, Rakiya took advantage of her access to the media by giving a number of interviews in which she denounced President Bush's offer of U.S. troops. Some of her interviews were broadcast on radio and television in the United States as well as in Britain.

When I returned to the office on the Monday after Thanksgiving, I was startled to discover what had happened. Human Rights Watch had no policy opposing the use of troops to protect the delivery of humanitarian assistance, and Rakiya's statements seemed to contradict the stand she had taken a few months earlier in our meetings with officials. As she was known to journalists as director of Africa Watch, and was identified as still occupying that post in the interviews denouncing President Bush's initiative, it appeared that she was speaking for Human Rights Watch. I tried to call her in London to get an explanation; we needed to dissociate her statements from Human Rights Watch. When I was unable to reach her or get her to return my calls, I faxed her a letter firing her from the consultancy that had another four months to run. It was the only time I ever fired anyone without doing it face to face.

As in the case of the resignation of Chuck Morgan in 1976, this episode was widely reported in the press. Internal disputes in righteous cause organizations readily attract media attention. It caused us some embarrassment, but in the end it did no damage. Some of my colleagues at Human Rights Watch who had clashed with Rakiya and were less admiring of her than I was let me know they were happy to see her go. I regretted the matter deeply, as I had valued her work during the three and a half years she directed Africa Watch and had wanted her to retain an association with Human Rights Watch.

When we established Middle East Watch in 1989, the first country we focused on was Iraq. That was both because of the severity of the abuses there and because I knew that our reports on the Israeli-Palestinian conflict would inevitably generate controversy in our own ranks and among our supporters. I wanted it to be clear that Middle East Watch would deal with the entire region. We would not pull our punches in reporting Israeli violations of human rights; nor would we focus on those abuses to the exclusion of what were often appalling abuses by other governments in the neighborhood. In 1990, we published a report in book form entitled *Human Rights in Iraq*.[5] The longest section discussed repression against the Kurds, focusing on chemical warfare against them in 1988 when Saddam Hussein's regime had attacked Halabja and other Kurdish towns with poison gas. We raised a question about 500,000 displaced Kurds. Where were they?

Over the next few years, we found out a great deal about what had happened to many of those people. The research we undertook was among the most ambitious and dramatic efforts of my tenure at Human Rights Watch. Immediately following the Gulf War in early 1991, the Kurds in northern Iraq rebelled and briefly gained control of several Iraqi cities. Saddam Hussein's forces that survived the war retaliated swiftly and decisively, suppressing the revolt and triggering an exodus of biblical proportions to neighboring Turkey and Iran. As many as 2 million Kurds, more than half the population of Iraqi Kurdistan, crossed the borders within a few weeks. The Western allies that had recently expelled Iraqi forces from Kuwait were able to repatriate the Kurds by establishing a security zone for them in northern Iraq (proposed by Fred Cuny, whom I got to know soon thereafter). Saddam's planes were barred from flying over this zone, and his ground forces were required to stay out. This permitted the infant Middle East Watch to establish a presence in Iraqi Kurdistan and to conduct a systematic investigation. We located several survivors of the events of 1988 and interviewed them; sent forensic scientists to the region to exhume mass grave sites; and, most significant, in May 1992, arranged for a U.S. Air Force transport plane to fly to the United States from Iraqi Kurdistan carrying 18 tons of Iraqi secret police documents. These had been captured by Kurdish guerrilla forces during their abortive uprising the previous year. We persuaded the guerrillas to turn the documents over to us, and when we got them to the United States, we set about the monumental task of analyzing the millions of pages in Arabic in which the security forces had recorded in great detail their persecution of the Kurds.

Our main focus was the Anfal, the Iraqi regime's name for a campaign it conducted over a six-month period in 1988 under the leadership of Ali Hassan al-Majid (known as "Ali Chemical" to the Kurds), a cousin of Saddam Hussein who was subsequently promoted to defense minister. In addition to destroying literally thousands of Kurdish villages and forcibly relocating hundreds of thousands of their residents, the Anfal had included the murder of about 100,000 Kurds. A large number, we established, had been taken by bus to a desert area in central Iraq where trenches were dug. The Kurds were forced into the trenches, machinegunned, and then covered with sand by bulldozers. Among the survivors we interviewed was Tamur, a twelve-year-old boy with a bullet in his back who had climbed out of one of the trenches ahead of a bulldozer and made his way across the desert until he was found by a Bedouin family who treated his wound and nursed him back to health. Two years later, he made his way back to Kurdistan, where he told us his story.

One of the researchers we employed to read and analyze the captured documents was an English-speaking Iraqi Kurdish engineer, Shorsh Resool. I met him in London where he was living at the time. He told me he had traveled around Kurdistan in the period of the Anfal and had compiled a list of 15,000 persons who had disappeared. Making his way to London, he had visited offices where he thought there might be interest in his list. One human rights group had greeted him with disbelief. It was not possible for 15,000 people to disappear without the organization knowing about it, he was told. I was glad to hire him to substantiate his findings through the Iraqi government's own documents.

Another participant in our research was the photographer Susan Meiselas, whose images of the wars of the 1970s and 1980s in Central America are sharply etched in the memories of many who recall that era (one of her photos, "Shadows," is on the wall in my office opposite my desk). Susan took part in several of our missions in Iraq and neighboring countries because we wanted a visual record of what happened in Kurdistan. Because of her work with us—including photos of Tamur's bullet-scarred back and of the bodies we exhumed—Susan developed a preoccupation with the Kurdish minorities throughout the region and eventually published a magnificent book that helped to reclaim a lost history.[6]

The first several years of my professional work for international human rights in the 1980s were particularly rewarding for me personally because we were figuring out how to have significant impact in a period that seemed inhospitable to our cause. It was a wonderful learning period in which my grasp of political processes expanded greatly. Despite severe repression by the Soviets, brutal military regimes in Latin America and East Asia, and "strong man" governments in many African countries, and even though the Reagan administration was more often than not antagonistic to our efforts, we made great headway.

I regard monitoring violations in armed conflict as my most significant contribution to the protection of human rights. This seems fitting to me, as my life span has exactly coincided with the era of deliberate bombardments of civilians. The Spanish market town Guernica was annihilated by aircraft of Hitler's Condor Legion and Mussolini's Aviazione Legionaria on April 26, 1937, four days after I was born. Thanks to Picasso's masterpiece, that episode has become the emblematic representation of a defining horror of our time.

The author of a book about the role of nongovernmental organizations in promoting human rights has said that I "virtually invented" the attempt to curb such crimes by denouncing them as violations of the laws of war.[7] "Virtually" is accurate, as I share responsibility with Robert Goldman, professor of international law at American University. I sought out Bob and invited him to become a founding member of Americas Watch because of his knowledge of human rights in Latin America. I wanted to draw especially on his expertise on Uruguay, a country once known as the "Switzerland of Latin America" (when that label sounded better than after revelations about Swiss conduct during World War II). Uruguay had been ruled by a nasty military dictatorship since 1973 and had the dubious distinction at the beginning of the 1980s of having what was said to be the highest ratio in the world of political prisoners to population. Goldman, subsequently a member of the Inter-American Commission on Human Rights of the Organization of American States and, for a period, that body's president, is a specialist in international humanitarian law, or the laws of war. From the outset, Bob urged the newly formed Americas Watch to apply that body of law to monitoring armed conflicts.

I found his argument appealing. The declarations, agreements, and treaties that make up international human rights law and that are the standards relied on by Amnesty International and all other groups that monitor human rights do not provide grounds for assessing many of the most abusive practices in military conflicts. I wanted a basis in international law to denounce indiscriminate attacks on civilian populations, disproportionate bombardments of population centers, forced displacement, and a host of other means by which the opposing sides in the wars then under way in El Salvador, Guatemala, and Nicaragua sought to prevail. The International Committee of the Red Cross (ICRC) intercedes with combatants and attempts to persuade them to respect international humanitarian law. It does not disseminate its findings publicly, however, as it believes that would interfere with its main mission: protecting the victims of armed conflict. The ICRC considers that confidentiality is the price it must pay for access to those who need its assistance. I have great respect for the ICRC and its delegates, who do excellent work in many countries, and I acknowledge their essential role. At the same time, I believe there is a need for another body that systematically monitors and publicly denounces violations of the laws of war. Americas Watch and, over time, Human Rights Watch became the preeminent institution meeting that need. During the last several years I spent at Human Rights Watch, and since then, I have been guided in my thinking on international humanitarian law by Theodor Meron, professor of law at New York University and, at this writing, a judge of the International Criminal Tribunal for the Former Yugoslavia.

Another attraction of monitoring armed conflicts against the criteria established by the laws of war is that those laws apply equally to both sides. In contrast, international human rights law only binds governments. Groups such as Amnesty International—which, eventually, shifted course to follow the lead of Human Rights Watch—limited themselves to reporting on government abuses. The opportunists in the Reagan administration seized on this to claim that groups reporting on death squad killings and disappearances by the Salvadoran armed forces were biased as they did not also denounce guerrilla crimes. Such allegations were so fierce that, in 1982, the Catholic Archdiocese of San Salvador disaffiliated its legal aid office, Socorro Juridico, and created a new body, Tutela Legal, to report on abuses by both sides. Neither the Reagan administration nor the San Salvador Archdiocese was aware that there was a basis in international law for this shift. The Reaganites did the "right deed for the wrong reason," which T. S. Eliot labeled "the greatest treason."[8] I recall a conversation I had at the time with a deputy assistant secretary of state for human rights in which I mentioned the Geneva Conventions. He responded that he was not a lawyer and therefore did not know anything about such matters. This comment, inconceivable today from one in such a post, reflected the pervasive ignorance of the laws of war when Americas Watch started its monitoring.

Reagan administration attacks on those who failed to report on guerrilla abuses in El Salvador were purely political. They were intended to impugn the anti-communism of critics of U.S. policy. The Salvadoran Archdiocese sought to shield itself against such attacks by starting fresh with a body that monitored both sides. Archbishop Arturo Rivera y Damas, successor to the murdered Archbishop Oscar Arnulfo Romero, and the woman he chose to head Tutela Legal, María Julia Hernández, expressed relief when I pointed out to them that there was a sound basis in international law for the step they had taken in self-defense.

Today, human rights groups worldwide have developed substantial expertise in the field, and governments, the media, and the informed public have become sensitive to laws-of-war issues. As a consequence, for example, the conduct of Slobodan Milošević's forces in Kosovo and the question of whether NATO did enough to minimize civilian casualties in its bombing campaign were widely discussed. More recently, the conduct of America's Afghan allies in the Northern Alliance in the treatment of captured Taliban combatants has become an issue. I believe this is one of the useful consequences of the innovation for which Bob Goldman and I were responsible at Americas Watch two decades ago. Another is that my focus on the laws of war led me in the mid-1980s to start monitoring the use of an indiscriminate weapon, landmines, and to initiate a proposal for the adoption of a treaty banning their use. It also led to a proposal I made in 1992 to establish an international criminal tribunal to try those who

committed war crimes during the conflicts in ex-Yugoslavia. Those proposals grew naturally out of our monitoring of compliance with international humanitarian law and, in turn, enhanced the significance of that
body of law for the protection of human rights.

My other important contribution to the international human rights
agenda involved an effort to incorporate issues I had focused on in promoting civil liberties in the United States: police practices, conditions for
common prisoners, and women's rights. (One of my regrets is that
Human Rights Watch did not also launch a campaign to deal with the
rights of the mentally disabled. Subsequently, however, at the Soros Foundations, I have been able to support such efforts.) The international human
rights movement was formed primarily to combat politically motivated
abuses. Its character in the 1960s and 1970s was shaped by Amnesty International. Human Rights Watch also had its origins in efforts to assist dissenters persecuted for their beliefs. My background in defending civil
liberties against abuses of power in a wide range of circumstances made
me reluctant to draw sharp distinctions between abuses against political
activists and other violations of the rights of the powerless that did comparable harm to the victims.

I encountered great resistance to making women's rights part of the international human rights agenda. Though its inclusion is widely accepted
today, as recently as the end of the 1980s, the issue was anathema to many
in the human rights movement—including a number of members of the
Human Rights Watch staff. For some reason, a few of the women on the
staff were among the most adamantly opposed. They argued that violence
against women, an issue I wanted to address, was mostly a consequence of
private conduct. Therefore, it should not be bracketed with state-spon-
sored crimes such as imprisonment for peaceable expression or torture. I
disagreed. Just as the state has a responsibility to prosecute and punish
those who engage in politically motivated crimes, such as death squad
killings, regardless of whether the murderers are public officials, so it has a
duty to protect women beaten or murdered by men who consider they
have a proprietary relationship to their spouses, lovers, or daughters. The
state action that the human rights movement should challenge is denial of
protection by the law based on the status of women. In many countries,
certain crimes against women are routinely ignored by law-enforcement
authorities. By applying the methods of the international human rights
movement—establishment of international norms, monitoring, dissemination of information, and campaigning in ways that embarrass responsi-

ble officials—it is possible to make significant headway in protecting women's rights.

William Korey, the author who has written about the part played by nongovernmental organizations in promoting human rights, has attributed Human Rights Watch's "preeminent global status" not only to its definition of its mandate and the quality of its reporting but to another factor. "Of equal, if not greater significance in Neier's pressing for a global agenda," according to Korey, "was the use of American power throughout the world."[9] I think Korey is right, but I would add a gloss. Unquestionably, Human Rights Watch's rise to international eminence derived in part from its role as an organization based in the United States that exercised influence over U.S. policy. We exploited the power of the United States around the world to promote our own agenda. What made our efforts effective was our insistence on holding the United States accountable for abuses by governments of other countries that held power because of U.S. support. Though U.S. officials were not the authors of those abuses, in circumstances where the United States acted as an apologist for torture, disappearances, or murder, we treated our government, as noted, as a "surrogate villain."

We succeeded, in part, because the Reagan administration—which held office when we developed this approach—made it easy for us. By denying or trying to explain away the abuses we documented, it justified our identification of Washington as the target of our denunciations. This made our efforts far more effective than they could have been at another time. Among the factors that contributed to the influence achieved by Human Rights Watch, I place high on the list the inadvertent boost we got from Ronald Reagan, Alexander Haig, Jeane Kirkpatrick, Elliott Abrams, and others who zealously defended the practices of despots aligned with the United States. Over time, as the organization has grown and established offices in all parts of the world, Human Rights Watch has become more global and less "American." This has proven fortuitous in the era of President George W. Bush, when a heightened U.S. refusal to abide by international agreements is provoking rapidly growing international resentment. Today, Human Rights Watch's global influence derives from its own prestige, whereas at an earlier stage in its development it reflected the influential position we established in Washington.

My critics in the international human rights movement were right, I now accept, in castigating me for my disdain of the United Nations. I acknowledged the world body's essential normative role, but I considered the UN of little value in dealing with governments about their disregard of its prescriptions. During my years at Human Rights Watch, I largely ignored the UN Commission on Human Rights, never attended its annual meetings in Geneva, never visited its offices there, and maintained little contact with UN functionaries concerned with rights. The commission had been silent, or virtually silent, about some of the greatest human rights abuses worldwide since its formation: Stalin's Gulag, the Great Leap Forward and the Cultural Revolution in China, the Cambodian Holocaust, and the crimes of Idi Amin and Milton Obote in Uganda among them. I thought many human rights groups wasted time and money in sending representatives to Geneva for a month each year to debate the language of resolutions little noted by the rest of the world. Human Rights Watch's travel budget should be expended on field research at the sites where abuses were committed, I insisted, not in Swiss hotels.

In retrospect, I overdid it. Resolutions by UN bodies carry weight in some countries. My successors at Human Rights Watch have adopted a more balanced approach. Though they do not delude themselves about the significance of actions by UN agencies, they have engaged with the world body in a manner that seems proportionate to its capacity to further their cause. My successor, Ken Roth, designated Joanna Weschler, a Polish émigré who joined the staff in the early 1980s because of her knowledge of and connections to the Solidarity movement, in which she was active before it was outlawed in December 1981, as HRW's UN representative. Her efforts there have paid off in ways that make clear this was a wise move.

This is not the only way that Ken, whom I hired as my deputy in 1987 and who has served as executive director of Human Rights Watch since my departure in 1993, has improved on what I did. I had not known him very long before I chose him but nevertheless felt confident in my choice. His obvious intelligence, and his care in the use of words, both in speaking and writing, to characterize abuses of human rights, made me believe that he could be trusted with responsibility for Human Rights Watch's reporting. Also, he seemed to me to combine boldness and prudence in ways that would serve us well. My expectations have been borne out. What pleases me most about the performance of the organization under Ken's leadership is that the quality of its reporting, which had already reached a high standard by the time I left, has gotten better.

Human Rights Watch's global monitoring today is incisive, focused, well-documented, path-breaking in its investigative quality, and reflects thoughtful judgments about abuses informed by a deep understanding of the historical, legal, cultural, and political contexts in which they take place. Time and again, as in Rwanda, Kosovo, Afghanistan, Chechnya, and Colombia, Human Rights Watch has obtained reliable information on abuses as they take place in war zones where no one else ventures. A high point, though not the only one, was Alison Des Forges's reporting on the Rwandan genocide.[10] A century from now, it will be the work that will be studied by those seeking to understand what took place. That is a rare achievement for an organization committed to engagement in the daily cut and thrust of public policy debates. Another outstanding example is the scrupulously detailed account that Human Rights Watch published in May 2002 of what happened when Israeli forces occupied the West Bank town of Jenin. It was published as a debate raged over whether a UN investigative team would get access to the town—from which the team was ultimately excluded—and just days after Israeli forces withdrew. None of its findings about events that had been hotly disputed has been seriously questioned. It is definitive.

Human Rights Watch's reporting gets attention because journalists who cover such conflicts and officials who monitor them know they can count on the researchers for Human Rights Watch to adhere to exacting standards. HRW is also publishing much of the best-documented material available on rights abuses in the United States, such as those that take place in the criminal justice system. In this, it is filling a gap left by the ACLU's failure to diversify its methodology. I know of no other institution anywhere in any field that publishes so large a quantity of excellent, research-based materials on contemporary events worldwide. Each time I see a new report by Human Rights Watch—that is, several times a month—I take pride in leaving behind an institution that has demonstrated the capacity to continue to raise its standards since my departure.

A special satisfaction of my years at Human Rights Watch is that we became effective without relying on litigation, the principal means used by the ACLU to protect rights in the United States. By the 1980s, I thought that efforts to defend civil liberties domestically by litigation were achieving diminishing returns. In certain fields—such as in free-speech cases—the courts remain the best forum to vindicate rights. In other areas, such as police practices and over-incarceration, I believe other means should be used to combat abuses. Litigation has a part to play, but only as a component of a broader effort. When it comes to upholding rights internationally, the option of litigation is rarely available. Human Rights Watch has had to generate political debates and embarrass the governments responsible for abuses to make them respect rights. It is not easy to do this worldwide, but I discovered it is often possible. My successors have demonstrated that by doing work of the highest quality the organization's modus operandi could continue to be effective long after the novelty had worn off.

It is unclear to me as I write how Human Rights Watch will solve the new challenges that it faces in the first decade of the twenty-first century, particularly those stemming from the events of September 11, 2001. In the aftermath of the terror attacks on the United States, the administration of President George W. Bush forged a number of new alliances and renewed some older ones to wage war upon the terrorists. Among the countries that were objects of the administration's efforts were such significant abusers of human rights as Pakistan, Uzbekistan, Russia, China, Saudi Arabia, and Egypt. In the process, the administration made it clear that a consequence would be further limits to its already relatively infrequent criticisms of human rights abuses by these governments. Indeed, in matters such as Russia's crimes against the Chechens and China's against the Uighurs, which could be conducted under the pretext that they are part of the global struggle against the al Qaeda network, the impact of September 11 was to provide a license for escalation.

As noted, a significant part of the influence that Human Rights Watch achieved in the 1980s and 1990s derived from its capacity to leverage U.S. governmental pressure on rights abusers. The new geopolitical considerations that take precedence in Washington, and the rising tide of anti-Americanism in much of the world, all but eliminate the value of this approach. The situation is not entirely bleak. After September 11, a country that hardly ever attracted the attention of the news media previously, Uzbekistan, became a focus of attention, including its human rights practices. For the first time that I recall, there were a number of stories in the press about its thousands of political prisoners and about the systematic torture they have suffered. This publicity provided Human Rights Watch an opportunity to seek reforms in a country previously insulated against pressure by its obscurity. But although new U.S. alliances can be exploited by shedding light on abuses that take place in dark corners, this benefit does not compensate for the loss of Washington's voice to speak out against severe violations.

Though the atmosphere in Washington is a daunting difficulty, I have no doubt that Human Rights Watch has the energy, the creativity, and the leadership to overcome it. The organization had a dynamic quality during the period when I led it that has been sustained and even strengthened since my departure. When new approaches are required, Human Rights Watch has demonstrated the capacity to find them and to show the way for the entire international human rights movement.

I believe our efforts at Human Rights Watch in an earlier era contributed to the extraordinary changes that took place in several parts of the world in the 1980s and the 1990s: the collapse of military regimes in most Latin American countries and in a few countries of East Asia; the fall of communism in Eastern Europe and the Soviet Union; the end of apartheid in South Africa and a turn to democracy in a few other countries in sub-Saharan Africa; and the emergence of signs of a human rights consciousness in parts of the Middle East. In recognition of our contribution to these developments, over time we were able to attract the resources needed to become a significant global organization. We also helped to inspire efforts in many countries to form the indigenous human rights groups that operate today and that have become an important force in world affairs. I consider the 1980s, especially the first few years of the decade, when I was learning every day how to be more effective internationally in dealing with issues of great consequence, as the most creative and rewarding time of my career.

CHAPTER NINE

Defeating Reagan

The election of Ronald Reagan in November 1980 as the fortieth president of the United States, and his designation of his principal foreign policy advisers, dismayed the small band of proponents of international human rights in the United States. Reagan's predecessor, Jimmy Carter, had embraced our cause. He was the first U.S. president to assert that promoting human rights would be a major concern of his administration's foreign policy. The new team of advisers repudiated the Carter policy.

Carter had been far from consistent. He did little for the human rights cause in Asia, where one of his notable foreign policy achievements, following up on the efforts of Nixon and Kissinger, was to resume full diplomatic relations with China. The long prison sentences imposed on Wei Jingsheng and other "Democracy Wall" activists in the late 1970s were not permitted to impinge on the new friendship with Deng Xiaoping's regime. To the chagrin of the Human Rights Bureau in the State Department—newly established by congressional mandate—the Carter administration was also a strong and resolute supporter of such Asian dictatorships as that of President Ferdinand Marcos in the Philippines.

To its credit, the Carter administration took a stand in favor of human rights in Latin America. A leading part was played by the State Department's assistant secretary of state for human rights, Patricia Derian. I had known Patt first as a civil rights activist in Jackson, Mississippi, where she had entered the struggle as a parent intent on keeping the schools of her city open when local officials closed them to thwart a federal court's desegregation order. She was also active in the ACLU, where I secured her election to the national organization's Executive Committee. Though we did not always see eye to eye—as in her backing of Charles Morgan—I admired her for her boldness, her tenacity, and her political savvy in the battles for racial equality in which she was a leader.

Patricia Derian took up her duties in the State Department with no background in international affairs. She was appointed to her post because she was a political ally of Jimmy Carter's in his struggle to secure the Democratic nomination for president. Her entry into politics was an outgrowth of her civil rights work. Patt had become a member of the Democratic National Committee for Mississippi when her integrated slate was accredited in place of the state's all-white party leadership. Carter enlisted southern liberals in the party to support his presidential bid. They became close during his campaign, as I became aware from the frequency with which ACLU Executive Committee meetings were interrupted by his calls to Patt. He must have assumed that the qualities she manifested in efforts to promote rights in the United States qualified her to play a similar role internationally. Against the odds, that assumption turned out to be correct, though her lack of experience in foreign policy undoubtedly exacerbated the difficulty she had in obtaining support from career professionals in the State Department.

Undaunted either by her lack of experience in international relations or by the novelty of her assignment, Patt traveled to Argentina shortly after taking office and personally confronted the generals and admirals who ruled the country over their abuses of human rights. In her first call to me after she was appointed, she had asked if I knew someone who knew about Argentina. It reflected her inability to get the help she needed from State Department professionals unenthusiastic about her or about the new policy initiative to promote human rights, or both. Overcoming the bureaucratic difficulties she encountered, Patt is credited by Argentine human rights advocates with saving many lives there. When democracy was restored in 1983 and Raul Alfonsín was elected president, I attended his inauguration and saw Patricia Derian—who had been out of office for three years—welcomed warmly as an honored guest. In contrast, the official emissary of the United States, Vice President George H.W. Bush, was received correctly but coldly.

With Patt often leading the way, the Carter administration took stands in support of human rights in several other Latin American countries. It cut off aid to the regime of General Augusto Pinochet in Chile, which had enjoyed the strong backing of the Nixon and Ford administrations, including extensive U.S. financial assistance to rebuild the economy shattered by the turmoil that had preceded Pinochet's 1973 coup. The Carter administration also terminated U.S. support for the Somoza dynasty in Nicaragua. And, it so outraged the military regime in Guatemala by condemning its violations of human rights that the Central American government renounced U.S. assistance.

Alexander Haig, Reagan's choice to serve as secretary of state, left us in no doubt that a new day had dawned in Washington. He told the Senate Foreign Relations Committee that in the new administration, a concern with terrorism would *replace* a concern for human rights. If anything, Reagan's appointee to serve as ambassador to the United Nations, Jeane Kirkpatrick, was even more outspoken. In an article in the November 1979 issue of *Commentary,* "Dictatorships and Double Standards," which Reagan read and which won her the post to which she was appointed, she blamed Carter's human rights policies for the downfall of "moderate autocrats friendly to American interests," such as the shah of Iran and General Anastasio Somoza of Nicaragua. In her reading of history, the rise of Khomeini in Iran and of the Sandinistas in Nicaragua was a direct consequence of U.S. protests against torture and murder by the Savak and the Guardia Nacional, security forces that were noted for their brutality.

The appointment of Haig and Kirkpatrick caused much hand-wringing by human rights advocates, but there was little we could do. When Reagan and Haig announced the choice of Ernest Lefever to serve as assistant secretary of state for human rights, however, a consensus quickly emerged among leaders of several small, recently formed groups—Helsinki Watch among them—that we should try to block his confirmation. (Amnesty USA, a more established body that had already developed a sizable grass roots membership by the beginning of the 1980s, had a policy against taking stands on nominees to public office and did not join the effort.)

Lefever was the director of an obscure right-wing Washington think tank, the Ethics and Public Policy Center. To the limited extent he was known by human rights organizations, it was as someone who showed up from time to time at congressional hearings to oppose all efforts to make promotion of human rights an object of U.S. foreign policy. Even after he was nominated, he said that: "Economic and military aid should be given or withheld to encourage sound external practices, but not to reform domestic institutions or practices, however obnoxious."[1] This statement directly contradicted the body of U.S. laws he would have to enforce. A series of measures adopted in the mid-1970s required the United States to "promote the increased observance of human rights by all countries" and provided that military and economic assistance must be denied to governments that practiced gross violations, including "torture or cruel, inhuman, or degrading treatment or punishment, prolonged detention without trial, causing the disappearance of persons by the abduction and clandestine detention of those persons, and other flagrant denial of the right to life, liberty or the security of person."[2] The law establishing the post to which Reagan had nominated Lefever required that official to gather detailed information on violations, report them to Congress, and present recommendations for compliance with the provisions denying military and economic assistance to gross violators.[3] In designating Lefever, who flatly opposed the legally mandated duties of the office he was slated to hold, Reagan spat in our face.

We knew we faced an uphill battle. In those days, the Senate hardly ever refused to confirm a presidential nominee. Not a single Carter appointment had been rejected. Nor was any Ford nominee defeated in the Senate. The last time the Senate had refused to confirm was when Nixon had nominated Harold Carswell and Clement Haynsworth to the U.S. Supreme Court more than a decade earlier. By comparison, Lefever had been nominated to a lowly office. If he were confirmed, he would be only one of a score or more assistant secretaries of state, all of them outranked by undersecretaries, the deputy secretary, and, of course, the secretary of state. We thought it vital for the future of the human rights cause to defeat him, but we could not even be sure the Senate would deal with the matter seriously. There were literally hundreds of positions of comparable or higher rank in various government agencies that required confirmation in the early months of the new administration. Most nominations at that level were, and are, dealt with routinely by the Senate. It is rare now, and was unheard of then, for such an appointment to become a cause célèbre. Moreover, Lefever had been nominated by a president who had just won a sweeping electoral victory and was at the height of his popularity in the first flush of victory. For good measure, his party controlled the Senate.

Yet our effort to block Lefever was not hopeless. Shortly after his nomination, the *Washington Post* reported that the Ethics and Public Policy Center had obtained a $25,000 tax-deductible contribution from Nestlé and had then launched a campaign to discredit the boycott of Nestlé's infant formula led by the World Council of Churches. (The boycott had been organized because children in Third World countries reportedly had been infected by water-borne diseases because their families did not have access to clean water to mix with the formula. Nestlé was accused of doing harm by promoting formula as a substitute for mother's milk.) Lefever's shoddy ethics as director of a self-proclaimed ethics center made him vulnerable.

Our determination to defeat Lefever was heightened by an episode that took place in Buenos Aires, Argentina, while his nomination was pending. On the evening of Friday, February 27, 1981, after the foreign press services had closed for the weekend, the Argentine national police arrested eight persons who made up much of what was left of the country's human rights leadership after years of persecution. Most prominent among them was Emilio Mignone, a lawyer and former university rector who was president of the country's leading human rights group, which was known by its Spanish-language acronym, CELS (Centro de Estudios Legales y Sociales). Mignone's daughter had been "disappeared" by the military several years earlier. As more than 9,000 disappearances, abductions in which the victims did not show up again alive, had taken place in Argentina since the armed forces had seized power in 1976, the friends and families of Mignone and the others taken into custody with him feared for their safety and quickly made calls to anyone who might be able to help.

One of the calls that evening was placed by Hector Timerman, the son of famed newspaper editor and publisher Jacobo Timerman, to his father in Israel. The elder Timerman had been stripped of his citizenship and deported from Argentina in September 1979 after two and a half years in prison and house arrest. In Israel, Timerman had written a memoir of his prison experience, *Prisoner Without a Name, Cell Without a Number,* which was soon to be published in the United States by Knopf, a division of Random House. He responded to his son's call by contacting Random House's CEO, my human rights colleague Robert Bernstein, who in turn called editors at the *New York Times* and the *Washington Post*. Front-page stories about the seizure of Mignone and his colleagues appeared in the U.S. press over the weekend. The resulting international outcry helped secure their release within a few days.

Though not yet confirmed, Lefever had already moved into the State Department and was carrying out the duties of the office to which he was appointed in a manner that contributed to the arrests in Argentina. Just before being seized, Mignone had been in Geneva attempting to persuade the United Nations Commission on Human Rights to continue the mandate of its working group on disappearances. In the Carter years, the United States had vigorously supported such efforts. In Geneva, however, Mignone got no help from the U.S. delegation. France, supported by other West European governments, took the lead in proposing a resolution to extend the life of the working group on disappearances. Argentina, as expected, opposed the resolution. So did the Soviet Union. Despite the purported anti-communism of the Argentine armed forces, the Soviets maintained cordial relations with the military junta in Buenos Aires, of which they were a principal trading partner. In addition, then as now, Moscow was an antagonist of international inquiries into its own human rights practices and could be counted on to rally to the support of evildoers worldwide eager to avoid such scrutiny.

I learned from friends at the State Department that there had been an internal dispute over the U.S. stand. The Latin American and European bureaus wanted to support the French and the other West Europeans, but Lefever opposed them. He argued that the United States should line up with Argentina and the Soviet Union. Eventually, a compromise was reached that the United States helped to work out. The working group on disappearances continued, but under conditions that the Argentines interpreted as prohibiting the UN body from issuing public reports. In the process, the United States signaled to the Argentines that the protection Mignone had enjoyed because of the Carter administration's solicitude for the human rights cause had come to an end. Even before he was confirmed, Lefever was doing harm.

Jacobo Timerman's small part in this episode foreshadowed a larger role he was to play in the weeks ahead. Just as his well-placed phone call helped foil what might have been a tragic consequence of Lefever's activities in the State Department, so he was to haunt Lefever's nomination. Eventually, some members of the Senate Foreign Relations Committee came to feel they were choosing between Timerman and Lefever in casting their votes on the latter's confirmation.

Jacobo Timerman, who like Emilio Mignone died in 1999, was a Jew born in Ukraine in 1923 who was brought to Argentina by his parents as a five-year-old boy. His father died soon thereafter, leaving behind an impoverished widow and two young sons. Eventually, he became a successful political journalist, and in 1971 he started his own newspaper, *La Opinión*. It was a turbulent period in Argentina marked by political violence by both leftists and rightists. Jacobo espoused a military takeover in the hope of restoring peace and security. When the armed forces did seize power in March 1976, things did not work out as he had imagined. The military launched a campaign of terror—the imprisonment of thousands without charge or trial, and worse, the kidnapping and disappearance of many thousands more. In his newspaper, Jacobo reported on the disappearances until, as he subsequently wrote:

At dawn one morning in April 1977, some twenty civilians besieged my apartment in midtown Buenos Aires. They said they were obeying orders from the Tenth Infantry Brigade of the First Army Corps. The following day my wife sought information at the First Army Corps and was informed they knew nothing of my whereabouts.

They uprooted our telephone lines, took possession of our automobile keys, handcuffed me from behind. They covered my head with a blanket, rode down with me to the basement, removed the blanket, and asked me to point out my automobile. They threw me to the floor of the back of the car, covered me with the blanket, stuck their feet on top of me, and jammed into me what felt like the butt of a gun. No one spoke.

We arrived at a certain place. A pair of large doors opened up. They squeaked. Dogs barked quite close by. Someone said, "I feel fulfilled." I was taken out of the car and flung onto the ground.

A long interval elapsed. I could hear only footsteps. Suddenly some bursts of laughter. Someone approached and placed what seemed to be the barrel of a revolver against my head. He put one hand on my head and from up close, perhaps leaning over me, said, "I'm going to count to ten. Say goodbye, Jacobo dear. It's all up to you." I said nothing. Again he spoke: "Don't you want to say your prayers?" I said nothing. He started to count.[4]

Jacobo Timerman was subjected to extended interrogations, painful confinement (for example, a period in which he was left by himself in a small cell for forty-eight hours, blindfolded with his hands tied behind him), and electric shock torture. Much of his interrogation focused on his Jewishness and on supposed Zionist plots against Argentina.

I first got to know Jacobo while Lefever's nomination was being considered. Over the years, we became friends, enjoying many long lunches and dinners together in which we talked about politics, literature, and life. He was a great storyteller. Telling stories and engaging in such conversations was so important to him that, while searching for a place to settle after exile from Argentina, he knew he needed to live in a city with cafés.

Several of his stories have become well known. Among those I particularly like is one about the time he was approached in prison by one of the guards who had participated in his torture some months earlier. By then the guard had become more friendly, and he said to him: "Mr. Timerman, you are an important man. I wonder if you would write a letter of recommendation for my son who is applying to college." Another concerned his house arrest. To keep an eye on him, military men actually moved into his apartment. This resulted in a letter from the board of his co-op complaining of unauthorized guests. Then there was the story of his apartment in Israel when he was deported there. It faced a courtyard where refuse tended to collect. One day, unable to stand it any longer, Jacobo took a broom and a pan and cleaned up the courtyard. Some time passed and a woman knocked at his door. When he answered, she pointed out that the courtyard had gotten dirty again and wondered if he would clean it up.

Argentina, Emilio Mignone, and Jacobo Timerman became a focus of the lobbying that Bob Bernstein, Orville Schell, and I did against the Lefever nomination. The three of us spent a lot of time in Washington in March and April 1981. Mignone's arrest on February 27 was only one of the reasons for our emphasis on Argentina. In preparing to publish Timerman's book, Bob Bernstein established a close friendship with his author, as noted, a man of exactly his own age. In the same manner that Bob identified on a very personal level with the Soviet dissidents whose cause he championed and on whose behalf he took the lead in establishing Helsinki Watch, he also shared vicariously in the humiliation and torture that Jacobo endured when he was imprisoned. Orville focused on Argentina because he had gone there a few months earlier as head of a Bar Association inquiry into the performance of Argentine lawyers in defending victims of repression. My own reason for concentrating on Argentina was that I was in the process of establishing Americas Watch as a sister organization to Helsinki Watch and I wanted the new group to address the dire human rights situation there.

In Washington, we met individually with almost all seventeen members of the Senate Foreign Relations Committee who would act on Lefever's nomination. I found the senators more accessible than was my experience previously. During my years directing the ACLU, except where matters of unusual significance were involved, my conversations with senators had generally been brief and hurried, and much of the time I had to make do with meetings with staff members if I wanted to talk at greater length. Yet in this case, which involved a nomination of a man with little public reputation to a third or fourth level post, senators were readily available to talk to us over lunch or dinner, or at length in their offices.

Initially puzzled, I eventually concluded that three factors combined to allow us to air our views about Lefever so fully to those who would decide his fate. First, though there was not much of an international human rights movement in the United States in 1981, our cause had disproportionate strength in Congress. For several years, Amnesty USA and newer groups such as Helsinki Watch had been persuading members of Congress to write letters to foreign governments on behalf of victims of abuse. From time to time, such efforts succeeded and prisoners were freed. Some beneficiaries subsequently traveled to the United States. The organizations that had campaigned for them usually arranged for them to see members of Congress who had written in their behalf. At such meetings, released prisoners occasionally exaggerated the impact of a congressional intervention. They would tell a congressperson: "You saved my life." The member might not even recall writing the letter that supposedly had this effect, as such matters are routinely handled by staff. Yet these declarations were very moving. The routine work of legislating provides few satisfactions comparable to meeting a brave dissenter who has stood up to a dictator and tells you that you saved her life. Such experiences made many members of Congress devoted advocates of human rights long before there was a significant public constituency for our cause. The nomination of Lefever, who opposed using the influence of the United States for such purposes, offended some senators.

Second was Helsinki Watch. Deservedly or not, the other small human rights groups opposing Lefever could be branded as leftists because they focused on abuses by rightist regimes supported by the United States. Helsinki Watch, in contrast, campaigned against abuses by the Soviet Union and its satellites. This was important in the climate created by the advent of the new administration. Senators discomfited by Reagan's nomination of Lefever were happy to hear from a group with impeccable anti-Communist credentials opposed to his nomination.

Third, but not necessarily least important, was Bob Bernstein. It was nothing personal. Up to then, he had been less involved in public affairs than Orville and I. Most senators did not recognize his name. It was his post as CEO of Random House, which we mentioned in requesting appointments. Our meetings with senators seemed to follow a script. We talked about Lefever for a while. As we were breaking up, the senator would stand up, take Bob aside, and say: "By the way, I've been thinking about writing a book." The opportunity to initiate this conversation with the head of the country's leading publishing house seemed irresistible. Bob responded graciously and even enthusiastically to all potential authors. To the best of my knowledge, however, no Random House books resulted.

Those we met for lunch or dinner included Senator Charles Percy, Republican of Illinois, the committee chairman, and Senator Claiborne Pell, Democrat of Rhode Island, ranking minority member. We saw Percy in March immediately after we met Lefever to tell the nominee we would oppose him. Percy had not yet met Lefever and was eager to get our impression. Though he listened to us carefully, he was noncommittal. I came away thinking we had scant hope of persuading him to oppose Lefever. A man of decent instincts who had intervened on behalf of a number of victims of human rights abuses, Percy was not noted for rocking any boats. As he had just become chairman of the Senate Foreign Relations Committee, with a chance for the first time to play an important role in shaping U.S. foreign policy, I did not think he would risk estranging himself from his own party's president over the nomination of an assistant secretary of state.

We had several meetings with Senator Pell. One took place on the afternoon of Friday, May 15. With the hearing on Lefever's nomination scheduled to begin the following Monday morning, Pell told us firmly he was not committed, spoke of his inclination to let the president have the appointee of his choice, and defended Lefever against some things we said. He told us he was leaving Washington for the weekend right after our meeting and said he would take along a copy of Timerman's just-published book. It was of great interest to him, he said, because he had twice extracted a pledge from President Roberto Eduardo Viola of Argentina to publish an accounting of the disappeared. Both times, Viola had repudiated the pledges. (A few years later, after democracy was restored in Argentina, Viola was convicted for his part in the disappearances. He was eventually released by President Carlos Saúl Menem, who pardoned all those convicted for this crime.) Pell was also particularly interested in Timerman's book because of its discussion of anti-Semitism. A front-page review in *The New York Times Book Review* the previous Sunday, May 10, by columnist Anthony Lewis—which was displayed more boldly than was customary at the time in the *Book Review* and attracted enormous attention—emphasized the anti-Semitic character of Timerman's treatment. As I knew well, Senator Pell took pride in the work of his father, Herbert Pell, one of the few U.S. officials to make a strenuous effort to save the Jews of Europe during World War II. The issue loomed large to Senator Pell.

Though Senator Percy had not met Lefever before our meeting to persuade Percy, he did meet him before the confirmation hearing, which began on Monday, May 18. What was said at that meeting became an issue at the hearing when Percy asked Lefever why he had said the opposition to his confirmation was "Communist-inspired" and "orchestrated" by Communists. Lefever denied he had used the word "Communism." Percy's voice rose—the only time I ever saw him display anger at any hearing: "There isn't any question you used the word 'Communism' to me. There is the White House staff sitting right behind you who was sitting with us, and a staff member of mine was sitting there. You used the word 'Communism' in connection with the opposition, and you did so to Senator Tsongas, and you did so in a separate conversation to our counsel, Charles Berk. There is no question of fact." Lefever waffled, said that *Izvestia* and a Dutch Communist newspaper opposed him, and divided the rest of his opponents into "people and organizations . . . generally opposed to the mainstream of American foreign policy for the last fifteen or so years, defense policy, intelligence policy and so on"; "another group of people who support revolutionary Marxist violence"; and "honest people who differ with the methods of the new Administration." He quickly qualified his reference to this last group, asserting, "There are people who have used human rights as a façade to promote certain political ideologies."

Pell evidently had read Timerman's book over the weekend and displayed the book repeatedly at the Monday hearing while questioning Lefever closely about abuses of human rights in Argentina. In particular, Pell wanted to know what part Lefever had played in shaping the Reagan administration's position in Geneva on the UN working group on disappearances. Lefever was evasive. He refused to acknowledge that Argentina had engaged in abuses. He did say, however, that he opposed making the working group's reports public.

That evening, Bob Bernstein hosted a dinner in Washington for Jacobo Timerman, whose visit to the nation's capital to promote his book had been timed by Random House to take place while the hearing on Lefever's nomination was under way. Random House's purpose was not to influence the hearings. It was done to suit Bob's schedule, as he wanted to attend the hearing and also to join Jacobo on some of his publicity visits in Washington. Several senators attended the dinner for Jacobo, including Senator Pell. The next day, the hearing on Lefever's nomination resumed. I attended while Bob and Jacobo went to the *Washington Post* to discuss the book with editors and the publisher, Katharine Graham. We agreed they would come by Capitol Hill when they were done to pick me up for lunch.

As the hearing did not recess at the expected time, someone passed a note to me in the crowded Senate Caucus Room, where the hearing was held to accommodate the large number of journalists and spectators who wanted to attend, to tell me that Jacobo and Bob were outside. I went out to see them. Jacobo told me that as he had never seen a U.S. congressional hearing, he would like to go inside for a few moments. As we went in, Senator Pell, who had been at dinner with us the night before, recognized Jacobo and interrupted the proceedings to welcome him to the hearing. This brought the crowd, including some senators, to their feet for a standing ovation. At that moment, I knew Lefever was defeated. The Senate Foreign Relations Committee voted against confirmation 13–4. In addition to all eight Democrats, five of the nine Republicans opposed him. It was, as best I could determine, the largest margin by which any presidential nominee was ever rejected by a Senate committee. The White House could have persisted and taken the nomination to the Senate floor. Wisely, it was withdrawn.

President Reagan did not rush to designate someone else to fill the post. Although it was established by a law stating that: "There shall be in the Department of State an Assistant Secretary of State for Human Rights," it seemed for a while that the president might leave the post vacant to pay us back for defeating his nominee. It was another way to demonstrate that human rights considerations would not affect U.S. foreign policy in the Reagan administration. We wondered whether there was any way to compel the president to fill the post. It could not be done by going to court, because any lawsuit would not survive a challenge to the standing of plaintiffs to bring such a case. No other way of requiring the president to comply with the law occurred to us.

The impasse was eventually broken more than half a year after Lefever was defeated by the president's nomination of Elliott Abrams to the post. A young, outspoken, and combative lawyer who had served as an aide to New York's Senator Daniel Patrick Moynihan and then entered the State Department at the outset of Reagan's term, Abrams had joined the first family of neoconservatism figuratively and literally by marrying the daughter of *Commentary* editor Norman Podhoretz and Committee on the Present Danger founder Midge Decter. Abrams, it was widely believed, was the actual author of a confidential memo to the secretary of state that fall arguing that: "Congressional belief that we have no consistent human rights policy threatens to disrupt important foreign policy initiatives." The memo suggested that human rights arguments could be turned to advantage by the new administration by making it clear that the Soviet Union was the principal threat to rights and "that the difference between East and West is the crucial political distinction of our time." It called on the administration to wage a "battle of ideas" under the human rights banner. At the same time, the memo acknowledged that the administration would need to criticize human rights abuses by friendly governments to maintain credibility.[5]

Although I believed then, as now, that the human rights cause should be promoted for its own sake, and not only as an ideological weapon against the Soviet Union, this was a lot better than Lefever, and better than I expected from an administration in which thinking about foreign policy was dominated by Alexander Haig and Jeane Kirkpatrick. I advised my colleagues that we should not oppose Abrams's appointment. Rather, we should try to work with him in the expectation that our concern for the intrinsic significance of human rights and his concern for its instrumental value might often lead us to find common ground in practice.

I went to see Abrams—whom I had not met previously—a few days before his confirmation hearing. We chatted in his office at the State Department for a couple of hours. Though our conversation was amicable, I realized there might be stormy times ahead from his response to what I described as the most important piece of advice I could give him. I urged him never to put himself in a position where he would act as a public apologist for abuses of human rights. His role should always be to serve as the advocate for human rights. Inevitably, there would be many situations when the administration would decide that other considerations, such as the economic or security interests of the United States, took precedence. When that happened, he should leave it to others to defend U.S. policy. The assistant secretary of state for human rights should not allow himself to be used to explain away or minimize abuses or to pretend they did not occur.

Abrams disagreed with me. He said he would be an advocate for human rights within the State Department. Once a policy decision was reached, however, he would be a team player. He would uphold the policy against those criticizing it on human rights grounds. In describing the role he intended to play, he spoke contemptuously of Patricia Derian. By not being a team player, he argued, she had not been an effective advocate inside the department. He was going to be effective. Abrams dismissed my contention that there was a qualitative difference between the post to which he was appointed and every other at the State Department.

The Abrams approach carried the day in the Reagan administration. It was taken further and articulated more fully by the president himself in a June 8, 1982, address to the British Parliament. At the time, the administration was preoccupied with developments in Central America, where it was assisting the Salvadoran armed forces in attempting to fend off a leftist insurgency and covertly organizing a rightist insurgency to overthrow the Sandinista regime in Nicaragua. In an attempt to demonstrate that the human rights situation was worse in Nicaragua than in El Salvador, Reagan ignored disappearances, death-squad killings, and massacres and instead focused on political developments. The Sandinistas had deferred elections until 1985, six years after they seized power. In contrast, El Salvador had just held elections for its National Assembly that produced televised images of long lines of people standing in the sun waiting their turn to cast their ballots. (A factor not often mentioned: There were too few polling places.) The president said Salvadorans "braved ambush and gunfire, trudging miles to vote for freedom." Building on this image, Reagan equated the promotion of human rights with elections and committed the United States to a global effort to promote democracy. "What I am describing now is a plan and a hope for the long term," the president told Parliament, "the march of freedom and democracy which will leave Marxism-Leninism on the ash heap of history as it has left other tyrannies which stifle the freedom and muzzle the self-expression of the people." He called the campaign for democracy that the United States would conduct worldwide "a crusade for freedom."

The administration had moved a long distance in the year and a half since Reagan took office. It went from repudiating the human rights cause to embracing it, even while attempting to redefine it as the promotion of democracy. The dire human rights situation in a democratic country such as Sri Lanka or Colombia—the latter proudly describes itself as "Latin America's oldest democracy"—was never allowed to interfere with the ideologically prescribed worldview of the Reaganites. Instead of saying the human rights issue did not matter, the administration shifted to arguing, no matter the facts, that the human rights situation was better in countries aligned with the United States than in countries our government opposed. These shifts turned out to be of enormous importance. Though the administration did not prevail in its attempted redefinition, or in its claim that a democratic form of government or alignment could be equated with respect for human rights, the inadvertent effect was to strengthen greatly the nongovernmental human rights movement. Helsinki Watch, Americas Watch, and the other regional Watch Committees yet to be born that formed Human Rights Watch were particular beneficiaries. By acknowledging human rights as an important issue, the Reaganites gave us the opportunity to challenge them on the facts. The administration was driven by its own rhetoric and by the effective human rights movement that it had helped to create to adopt policies that would have been anathema to Reagan, Haig, and Kirkpatrick if they could have imagined them when they took office in 1981.

Having committed his administration to promoting democracy worldwide, Reagan was ultimately driven to abandon such "moderate autocrats friendly to American interests"—in Kirkpatrick's words—as Generalissimo Ferdinand Marcos in the Philippines, president-for-life Jean Claude "Baby Doc" Duvalier in Haiti, and General Augusto Pinochet in Chile. (I differentiate Abrams from some of his fellow Reaganites. It seems possible to me that he both anticipated and welcomed the consequences of the policies he advocated.) Efforts to sustain these dictators in power, which the Reagan administration pursued throughout its first term, could not be reconciled indefinitely with a worldwide crusade to promote democracy. Human rights groups and others had an easy time scoring points against the administration for failing to live up to its rhetoric and eventually embarrassed the Reagan crowd into making good on the commitments undertaken in the president's 1982 speech to the British Parliament.

Although the question of the relative significance of physical abuses and democratic development was debated throughout the Reagan years, no one argued any longer about the importance of human rights. After the defeat of Lefever and the rise of Elliott Abrams, that was a given. Not only Lefever's nomination but his views were put to rest. In combination, Lefever and Abrams, who were as opposed to each other in their approach to human rights as each was opposed to the views I espoused, did as much to establish the legitimacy of the human rights cause as anyone.

Abrams's further contribution was to shape the methodology that enabled Human Rights Watch to emerge as an important institution. His insistence on the instrumental significance of human rights led him to distort facts when necessary to argue that governments aligned with the United States did not commit abuses. Accordingly, Human Rights Watch developed an investigatory approach to promoting human rights. We took great care in gathering information and set forth in detail the evidentiary basis for our findings. Where warranted, we then entered into debates with Abrams and other Reagan administration spokespersons over the facts. It was this fact-finding, and the debates it engendered, that permitted us to build our reputation.

Once or twice as the battle to defeat Lefever was under way, I wondered whether such an enormous effort was warranted to block the appointment of a low-level official. It seemed important at the time, but what would we achieve if Reagan just designated someone else with similar views? In retrospect, that struggle was far more significant than I realized. It was, I now believe, the turning point in establishing the human rights cause as a factor in U.S. foreign policy and not the passing fad or even folly of the Carter administration, as it was considered in 1981 by the man who nominated Lefever and by his foreign policy team.

CHAPTER TEN

Americas Watch:
A Testing by Fire

A tiny, densely populated country that few Americans could locate on a map prior to the 1980s and that has since relapsed into obscurity, El Salvador was the focus of U.S. attention when Ronald Reagan became president in 1981 because war had broken out the previous year between leftist guerrillas and the country's military regime. As Reagan associates such as Jeane Kirkpatrick blamed former President Jimmy Carter for allowing nearby Nicaragua to fall to the Communist-backed Sandinistas in 1979, the new administration would not allow a repetition in El Salvador. By assisting the Salvadoran military in defeating the insurgent FMLN—the acronym for the leftist guerrillas[1]—Reagan would "draw the line" (in the words of Secretary of State Alexander Haig) against the advance of communism in the Western hemisphere. Though this only became known later, the new administration also prepared plans to overturn the Sandinista victory in Nicaragua. Reagan's policies placed Central America at the top of the agenda for debates over U.S. foreign policy throughout the decade.

El Salvador also gained notoriety in 1981 because of the extreme brutality of its armed forces and the extraordinary number of violent abuses of human rights they committed before the outbreak of war in 1980 and, to an even greater extent, once the war began. These included the assassination of Archbishop Oscar Arnulfo Romero in March 1980 as he was saying mass at a memorial service; later the same year, the kidnapping of six leftist political leaders from a press conference and their murder; and a seeming unending stream of gruesome killings by shadowy groups known as "death squads" that everybody knew—though this was hotly denied by Reagan administration officials—were military men dressed in civilian clothes who traveled in unmarked vehicles to do their dirty work. The abuses that riveted public attention the most in the United States on El Salvador in the early 1980s were the murders of seven Americans: four churchwomen (three Maryknoll nuns and a lay church worker), two labor advisers associated with the AFL-CIO (murdered in the restaurant of the Sheraton Hotel in the capital along with the Salvadoran who directed the country's land-reform agency), and a freelance journalist.

These seven murders all took place between the time Reagan was elected president in November 1980 and his inauguration in January 1981. I suspect that the murders, along with a larger number of death squad killings than during any other period of that duration throughout the Salvadoran conflict, manifested exuberance by Salvadoran military officers who felt that the transition from Carter to Reagan liberated them from continuing strictures about human rights abuses. (In other countries in the region, among them Guatemala and Haiti, the transition period was also marked by especially high levels of political violence.) As the murders of Americans stopped when Reagan was inaugurated, I imagine someone in the new administration passed the word that this was going too far.

No more Americans were being murdered by the military in El Salvador when Americas Watch was formed in the spring of 1981. Yet the overall rights situation was ghastly; 1981 was the bloodiest year of the conflict. In addition to the death squad killings, hundreds of peasants at a time were being slaughtered in military operations. The carnage made El Salvador our first priority. El Salvador was also a priority in the U.S. Congress, which adopted legislation in 1981 conditioning U.S. assistance on a presidential certification every six months that certain human rights conditions had been met. The first certification was required on January 28, 1982. That was an opportunity. I decided the new Americas Watch should publish a report just before the presidential certification was due to document the situation in El Salvador. Our report would demonstrate that certification was not warranted.

A lot of people, outraged by the administration's backing for the murderous Salvadoran military, contributed their expertise to enable us to publish a book-length report on January 26, 1982, two days prior to the presidential certification.[2] The timing and the frontal challenge to the administration caused a sensation, greatly heightening attention to the certification itself. It put Americas Watch on the map just months after it was born. By making Reagan's policy the issue, our report also pioneered in exploiting the potential for bringing about change by identifying our own government as the surrogate villain.

The law on certification required Reagan to assert that the Salvadoran government was "making a concerted and significant effort to comply with internationally recognized human rights" and was "achieving substantial control over all elements of its armed forces" so as to end human rights abuses. If it did not, U.S. military assistance would end. Given his administration's determination not to allow El Salvador to go the way of Nicaragua, there was never a question how Reagan would act. Yet he could not certify truthfully. The report he submitted to Congress in support of certification misstated what was happening in El Salvador. By collecting and documenting the facts, Americas Watch demonstrated the mendacity of the presidential certification.

In retrospect, it seems astonishing that a newly established organization aspiring to be taken seriously had the temerity to dispute the facts with a popular president riding high in public support a year after he took office. In effect, we called President Reagan a liar. Predictably, his administration reacted furiously,[3] as did his allies in the media. On the editorial page of the *Wall Street Journal,* we were the subject of regular defamatory attacks. Yet Bernstein and Schell never flinched. Their staunch backing permitted me to battle the Reaganites without worrying whether the lay leaders of Helsinki Watch and Americas Watch could stand the heat. As an organization, we had no track record in Latin America. All we had going for us were Helsinki Watch's work on Soviet abuses, our individual reputations, and our own fact-gathering in El Salvador. Yet we stood up to the president and the foreign policy apparatus of the U.S. government in that debate. Americas Watch not only survived the attacks by the Reagan administration and its allies in Congress and the media. We flourished.

That could not have happened at any earlier time. It was possible at the beginning of the 1980s because of the country's experiences in the previous decade. After Vietnam, Watergate, and the disclosures by the Church Committee about CIA efforts to overthrow foreign governments and to assassinate their leaders, presidential credibility was at low ebb. Though Reagan was wildly popular in the immediate aftermath of his electoral triumph, many Americans were persuaded by us when we showed that the president was not telling the truth. Johnson and Nixon had lied, and it did not seem outlandish when we suggested Reagan was lying to achieve one of his foremost foreign policy goals.

Every six months, when it came time for Reagan to certify again, we did it again. A few days before the presidential certification, we published lengthy and ever better-documented reports of the human rights situation in El Salvador. We never expected to stop the president from certifying; it was a way of building pressure in Congress on the administration and, over time, getting the administration to put pressure on the Salvadoran military to curb abuses so the president could certify with less embarrassment.

The Reagan administration shaped our course. Its approach to human rights was typified by its periodic certifications of El Salvador. Governments supported by the United States—El Salvador, Guatemala, Turkey, Argentina under the generals, the Philippines under Marcos, Haiti under Jean Claude Duvalier, Liberia under Samuel Doe, and others of that murderous ilk—were portrayed as respectful of human rights, or at least as making progress on human rights. The designated enemies of the United States—first and foremost, the Sandinistas in Nicaragua—were supposedly the greatest violators. After Reagan's first year in office, we did not debate administration officials about the importance of human rights. That was a given, a legacy of our triumph in sinking Lefever. We disputed them on the facts. In the lengthy, meticulous reports that were our hallmark, we pointed out the discrepancies between the claims by governments to respect human rights and their practices. The Reagan administration supported many abusive governments solely because they were aligned with the United States in the global struggle against the Soviet Union. With the pretense it had adopted by the end of 1981 to be a proponent of human rights, it became the foremost public apologist for many ghastly regimes. As a result, our debates with the administration were frequently more intense, and more acrimonious, than those with governments that actually committed the abuses.

I enjoyed these debates with the Reagan administration, which trapped itself into becoming our foil. Our exchanges had a salutary effect on our work as they forced us to take great care in our fact-gathering to ensure that our findings could stand close scrutiny and systematic efforts to discredit us. When we made mistakes, we were quick to acknowledge them, attempting to do so before they were spotted by our foes. Disputing us, the administration became our inadvertent ally in calling attention to abuses and thereby, over time, in helping to curb them. Debates with our own government over its support for a dictatorship's death squad killings, disappearances, or systematic torture were far more newsworthy than criticism of the governments directly responsible. The more the Reaganites attacked us, the greater the attention to the violations of human rights. As we debated whether those practices took place, to what extent, and who was responsible, the focus of press coverage was exactly where we wanted it. Those debates led foreign correspondents to make their own inquiries. Human rights abuses became a bigger topic for the press than previously, and findings by journalists regularly buttressed our arguments.

We saw a pattern emerge. At the outset, a government that committed abuses usually tried to ignore our reports. Where we also challenged U.S. aid to that government, however, and the Reagan administration felt obliged to defend its support, it would become difficult for the target government to remain silent. Its next response was to try to discredit us as partisans of opposition forces. This did not work for three reasons. First, we took great care in our reporting. Second, in embracing international humanitarian law, we had broken with previous practices in the human rights field by reporting human rights abuses by guerrillas fighting governments as well as government abuses. Third, Americas Watch was the same organization as Helsinki Watch. It was difficult to impugn our anti-Communist credentials.

One reason we were able to fare well in those debates in the early 1980s was that I had enlisted an outstanding staff. The first person I hired for Americas Watch was Juan Méndez, an Argentine lawyer who had defended political prisoners in his own country. Juan became my closest collaborator in my efforts to promote human rights internationally.

For his efforts to defend the rights of Argentine dissenters in his own country in the 1970s, Juan had been imprisoned and tortured. He might have been added to the list of the disappeared were it not for an international campaign in his behalf. Juan may owe his life to his participation in a student exchange program when he was in high school that brought him to the United States for a year. His "Iowa family" devoted themselves to securing his release, enlisting members of the U.S. Congress to bring pressure on the Argentine government. The military released him by sending him into exile in this country. He went back to law school to get an American law degree and also served as a frequent spokesman for Amnesty International, which had designated him a "prisoner of conscience" and campaigned for his release.

Juan quickly established our credibility in dealing with human rights issues in Latin America. Over the years I worked with him, he also contributed much to my own thinking about how to cope with the complex issues that confronted us. Early on, for example, it was Juan who helped me to grasp the significance, both in our work and in the evolution of a human rights consciousness internationally, of holding officials accountable for past crimes.

I also enlisted a group of remarkable young women to gather information for us in Central America, write reports, and persuade members of Congress to join us in challenging the Reagan administration's policies on human rights. Four who started working for us in 1982 and 1983 when they were in their twenties or had just turned thirty—Cynthia Brown, Cynthia Arnson, Jean-Marie Simon, and Holly Burkhalter—played a crucial role in establishing our modus operandi. Entrusting much of our field research and reporting to women too young to have long track records was taking a risk. Yet I judged that each had a personal commitment to getting the story right on Central America that complemented our institutional need to prevail in battles with the Reagan administration over facts. Though we were an upstart organization, I entered into debates with top government officials with confidence as I knew I could count on our researchers. The government had vastly greater resources to draw on in gathering information, but if our twenty-something field researchers told me that military men had carried out a disappearance that the administration attributed to "extremists of the right or the left," or that a massacre of peasants had taken place where the administration denied anything happened, I always found their reporting reliable.

Cynthia Brown's commitment to accuracy seemed to me to reflect her passion for language. She used words sparingly. Her reports were detailed and long, but I never thought anything could be cut. Every sentence was a model of clarity. This was as true of her speaking as her writing. A tightly coiled spring of a woman whose appearance and manner reflected the orderliness of her intelligence, her dedication to getting the facts straight was as much aesthetic as political. After I left Human Rights Watch, Ken Roth appointed her as his principal deputy, program director. In that post, I heard, she inspired some terror among newer members of the staff. Though I had one or two difficult arguments with her, I never saw her mistreat a subordinate. Yet it did not surprise me to hear she was feared. She applied the same demanding standards to the work of others as to her own reporting.

Cindy Arnson (nobody called the other Cynthia "Cindy") is a gentler personality but, for different reasons, just as rigorous in her writing. In Cindy's case, a commitment to scholarship is reflected in her articles and books on Latin America as well as in her human rights reports. Though not given to bravado, she conducted investigations for us in El Salvador when it was particularly dangerous for her to go there, as her writing on the country was well known. (In recent years, her scholarly focus at the Woodrow Wilson Center, where she is now based, has shifted to another country where field research has more than its share of perils, Colombia.) Fortunately, she did not encounter any difficulties, though I recall one false alarm. She visited El Salvador at a time when there were many violent attacks on journalists and humanitarian relief workers taking place. As human rights monitoring was even more suspect than journalism or relief work from the standpoint of the Salvadoran armed forces, I was nervous about sending her there just then. Returning, she flew to New York to work with me on the report, which we were eager to publish right away. I drove to the airport to pick her up and that evening she sat with Yvette and me in our living room talking about her visit. Had she encountered any problems? No, but there was one scary moment. Answering a knock on the door of her hotel room, she had been startled to find two men outside in uniforms she did not instantly recognize. It took a few heart-stopping seconds before she realized they were hotel maintenance men sent to repair the air conditioning.

Jean-Marie Simon's connection to us was only known by a handful of people in the early 1980s. She lived in Guatemala and could not have survived there in that era if we had disclosed that she documented human rights violations for Americas Watch. Ostensibly, she was there as a freelance photographer, and later she became a stringer there for *Time* magazine. Her stunning photos of Guatemala were exhibited in art galleries and appeared in magazines as well as in her book, *Eternal Spring, Eternal Tyranny*.[4]

Living in Guatemala and traveling to remote places to take photos, and in the process conducting interviews on human rights abuses, she looked down on those who based their findings on visits that lasted a week or two at a time. That might suffice in El Salvador or Nicaragua. Domestic human rights groups, though beleaguered, assisted visiting researchers in those countries, and foreign journalists based there shared information with us. Not in Guatemala. No Guatemalan could have monitored human rights in the country in the early 1980s and no major media organization had a bureau there. Guatemala was also harder because of the difficult terrain, because of its twenty-two indigenous languages, and, above all, because of the reluctance of Mayan Indian peasants to tell their stories to strangers at a time of pervasive terror. Without Jean-Marie, we could not have assembled the kind of information we published on Guatemala. She felt that her fact-gathering was much more reliable than anything that could have been obtained by "tourists."

The UN special rapporteur on human rights in Guatemala, Lord Colville, a political ally of Prime Minister Margaret Thatcher whose UN post appointment had been engineered by the Reagan administration, got a sense of Jean-Marie's research when I introduced them over lunch in New York. I did not tell Colville she was working for us; only that she lived in Guatemala and knew a lot about the human rights situation. Colville had just published a report that he had compiled by traveling around Guatemala in a vehicle flying a UN flag with an escort of Guatemalan troops to assure his security. As he must have known, this was hardly the way to get Mayans to tell him about abuses they suffered. Unsurprisingly, his report was a whitewash. Jean-Marie, who could be salty-tongued— even Archbishop Próspero del Barrio Penados of Guatemala City had chided her about her vivid Spanish on one of my visits to him with Jean-Marie—had promised me in advance that she would be on her best behavior at lunch. Indeed, I could not fault her manners. Even so, Colville ended lunch somewhat abruptly in annoyance at the questions she asked him. It was plain she was familiar with all the sites he had visited and kept asking about things he left out. After an hour or so, he'd had enough. (A few years later, Colville was appointed by Thatcher to a post dealing with Northern Ireland. I reported our experience with him in Guatemala to a human rights colleague in Belfast. His performance there was true to form, I subsequently learned.)

Holly Burkhalter represented us in Washington. An Iowan who had come to Washington to work for a member of Congress from her home state, then Representative and subsequently Senator Tom Harkin, she was working for the Human Rights Subcommittee of the House Foreign Affairs Committee when I met her. The subcommittee chair was perfunctory in his espousal of human rights. He cared more about wildlife, prompting a couple of staff members to concoct a report that whales were being tortured so they could see him really angry. Holly compensated for the chairman's lethargy by her spirited staff work. As Washington was the principal battleground for the newly established Americas Watch, I knew that choosing the right lobbyist was all-important. More senior people were available, but the only person I considered for the job was Holly. I persuaded her she could do more for human rights representing Americas Watch than working for Congress.

Holly did not do field research. She only traveled to Central America once, for a quick tour of the region as a participant in a delegation that included members of Congress and other prominent persons (among them, George Soros). She made good use of this visit, however. In El Salvador, she learned that a kidnapping had just taken place of a young couple employed as relief workers by a Catholic Church agency. They had been abducted together with their infant children. Mobilizing the delegation and calling me in New York to launch a campaign in the United States, Holly's efforts paid off in the early release of the family. She probably saved their lives.

Several years later, when we established Africa Watch, I suggested to Holly that she take part in a mission to look into the situation of Liberian refugees in Sierra Leone and Guinea. If possible, she had devoted herself even more passionately to the cause of human rights in Liberia than was her custom in other projects involving terrible abuses. I thought that, like others who dealt with such issues from afar, she would welcome an opportunity to get a closer look. She gamely accepted my suggestion. It was a mistake. The climate, the food, the amenities, and everything about the surroundings were nothing like Iowa. Sick and unhappy, she made it through in large part because our mission was undertaken jointly with Refugees International and its president, Lionel Rosenblatt. As I discovered when Lionel joined me on a number of visits to besieged Sarajevo during the Bosnian War, one couldn't ask for a better traveling companion in difficult circumstances.

Holly was at home in Washington, particularly in the halls of Congress. As she did everything at great speed, I sometimes thought members and their staffs had advance notice that they were about to get their arms gently twisted for the human rights cause when they heard the distinctive rapid click of her heels approaching on the marble floors of the corridors.

In that era, several veteran lobbyists for rights were badly battered by the Reagan administration. Red-baiting of a sort unknown since the McCarthy era was the rule of the day. Officials such as Jeane Kirkpatrick— who told the *Tampa Tribune* in December 1980, without basis, that the four U.S. churchwomen just raped and murdered in El Salvador "were not just nuns. The nuns were also political activists . . . on behalf of the *Frente*"— were always ready to traduce not only victims but also those who reported human rights abuses by governments aligned with the United States. Holly took on the Reaganites, but she insisted the information she presented should be solid. It was a political imperative. She would not allow *her* organization to suffer the fate of others whose minor errors had been blown out of all proportion by an administration that seized every opportunity to smear critics of its human rights policies or those of America's client states.

A little later, a number of other women also contributed to Americas Watch's reporting on Central America. We commissioned a freelancer, Anne Nelson—subsequently director of another human rights group, the Committee to Protect Journalists and, after September 11, celebrated for a play, *The Guys,* that she wrote about the firefighters—to help us gather information from Guatemalan refugees across the border in Chiapas, Mexico. Beatriz Manz, then a professor of anthropology at Wellesley and now at Berkeley, whose scholarly work focused on Guatemala, also played an important part in our reporting on that country, as did Anne Manuel, who joined our staff later in the 1980s. In 1985, I hired Jemera Rone, an attorney, to open an office for us in El Salvador and to report on that country and Nicaragua. All of these women added to our reputation for comprehensive and trustworthy reporting. Fortunately, despite the risks they took, none came to harm. Perhaps the closest call involved Beatriz Manz.

Visiting Santa Cruz del Quiché, a Guatemalan highlands town that had been the subject of her Ph.D. thesis, in the center of an area ravaged by abuses, her movements apparently aroused the suspicions of some military men. They took her into custody. At a nearby military base, they searched her belongings and discovered the business card of the country's economics minister in her wallet. She had interviewed him in the capital earlier in the week. The business card persuaded the soldiers to call a higher officer for instructions. Apparently, he directed she should be released. But for the card, she might have suffered the fate of others taken to Guatemalan military bases in that era.

When I enlisted these talented individuals to report on Central America, some of my colleagues asked me why I had hired so many women. I thought it was a product of the times. In the 1960s, all the lawyers I hired at the New York Civil Liberties Union were men. At the beginning of the 1970s at the parent ACLU, males still made up the majority of the professionals I brought on to the staff, but later in the decade, the division became roughly equal. By the early 1980s, a disproportionate number of the ablest researchers and advocates I could find were female. That most were young reflected the fact that the cause was new. Experience could not be a significant factor in my hiring decisions, as it was rarely available. I had to make judgments based on potential. I could attract the best because in those heady days of combat with the Reagan administration, Americas Watch crackled with excitement.

Of course, we did not invent human rights reporting. Amnesty International's London-based researchers had compiled many valuable reports during the 1960s and 1970s chronicling abuses worldwide. We added some new elements: identification of the evidence on which our findings were based; reporting on violations by both sides in armed conflicts; assessments that cited international humanitarian law covering such practices as indiscriminate attacks; speed in issuing our reports to ensure their timeliness; and political context. These additions were needed for our reports to carry weight in Washington. The reports made it possible for Holly Burkhalter to mobilize members of Congress to confront the Reagan administration over the human rights abuses it tolerated or supported in a region it identified as a primary Cold War battleground.

No doubt, there were also some jocular comments. Attending Anne Nelson's wedding reception, I posed for a photograph with a group of them and heard someone across the room say, "Aryeh's angels." I had never watched the popular television series of that era called *Charlie's Angels*, but from what I knew, it was a fair comment. My angels did not wear skimpy clothes, but they faced dangers and got the job done.

As Americas Watch built its reputation, it became ever more difficult for abusive governments to discredit us. They did not stop trying. Rather than focusing on us directly, however, they attacked our sources—or our supposed sources—within the country, claiming they were associated with opposition forces. This tactic concerned us as human rights monitors in those countries were vulnerable to reprisals.

Reflecting Americas Watch's origins in Helsinki Watch, which we had established to protect human rights monitors, we made the safety of monitors wherever we worked our topmost concern. Many all over the world who gather and disseminate information on human rights abuses by their governments suffer imprisonment, torture, or even death. We had to protect them. In some circumstances, we maintained the confidentiality of our sources. At other times, we celebrated local human rights monitors to inform governments they would pay dearly if they harmed them. Choosing which course to follow was not easy for us. We did not want the responsibility for making decisions that could have life-or-death consequences. Our sources told us whether they thought they were better protected by confidentiality or publicity. Their lives were at stake. They had to choose.

We made sure not to depend on the fact gathering of local human rights monitors too much. They were indispensable to our work in countless ways, especially in identifying issues to examine and episodes to investigate. Yet in most cases, we avoided reliance on their findings. We went to the sites of abuses. We located and interviewed victims, family members, witnesses, and officials, where they would talk to us. We gathered physical, documentary, and circumstantial evidence. Through painstaking and laborious research, we raised the standard of human rights reporting. We shielded local monitors by reporting our own findings, not the information they passed on to us. When they came under attack, we did all we could to defend them. Sometimes, this was not enough. If they were exiled, imprisoned, assaulted, or killed, we made sure the responsible government paid a heavy price.

When governments realized they could not succeed in ignoring us, and failed to discredit us or our sources, they sometimes altered their practices to improve their side of the argument. This was what we sought. When we made headway, it was often because the Reagan administration pressured client governments to clean up their act so it could defend them more effectively. This happened in El Salvador. In December 1983, the administration sent Vice President George Bush to San Salvador—on his way back from the inauguration of President Raul Alfonsín in Buenos Aires—to meet with the military high command. Not long before, a new U.S. ambassador, Thomas Pickering, had been sent to El Salvador. He exerted pressure to curb death squad killings. His efforts had been undercut, how-ever, when two other administration officials, Undersecretary of Defense Fred Ikle and Assistant Secretary of State Elliott Abrams, visited El Sal-vador and held a press conference. Ikle said the death squads were "in fact enjoying the protection of the Communist guerrillas," and Abrams added that the members of the death squads were "fairly well known" but "there's no action taken by the far left because they like to see Salvadoran society divided."[5] This was an astonishing statement as it implied the death squad problem should be solved by assassinations by the guerrillas. Also, it was an indirect acknowledgment that the government knew the identity of the death squads but did nothing about them. In a widely pub-licized address to a Salvadoran business group two weeks later, Pickering tried to undo the damage: "There has been little doubt of the commit-ment of the authorities to dealing with terror by the FMLN," he said. "There may be lack of means, but there is no lack of resolve. What has distressed my government is the lack of parallel activity against those who murder and kidnap university professors, doctors, labor leaders, *campesinos* and government workers. We know by their selection of victims . . . [that they] are not guerrilla organizations."[6] The vice president's visit was sought by Pickering to drive home the point.

Bush demanded the removal or arrest and prosecution of officers to be named on a list provided by Pickering; it had to be done by someone suffi-ciently senior to Ikle and Abrams so as to erase their impact. Action was required by January 10, 1984, a few days before Congress was to recon-vene. The point was driven home in a public speech the vice president made at a state dinner in San Salvador: "These cowardly death squad ter-rorists are just as repugnant to me, to President Reagan, to the US Con-gress, and to the American people as the terrorists of the left. . . . If these death squad murders continue, you will lose the support of the American people."[7] Though many abuses persisted, the efforts of Pickering and the Bush visit produced a dramatic reduction in death squad killings. (Publicly, however, the Reagan administration continued to deny that the armed forces controlled the death squads, even as it curbed their activities by put-ting pressure on the military.) My Americas Watch colleagues and I had a sense of satisfaction. We believed that our repeated confrontations with the administration through publication of our reports on the eve of each periodic certification, and our persistence in the face of efforts to ignore us and discredit us and our sources, despite the damage done by apologists for the Salvadoran military such as Ikle and Abrams, had paid off.

Our certification battles with the administration over El Salvador also had collateral value. The legislation that required the president to certify every six months that certain human rights conditions were being met in El Salvador also made U.S. military and economic assistance to two other Latin American countries, Argentina and Chile, dependent upon presidential certifications. In those cases, however, periodic certifications were not required. If the president once certified that the conditions in the law were met, U.S. aid could flow. Though the administration early manifested its intent to support the military regimes in both Argentina and Chile, neither was ever certified by Reagan. As Elliott Abrams once admitted to me, El Salvador was the administration's top priority in the hemisphere. No matter the facts, Reagan would certify Salvadoran compliance with the human rights conditions for U.S. assistance—which, in the dozen years of war in that country, amounted to about $4.5 billion. The administration was not eager to engage simultaneously in intense struggles over certifying two other Latin American countries where we could challenge its truthfulness.

In the Argentine case, the administration had a compelling reason to certify that did not become clear to us until later. At the behest of the United States, Argentine military officers had gone to Honduras in 1981 and 1982 to help establish the Contras, who engaged in an armed struggle throughout the decade to overthrow the Sandinista regime in Nicaragua. (Juan Méndez spotted the Argentine impact on human rights in Honduras before it was disclosed publicly. We subtitled the first report he wrote for us on Honduras in 1982 "Signs of the Argentine Method." His background, of course, made him especially alert to that methodology. Several years later, Juan had the satisfaction of arguing before the Inter-American Court of Human Rights in a case brought by families of the disappeared against the government of Honduras that resulted in a landmark decision requiring the government to pay them damages.[8]) Secret arrangements for the Argentines to assist the Reagan administration in its effort to oust the Sandinistas had been made with General Leopoldo Galtieri, who later led the ill-fated invasion of the Falklands in 1982, when he was president of the military junta governing Argentina. Administration officials such as Jeane Kirkpatrick, who had obtained Galtieri's cooperation in launching the Contras, were eager to repay him with certification. Indeed, Galtieri seems to have imagined that America's debt to him for helping to establish the Contras would be paid off in support in his war with Britain, or at least neutrality. That notion may have encouraged his reckless behavior in starting a war he could not win.

The law setting the conditions for certification was an obstacle for those seeking to reward Galtieri. It required the Argentine government to account for the fate of the disappeared, the human rights abuse for which it was notorious. During its years in power, the Argentine military engaged in more than 9,000 disappearances: kidnappings by men in civilian clothes traveling in unmarked vehicles (in Argentina, Ford Falcons acquired a sinister reputation, as they were used in these abductions), followed by torture of the victims in secret places, murder, clandestine disposal of the bodies (some were dumped out of planes over the South Atlantic), and subsequent denial of any knowledge of their whereabouts. Everything was designed for deniability. Accounting for the victims required a transformation of the regime that was responsible. That did not happen so long as the military remained in power.

Nevertheless, the Reagan administration claimed that the military regime was complying. In its annual country report on human rights for 1982, for example, the State Department credited the Argentines with furnishing data to 1,450 families on the fate of their disappeared relatives. Working with CELS in Buenos Aires, Emilio Mignone's organization, Americas Watch commissioned a team of sociologists to interview families of the disappeared. I testified before a congressional committee on the results: We found no shred of evidence to support the claim that any families had been informed. In retrospect, Reagan administration officials may have been thankful they could not go forward with certification. If they had done so prior to the Falklands War, U.S. military assistance to Argentina would have been used against a NATO ally, Britain. No doubt Prime Minister Margaret Thatcher would have had a few choice words to say on the subject to her good friend, President Ronald Reagan.

The case of Chile was somewhat different. General Vernon Walters, former deputy director of the CIA under Nixon and, a decade and a half later, the Reagan administration's ambassador to the UN, went soon after Reagan took office to get Pinochet's shopping list. Jeane Kirkpatrick traveled there in August 1981 to inform the dictator directly of the Reagan administration's friendship. Everett Briggs, a deputy assistant secretary of state for inter-American affairs, went the following year to express publicly a desire to resume U.S. military aid. Yet there was an insurmountable hurdle. The certification law required Chile to cooperate in bringing to justice those indicted by a U.S. grand jury for the 1976 murders in Washington, D.C., of its former defense minister, Orlando Letelier, and a U.S.

associate, Ronni Karpen Moffitt. They had been killed by a bomb that exploded in their car as they were driving on Embassy Row.

One of those indicted was the former head of the Chilean secret police, General Manuel Contreras. Documents declassified in 2000 revealed that he was on the CIA payroll at the time of the assassination of Letelier and Moffitt and that Pinochet had personally called on Paraguayan dictator Alfredo Stroessner to issue "cover" passports to two Chilean military operatives who eventually pleaded guilty to the murder and were convicted. There was no chance Pinochet would allow Contreras to be brought to justice, as he could testify to the dictator's own part in the murders. What made it impossible for the Reagan administration to ignore or finesse this condition was that career prosecutors in the Justice Department had worked on the Letelier-Moffitt murders. They would denounce certification. The administration could not risk this at a time it was embroiled in controversy over its certifications of El Salvador.

Even among the Reaganites, some wanted to keep a distance from Chile and Pinochet. One such skeptic was Elliott Abrams. Over time, my relations with Abrams had deteriorated and we no longer spoke. *The Columbia Journalism Review* reported that Abrams had informed television talk shows, such as Ted Koppel's *Nightline,* that he would no longer go on the air with me. One of our clashes on that show in 1985 had particularly discomfited him. Earlier, however, Abrams and I had maintained friendly contact. He even assisted me on my first visit to Chile.

I went to Santiago in December 1981 because the secret police had seized several leaders of the Chilean Commission of Human Rights. The men had been taken into custody at an event marking the anniversary of the Universal Declaration of Human Rights, December 10. In accordance with the priority we gave to defending local monitors, I went to Chile right away to gather information about the detention of the commission officers and, through my visit, to call attention to their imprisonment and thereby try to free them.

With the help of the commission's president, Máximo Pacheco, I got into the jail where his colleagues were being held. Pacheco was a cabinet member of the last Christian Democratic government of Chile before Allende and Pinochet had taken over, serving both as education minister and foreign minister. A well-known figure in Chile, he got me into the jail by telling the commandant that a prominent law professor from New York wanted to look around. In the jail, I talked to three imprisoned commission members. Two had been tortured, Pablo Fuenzalida, the commission's field secretary, especially severely. He had been strapped to a bedspring and given electric shocks to sensitive parts of his body. When I saw him in jail a week later, he was still partially paralyzed from the effects.

As a result of Abrams's intercession, U.S. Ambassador George Landau arranged for me to meet with government officials, including the secretary general of the Foreign Ministry, to discuss the assault on the commission officers. He listened impassively as I talked to him about the torture but arranged to deliver to my hotel statements by doctors—with indecipherable signatures and no other indication of their authorship—saying they had examined the men when they were turned over by the secret police to the regular jail where I saw them. The doctors said the men had been in good health and had shown no signs of mistreatment. There was no mention of the paralysis I saw. Some time later, I learned that the secretary general of the Foreign Ministry was a first cousin to Pablo Fuenzalida.

When I talked to Fuenzalida in the jail, he told me he had been blindfolded by the secret police. He believed that several times during his torture on the bedspring he had been examined by a doctor who ascertained that the electric shocks could continue. I arranged to see the president of the Chilean medical society and a few of his colleagues. They expressed concern but said there was little they could do because Pinochet had stripped the professional societies of the power to discipline members for ethical violations. Several years later, however, while Pinochet continued in power, the medical society did investigate the role of doctors in torture; they denounced the practice and expelled some doctors for their involvement. In taking this stand, the medical society propelled itself into the forefront of efforts to end the dictatorship and restore democratic government.

Abrams was not the only Reagan appointee to oppose Pinochet. The most effective was Harry Barnes, who served as U.S. ambassador to Chile during Reagan's second term. He visited me before taking up his post in Santiago to discuss how best to promote the human rights cause and seemed to make that his highest priority during his tenure in Chile. Barnes clashed with Pinochet when he presented his credentials. Responding to a remark by the dictator critical of the permissive character of democracy, Barnes told him that "the ills of democracy can best be cured by more democracy." Like Pickering's efforts in El Salvador, his performance made it clear to me that personal commitment to human rights by a U.S. ambassador, regardless of the overall policy of the administration, has an important impact. In October 1988, as the date for the plebiscite that ended Pinochet's rule approached, word circulated that the dictator planned to provoke riots that would provide a pretext for a coup canceling the vote. Barnes persuaded the State Department to call in the Chilean ambassador to inform him that it knew what was planned and that such tactics would not be tolerated. The message was delivered by Deputy Secretary of State John Whitehead. (As Abrams was then assistant secretary of state for inter-American affairs, he must have played a part in this.) I believe Harry Barnes deserves as much credit as any non-Chilean for bringing about a peaceful end to the Pinochet dictatorship.

From time to time, I glimpsed the frustrations experienced by U.S. ambassadors who were proponents of human rights during the Reagan years. One episode involved Pickering. The Robert F. Kennedy Memorial Foundation chose a group of Salvadoran women to receive its annual human rights prize, but they were denied visas to the United States to receive the award. Rumor had it that Pickering favored granting them visas but was opposed by his deputy, reportedly the CIA station chief in El Salvador. The deputy prevailed. In a meeting with Pickering I asked why the women were denied visas. He responded, "Because we had information that they are connected to the FMLN." A colleague followed up: "Is the information reliable?" Pickering: "No."

Though Elliott Abrams assisted me on Chile, from the start he fought me tooth and nail on Central America. We had frequent and increasingly acrimonious arguments—while we were still speaking—not only about El Salvador but also about three other countries where there were major human rights concerns: Guatemala, Honduras, and Nicaragua.

In El Salvador, one disagreement concerned indiscriminate bombing and strafing by the Salvadoran Air Force. Frustrated by its inability to defeat the FMLN, the Salvadoran military had begun to attack peasants because they considered them supporters of the guerrillas. In the early years of the war, most such attacks were ground assaults. Many thousands of Salvadorans were killed, including close to a thousand in a single episode in December 1981 known as "El Mozote." By 1983, with planes furnished by the United States and pilots trained by our government, much of the war on the peasants was waged from the air.

In response to our criticism, Abrams's office at the State Department circulated to members of Congress a January 25, 1984, cable it had obtained from the U.S. embassy in San Salvador justifying the practice. The cable, reflecting the views of the Salvadoran military, disputed our classification of the peasant deaths attributable to the bombings as human rights abuses. Those killed "were something other than innocent civilian bystanders," the cable said. It called them *masas,* a term the Salvadoran guerrillas used for those they considered their civilian supporters. They were described in the cable as persons who "live in close proximity of and travel in the company of armed guerrillas."

The State Department was arguing for the legitimacy of a widely used counterinsurgency strategy that has been responsible for much of the slaughter in internal armed conflicts in the post–World War II era. Turning around Mao's dictum that guerrillas are like fish who swim in the sea of a civilian population, this strategy aims to drain the sea to get at the fish. Its purpose is to make a territory where guerrillas operate uninhabitable by civilians. That way, the guerrillas are unable to live off the land. An entire territory becomes a free fire zone. It is possible that many peasants in such a zone support the guerrillas. Others oppose them, and still others may be neutral, or may wish to remain neutral, like those slaughtered at El Mozote, who were mainly evangelical Christians. There is no room for distinctions, however, when such a strategy is employed. What matters is the location of a peasant's home, not whether the peasant engages in conduct that warrants identification as a combatant. El Mozote was in a region controlled by the FMLN. That was enough cause for the U.S.-trained Atlacatl battalion to kill its residents, most of them young children.

Juan Méndez and I made a quick trip to El Salvador to discuss the cable with U.S. embassy officials, including Ambassador Pickering, and to get more information on the bombing. Within days after our visit in February 1984, we published a report, "Protection of the Weak and Unarmed," analyzing the cable and demonstrating the invalidity of its arguments under the international laws of war applicable to the Salvadoran conflict. We denounced the State Department's attempt to invent a new category of "something other than innocent civilian bystanders." The laws of war, we said, recognize only two categories: combatants, who may be attacked; and noncombatants, who may not be attacked. The third category was invented by the State Department to legitimize attacks on noncombatants by reason of their presumed sympathies or their residence.

Our report forced the State Department to back away from its explicit justification of indiscriminate bombing, but it did not halt the practice. A little later in 1984, on another of my frequent trips to El Salvador, I learned about some aerial attacks that particularly infuriated me when I went to talk to the International Committee of the Red Cross delegates in San Salvador. They told me their own work had been directly affected by the aerial attacks on civilians. The ICRC in the past had sent mobile clinics into territory controlled by the guerrillas to provide medical care for civilians. They had decided to discontinue the practice, they told me, because on several occasions, as their mobile units moved on, Salvadoran Air Force planes had attacked the peasants who had gathered to visit the clinics. I asked whether I could discuss the matter with Ambassador Pickering. They said yes. Later the same afternoon, I told Pickering about the problem. He promised to halt such attacks, and did. The Salvadoran military continued to attack presumed civilian supporters of the guerrillas throughout the war, though never again with the same intensity as in late 1983 and early 1984, and without a renewed attempt by the U.S. government to justify the practice.

The debate on Ted Koppel's *Nightline* in February 1985 that apparently caused Abrams to decline to take part in further discussions with me concerned two massacres, one the previous July at a hamlet known as Los Llanitos, in which at least sixty-eight civilians were killed, and another the following month at the Gualsinga River, where a minimum of fifty noncombatants were killed and probably a great many more. Americas Watch had investigated both massacres. The following exchange took place:

KOPPEL: Secretary Abrams, why was neither of those incidents reported [in the State Department's country report on El Salvador]?

ABRAMS: Because neither of them happened. Because it is a tactic of the guerrillas every time there is a battle and a significant number of people are killed to say that they're all victims of human rights abuses.

NEIER: That's why *The New York Times*—

ABRAMS: Ted, there's one very important point here.

NEIER: —and *The Boston Globe* and *The Miami Herald* and *The Christian Science Monitor* and Reuters and all the other reporters who went to the scene and looked at what took place, they were simply being propagandists for the guerrillas? Is that right?

ABRAMS: I'm telling you that there were no significant—there were no massacres in El Salvador in 1984.

After I pressed the issue of the newspaper reports, our debate continued as follows:

ABRAMS: I would have to tell you that the US Embassy is in a better position than a newspaper which has a one-man bureau to investigate what is going on in El Salvador.

NEIER: The US Embassy says it's not an investigative agency. When I've asked the US Embassy about this, they say they're not an investigative agency; they aren't capable of doing this; they don't do this sort of thing. Therefore, they may have more resources. But they don't do it.

ABRAMS: Well, I think that's false. Whenever there are accusations like this we do look at them . . .

KOPPEL: All right, but do you also send out independent investigative teams then to check on something like a report of a massacre?

ABRAMS: Frequently, we do whenever there is a—

KOPPEL: Did you in these instances?

ABRAMS: My memory is that we did, but I don't want to swear to it because I'd have to go back and look at the cablegram—[9]

After this, Americas Watch went back to the U.S. embassy in San Salvador to ask if any investigator had been sent either to Los Llanitos or the Gualsinga River. The answer, as we knew full well, was no in both cases. Typically, massacres were committed in territories where the FMLN guerrillas were active, as civilians in those areas were considered guerrilla sympathizers by the military. As Abrams must have known, the embassy had a policy against sending its personnel to such places. Journalists and human rights investigators did not operate under such restrictions.

During this period, I was also deeply engaged in efforts to deal with Guatemala. It was the country where the disappearances that became a hallmark of many repressive regimes were invented in 1966. The worst violence took place in the late 1970s and the early 1980s during the presidencies of General Romeo Lucas García (1978–1982) and General Efrain Rios Montt (1982–1983). Under Lucas García, disappearances hit their peak; under Rios Montt, that practice was curtailed but the intensity of the government's counterinsurgency campaign against leftist guerrillas escalated greatly. About 400 Mayan Indian villages were wiped out. In 1999, a "Clarification Commission," established by the United Nations as part of a peace settlement negotiated three years earlier that ended Guatemala's prolonged guerrilla war, issued a nine-volume report. It concluded that some 200,000 persons had been killed in human rights abuses that reached genocidal proportions under Rios Montt.

At the height of Rios Montt's bloody counterinsurgency campaign, in December 1982, President Reagan met with the Guatemalan leader in Honduras and hailed him as "a man of great personal integrity and commitment." The U.S. president said human rights reports documenting his abuses were "a bum rap." Reagan's obscene comment reflected the consistent stand of his administration. More than two years after Rios Montt was deposed, at a point when extensive documentation of his crimes was available, Jeane Kirkpatrick continued to sing his praises, writing that he "offered new powers of self-government and self-defense to the Indians" and that his rule "included a strong effort to end human rights abuses by government forces."[10] The State Department and its embassy in Guatemala City strongly backed successive Guatemalan military regimes. They denied or tried to explain away the most blatant abuses. Guatemala, I believe, was the most shameful chapter of all in the Reagan administration's human rights record. I have never wavered in my scorn and loathing for the officials—Reagan himself, Haig, Kirkpatrick, Abrams, and others—for their apologias for Rios Montt.

After Rios Montt was deposed by General Oscar Humberto Mejía Victores in an August 8, 1983, coup, the pace of the counterinsurgency campaign slowed, and massacres in the countryside largely stopped, but disappearances picked up again. In 1984, several wives of disappeared men —who had met in the Guatemala City morgue while searching for their missing husbands—organized the Group for Mutual Support, or GAM in its Spanish-language acronym.[11] Like similar groups in other Latin American countries where there were disappearances, the members sought information on their missing relatives and staged demonstrations in front of public buildings. At the time, GAM was the only human rights group in Guatemala; several previous efforts to form such organizations had been snuffed out quickly by the murder or disappearance of their leaders.

GAM held its first meeting on June 5, 1984, at the home of Archbishop Penados of Guatemala City. Over the next nine months, it enlisted several hundred members and organized a few peaceful protests that attracted a lot of attention. Then, in quick succession, on March 30 and April 4, 1985, two of its six leaders, Hector Gómez Calito and Rosario Godoy de Cuevas, were murdered. Godoy was killed with her two-year-old son and her twenty-one-year-old brother. It seemed GAM would be destroyed in the same way as every previous human rights group in Guatemala. I was in Europe at the time, but I got a call informing me that GAM would hold a memorial march in Guatemala City on April 13. Two U.S. congressmen, Representatives Ted Weiss (D-New York) and Bob Edgar (D-Pennsylvania) said they would attend, but they wanted me to join them. I agreed.

I arrived in Guatemala City the day before the march and made the U.S. embassy my first stop. There, the chargé told me the congressmen were not coming. The State Department had received information that it would be dangerous for them to attend the demonstration and had contacted House Speaker Tip O'Neill. Though the Speaker was an outspoken critic of the administration's policies in Central America, the warning put him in an awkward position and he instructed the two representatives not to go. The chargé told me the embassy had also learned of specific threats against me and advised me to leave Guatemala. I responded that since I had made the trip, I planned to stay. I would be at the demonstration the next day. Though I did not say this to the chargé, I was unhappy that the congressmen had stayed away. If there was any danger, their presence would have required the embassy to furnish security. I could have benefited from the protection offered to them.

After leaving the embassy, I went to the small, inexpensive, but clean hotel in the city center, the Pan American, where I customarily stayed in Guatemala City. There, I met in my tiny room with three frightened women, the surviving leaders of the GAM (the fourth survivor had fled the country immediately following the two assassinations). They had been brought to see me by Jean-Marie Simon, whose role as Americas Watch's representative in Guatemala was still secret.

The surviving leaders of GAM were scared. They knew that, like their murdered colleagues, they were easy targets. All three were wives of men who had disappeared during the year and a half since the Mejía Victores coup, leaving them in no doubt about how dangerous it was to be identified as an enemy by the country's military. They also had a more mundane concern. Would anyone show up for the demonstration the next day? The U.S. congressmen I was supposed to accompany had been frightened off. What about Guatemalans? They were far more vulnerable, as they would remain in the country when the demonstration was over. With so many killings, a few more deaths of ordinary Guatemalans would be of little note.

The next morning, much to our surprise, about a thousand people turned up to take part in the demonstration. Though not a large number by standards elsewhere, it was many more than anyone remembered taking part in a protest in Guatemala. They walked peacefully for about a mile along the city's busiest avenue to the presidential palace, carrying placards with blown-up photographs of Rosario Godoy and Hector Gómez, the murdered GAM leaders. Most marchers were Indian women wearing the distinctive *huipiles* that identified their communities to those familiar with Mayan textiles. They had traveled long distances by bus to take part and, as they had no place to stay in the city, had slept in churches or in the streets overnight. Paying the bus fare and missing three or four days of work was a hardship for these women, but they were wives and mothers of disappeared men. They wanted to register their protest. Many marched barefoot.

The demonstration took place without incident. One of the most visible participants was a young girl with a bullhorn who kept everybody in line. When it was over, Jean-Marie—who photographed the march for *Time*—suggested that I interview Eva, the girl with the bullhorn. We went to a nearby coffee shop. For about two hours, Eva told me about family members who had disappeared. As we left the coffee shop, I noticed a couple of men waiting outside and thought they were probably following me. I went off to the Pan American Hotel and thought no more about them.

Early the next morning, I was awakened by a call from a young man who said he was a neighbor of Eva's. She had spotted the same two men outside the coffee shop the day before, and that morning she had noticed them near her home. She had sent her neighbor to a place in the neighborhood where there was a phone to call me. I roused a journalist and Beatriz Manz, who were also staying in my hotel, and we took a taxi to Eva's home on the outskirts of the city, where she lived with her grandmother and a younger brother, collected her, and took her back with us. Later that day, Eva moved into Jean-Marie's one-room apartment. She lived there for several months until I could arrange for her admission to the United States, where Yvette instructed her in English. Today, Eva is a labor organizer in Los Angeles.

I also arranged for another woman connected to the demonstration to go to the United States. A month or so after the GAM demonstration, in May 1985, I went to Guatemala again. This time my purpose was to visit highland communities, such as Rabinal, where many hundreds had been killed by the military two or three years earlier. Passing through Guatemala City, I went to see the three remaining GAM leaders. They told me about continuing threats. These particularly terrified Blanca, whose husband, an agronomist, had disappeared the previous August. I went to the U.S. embassy to ask about admitting Blanca and her two infant children as refugees. A consular official seemed eager to help but told me no one at the embassy knew how to go about it. They had never processed a refugee application. (At the time, Canada and Australia were admitting hundreds of refugees each year from Guatemala to save the lives of those threatened by political repression; indeed, the Canadian ambassador told me that admitting refugees was virtually the full-time business of his embassy.) The consular official and I got on the phone to Washington together to figure out the process and obtained a visa to allow Blanca and her children to accompany me when I returned to the United States. Yvette, who drove to the airport in New York to greet me on my return, was startled to see me arrive carrying the two children. Eventually, with the help of an affidavit that I provided her, Blanca was one of the rare Guatemalans to obtain asylum in the United States. It was difficult to deny she had a well-founded fear of persecution.

Another of my visits to Guatemala touched off one of my many battles with Elliott Abrams, who had, by this time, shifted to the post of assistant secretary of state for inter-American affairs. I coordinated my travel with Beatriz Manz. One afternoon, I was conducting an interview in the lobby of the Pan American Hotel when Beatriz came in ashen-faced. She told me she had just witnessed a nearby sidewalk execution: Two men had approached a young man, shot him in the head, and calmly walked away. Beatriz had stayed at the scene until an ambulance arrived to take away the body.

Jean-Marie Simon, who was with me in the hotel lobby, suggested we go to the hospital where the body had been taken. There, we discovered the identity of the victim, a twenty-nine-year-old architecture student, and ascertained that he had died from a bullet wound to the neck shortly after arriving in the hospital. Beatriz telephoned the family, told them she had witnessed the execution-style murder, arranged to talk to them, and later went to the funeral. She also visited national police headquarters to report what she had seen. No one was interested in taking her statement. Subsequently, she wrote an op-ed article about the episode for the *New York Times*.[12]

My dispute with Abrams involved one of the points Beatriz made in her article. At the time, the State Department based its reporting on deaths due to human rights abuses in Guatemala on newspaper accounts. As in El Salvador, the U.S. embassy refrained from conducting its own investigations. Americas Watch pointed out that this method grossly understated the violence, particularly in highland Indian areas to which the newspapers had little access. Beatriz noted in her article that even the execution she witnessed in the center of Guatemala City in broad daylight was not reported in any newspaper, though one of the major dailies had its offices two blocks away. We scoured all the papers for several days after the murder and saw no account of it.

Abrams wrote a letter to the editor of the *Times* saying Beatriz Manz was mistaken and the murder had been reported. Though the *Times* did not publish his letter, we saw it because he circulated copies to members of Congress and others who inquired about Beatriz's article. Concerned we might have overlooked something, we went back to the newspapers, but could find no report of the murder. We did find something else we had not noticed previously, however. The young man's family had placed a small advertisement as a death notice; it did not say how he died, only his name and the date of his death. It was one of many similar death notices in the newspaper. Publishing these is a common practice in Guatemala. Neither the State Department nor anyone else tabulated these as human rights abuses, as they provided no information about the cause of death. Most referred to people who died of natural causes.

I carried on a lengthy correspondence with the State Department over this matter and eventually got a concession that it was this death notice to which Abrams had referred. Neither Abrams nor anyone else at the department acknowledged that they had erred—or lied—in purporting to rebut Beatriz Manz's article on this basis.

When Abrams moved to Inter-American Affairs from his previous post as assistant secretary for human rights, he was succeeded in the human rights post by Richard Schifter, with whom Americas Watch also clashed. One episode involved Schifter's attempt to secure the dismissal of a Salvadoran lawyer, Roberto Cuellar, from the staff of a body that received funding from the United States, the Inter-American Institute of Human Rights in San José, Costa Rica. Roberto had been the first director of the Catholic Church's human rights office in his own country when it was established by Archbishop Oscar Romero. Not long after the archbishop was assassinated in March 1980 by a death squad connected to the country's military forces, Roberto's own name had appeared on a death list. He fled to Costa Rica, where he was employed by the institute. With the United States strongly backing the armed forces that controlled the death squads in El Salvador, Schifter demanded that Roberto should be fired in exchange for continuation of the $900,000 a year the United States provided to the institute. As this was a sizable portion of the institute's budget, its very existence was threatened.

The director of the institute at the time was Sonia Picado, an elegant and aristocratic woman who had previously served as dean of the law school of the national university and subsequently as a member of her country's Supreme Court and as ambassador to the United States. As I discovered when the threat involving Roberto took place, her lady-like manner masked a core of steel.

Sonia flew to the United States to enlist her friends in resisting Schifter. She contacted me, and as it turned out, I was able to help. As in other cases where we needed to counter the efforts of the Reagan administration, we turned to our friends in Congress. Holly Burkhalter and I got in touch with Meg Donovan, an aide to Representative Dante Fascell of Florida, chairman of the House Foreign Affairs Committee. I had known Meg since the early days of Helsinki Watch; she then worked for the congressional Helsinki Commission chaired by Fascell, and she joined the Foreign Affairs Committee when he became chairman of that body. She was as reliable and effective an ally as we had among congressional staff members. Meg went to Fascell, and he summoned Schifter to his office. As I was not present, I do not know exactly what transpired. Knowing Fascell, however, I imagine he was plainspoken. The effect was all I could have wished. There were no further threats to terminate the funding of the institute. Roberto remained on its staff, and today he is its executive director, succeeding Juan Méndez in that post. Sonia Picado was a finalist for the post of United Nations high commissioner for human rights but was passed over for that post in favor of the former President of Ireland, Mary Robinson. Before the decision was made to appoint Robinson, I wrote to Kofi Annan urging him to choose Sonia Picado. Her refusal to buckle under Schifter's pressure figured in my support. It demonstrated she had the toughness that is needed to deal with governments that abuse human rights.

Dealing with the human rights situation in Nicaragua was the trickiest problem I encountered in the 1980s. It required careful attention to every word in our reports and every nuance the words conveyed. On the one hand, the Sandinistas engaged in many abuses: severe restrictions of freedom of expression; denial of due process of law in their police courts and "popular tribunals"; abusive methods of interrogation and pretrial detention; forced relocation and violence—including at least one massacre—against the Miskito Indians and other indigenous groups, especially during the early part of the decade; and, particularly in the latter stages of the war against the Contras, a number of targeted killings of presumed civilian supporters of the Contras. Their record was very poor. On the other hand, it was not nearly so violent as portrayed by the Reagan administration. To the Reaganites, the Sandinistas were the devil incarnate. The United States was intent on overthrowing the Sandinistas, organized a war to achieve this aim, and used human rights information as an instrument of warfare. The greater the abuses attributed to the Sandinistas, the more the administration believed it could persuade the U.S. public and the Congress to support the Contras. Because political violence was so great in nearby El Salvador and Guatemala, and those governments were backed by the United States, the State Department portrayed the Sandinistas as worse. That led to extremes of exaggeration.

To report accurately and fairly on abuses committed by the Sandinistas, we had to walk a thin line. We didn't want to fall into the trap of overstating them in a way that would further the war aims of the Reagan administration. At the same time, we had to make sure we didn't understate abuses, as that would make us an apologist for them. Also, it would undermine our credibility in reporting on other countries. Predictably, that made us—and me in particular—a target for regular attacks by leftists such as Alexander Cockburn in *The Nation*. He could be counted on to deny or explain away abuses by leftist regimes in the same manner that Jeane Kirkpatrick or Elliott Abrams served as an apologist for Central American governments aligned with the United States. In line with our policy of reporting on insurgent abuses as well as those by governments in armed conflicts—which we applied first to the FMLN in El Salvador—we also reported on Contra violations of the laws of war. Here, too, we carefully weighed our words so as not to seem to take sides in the conflict.

I traveled to Nicaragua frequently during the 1980s. During my first visit, in 1981, I got into sharp arguments with the interior minister, Tomás Borge, a Sandinista hard-liner to whom I took a strong dislike, over the justice system established under his direction. (Part of my dislike for

Borge was visceral: The combination of several crucifixes on the wall of his office, a hand grenade on the coffee table around which we met, and his Leninist rhetoric offended me.) Thereafter, it did not surprise me that almost every time we encountered severely abusive practices by the Sandinistas, Borge was involved. On that same trip, I accidentally encountered what may have been part of an early effort to form the Contras, though I did not realize it at the time.

I flew into Managua on the same flight as a prominent scholar of Latin American studies who I knew had long-term connections to the CIA. When we arrived at the airport, he told me he was being picked up by a friend. As taxis were unreliable, and as we were both staying at the Intercontinental Hotel—a pyramidal building with the top sliced off, famous as a one-time residence of Howard Hughes and one of the few structures in Managua to survive the 1972 earthquake intact—he offered me a lift. I accepted. It turned out that the friend who drove us to the hotel was Adolfo Calero, the local bottler and distributor of Coca Cola and the leader of Nicaragua's Conservative Party. The following year, Calero left Nicaragua to become civilian chief of the newly formed Contras organized by the CIA.

Of the many disputes in which I engaged with the State Department over Nicaragua, one that stands out in my memory resembled the controversy over the Salvadoran military's attacks on peasants. It involved attacks by the Contras on farm cooperatives. Like other guerrillas, the Contras avoided direct confrontations with the Nicaraguan armed forces. Their attacks concentrated on economic enterprises. The economy of Nicaragua was extremely weak, and disrupting the cooperatives was calculated to do great damage. As the cooperatives were scattered throughout the countryside, they were easy targets. Attacking them was attractive, as their collectivist character symbolized the ideology against which the Contras were fighting. Also, some of the land farmed by the cooperatives had been confiscated from well-to-do Nicaraguans who had left the country but still supported the Contras. They had scores to settle against those occupying their land.

Though the Contras occasionally killed military men sent to guard the cooperatives from attack, most casualties were civilians. We gathered information on many such killings and identified those that were deliberate or indiscriminate as violations of the laws of war by the Contras. The State Department challenged us on this matter. A July 1, 1986, press statement by the department was typical:

It is not the policy of the resistance [i.e., the Contras] to attack civilian targets. However, the allegation that the resistance attacks civilians is a consistent propaganda theme of the Sandinista government. These cooperatives, this was what was attacked in Nicaragua, often have a dual military-economic purpose and are part of the Sandinistas' strategy of population control designed to keep the resistance away from its supporters. To that end, most of these cooperatives are located in conflictive or potentially conflictive areas. The inhabitants of the cooperatives are armed and receive regular military training. Unfortunately, due to the intermingling of civilian and military functions, there are sometimes civilian casualties.

Traveling with Jemera Rone—who had a theory that if she drove very fast over the deeply rutted dirt roads, it smoothed out the bumps—I visited a number of cooperatives in different parts of the country shortly after they were attacked. Often, the casualties included young children. None had military fortifications, and only one was defended by a military unit. Because they were so vulnerable and it was known they were targets, the men who worked the fields took turns doing guard duty and fired back when attacks began. Some men who did guard duty received training and were members of militia units. They were not deployed to engage in combat, only to protect the cooperatives where they lived and worked. As best I could determine, this was the closest they came to fulfilling a military role. We had disputes within Americas Watch about whether these men could be considered combatants, and therefore legitimate targets, but there were no doubts about the killing of women, children, and the disabled who were murdered after a cooperative was overrun. At most cooperatives I saw, the Contras also set fire to homes and food storage buildings and destroyed farm machinery to end their economic viability. (In making these trips, we were occasionally flagged down by Sandinista soldiers seeking rides. Jemera politely explained that we could not oblige as that would compromise our neutrality as human rights investigators. It would also make us legitimate targets for any Contras around. Fortunately, the soldiers accepted these explanations.)

A conversation I had with a journalist in Managua suggests how controversial the attacks on the cooperatives became as a consequence of efforts by the Reagan administration to discredit any information that cast doubt on its policies. I was at the Intercontinental Hotel, which also housed the foreign press offices in Managua, when Julia Preston, then a reporter for the *Washington Post* and now with the *New York Times*, came in looking tired and begrimed. I regarded Julia as one of the best journalists covering the region: hard-working, tough-minded, and thoroughly reliable in her reporting. (When I mentioned to her that Elliott Abrams had denied on *Nightline* that the Los Llanitos massacre in El Salvador had ever happened, she pointed out that she still limped months later because she twisted her foot getting to the site to view the bodies.) Julia told me she had just returned from the scene of a Contra attack on a cooperative about a hundred miles from Managua—a long distance on the terrible roads of Nicaragua. Though ready to file her story, she was worried about one thing. She had arrived on the scene in time to witness the funeral of two children who had been killed in the attack, but she did not see the bodies. Julia said she could not bring herself to ask the grieving parents to open the small coffins so she could examine the corpses. She asked whether I thought she had made a mistake.

I am unsure whether Americas Watch's reporting on the attacks on the cooperatives had any impact. It did not seem to affect the practices of the Contras. But it is possible that it affected the support they obtained from the United States. Over time, even many bitter opponents of the Sandinistas became sick of the Contras because of their corruption and brutality. Our reporting helped them acquire their well-deserved reputation.

Our politically charged struggle with the Reagan administration was a testing by fire. Because we survived, we were toughened. It gave Human Rights Watch a degree of prestige that would normally take much longer to achieve, and that we might never have achieved otherwise. When we began, Amnesty International was the household name. By the time the Reagan years drew to a close, Human Rights Watch was just as significant. The attention we garnered transformed the human rights field. It legitimized a focus on violations of the laws of wars, reporting on abuses by both sides in situations of armed conflict, efforts to hold accountable those responsible for abuses, and confrontations with surrogate villains over their support for those directly responsible.

There were moments when our strife with the U.S. government was very unpleasant for an infant organization. Administration officials denounced us; members of Congress harangued us at hearings (I clashed sharply with several House Republicans at hearings where I testified. Among them were Michael DeWine of Ohio and John McCain of Arizona, both now members of the Senate. I have come to admire the latter for his leadership on such matters as campaign finance reform. But two decades earlier, I thought he was obnoxious. Another, Jack Kemp of New York, was so infuriated by my insistence on giving back as good as I got that he stalked out of a hearing). The editorial pages of the *Wall Street Journal* were unfailingly creative in cataloguing our supposed sins. But the attacks helped us grow up fast and made us strong.

CHAPTER ELEVEN

Promoting Accountability

I was in Buenos Aires, Argentina, on December 10, 1983, for the inauguration of Raul Alfonsín as that country's democratically elected president ending seven and a half years of military rule. It was a thrilling occasion, what seemed even then the beginning of the end of an era of brutal military dictatorships in Latin America and the most fitting way I could imagine to mark the thirty-fifth anniversary of the adoption of the Universal Declaration of Human Rights by the United Nations. The armed forces had to give up power and allow the restoration of democratic government because they could no longer govern. They had been thoroughly discredited by their inability to manage the economy, by the cowardly performance of many of their commanders during the war they had started and lost against Britain the previous year for control of the Falkland Islands (known to Argentines as the Malvinas), and by their well-earned reputation for murderous cruelty. A resolute group of human rights campaigners who were not intimidated when they themselves became targets—especially Emilio Mignone, my host on that visit—had made certain that the military's dirty deeds were widely known both internationally and at home. They deserve a large part of the credit for the transition to civilian rule I came to celebrate.

The military had seized control of Argentina in March 1976 from the corrupt and incompetent government of President Isabel Perón (the widow of Juan Domingo Perón whom he had married after the death of Evita) at a time when several leftist groups were engaged in urban guerrilla warfare. Paramilitary gangs supported by the Perón government had used terror tactics against the terror of the Left. When the armed forces took power, these efforts were redoubled and terror became the central mission of the armed forces. In their words, they fought a "dirty war." The guerrilla threat was soon eliminated. But the military did not stop. Thousands of Argentines suspected of supporting the leftists, sympathizing with them, defending their rights, or otherwise opposing the armed forces—among them Jacobo Timerman, who had initially favored a military takeover to end the chaos but then became a critic of military abuses—also became the victims of military action. Disappearances became the hallmark of Argentina's military. In addition, many thousands were imprisoned for long periods without charge or trial.

In April 1983, as the end of its rule approached, the Argentine military issued its "Final Document on the Struggle Against Subversion and Terrorism." In it, the armed forces denied any use of the methods characteristic of disappearances. There were no abductions, no clandestine detention centers, no torture, and no prisoners were secretly executed. At Americas Watch, we promptly denounced the "Final Document."[1] Several European governments, the European Economic Community, and the Vatican also condemned it. The Reagan administration, however, consistently an apologist for the Argentine military—except, briefly, during the Falklands War, when it felt obliged to side with its NATO ally, Britain—could only muster a bland expression "of disappointment . . . that an occasion has been lost to begin a resolution of this question [the disappearances]." Then, in September, a month before the elections that would terminate its rule, the military, following the example of General Augusto Pinochet in neighboring Chile, who had pioneered in this approach five years earlier, decreed an amnesty for its own crimes—which it still refused to acknowledge—during the "war against subversion." Both leading presidential candidates denounced the amnesty, but Italo Luder, the Peronist candidate, said it would be binding.

His opponent, Alfonsín, who was trailing, said he would annul the decree. Alfonsín's response propelled him to victory and brought me to Buenos Aires to celebrate. It also launched Americas Watch's campaign to hold accountable those responsible for the most severe human rights abuses: war crimes, crimes against humanity, and genocide. Over time, the struggle for accountability we initiated became a dominant theme of the work of the human rights movement worldwide. It led to the formation of "truth commissions" in many countries; major advances in international law, including, for example, widespread acceptance of the doctrine of "universal jurisdiction," which permits courts everywhere to sit in judgment of crimes such as those of Pinochet in Chile; the creation of a number of ad hoc international criminal tribunals by the United Nations

Security Council; and now, despite strenuous opposition by the Bush administration, the establishment of a permanent International Criminal Court with worldwide jurisdiction.

My own engagement with accountability was a natural outgrowth of my work at the ACLU. Two decades earlier, establishing civilian review of police abuses had been one of my major concerns. A decade after that, impeaching Richard Nixon was a focus of my work. The big difference in the international human rights field is that the crimes at issue are of incomparably greater magnitude. Yet the principle is the same: Those who wield authority must themselves obey the law. When they do not, they must be answerable, especially when they commit the most egregious crimes.

Another factor that made developments in Argentina the starting point for my work on accountability internationally was that I had been influenced by my Argentine colleague at Americas Watch, Juan Méndez. His familiarity with developments in Argentina, and his close ties to colleagues there who led the struggle for human rights, made Americas Watch the leading source for information on accountability in that country. Emilio Mignone, whose own detention in February 1981 had aroused an international outcry, thus helping to defeat Reagan's plan to jettison the U.S. commitment to human rights internationally, wanted Juan to return to Argentina to succeed him as director of that country's leading human rights group, CELS. Juan was inclined to accept that offer, but could not persuade his wife, Sylvia, also a lawyer, to return to their native land. His abduction, imprisonment, and torture had left scars on his wife that did not heal. She would not go back. In my eagerness to hold on to Juan, I told him we would gladly enter into an arrangement with CELS that would allow him to retain a leading role in Americas Watch while serving as director of the Argentine group. Sylvia's resistance mooted that plan. Remaining with us, Juan helped Human Rights Watch to emerge as the foremost proponent of accountability internationally. It is a cause he continues to champion today as a professor of law at Notre Dame and as first a commissioner, and now president, of the Inter-American Commission on Human Rights of the Organization of American States.

In Argentina, immediately upon taking office President Alfonsín appointed a commission to investigate and disclose the truth about the disappearances. Truth was at issue because the essence of these crimes is that they were designed to be deniable; because the military claimed in its

"Final Document" that it had not engaged in such practices; and because families demanded to know what happened to their missing children. Of course, most Argentines knew the men in the unmarked Ford Falcons wearing civilian clothes had been military, but they wanted an end to the lies by which the regime had maintained a pretense of legality. The commission would penetrate the falsehoods. Alfonsín also ordered the prosecution of the nine members of the first three military juntas that governed Argentina after the armed forces seized power in 1976. Among them were three generals—Jorge Rafael Videla, Roberto Eduardo Viola, and Leopoldo Galtieri—who had served as successive presidents. The commission would establish truth and the prosecutions would do justice.

The commission was headed by novelist Ernesto Sabato, a man of political integrity as well as literary distinction. I visited him at his beautiful home in an incongruously dreary industrial suburb of Buenos Aires just days before his appointment. He eventually documented 8,960 disappearances by the armed forces, but pointed out that the actual number was higher. The prosecutions secured convictions of five of the nine junta members, including former presidents Videla and Viola. Thereafter, justice ran into trouble. The generals and the admirals in the juntas did not act alone. When prosecutions were launched against hundreds of lower ranking officers for their part in the disappearances, they rebelled. Though the civilian democratic government was probably not in grave jeopardy, as it enjoyed popular support, it had to suppress a number of uprisings by segments of the armed forces. Placating the military, President Alfonsín pushed through Congress a Due Obedience Law exonerating officers below the rank of colonel if they were following orders and a Full Stop Law barring new prosecutions. In October 1989, Alfonsín's successor, President Carlos Saúl Menem, pardoned those officers still awaiting trial, and the following year he extended the pardons to those already convicted, including the five junta members and two former police chiefs of Buenos Aires serving sentences for mass murder.

One of those pardoned was General Carlos Guillermo Suárez Mason, the former chief of the First Army Corps. His exoneration was an especially bitter pill for Juan Méndez to swallow. As military commander of the greater Buenos Aires area, Suárez Mason had presided over several thousand disappearances. Juan's own abduction, detention, and torture had taken place under his jurisdiction. Suárez Mason called himself the "Lord of Life and Death" while the military held power. In 1980, he presided over the Buenos Aires conference of the World Anti-Communist League; the participants included aides to Senators Jesse Helms and James McClure from the United States as well as the leaders of the Salvadoran and Guatemalan death squads.[2] When the transition to democratic rule took place in 1983, however, Suárez Mason was the only senior officer to flee Argentina in an effort to avoid prosecution. He entered the United States illegally by using a forged passport, but in 1987 was discovered in California and held for extradition to Argentina. While he was jailed in California, some of his surviving victims, also in the United States, filed a civil suit against him. Juan acted as one of the lawyers bringing the action against his former tormentor, and a federal court awarded $21 million to the plaintiffs.[3]

The triumph was sweet but brief. None of the court's judgment was ever collected. Extradited to Argentina in 1988 to face criminal charges and then freed by Menem, Suárez Mason also managed to evade payment of the civil judgment against him even though it was widely known he had acquired considerable wealth by looting the state oil company, which he headed during the final period of the military dictatorship, and by engaging in corrupt transactions with an Italian armaments firm. He was one of a group of Argentines connected to the military regime who held a numbered account at Banco Ambrosiano of Milan, which was forced to close in a scandal in 1982 that brought down the Italian government and exposed corruption in the Vatican, a major shareholder in the bank. (Suárez Mason was later rearrested along with General Leopoldo Galtieri under the orders of an Argentine judge who held the laws under which they were freed to be unconstitutional.)

The collapse of the justice process in Argentina after a number of abortive military rebellions reverberated throughout Latin America. In neighboring Uruguay, where a democratic transition took place in 1995 after twelve years of military rule marked by an extraordinarily high rate of political imprisonment and the prolonged torture of detainees, an amnesty was adopted by Congress in 1986 and upheld three years later in a popular referendum. A critical factor in the outcome of the 1989 referendum was concern about the military revolts in Argentina. Though the prohibition on justice was unpopular, many Uruguayans feared their armed forces might stir up comparable turmoil. Statements by military leaders that they would not stand for prosecutions fostered public apprehension.

There were also repercussions in Chile. In 1988, fifteen years after seizing power and a decade after he decreed an amnesty forgiving himself and his associates for their crimes, Pinochet lost a plebiscite required under the constitution that he had put in place. This set in motion a democratic transition that took place in March 1990. An important question for officials of the incoming democratic regime was whether to accept Pinochet's self-amnesty. What happened in Argentina was undoubtedly in the forefront of their thinking. Also, the new democracy in Chile had little choice. It governed under Pinochet's constitution, which left him in control of the armed forces and gave him a lifetime seat in the Senate and immunity from prosecution (eventually lifted by the Chilean Supreme Court after the proceedings against him in Britain; Pinochet resigned his lifetime appointment in 2002 when he could no longer sustain the claim that he was too ill to stand trial but fit enough to remain a senator). The Chilean armed forces had not been disgraced by their conduct on the battlefield; they had not left the economy in a shambles; and they remained a formidable force. The infant democracy could not do what Alfonsín had done in Argentina seven years earlier.

Though I readily acknowledge that the new Chilean government at that moment could not have taken on Pinochet and the armed forces by bringing prosecutions, I disagree with its rationale for going along with the amnesty it inherited. Transforming necessity into a virtue, Chile's democratic leaders proclaimed their commitment to "reconciliation." Borrowing the popular term for the Argentine National Commission on Disappeared Persons (called the "Truth Commission," though the word "truth" did not appear in its title), Chile established a Truth and Reconciliation Commission. Its architect and one of its members was José ("Pepe") Zalaquett, a lawyer and leading human rights advocate.

Vice rector of Chile's Catholic University at the time of Pinochet's coup in 1973, Zalaquett was an organizer of a Committee for Peace in the days immediately following the coup that evacuated to safety thousands of foreigners who had been attracted to Chile by the leftist Allende regime. The committee also helped establish the Vicariate of Solidarity under the sponsorship of Chile's Cardinal Raúl Silva Henríquez to defend the rights of Chileans. Zalaquett became the vicariate's legal director until Pinochet had him arrested and expelled from the country in 1975. In exile, where I got to know him, he became chairman of Amnesty International and one of the most universally respected leaders of the international human rights movement, as much for his generosity of spirit as for his courage in challenging Pinochet. Though Zalaquett is a friend whom I admire greatly, he and I had many arguments about the Chilean approach.

One of our debates took place at a meeting at the Aspen Institute's Wye River Plantation in Maryland in November 1988. This meeting, which took place a month after Pinochet's defeat in the plebiscite by a margin of 55 to 43 percent, played a seminal role in shaping the global struggle for accountability. The question of how to hold the Chilean military accountable was at the forefront of the thinking of the thirty or so human rights leaders, journalists, political scientists, and legal philosophers who participated. Lawrence Weschler captured the essence of my debate with Zalaquett in his 1990 book, *A Miracle, A Universe:*

> Zalaquett noted that any policy regarding past abuses would have two central objectives—first, with regard to the past, reparation, repairing the damage wrought by the earlier abuses; and second, with regard to the future, prevention, promotion of a stable democratic future in which such abuses wouldn't recur. He argued that any such policy would have to meet certain minimum requirements to be considered legitimate. First, the truth would have to be known, complete, officially sanctioned and publicly exposed ("put in the record of the nation's memory"). Second, the policy would have to represent the will of the people. This might admittedly prove difficult to achieve, but a self-amnesty on its face would always be illegitimate both because it violated this principle and because nobody ought ever to profit from his own bad faith. Third, the policy would have to be such that it did not violate standards of international law, either by exacting punishments that were too severe or lavishing clemencies that were too broad. . . . "But if those three conditions are met," Zalaquett continued, "whether a policy leans more toward clemency or severity should be up to the nation in question"—that is, not subject to absolute outside standards. "And clemency can be just as valuable a preventive as severity," Zalaquett concluded. "I insist on that." . . .
>
> He got an argument on that from Aryeh Neier, the executive director of Human Rights Watch in New York. To begin with, Neier demurred from the notion that "the will of the people" has anything to do with the proper application of justice. "If Pepe hits me," Neier proposed, "I have a right to forgive him, but does everybody else in this room have the right to forgive him in my stead?" Neier then went on to an even more fundamental disagreement. "I want to quarrel," he said, "with the assumption

that a principal reason for seeking justice, or criterion for evaluating its ef-
ficacy, should be the future stability of the reconstituted democracy. Such
predictions are highly speculative. Who's to say that clemency won't simply further embolden the torturers, thereby inviting rather than preventing future abuses ... ? The human capacity to look backward is frail
enough. The human capacity to look forward is frailer yet. Rather, punishment is the absolute duty of society to honor and redeem the suffering of
the individual victim. In a society of law, we say it is not up to individual
victims to exercise vengeance, but rather up to society to demonstrate
respect for the victim, for the one who suffered, by rendering the victim-
izer accountable. As a matter of law we simply have to say we are not
going to grant clemency to the most grotesque criminals. We may be
forced to do so on the basis of *force majeure*, but we should never do so as a
matter of law."[4]

Another objection I made to leaving determinations to the will of the
people was that victims of abuses are often hated or despised minorities:
Jews in Nazi Germany, Kosovars in Serbia, Chechens in Russia, Tutsis in
Rwanda, and so forth. If popular majorities decide such matters, there is
little chance perpetrators will ever pay a penalty. Human rights must be
protected against democratic majorities as well as against dictators. (In the
Argentine and Chilean circumstances that were Pepe Zalaquett's focus,
the question of bias against a minority did not arise, as victims, perpetrators, and bystanders mostly came from the same ethnic and religious backgrounds.)

The Chilean Truth and Reconciliation Commission embodied Zalaquett's approach. It documented more than 2,000 political killings by the
Pinochet regime. Many of the victims had been tortured to death by the
secret police agency, the DINA (later known as the CNI).[5] The commission said that body's "internal organization, composition, resources, personnel and actions escaped not only public knowledge but also the control
of any legality. ... Although formally the DINA was subordinate to the
Junta, in practice it was responsible only to the President of the Governing Junta, later President of the Republic." That is, Pinochet was personally responsible for the crimes the commission described in chilling detail.
The commission refrained, however, from identifying the military officers
who carried out these crimes. Zalaquett said naming them would violate
their rights. I disagree. They were protected against judicial process by the

new government's acceptance of Pinochet's amnesty. Not naming them extended this protection. It was another case, I believe, of justifying an accommodation based on the continuing power of the military on seemingly benign grounds.

The commission published its report in March 1991. That same month, in another part of the world, it became clear that war would break out in Yugoslavia as President Slobodan Milošević of Serbia sent tanks into his own capital in a show of force. By June, fighting was under way in Slovenia and Croatia and, the following April, in Bosnia. Probably no one in Argentina or Chile suspected that events in far-off ex-Yugoslavia would one day help put behind bars the Latin American military men who escaped justice in the late 1980s and early 1990s by intimidating the new democratic governments of their countries.

The development involving ex-Yugoslavia that altered the way Argentina, Chile, and many other countries approached accountability was the decision by the United Nations Security Council in 1993 to deal with the crimes there by establishing an International Criminal Tribunal. I initiated the call to establish the Tribunal in the summer of 1992. Several factors came together that made me decide to take this step. First, of course, was the severity of the crimes in Bosnia. Though the war that lasted more than three and a half years had only been under way three and a half months when I made the call in July 1992, tens of thousands of Bosnians had already been killed and hundreds of thousands had been forced to flee their homes. Second was that the ethnic basis for these crimes was explicit. "Ethnic cleansing," the emblematic coinage of an awful decade that ended an awful century, was not a pejorative label invented by critics; the term originated in August 1991 when Serb forces launched assaults in a region of Croatia largely populated by ethnic Serbs. It was a euphemism by Serb leaders for their modus operandi in Bosnia as well as Croatia. Non-Serbs in a town or village were rounded up. A few prominent citizens—the mayor, doctors, lawyers, engineers—were executed. Women were raped publicly. Men of military age were taken away to a detention camp. Everyone else fled. This was "cleansing." The racial or ethnic/religious character made it appropriate to follow the Nuremberg precedent in responding to crimes reminiscent of those by the Nazis.

The third factor, and one that was crucial, was that there were good legal grounds to establish an international criminal tribunal. Elsewhere, the most severe abuses that Human Rights Watch monitored took place in internal conflicts, the characteristic form of warfare in our time. Yet as Bosnia and Croatia were recognized internationally, and as the forces of the Federal Republic of Yugoslavia (Serbia and Montenegro) were involved, the wars in ex-Yugoslavia were international. Later in the 1990s, international humanitarian law evolved rapidly. As a result, it is now established that certain crimes committed in internal armed conflicts are war crimes punishable by an international criminal tribunal. That was not the case as recently as 1992, when I issued the call for Human Rights Watch. As the law stood then, the only clear jurisdiction for an international tribunal was over war crimes committed in an international armed conflict. In our call, I cited provisions of the Third and Fourth Geneva Conventions of 1949 and of Protocol I of 1977 designating certain crimes as "grave breaches" of the laws of war. The concept of grave breaches only applies in international armed conflicts.

As noted in the chapter on Sarajevo (see Chapter 15, "Relieving Misery in Sarajevo and Chechnya and the Loss of Fred Cuny"), the timing of Human Rights Watch's call for a tribunal was fortuitous as it coincided with the world's discovery of the ghastly camps maintained by Serb forces in Bosnia. To many, camps meant Nazis, reinforcing our argument for a Nuremberg-style tribunal. In October 1992, the UN Security Council established a Commission of Experts to collect evidence of war crimes; in December, U.S. Acting Secretary of State Lawrence Eagleburger joined the call to establish a tribunal; in January 1993, Bill Clinton was inaugurated as president and his appointee to serve as ambassador to the United Nations, Madeleine Albright, took up the effort to create the tribunal and made it her cause, taking pride in becoming known as "the mother of the tribunal"; in February, the UN Security Council authorized the creation of the International Criminal Tribunal for the former Yugoslavia (ICTY); and in May the Security Council approved a specific plan for its operation.

Then things ground to a halt. It took fourteen months from its approval of a plan until the United Nations designated a chief prosecutor. The delay was nearly fatal. Victims and perpetrators alike shrugged off the possibility that justice would be done. If anyone paid attention elsewhere in the world—say, in Rwanda, where the genocide began after the UN dilly-dallied for nearly a year and ended before a prosecutor was appointed—they would have concluded that the Security Council was not serious about bringing to justice those who commit genocidal crimes. The effort lost credibility among Western governments and the Western public. As the Tribunal depended on their support if its bills were to be paid and if UN and NATO troops in Bosnia were to arrest those indicted and bring them to The Hague for trial, it urgently needed to make its mark. It could not do so without someone in charge of bringing indictments.

Conflicting agendas of important member states of the UN were largely responsible for the delay. Russia blocked designation of anyone from a NATO state. Pakistan blocked appointment of a former attorney general of India. An Egyptian-American authority on international criminal law was passed over as a Muslim who might appear biased. Several potential appointees were rejected because their own governments failed to back them. At one point, the Security Council seemed ready to designate a Brazilian lawyer proposed by the Brazilian ambassador to the UN. Checking with human rights colleagues in Brazil, I discovered they considered him third-rate; worse, he was closely identified with the country's former military dictatorship. I called my longtime ACLU colleague John Shattuck, then assistant secretary of state for human rights, and through him, arranged for the United States to block his appointment.

Eventually, in July 1994, the deadlock was broken. Judge Richard Goldstone of South Africa became the chief prosecutor for ICTY. Though I knew and admired Goldstone, it had not occurred to me to propose him. Up to then, it was not possible for a South African to be appointed to a UN post. That had changed, however, when Nelson Mandela became president two months earlier. Goldstone's name was suggested by a prominent French lawyer, Roger Herrera. As Goldstone had Mandela's strong backing, Russia did not stand in the way.

Though Goldstone was not a prosecutor in South Africa and lacked a background in the laws of war, he turned out to be an inspired choice as he gave the Tribunal what it needed most: credibility. A successful commercial litigator in South Africa, Richard was appointed a High Court judge during the apartheid era. His performance in that post, in which his decisions were constrained by the requirement of his country's legal system whereby judges must enforce the laws enacted by Parliament and may not invalidate legislative enactments because they conflict with a higher law, had earned him wide acclaim. In 1991, the year following the release of Nelson Mandela from prison, Richard's record made him the unanimous choice of all the groups in a National Peace Accord of political, church, and civic groups to head a Standing Commission of Inquiry Regarding the Prevention of Public Violence and Intimidation. That body became known as the Goldstone Commission. It had a crucial part in making possible the mostly peaceful transition to majority rule in 1994 that ended apartheid and resulted in the election of Mandela as president.

Richard Goldstone's commission uncovered the role of the police in fomenting and organizing much of the "black on black" violence between the Inkatha Freedom Party and the African National Congress that had cost as many as 20,000 lives. By chance, I happened to visit Richard in the commission's office in Johannesburg on the morning in February 1994, two months before the election, when he telephoned Mandela to let him know about an important development. Richard was about to announce that he had identified the number two officer of the South Africa Police Service as the leader of this deadly covert campaign.

Richard's reputation in South Africa for fairness and firmness served him well at the Tribunal. As chief prosecutor, he spent much of his time on the road meeting with governments, intergovernmental bodies, bar associations, human rights groups, and journalists. He was also needed in The Hague to give day-to-day direction to the international staff of lawyers and investigators assembled for the Tribunal, and his frequent absences created certain difficulties. I often wished he could clone himself so his double would stick to the office. Yet I believe he made the right choice in devoting much of his time to building the image of the Tribunal and to negotiating with the officials whose cooperation the Tribunal required. This salesmanship was essential if the Tribunal was to succeed. Governments had to pay its bills, and the cooperation of those that furnished troops to the UN and to NATO in Bosnia was required if indicted defendants were to be apprehended and brought to The Hague to stand trial. More than almost anyone I know, Richard projects bulldog tenacity. At that moment, being a white South African who had contributed mightily to an historic transition and who enjoyed Mandela's confidence was of no small significance. Though the Tribunal had accomplished little, he inspired confidence that it would succeed, just as, against all odds, the opponents of apartheid had succeeded in their peaceful revolution.

Notwithstanding Richard's persuasive gifts, the Tribunal also urgently needed to show tangible results. It did not hand down its first indictment until November 8, 1994, a year and a half after it was established. The same day, the Tribunal announced it would ask Germany to turn over to it for trial Duško Tadić, a former middle-level official at Omarska, the most notorious of the detention camps maintained by the Bosnian Serbs. Tadić, who was accused of many atrocities, was, fortuitously, apprehended by German authorities in Munich the previous February after he was recognized on the street by survivors of Omarska. For a long time, he was the only defendant in the custody of the Tribunal. It appeared for a while he might remain the only one.

I kept in close touch with Richard during this period and urged him to seek indictments against the main architects of ethnic cleansing. The indictments handed down in the first year following his appointment focused on low-ranking officials—"corporals," in the dismissive comment I heard from one of the Tribunal's critics. This order of business may be appropriate in ordinary organized crime cases, as it is a way to make deals that inculpate mob leaders. It was a mistake for ICTY, however, because the Tribunal lacked custody over those whom it indicted and could make no deals; moreover, it could not be sure it ever would get custody of those who were implicated. If it did get hold of them, deals might still be inappropriate because of the nature of the crimes committed. The leaders who bore the highest responsibility for criminality needed to be named in indictments. This would discredit them and increase the credibility of the Tribunal by showing it would go after the main authors of the bestiality in ex-Yugoslavia.

Richard invited me to The Hague to discuss the issue with his senior prosecutors. I met in his office with about ten of them. We talked for two hours about the legal criteria for establishing command responsibility for war crimes. Subsequently, I enlisted others familiar with international humanitarian law issues to take part in such conversations with the prosecutors, most of whom had no background in this field. Eventually, in July 1995, Richard announced the indictment of Bosnian Serb "President" Radovan Karadzić and military chieftain General Ratko Mladić. I believe those indictments were crucial in complementing Richard's public advocacy by demonstrating that the Tribunal meant business. Yet I wish those indictments had come a bit sooner. The massacre of 8,000 Bosnian Muslim men and boys at Srebrenica, the worst crime in Europe since World War II, took place in the two weeks prior to the indictment under the direct supervision of General Mladić. I can't help wondering whether some who took part might have thought twice about carrying out his orders if he had already been indicted for genocide. Some months later, Karadzić and Mladić were indicted again for Srebrenica, and one of Mladić's confederates, General Radislav Krstić, subsequently got a forty-six-year prison sentence for his part in the massacre. It was the first conviction for genocide by the Yugoslav Tribunal.

During the period that Richard was promoting the Tribunal, I was doing what I could to back his effort. I gave many talks about the Tribunal, including in Sarajevo (where I conducted a seminar for lawyers on the Tribunal in April 1993, the month before the Security Council approved a plan for its operation), Zagreb, and Belgrade. Those who listened to me in places such as Sarajevo were polite, but I know they were skeptical. They were besieged, the Serbs were winning the war, so how was it possible their triumphant tormentors would ever be put on trial for their crimes? Probably they thought I was just trying to cheer them up. I also helped form new organizations that supported the work of the Tribunal—such as a group called the Coalition for International Justice, which a division of the American Bar Association agreed to sponsor—and persuaded a number of established groups to assist it. When the Tribunal was derided as ineffectual, I rose to its defense. An example was an exchange in *The New York Review of Books* with Columbia University historian Istvan Deak. In an article on Nuremberg, Deak scoffed at the Tribunal for ex-Yugoslavia, saying its establishment by the UN "smacks of cynicism and hypocrisy."[6] I wrote a lengthy response defending the Tribunal to which Deak responded in turn, comparing it to "the sorry example of the 1967 Stockholm War-Crimes Trial when, under the presidency of Jean-Paul Sartre, a seventeen-person jury listened to charges against the United States."[7]

Several years later, I was pleased to get a letter from Professor Deak acknowledging that he had been mistaken and that events had proved me right about the Tribunal. I answered, confessing that, when we debated, I had my own doubts. Yet I thought I had to rise to the Tribunal's defense if it was to get a chance to fulfill my hopes for it. The same concerns lay behind my talks about the Tribunal in war-torn ex-Yugoslavia. It could only succeed if Richard Goldstone and those like me who were committed to its success could persuade others that it should be taken seriously.

By the time Richard stepped down as chief prosecutor in late 1996, fulfilling a commitment he'd made to President Nelson Mandela to resume his place on the South African Constitutional Court, the Tribunal had achieved a measure of credibility. Its reputation was enhanced by the support of Tony Blair in Britain, who became prime minister in 1997. The previous British government under Prime Minister John Major had provided only token support for the Tribunal and seemed ready to negotiate away its existence as part of the effort to settle the Bosnian War. When Blair and his foreign secretary, Robin Cook, assumed office, British troops in Bosnia took the lead in arresting those indicted by the Tribunal. Other governments, including the United States and, at a later point, even France—which had been actively hostile—were embarrassed into following the British lead, though they did not do much. U.S. Secretary of State Madeleine Albright wanted the United States to do more, but the Department of Defense under William Cohen was reluctant to risk retaliation against U.S. troops stationed in Bosnia. Albright could not get the backing from President Clinton that Prime Minister Blair gave to Cook. Despite such difficulties, at this writing, most of those publicly indicted by the Tribunal have been taken into custody, including, of course, Slobodan Milošević. Some are serving sentences, while others, such as the former Yugoslav president, are on trial or still awaiting it. In the period right after they were indicted, Karadzić and Mladić moved about Bosnia freely, flaunting their invulnerability. No longer. The change of NATO policy led by Britain forced Mladić to flee to Serbia and Karadzić into hiding. Since Milošević's arrest, Mladić's whereabouts have not been known. He may be back in Bosnia.

From the mid-1980s to the mid-1990s, the global trend, following events in Argentina, was to avoid justice and to focus on official disclosure of the truth. In the late 1990s and at the beginning of the twenty-first century, the prestige achieved by the Tribunal for ex-Yugoslavia has made doing justice again the focus of many efforts to establish accountability. In some countries, among them South Africa and Guatemala, the political arrangements that accompanied negotiated settlements blocked most prosecutions. Yet even in those countries, they were not ruled out, and a few prosecutions and convictions have taken place.

Though long delayed, a justice process is now under way in Chile. It was set in motion by the arrest of Pinochet in London in October 1998 for possible extradition to Spain to stand trial for his crimes in Chile. The detention of the former dictator, and the subsequent ruling by the British Law Lords that his status as a former head of state did not confer immunity on him and upholding universal jurisdiction to try those who commit such crimes as torture, seemed to embolden and liberate the Chilean judiciary. Secret-police officials were arrested for crimes committed subsequent to—and therefore not covered by—Pinochet's amnesty decree. Among them was General Humberto Gordon, former director of the secret police. Military officers were arrested for disappearances during the period covered by the amnesty; as the bodies of the disappeared were never found, the courts held that the abductions were continuing crimes therefore not covered by the amnesty. (In an effort to evade such prosecutions, military officials have revealed what happened to some of their victims and have disclosed the location of their remains, contradicting their previous denials of knowledge or culpability.)

Those jailed include senior officers involved in notorious crimes of the Pinochet era, such as the so-called "Caravan of Death." Other courts found new ways to limit application of the amnesty decree, and Pinochet himself was stripped of his immunity from prosecution by a judicial ruling upheld by the country's Supreme Court. "The mere witnessing of Pinochet's arrest and arraignment, his submission to the law like any mortal, broke his aura of invulnerability, shattering the terror with which he had poisoned our hearts," according to Chilean novelist Ariel Dorfman.[8] Though the aging former dictator has avoided trial due to mental incompetence (dementia), the court cases against him have already yielded most of the results they could achieve by demonstrating that he is not above the law and by humiliating him.

A justice process also resumed in Argentina, where a number of senior military officers were arrested in 1999 and 2000 for a crime not covered by the pardons a decade earlier: kidnapping the children of the disappeared. It was the practice in Argentina when pregnant women were abducted to allow the mothers to give birth and then to execute them immediately. The newborn infants were given to military families seeking children to adopt. A group known as the Grandmothers of the Plaza de Mayo pursued a demand for information on more than 200 such cases and, with the help of DNA testing, secured the return of some children to their natural families. Among the officers arrested were two former junta members pardoned by President Menem: former President Videla and Admiral Emilio Massera, the former commander of the Navy and one of those with the most blood on his hands. A leading Navy torturer, Ricardo Miguel Cavallo, was arrested in Cancun, Mexico, on August 24, 2000, for extradition to Spain to stand trial for his crimes two decades earlier. He was indicted there by Baltasar Garzón, the prosecutor who had launched the criminal proceedings against Pinochet two years earlier. After democracy was restored to Argentina in 1983, Cavallo had moved to Mexico, where he entered government service. He was apprehended after a local newspaper carried a photo of him in connection with his appointment to direct the country's national motor vehicle bureau. Torture victims living in Mexico recognized him from the photo. When he realized he faced extradition, he caught a plane to Argentina in an attempt to take advantage of the pardons issued by President Menem, but he was arrested by Mexican police when his flight stopped at Cancun. Cavallo's arrest highlighted the irony that, in the era of universal jurisdiction, amnesties and pardons make the authors of great crimes safer in the countries where their crimes were committed than in the lands where they seek new identities or attempt to take refuge.

Developments in Argentina and Chile, and the readiness of Mexican authorities to comply with an arrest warrant issued by a Spanish judge, reflect the momentum internationally to prosecute and punish those responsible for the gravest crimes. Building directly on the precedent of the Tribunal for ex-Yugoslavia, in November 1994 the UN Security Council established a Tribunal for Rwanda. It, too, got off to a bad start but, over time, righted itself. Most of those who organized and directed the 1994 genocide are now behind bars, either awaiting trial or serving long sentences. The Rwanda Tribunal's work now contributes to the growing support for efforts to do justice. The success of the first two ad hoc criminal tribunals paved the way for establishment of the permanent International Criminal Court and for the proceedings against General Pinochet. Another special tribunal with international participation has been established in Sierra Leone to deal with the horrible crimes that devastated that country. Though its birth process has been difficult, yet another such tribunal may come into existence in Cambodia to deal with the crimes of the Khmer Rouge going back to the 1970s.

In this climate, a number of European governments have demonstrated renewed interest in prosecuting some of those still alive who committed war crimes during World War II. In 1999, a British court exercising universal jurisdiction convicted Anthony Sawoniuk, an immigrant from Belarus, for Nazi war crimes in his homeland in 1942. France convicted a former high-ranking official, Maurice Papon, for crimes against humanity (only the second Frenchman convicted on such charges and the first case in which a French court recognized that the crimes were committed under French authority). And Croatia convicted Dinko Šakić for his crimes at the Jasenovac death camp more than a half century earlier.

The last of these is the most remarkable. Jasenovac was the Auschwitz of Yugoslavia. Tens of thousands of Serbs, Jews, and Gypsies were burned alive, clubbed to death, gassed, or murdered in other ways at Jasenovac by Croatian officials of the fascist Ustasha regime that collaborated with the Nazis. Before 1999, no one associated with Jasenovac was ever prosecuted and punished for the crimes there. Though Croatia's late strongman, Franjo Tudjman, fought the Ustashas as a young partisan, as president he never acknowledged what happened at Jasenovac and did not allow the site to be marked as a memorial to its victims. When Šakić, who commanded Jasenovac, was apprehended in Argentina, he may have expected a hero's welcome when he was returned to Croatia. Instead, under international scrutiny, the Tudjman government put him on trial. For a time, it seemed nothing would come of this as the prosecution presented little evidence against Šakić. The case was transformed, however, by the intervention of survivors of Jasenovac, as is their right under Croatian law. Represented by a prominent Zagreb attorney, Cedo Prodanovic, they testified against Šakić, presenting a strong case against him. With Tudjman's nationalist government still in power, Šakić was convicted and got the maximum sentence.

On April 11, 2002, the requirement for sixty countries to ratify the treaty for the International Criminal Court (ICC) adopted in Rome in July 1998 was surpassed, allowing establishment of the court. The major obstacle to ratification was the hostility of the United States, which claimed that a politicized prosecutor could run amok and indict U.S. soldiers, who have a special role to play worldwide as the guarantors of international security. In fact, the treaty for the court has many safeguards against politically motivated prosecutions. Its jurisdiction is limited to genocide, crimes against humanity (by definition, crimes committed on a large scale), or war crimes. The latter are only subject to the court's jurisdiction if committed on a large scale or pursuant to policy in circumstances of armed conflict. The ICC is required to abstain if a government acts in good faith to investigate and try its own nationals for these offenses. One three-judge panel must authorize investigations by the prosecutor, and another must act before charges may be brought. The judges and the prosecutor are chosen by the governments that accept the jurisdiction of the ICC. This means the rogue governments most likely to favor politically motivated prosecutions are excluded from the process.

The claim that the United States is particularly vulnerable because of its global role is misleading. U.S. troops are stationed in countries such as Germany, Japan, and South Korea under long-standing security agreements. But as these countries are at peace, crimes that Americans may commit there are not war crimes and it is inconceivable that U.S. troops based there would commit crimes against humanity or genocide. The United States infrequently contributes troops for peacekeeping purposes; at this writing, there are fewer than 700 Americans participating in United Nations peacekeeping missions worldwide. This role is taken up far more often by governments that are among the foremost supporters of the ICC, such as Australia, Canada, the Netherlands, Norway, and Sweden. Britain and France, which are also leading advocates of the ICC, provided most of the troops that served in Bosnia while the war there was under way. U.S. troops were first dispatched there after the 1995 Dayton Accords ended the conflict.

The most effective argument I have seen against universal jurisdiction and the International Criminal Court was made in an essay by Henry Kissinger in *Foreign Affairs*.[9] Kissinger is particularly critical of the decision of the British Law Lords in the Pinochet case. Noting that the request to extradite Pinochet was initiated by a Spanish judge, Kissinger pointed out

> the incongruity of a request by Spain itself haunted by transgressions committed during the Spanish Civil War and the regime of General Francisco Franco, to try in Spanish courts alleged crimes against humanity committed elsewhere. The decision of post-Franco Spain to avoid wholesale criminal trials for the human rights violations of the recent past was designed explicitly to foster a process of national reconciliation that undoubtedly contributed much to the present vigor of Spanish democracy. Why should Chile's attempt at national reconciliation not have been given the same opportunity?

Another issue raised by Kissinger is selectivity. He wrote, "When discretion on what crimes are subject to universal jurisdiction and whom to prosecute is left to national prosecutors, the scope for arbitrariness is wide indeed. So far, universal jurisdiction has involved the prosecution of one fashionably reviled man of the right while scores of East European communist leaders—not to speak of Caribbean, Middle Eastern, or African leaders who inflicted their own full measures of torture and suffering—have not had to face similar prosecutions." Above all, Kissinger opposed the effort to replace politics with law, arguing that, "The role of the statesman is to choose the best option when seeking to advance peace and justice, realizing that there is frequently a tension between the two." Though unenthusiastic about the International Criminal Court because of what he terms "prosecutorial discretion without accountability," Kissinger acknowledged that, "To the extent that the ICC replaces the claim of national judges to universal jurisdiction, it greatly improves the state of international law."

Though these are serious objections, there are answers to them. In the case of Spain, a transition did not occur until nearly four decades after the crimes of the Spanish Civil War. By then many of the perpetrators—including the arch perpetrator—victims, and witnesses, were dead. A new constitution, which first provided the possibility of choice, was not adopted until December 1978, more than three years after Franco's death. The situation in Chile was very different. A transition took place when Pinochet's crimes were much fresher, in circumstances in which the principal author of those crimes had unilaterally decreed an amnesty for his own offenses, retained his military command under a constitution he put in place, and threatened reprisals against anyone who sought to hold him or the armed forces accountable. Whereas reconciliation took place gradually in Spain in circumstances in which a *ruptura* (to use the Spanish term) was avoided, it was taken under duress in Chile. Thereby, Pinochet rubbed salt in the wounds of his victims.

Kissinger is mistaken in asserting that the prosecution of Pinochet was unique. In addition to the United Kingdom and Spain, both of which have invoked universal jurisdiction in cases other than Pinochet's, Belgium, Germany, and Switzerland are among the European governments that have brought such prosecutions. Though the case has not fared well, a former African dictator, Hissein Habré of Chad, has been prosecuted in another African country, Senegal, under principles of universal jurisdiction. Those principles were endorsed by the United States in 1990 in ratifying the Convention Against Torture, which obligates parties to adopt measures to ensure that torturers within their territory are held legally ac-

countable for their acts. Though our country lacks implementing legislation providing criminal sanctions, Congress did adopt, and President
George H.W. Bush signed, the Torture Victims Protection Act in 1992,
which provides civil remedies for victims of torture in other countries.
Even before the law was adopted, a number of such cases were brought
successfully in U.S. courts.

I think there is merit to the concern Kissinger expressed about bringing
the policy role of officials into the judicial process. On those grounds,
among others, I have declined to join those such as journalist Christopher
Hitchens who call for the prosecution of Kissinger himself as a war criminal. There is a need to distinguish, I believe, between policies that lead to
the commission of war crimes and criminal responsibility for those crimes.
Also, some of the crimes in Vietnam of which Kissinger is accused were
not generally recognized internationally as war crimes until the adoption
in 1977 of the Protocols additional to the Geneva Conventions. By then,
of course, the Vietnam War had ended. I condemn Kissinger for the policies he promoted in Vietnam, East Timor, and Chile, but given what is
known about his activities, I am uncertain they form the basis for criminal
charges.

Kissinger's implicit proposal that the International Criminal Court
should replace national judges in exercising universal jurisdiction is worthy of consideration. This resembles a suggestion by Ken Roth that the
ICC should have a role in determining whether national prosecutions
should go forward. It would help ensure that the jurisprudence in a novel
but extremely important area of the law develops in coherent rather than
arbitrary fashion. (From Kissinger's personal perspective, there is another
advantage to leaving such matters to the ICC that he does not mention.
The ICC's jurisdiction is exclusively prospective. It cannot consider crimes,
such as those of which Kissinger is accused, committed prior to the ratification of the treaty creating it.)

I n recent years, my position at the Open Society Institute has afforded me the opportunity to assist those worldwide promoting accountability. It is clear that no single formula is appropriate in all
circumstances. In many situations there are constraints that limit the capacity to do justice. I agree with José Zalaquett, who has argued that truth

must be "known, complete, officially sanctioned and publicly exposed." At the same time, I am gratified that, increasingly in the past several years, after a decade in which many argued that it was impossible or inappropriate to prosecute, try, and punish the authors of even the gravest crimes, it is also possible to do justice.

CHAPTER TWELVE

Contacting the Underground in Poland

T he only time Yvette accompanied me on a human rights mission was on a visit to Poland in March 1984. Though Warsaw in March in that grim era shortly after the end of martial law was not a popular holiday destination, we pretended to be tourists. Her presence helped mask my purpose in going. As Yvette is of French origin, her fluency aided in conversations with older intellectuals, many of whom spoke the traditional language of the Polish elite.

Martial law was imposed in Poland in December 1981 to crush the Solidarity movement that had functioned openly for the previous sixteen months. The movement had enlisted an amazing 10 million members and had given the country its first experience of freedom in the more than four decades since the beginning of World War II. The decree of a state of war was formally lifted on the Polish national holiday in July 1983, and some political prisoners were released. In practice, little changed. A week before martial law ended, a new law on the operation of the Ministry of Internal Affairs and its organs provided that the Security Service (secret police) and the Citizens Militia (civil police) were not only to prevent and prosecute crimes but also to maintain surveillance over citizens and all aspects of public life.

The Penal Code was amended to add a number of new crimes, including "activity aimed at provoking public disorder or riots"; "organizing or leading a protest action carried out contrary to the legal regulations"; "participating in an association which has been dissolved or which has been refused legal status"; and "publishing or distributing a newspaper, magazine or other publication without necessary permission." Violations carried three-year prison sentences. Several new misdemeanor offenses were also enacted: putting up advertisements, posters, signs, or drawings in a public place without permission of the authorities; paying a fine for another person or organizing the collection of money for such a purpose; and taking part in an assembly organized without permission of the authorities. Another provision of the Code of Misdemeanors, previously enacted, prohibited wearing insignia or uniforms that did not have official sanction. This was used to prosecute those found wearing a button or an article of clothing with Solidarity's distinctive logo. Offenses were tried in Misdemeanor Courts, administrative tribunals attached to local government bodies operating under the supervision of the Ministry of the Interior that afforded no protections for the rights of defendants. Those convicted could be jailed for three-month periods.

Despite severe repression, there were signs that a lively underground movement was flourishing. My purpose in going to Poland was to contact leaders of this movement to determine how we might provide support and to call attention in the West to its existence and its activities. It was, I believe, the first visit to Poland by anyone associated with an international human rights group in the more than two years since martial law had been declared. No one had wanted to take the risk of endangering the Poles who would be contacted. I decided to go because we had received a message that it was time to break the isolation.

En route, Yvette and I stopped in Paris to see several Polish émigrés. As we sat talking to one of them, he used a paper clip to pull the tobacco out of a cigarette. This seemed odd, but we did not say anything. Eventually, we realized what he was doing. Taking a long, narrow sheet of very fine paper, he wrote out a message in tiny script, rolled it tight, fit it into the cigarette, tamped some tobacco back over the message, and put the cigarette back into a pack of Gauloises. He repeated this with another cigarette from a pack of Gitanes. The cigarettes were to be given to designated contacts in Warsaw.

Our first stop in Warsaw was the home of the man who got the Gauloises. As in all our visits, we took great care in going to see him. I carried his address and those of the others I was to see in encrypted form. We made no contact with him in advance. Using a detailed map of Warsaw I had brought with me, we picked a spot some distance from his home. Instead of taking a taxi there from our hotel, we flagged one down on the street, then waved it off and took another. All the time, we kept a lookout to see if we were being followed. Yet when we reached his apartment, I soon realized I was not cut out for this sort of thing. As I handed him the pack of Gauloises, he ripped it open and before either of us could say a word, lit up. With visions of the carefully written message going up in smoke, I tried to stop him without saying why in case his apartment was bugged. Fortunately, the lit cigarette was not the one with the message.

The recipient of the Gauloises was Konstanty ("Kostek") Gebert, a journalist with whom I have worked on a number of projects sponsored by the Open Society Institute in recent years. That was my first encounter with him. He spoke perfect idiomatic English as his parents were Americans of Polish origin and Communists who had returned to Poland after World War II to take part in building the workers' state. Their son had become a dissident against communism and was then a columnist for the underground Solidarity press under the pen name David Warshawski. If Yvette and I had been followed despite our precautions, our visit to Kostek could fit the pretense of tourism. Some American Jews went to Poland to see what was left of the homes of their parents or grandparents and to visit such sites as the Warsaw Ghetto. Going to see Kostek was a logical stop on such an itinerary as he led the country's tiny Jewish consciousness movement. This made it natural for him to receive foreign visitors. It was the reason I chose to see him first.

Over the next several days, we went to many homes—always unannounced and, therefore, not always finding at home those whom we wished to see. We aborted one visit when our taxi driver, who had indicated that he spoke no English, seemed to understand what we were saying. As we passed a drunk, Yvette said, "Poor man. He'll have such a headache." In the rearview mirror, we saw a small smile cross the driver's face. That was enough. We reserved until the end of our visit stops where we were sure to come under surveillance, such as those to families of prominent political prisoners.

One of the family members we went to see was Zofia Romaszewska, wife of Zbigniew Romaszewski, a scientist who had founded the Polish Helsinki Committee three years earlier at the suggestion of Jeri Laber and today a member of the Polish Senate. He was then among those facing the gravest charges for his leading role in Solidarity. Shortly before I went to Poland, I had lunch with an American lawyer friend, the late Alan Finberg, general counsel of the *Washington Post*, who told me that as a member of Amnesty, he had "adopted" a prisoner of conscience in Poland, Romaszewski. In the fashion of such adoptions, Alan regularly wrote letters on Romaszewski's behalf. He was delighted when I told him Romaszewski's wife was on the list of those whom I planned to see in Warsaw.

Sitting at her dining table, I asked Zofia whether she was aware of any foreign efforts on her husband's behalf. Yes, she said, she knew of two people who had written letters for her husband: One was a man in the Falkland Islands and another was an American lawyer, Alan Finberg. It felt very good to be able to say I knew him and to tell her something about a person who had dedicated himself to looking out for Zbigniew's welfare though he had never met him. Whether or not the letters by Alan and the man in the Falklands ever made a difference in his treatment, the fact that two people in remote parts of the world had engaged in efforts on his behalf plainly mattered to his wife. The episode deepened my appreciation for Amnesty's way of enlisting its members in its work.

Most of the people we dropped in on were very pleased to see us and all quickly sized up the purpose of our visit and invited us in. Several visits were to the homes of lawyers, some associated with the Helsinki Committee, which had been founded by Romaszewski. In contrast to other Communist countries, Poland had never completely corrupted its legal profession. Some lawyers practiced independently and provided effective legal representation to those charged with political crimes. Others we went to see were journalists like Kostek Gebert. One who made a particularly strong impression on us was Darius Fikusz, the editor of a magazine for the blind published in Braille. He had been a leader of the journalists association but, as a critic of the regime and its abuses of human rights, he had been removed from his post by the state. The only publication where he had been able to find employment was the magazine for the blind. I was told that under Fikusz, this journal was the most outspoken published legally. Perhaps there was a shortage of censors who could read Braille. Fikusz was arrested a few days after we left Warsaw. We worried that his arrest could have been due to our visit, but as best we could discover, it was unconnected.

One visit seemed to take place at an inopportune moment. We arrived at the home of the leading underground book publisher, Grzegorz Boguta, in the middle of a birthday party for his young son. Boguta was momentarily upset, but on reflection he decided our timing was good. A number of couples were coming and going to drop off and pick up children; anyone watching his apartment might think we were among them.

Covered up against the cold and rain of Warsaw in March, and carrying umbrellas, our appearance did not immediately give us away. With the party under way in the next room, Boguta talked to me in the kitchen with the water running. At another home, we met with lawyers active in the underground Polish Helsinki Committee, whose well-researched reports we published in the United States in English translation before, during, and after martial law. Our host pointed to the ceiling—a gesture used in much of the world to indicate the presence of bugging devices—and played a record of a Tchaikovsky symphony very loud as we talked. This made me appreciate the advantage that International Committee of the Red Cross delegates derived from speaking to each other in "Swiss German," a kitchen language unintelligible to anyone else, or the ability of an Irish priest in El Salvador whom I once visited to conduct a phone conversation with a fellow priest in Gaelic.

Leaving Poland, Yvette and I traveled separately. I carried her suitcase as I had discovered I could hide some documents I wanted to take out of the country in its lining. At the airport all bags of travelers leaving the country were searched. I had a choice of two lines. At both, the uniformed guards searching the bags were women. One was young and pretty; the other, large, tough looking, and scowling. I mentally identified her as Ana Pauker for the formidable, unsmiling Comintern leader of the 1950s. Watching both women methodically searching the luggage of those ahead of me in line, I had ample time to grow increasingly pessimistic about my prospects of getting through with the documents. Just as my turn came, Ana Pauker accidentally dropped her rubber stamp on the floor. Without thinking, I bent down and picked it up for her. She gave me a big smile and waved me through.

When I returned to the United States, I published several articles about the underground movement in Poland. In one that appeared in the *New York Times*,[1] I argued that Solidarity had not been destroyed by martial law, but its struggle had entered a new phase. "The current phase," I wrote,

> is not marked by the effort to build democratic institutions that was the essential aim of Solidarity in the 16 months prior to martial law. . . . Their main aim is to enlist other Poles in 'independent' underground activities. Hundreds of underground periodicals are being published more or less regularly. Scores of new titles are added annually to the already rich library of underground book publishing, some of them in quantities that would

seem respectable to Western commercial publishers. Living room theater, underground cabaret and unofficial art exhibits are flourishing. Tens of thousands of Poles attend unofficial adult education classes.

A crucial feature of Solidarity was that it was a worker-led labor union in which intellectuals played important roles. Their alliance had been formed a few years before the emergence of Solidarity, in 1976, when worker protests against a government announcement of dramatic increases in food prices led to hundreds of arrests. In response, a small group of prominent intellectuals, including the philosopher Leszek Kołakowski, the historians Jacek Kuroń and Adam Michnik, and the journalist Thadeusz Mazowiecki, formed the Workers Defense Committee, known by its Polish initials, KOR. Kołakowski left Poland, but when Solidarity was formed, Kuroń, Michnik, Mazowiecki, and such leading scholars as the medievalist Bronislaw Geremek became key advisers. When martial law was declared, many intellectuals were arrested. At the time of my March 1984 visit two years later, Kuroń and Michnik were among those still in prison. They were released not long thereafter but were rearrested six months later on charges of attempting to overthrow the government. The regime made a strategic mistake in persecuting them, I thought, as it reinforced the view among Polish workers that intellectuals were ready to endure the same suffering they faced. They were united in struggle. This was especially significant in Poland where the gulf dividing workers and intellectuals had historically been far wider than elsewhere.

In 1978, Adam Michnik helped to found Poland's famed "Flying University," which presented uncensored lectures in private apartments. In my *Times* article, however, I pointed out that:

The term 'flying university,' which antedates Solidarity, is no longer used because most of the students in today's unofficial classes are not taking university-level courses. Many are factory workers—a matter of some pride to the organizers of the classes. Indeed they regard the links that were forged between workers and intellectuals as one of the great achievements of the period before martial law.

How many people take part regularly in such independent activity? It is impossible to say for certain, but the estimates one hears in Poland range from 200,000 to about one million. The higher figure represents those who are thought to pay monthly dues to underground Solidarity; the lower number represents those who go further and spend some time each month putting out or distributing an independent book or periodical, or attending a class or in some other way acting outside the institutions of the state.

The underground periodicals impressed me the most. In several homes I visited in Warsaw, a prominent artifact was a large magnifying glass. This was needed to read newspapers such as *Tygodnik Mazowse* (Warsaw Weekly), probably the most influential, and the most enduring, of the underground periodicals that began appearing under martial law. To conserve paper and to facilitate clandestine distribution, as much information as possible was crammed on a page. It was virtually unreadable without a magnifying glass. As many as 60,000 copies of each issue were distributed.

I got a glimpse of how information was circulated to provincial towns when I visited a bookstore near Warsaw's central railroad station. Visitors from around the country came to Warsaw by train, stopped in the bookstore, bought a book, and in the process picked up copies of feature articles, columns, and cartoons they could reproduce in their local publications. In 1984 and 1985, according to an archivist for *Tygodnik Mazowse*, 650 titles were published, though only some 210 endured throughout this period. At any given time, about 400 periodicals were being published. Police activity was but one factor in the demise of many of these publications. Some fell by the wayside simply because of competition from other better-produced periodicals.

To Poles, this phenomenon had a particular historic resonance. It meant a new generation was following in the footsteps of the World War II resistance to the Nazis. As Czeslaw Milosz has pointed out, "The underground press in occupied Poland was a phenomenon unique in Europe, both for its wide circulation and for the number of its printing shops. It reflected a large spectrum of political opinions, including those of the right and the extreme right. This did not happen in other countries where the extreme right collaborated with the Nazis."[2] Kostek Gebert proudly told me on that March 1984 visit that a printing press the British had brought into Poland during World War II for use by the underground press of that era was still functional and back in use by underground Solidarity.

One way we tried to assist the Polish underground was by supporting economic sanctions. Although Americas Watch was at sword's point with the Reagan administration over human rights in Latin America, Helsinki Watch found officials in the State Department and the National Security Council more than ready to take strong stands on abuses by Communist regimes. I believe the manner in which sanctions were imposed against Poland by the Reagan administration is a textbook example.

The administration announced the sanctions in early 1982, soon after martial law was declared, at a time when an estimated 30,000 Poles had been rounded up and summarily imprisoned. The sanctions included denial of most-favored-nation trading status, purchases of grain on credit, direct financial assistance, transfer of high technology, fishing rights in American waters, and landing rights for LOT Polish Airlines at American airports. Most important, the United States canceled talks on rescheduling the Polish debt and said it would oppose Polish access to the International Monetary Fund (IMF).

Prior to martial law, Poland had enjoyed closer economic relations with the United States than any other Soviet bloc state. This connection reflected the influence of a large Polish immigrant population that maintained ties to the homeland. It also derived from the policies of the Communist leader of the 1970s, Edward Gierek, who was much more sympathetic to the import of Western consumer products than other Soviet bloc leaders. In addition, Washington recognized that Poland, where agriculture was never collectivized and where the Catholic Church was a powerful institution preserving independent space for its own activities, was not as monolithic as other Communist countries. The Reagan administration attempted to enlist European collaboration in imposing sanctions, but this effort was largely a failure. A publicity campaign by the United States on the theme "Let Poland Be Poland" was mocked in Europe by demonstrators chanting, "Let Central America Be Central America." Yet Poland's economic ties to the United States made the country vulnerable to unilateral sanctions.

The Reagan administration gave Poland specific conditions for the removal of sanctions: lifting martial law; releasing all political prisoners; and entering into a dialogue with Solidarity and the Catholic Church. Our one significant quarrel with the administration over sanctions took place in June 1983 when the reference to Solidarity was dropped. Instead, the administration said sanctions would be eased if Poland "took meaningful liberalizing measures."

When martial law was formally lifted and some political prisoners were

252 TAKING LIBERTIES

released, the administration responded with minor concessions. The most significant ended exclusion of the Polish fishing fleet from American waters. Given the harsh new laws introduced at the same time, no more was warranted. In July 1984, however, again on Poland's national holiday, a large number of the remaining political prisoners were released, reducing the number still confined for their role in Solidarity to about thirty. The administration responded that LOT could land at Kennedy Airport in New York and, more significantly, suggested it might withdraw its objections to Polish entry into the IMF. Such measured responses continued until all the political prisoners were released. Eventually, on February 17, 1987, the Reagan administration announced an end to all sanctions.

What made these sanctions effective, I believe, is that they were based on specific, declared human rights objectives that the Polish government could meet, and they were not maintained on an all-or-nothing basis. They were calibrated. Progress in meeting the objectives was rewarded by modification of the sanctions. The contrast with the performance of the Bush and Clinton administrations with respect to China after Tiananmen Square (see Chapter 14, "Suffering Defeat Over China") is striking.

Though the requirement for new negotiations with Solidarity was deleted early as an explicit goal of the sanctions, the changes brought about by the end to political imprisonment created an opening that led to new negotiations anyway. These in turn led to elections, which Solidarity contested and won overwhelmingly, bringing a peaceful end to the Communist regime. As is widely recognized, Poland was the pacesetter for the region. The transition there paved the way for the revolutions of 1989 throughout Eastern Europe.

I believe that the underground newspaper and book publishers, the participants in Poland's rich underground cultural life, and all those who took part in myriad other unofficial activities of Poland's parallel society contributed to the downfall of communism and the end of the Cold War. Among them, it seems to me, the greatest credit belongs to the intellectuals who organized KOR and helped to give the Solidarity of 1980–1981 and underground Solidarity from 1982 on their special character, and to the labor leaders, who welcomed the intellectuals into their midst. Bridging the divide between workers and intellectuals was crucial.

Some partisans of the Reagan administration have claimed that it caused the collapse of communism and so ended the Cold War. Most of those making this argument have focused on the administration's huge increases in military spending, particularly for projects such as "Star Wars."

They suggest that the Soviets could not keep up and therefore had to sue for peace. Others ridicule these claims, pointing out that the United States may have spent a lot on Star Wars, but the project never got off the ground, and it shows no prospect of adding to the military capability of the United States even now long after the end of the Reagan era, despite the eagerness of a new administration to spend vast sums on it before its technological effectiveness is proven. Many analysts have derided the contention that the Soviet Union was nevertheless fooled into surrendering by the prospect of a Maginot Line in space as ludicrous. They believe that military spending by the Reagan administration had little or nothing to do with the rise of Mikhail Gorbachev, his policies of glasnost and perestroika, and his decision not to intervene as his predecessors had done to prevent changes in Eastern Europe. Though I count myself among those skeptical that policies formulated in Washington were prime causes of the changes in the Soviet Union, I believe the Reagan administration's steady management of sanctions against Poland did play a part in the end to communism in that country. Freed from the threat of imprisonment, the underground movement could surface, and the regime had no choice but to enter into the negotiations that transformed the country. As Poland played so large a part in the changes elsewhere in the region, this was a policy with significant consequences.

Puzzlingly, the Polish case hardly ever figures in discussions about sanctions. It is not even mentioned, for example, in a leading work published by the Council on Foreign Relations in 1998, *Economic Sanctions and American Diplomacy*.[3] That book includes extended discussions of China, Cuba, Haiti, Iran, Iraq, Libya, Pakistan, and the former Yugoslavia. Several other examples are noted in the introductory and concluding chapters, but not Poland. Similarly, Henry Kissinger has written, "The most successful example [of sanctions]—and so far the only unambiguously successful one—was the economic embargo against South Africa passed by Congress in 1986."[4] Poland is one of the Reagan administration's great successes, but it is rarely cited even by admirers of the fortieth president's foreign policy.

The contribution of the underground activists is enduring. Among the former Communist states, Poland stands out for the vigor of its democracy. Its economy is strong. It has developed stable democratic institutions that function effectively. The rule of law prevails. And, Poland has an array of nongovernmental institutions that assure that public policies are thoroughly and intelligently debated. The intellectuals who played crucial roles in KOR, Solidarity, and underground Solidarity are now central figures both in government and in private enterprises that contribute to public discourse. Thadeusz Mazowiecki served as prime minister. Until 2000, Bronislaw Geremek was foreign minister. Grzegorz Boguta—the underground book publisher, a biochemist by training—heads a large scientific publishing house with several hundred employees. Adam Michnik and Helena Luczywo—who edited *Tygodnik Mazowse*—now edit *Gazeta Wyborcza,* the largest and most successful newspaper in any of the former Communist countries. Darius Fikusz died a few years ago but, until his death, he edited another major newspaper, *Rzeczpospolita.*

In some respects, the success of *Gazeta Wyborcza* is emblematic of the transition in Poland. It evolved directly out of *Tygodnik Mazowse.* Many of those associated with it today were contributors to its underground predecessor. As a consequence of their connection to the newspaper, they have become well-to-do, or even rich. *Gazeta* today has a daily circulation of 600,000, a weekend circulation of 800,000, many regional editions, color supplements, a variety of Internet ventures, and 2,400 employees. Two or three years after the transition, I got a call in New York from Helena Luczywo, with whom I had established a friendship when she was an underground editor, to tell me that an Italian business tycoon wanted to buy shares in the newspaper. She asked me, "What's a share?" I put her in touch with a lawyer I knew who handled business transactions in Italy. That proposed investment came to naught, but in 1999 *Gazeta* went public in an offering handled by Credit Suisse/First Boston and reached a market value in the vicinity of a billion dollars. Today, Helena Luczywo speaks with pride of all those associated with *Gazeta* who have been able to purchase apartments because the newspaper provided them with stock in the company. (Adam Michnik declined to take shares on the grounds that he is well paid as editor and his editorial independence might be compromised if he also had a stake in the newspaper's business success. Responding to a question about the newspaper's prosperity and his own, he said, "The only time I feel like Rockefeller is when I walk into a bookstore and realize I can buy every book I want.")

Writing in *The New Yorker* about Helena Luczywo and the success of *Gazeta Wyborcza,* Timothy Garton Ash said:

> I find myself wondering where the paper will be in ten years. . . . I would like to think that some positive singularities will remain. But if I had to lay

a wager, I would bet they will go. The pressures of a Western consumerist, entertainment model of "normality" may prove more difficult to resist than those of the Soviet-type communist "normalization" that Solidarity so roundly and unexpectedly defeated. Perhaps this is the last irony of freedom's battle: the compulsory could be defied, but the voluntary may be irresistible.[5]

Garton Ash's cynicism may or may not be warranted. I have no way of knowing. Perhaps every triumph carries within itself the seeds of corruption. Yet such speculation seems to me no reason to refrain from celebrating the transformation of a clandestine news sheet whose editors, printers, and distributors constantly risked imprisonment into a thriving media enterprise that plays a role that is critical—in both senses of the word—to what has become an open democratic society.

CHAPTER THIRTEEN

Visiting Prisons in Cuba

I went to Cuba in 1988 to see the country's prisons and to interview prisoners about the conditions of their confinement. It was my first and only visit. Previously, I had not been permitted to enter the country. That changed when the Reagan administration launched an intense attack on Cuba's human rights practices at the United Nations. Though staunchly insistent that its treatment of its own citizens was no one else's business, the Cuban government decided it was in its interest to permit inspection of its prisons by a few Americans who would enjoy credibility internationally in discussing the conditions in which prisoners were kept.

Throughout the decade, the Reagan administration responded to accounts of abuses of human rights in countries it supported, particularly El Salvador and Guatemala, by claiming that more severe violations were committed by left-wing governments. The main villain for the administration was the Sandinista government in Nicaragua. This strategy was not very successful. Though human rights groups and the small army of U.S. journalists covering the wars in Central America documented many abuses by the Sandinistas, these were overshadowed by the widely reported brutality of the Contra army that was attempting to overthrow Nicaragua's left-wing regime and by the disappearances, summary executions, and massacres committed by the armed forces in nearby Central American countries attempting to put down left-wing insurgencies. Accordingly, the administration decided to mount a campaign against Cuba. Given the Castro regime's totalitarian character, this plan was calculated to bolster the administration's contention that the Left was a greater threat to human rights than the Right. In addition, because the Cubans were the main regional backers of the Sandinistas in Nicaragua and of the FMLN rebels in El Salvador, a campaign against Cuba would also tarnish these enemies of the United States in Central America.

The importance of this campaign to the Reagan administration was signified by its choice of Armando Valladares to serve as the U.S. representative to the UN Human Rights Commission. Valladares had spent twenty-two years as a prisoner in Cuba, from 1960 to 1982, when he was released in response to a plea to Fidel Castro from French President François Mitterrand. Five years later, he published a memoir, *Against All Hope*,[1] chronicling the horrors of his treatment in prison. His appointment was unusual. Valladares became a U.S. citizen by an act of Congress in 1987 but lived in Madrid and was probably the only person ever to serve as an ambassador of the United States who could not speak English. Given his long years in prison cut off from information about developments in the rest of the world, he had little knowledge of most issues that came before the Human Rights Commission. The only matter he could address knowledgeably was the human rights situation in Cuba. As this was what the Reagan administration cared about, he was deemed an appropriate choice to serve as its representative.

Though Valladares's appointment was galling to the Cubans—who attacked him as a one-time policeman for the Batista regime, a convicted terrorist, and a man who fraudulently pretended to be crippled in prison as a consequence of ill treatment (charges vigorously disputed by Valladares)—he was not the central figure in the campaign against the Castro regime's human rights practices. That role was played by the U.S. ambassador to the United Nations, General Vernon Walters, a former deputy director of the Central Intelligence Agency, a talented linguist and long a central figure in U.S. efforts to defeat left-wing insurgencies and to assist military leaders in overthrowing left-wing civilian governments in such Latin American countries as Brazil, Chile, and Guatemala. In a 1987 speech to the United Nations Human Rights Commission, Walters charged that "15,000 or more" political prisoners were being held in Cuba under cruel conditions and also accused the Castro regime of practicing the abuses that were the hallmarks of repression in Central America: torture, disappearances, and summary executions. To try to rebut the allegations about its prisons, the main focus of Walters's charges and of Valladares's book, the Cuban government decided to grant me a visa and to give me unprecedented access to its prisons and their inmates.

I very much wanted to see the Cuban prisons. One reason was that I had formed a friendship with a former prisoner, Jorge Valls. We had met in New York a few months after he was released in June 1984. Over lunch,

I asked how long he had been in prison. "Twenty years and forty days," he told me. I had encountered many men and women who had been imprisoned for dissenting peaceably, but I don't recall ever being struck so forcibly by the perversity and cruelty of such extended sentences. It was the forty days. The exactness of his answer made me realize how little I could imagine what it would be like to be confined for such a long time with virtually no contact with anyone or anything outside the prison walls. It was also Valls. He seemed a gentle and unpretentious man with a somewhat mystical air about him and a deep commitment to ethical behavior. It says a lot about a regime when it chooses such a person as one of its enemies.

In the 1950s, Valls had been a leading activist in the student movement at the University of Havana, where he studied philosophy. He was imprisoned several times by the Batista regime for leading protests. In 1958, after one of his terms in prison, where he was severely beaten, he left Cuba and went into exile in Mexico—the second time he took refuge there—and so was out of the country on January 1, 1959, when the Batista regime collapsed and Fidel Castro's small revolutionary force triumphed. Valls returned to Cuba three weeks later but soon became a critic of Castro's violations of human rights. As under Batista, he was frequently arrested. In 1964, he attempted to testify at the trial of a friend, but he was prevented from doing so and taken from the courthouse by security agents to Fidel Castro's apartment. Castro interrogated him about his association with the friend who was being tried. His friend was convicted and promptly executed. Two weeks later, Valls was arrested. After a cursory trial behind closed doors before a military tribunal, he was convicted of leading several antigovernment organizations and of activities "against the powers of the state." At the time, he was not even informed of his sentence. He learned how long he would have to spend in prison from a note slipped to him by his fiancée. Like some of his fellow political prisoners, Valls devoted himself to writing in prison and managed to smuggle out some of his writings. He was awarded several literary prizes—that he could not collect—including the Grand Prix at the 1983 International Poetry Festival in Rotterdam.

I proposed to Valls that he write a memoir of his prison experiences that we would publish. It was the only time Americas Watch or any division of Human Rights Watch published such a work. The title, of course, was *Twenty Years and Forty Days* (1986). We sold far more copies of it than we had of any of our other reports, and translations were published in several languages. Armando Valladares's book was published at about the same time. Though it was much more sensational than Jorge Valls's memoir covering the same period, I thought it was inferior both as a portrait of prison life and as literature.

Another person who influenced my thinking about Cuba and its prisons was a Cuban-American airline flight attendant, Gisela Hidalgo. She came to see me not long after I met Jorge Valls to talk about her brother, Ariel Hidalgo, who was serving an eight-year sentence in Combinado del Este, a large prison near Havana. A Marxist historian and a professor of socioeconomics at the University of Havana, he had been arrested in 1981 for possession of "enemy propaganda." The "propaganda" was his own unpublished manuscript, *Cuba, The Marxist State and the New Class: A Dialectical Materialist Study.* Having no place to publish it, Hidalgo had consigned it to a desk drawer, where it was discovered during a police search of his home. Gisela Hidalgo, taking full advantage of her ability to get free rides on planes to many locations, devoted herself to a campaign to free Ariel Hidalgo. Her soft-spoken manner and her great personal charm, combined with her unflagging dedication to securing her brother's freedom, made her a formidable advocate. On several occasions, I heard comments from those who met Gisela Hidalgo along the lines of, "What every prisoner of conscience needs is a sister like that." She was a frequent visitor to my office, along with several other Cuban Americans who shared a commitment to human rights and a dislike of the right-wing Cuban groups that seemed to them (and to me) to manifest some of the authoritarian characteristics of the Communist government they denounced as their enemy. As time went by, Gisela Hidalgo became more and more absorbed in the human rights cause, eventually leaving her airline job to devote full time to a small organization she established with some of the others who used to visit me, Human Rights in Cuba.

To save face, the Castro regime did not allow me to go to Cuba as a representative of Human Rights Watch or its Americas Watch division. I had to go under the auspices of a left-wing group that had long enjoyed friendly relations with the Cuban government, the Institute for Policy Studies (IPS). Under the arrangement worked out by IPS, my visit to Cuba was purportedly part of an exchange that also included plans for a Cuban delegation to visit U.S. prisons. Accompanying me were three other Americans not connected to IPS who would also have credibility in discussing the conditions they saw in the prisons.[2] The visit by the Cubans never took place because the United States denied them visas. The fact that it was part of the agreement with IPS, however, permitted the Cubans to avoid an embarrassing situation where their prisons would be portrayed as being particularly in need of external inspection.

I had misgivings about going to Cuba under the auspices of the IPS, as one or two of those associated with it seemed to me apologists for the Castro regime, but decided to do so because the arrangements for the prison visits were satisfactory. We could go to six prisons of our choice and interview 100 prisoners of our choice in circumstances that would permit them to speak to us confidentially. Also, I knew the other outsiders invited by IPS and had confidence in their readiness to conduct an impartial investigation of the Cuban prisons and to speak out honestly about what they found. The ground rules for the visit imposed no restraints on my own right to report my findings. Finally, I knew I could rely on the research Americas Watch had been doing on the Cuban prisons and that I would be well prepared.[3]

The arrangements the Cuban government officials made for the visit suggested its importance to them. Though I was the only member of the delegation to travel all around the country to see the prisons—the others only saw institutions in the vicinity of Havana—a plane and its crew were put at my disposal for the entire trip. It was prepared to take off whenever I was ready to go on to the next prison. The others who accompanied me on the plane were an IPS officer, a translator,[4] and two officials of the Cuban Ministry of the Interior: a Colonel Guzmán, who spoke fluent English and Russian as well as Spanish, and a sergeant who served as his aide-de-camp. Guzmán proved a useful travel companion because he was well informed about the Cuban prisons and versed in the history and philosophy of prisons internationally. He readily grasped the import of my many questions and provided answers that were generally helpful. I knew his role was to steer me away from sections of the prisons the government did not want me to see, to put the best face on what I did see, and to report back on my activities. Yet we quickly established a modus vivendi in which he kept clear of my visits with individual prisoners and did not try to control my movements.

Our accommodations were mostly in what the Cuban government referred to as "protocol houses." These were very comfortable lodgings. I recall particularly one I stayed in outside Santiago de Cuba, the city at the far eastern end of the island that I visited to see Boniato Prison. It consisted of a compound with a dozen or so chalet-like houses; a dining hall ready to serve a wide range of superb meals twenty-four hours a day; a glass-enclosed building devoted to state-of-the-art exercise equipment; and a swimming pool. Though colleagues subsequently told me that there were swimming pools like this at various Caribbean resorts, I had not seen its like. On one side, water cascaded into the pool from an overhanging shelf. Through the falling water, I could see a well-stocked bar; drinks were served in the pool itself. Reportedly, this particular compound was a favorite gathering place for Fidel Castro and his military commanders.

The general who served as commander of the province of Santiago seemed eager to show me the sights; I realized, however, that he was probably hoping to cut into the time I had available to spend in Boniato. I put up with a few hours of the tourism he foisted upon me. He took me to two places in which he manifestly took great delight. One was a museum devoted to cars, or, rather, miniature models of cars of every imaginable make, thousands of them, of the kind manufactured as toys by firms such as Matchbox and Corgi. The other was a building, perhaps 80 feet by 30 feet, entirely filled by an electric train set that could be viewed from a balcony above it. Though he described these as museums for the children of Cuba, I got the impression that the general—whose photo examining the train set with Fidel Castro hung in the building housing it—was the most devoted visitor.

At the start of my visits to the Cuban prisons, Colonel Guzmán told me that the central principle of the system was "reeducation." As my visits proceeded, I found myself thinking that this was the central principle of the Cuban state. Reeducation is not the same as education. The concept suggests a person has gone wrong. The state reeducates someone to set her straight. Her bad behavior does not reflect her true nature; it is external influences that have led her astray. She is reeducated to eliminate deviance. A corollary is that the possibility of contact with corrupting forces must be foreclosed. The state cannot be too vigilant.

This was, of course, the philosophy of the early nineteenth-century reformers in the United States who invented the asylums that spread universally over the next two centuries. They argued that criminals and the mentally ill should be confined so they could be rehabilitated. What gave reeducation a particularly sinister cast in Cuba and other Communist countries where it was practiced is that ideological deviance was one of its targets. As many as 20,000 "counterrevolutionary" prisoners at a time were confined in Cuban prisons in the early 1960s. They were reeducated to make them accept Fidel Castro's revolution. By the time I visited in 1988, however, the number of those considered to be counterrevolutionaries in the prisons—whether on account of violent or nonviolent resistance to the government—had dwindled to fewer than 1,000 in a total prison population of about 32,000. Ambassador Vernon Walters's claim that "15,000 or more" political prisoners were being held in Cuba was insupportable. Cuba was and is now a totalitarian state, but by the late 1980s, Fidel Castro no longer needed to incarcerate such large numbers to maintain control.

A few words are in order about how I ascertained the approximate number of prisoners in Cuba. The number 32,000 came from Colonel Guzmán. When I visited the prisons and talked to prisoners, it was apparent that the general practice was to send prisoners to prisons in their own provinces. Everywhere I went, I tested Guzmán's figure by asking local officials about the number of prisoners in their complex. At times, there was only one prison in the province. The figures were consistent with the nationwide total I obtained from Guzmán. I could see for myself that the numbers given to me concerning those prisons were realistic. As those who compiled lists of political prisoners were able to identify the prisons where they were held, I discounted suggestions that there were secret prisons, as this would mean they confined prisoners unknown to anyone else. The number of prisoners might have been larger than Guzmán's figure, but not by an order of magnitude. (Among groups that echoed Ambassador Walters's contention that there were 15,000 political prisoners in 1988, it was customary to contend that the total prison population in Cuba was at least 100,000, out of a total population in the country of 10 million; if this were true, it would be a far higher proportion of the population in prison than is known anywhere in the world.) As for the number of counterrevolutionaries or political prisoners, I learned from the dissidents in the prisons that they made up only a small portion of the population of the various institutions I visited. They knew very well the identities of their fellow "counterrevolutionaries." The great majority of those subjected to reeducation were held for common crimes.

My findings were mixed. The attempt to reeducate prisoners in Cuba is pursued with zeal. The result is a prison system that has some humane features and that is clearly regarded with considerable pride by Cuban officials. The system also produced cruelties. These were not aberrations, or contradictions of its humane elements; the two sides were closely related.

How was reeducation to be achieved? In the Cuban prisons I visited, work was central—regular, disciplined, productive work over a prolonged period. Several of the prison officials with whom I spoke quoted Fidel Castro: "In reeducation, as in education, work is the great teacher." They reported that 85 percent of all their prisoners worked. It was apparent that this figure was more or less accurate. Unlike prisoners in most countries where I have visited prisons, including those in many prisons in the United States, Cuban prisoners were not as a rule idle. (The only other prison I have visited where almost all the prisoners worked was in China.) Large industrial enterprises are connected to the prisons in Cuba, and it appeared that the prefabricated housing industry depended on prison labor.

The conditions of labor seemed similar to those of other Cubans. Also, remarkably, prisoners were paid the same as workers outside the prisons, with discounts to cover the cost of confining them, amounting, at the time, to 35 percent of the first 100 pesos a month and 50 percent of the rest. They could use what remained to support their families or, if they did not have such responsibilities, to accumulate what could amount to substantial savings—by Cuban standards—during the long prison terms that were characteristic of their sentences. In contrast, U.S. prisoners who worked in prison at that time typically earned ten or fifteen cents an hour—enough to buy an occasional soda or a pack of cigarettes, but of no use in supporting a family or in building up savings. (Wages for prison laborers in the United States have gone up in some places to keep pace with inflation, but, overall, are no better than in the 1980s.)

The opportunity for productive, paid labor in decent conditions seemed to me much the most humane feature of imprisonment in Cuba. Some former prisoners kept their prison jobs after release—perhaps because they lacked other choices—getting the same pay as prisoners but without the discounts. They could be distinguished from those serving sentences because, like the skilled carpenters, machinists, and others hired to train the prison laborers, the former prisoners wore civilian clothes.

In addition to working, Cuban prisoners received political education. I did not sit through any classes, but it was possible to get a sense of what this was like from the wall paintings and slogans I saw in the prisons. The wall paintings were glorified likenesses of the heroes and martyrs of the revolution, and the slogans were exhortations to work and to persevere.

The same messages were conveyed in the patriotic finale to an evening spectacle performed for a steady stream of visitors to Cuba's showplace prison that was then a required stop for political tourists to Cuba, the Women's Prison in Havana, an institution with 600–700 inmates. It is a prison where the cells were decorated with dolls in satin costumes with buttons and bows of the sort that might be prizes at an amusement park. The show I saw there ended with all its talented inmate singers and dancers (including the star, a long-legged beauty who, I was told, had been a chorus girl at the Tropicana night club until some offense landed her in prison) on stage. They sang "Here, Nobody Surrenders" as the screen behind them filled with scenes of Cuban guerrillas battling what looked like Yankee troops and taking them prisoner. The audience for this show consisted of about 200 of the inmates, a few guards, and the energetic, back-slapping female warden. They cheered, applauded, sang at deafening volume, and danced in the aisles.

Watching this made me extremely uneasy as I sensed the pressure to join in the singing and cheering. Turning around from my front-row seat, however, I was unable to discern any sign of discomfiture or strain on most faces. Only a handful of prisoners sat stoically still, resolutely demonstrating their disenchantment. With the exception of a few women who were confined because they had been apprehended for trying to leave the country without permission—a leading cause of political imprisonment in Cuba—all the inmates who spoke with me in private interviews in this prison expressed the same enthusiasm for the general conditions there as they demonstrated at the evening performance.

Discipline, like the other elements of reeducation, is taken seriously in the Cuban prisons. As I walked through the corridors and dormitories of the men's prisons, which were the main focus of my inquiry, all the inmates snapped to a rigid version of the position known as "parade rest." Though I saw literally thousands of prisoners' beds during my tour of the prisons, I did not see one that seemed less than perfectly made up. The prisons I saw were spotlessly clean. Prisoners who resist such discipline were dealt with harshly, as I found when I visited the punishment cells of several prisons. The only cell block where I saw less than perfect discipline was one reserved for psychotic inmates at Boniato prison. I was told those prisoners would shortly be transferred to a new facility I also visited that was just then being completed at a nearby psychiatric hospital.

Another of the humane features of each of the prisons I visited in Cuba was the conjugal pavilion where prisoners could have twenty-four-hour private visits with their spouses. In one of the prisons I saw, Nievo Morejon in Sancti Spiritus, some 300 kilometers from Havana—an institution not on the tourist circuit—the pavilion was set in a part of the prison that had a small wildlife park with a few tame deer, a flamingo, and a number of other exotic birds. The conjugal facilities were attractive in all the prisons I saw. A contrast that comes to mind is the arrangement for conjugal visiting I saw at a large prison in the state of São Paulo, Brazil. At that overcrowded institution, prisoners typically had between ten and twenty square feet of space each in cells they shared with several other inmates. Some slept on mattresses on the floor; others on bunks, with hanging sheets or strips of cloth partitioning each cell. In the most crowded cells, not all the prisoners could sleep at the same time. During the daytime, these cells were not locked, and when a prisoner had a conjugal visit, his cellmates would clear out and the hanging sheets provided the couple with a modicum of privacy. Whatever the circumstances of such visits, in this respect prisons in either Cuba or Brazil are more humane than in the United States, where conjugal visiting remains uncommon. When I started dealing with prisons, it was available only at Parchman State Penitentiary in Mississippi.

Although conjugal visiting was permitted in Cuba two to four times a year for eligible prisoners, other types of visits were less frequent than elsewhere. During the 1960s and 1970s, many "counterrevolutionary" prisoners were denied visits for years. Even in the late 1980s when I visited, some prisoners were permitted only one visit every six months. It was only when prison officials decided that prisoners were doing well in reeducation that they were permitted more frequent visits. It was the same with correspondence. The rules demonstrated an intent to isolate prisoners from the outside world as part of the process of reeducation. They were to be kept away from the influences that had made them deviant, just as Cubans generally were kept away from what were considered the corrupting influences of the outside world until the regime decided to promote the island's tourist attractions to relieve its economic woes.

Before going to Cuba, I had asked some former prisoners, including Jorge Valls, to draw maps of the prisons I would visit. These proved indispensable. In the first prison I saw, Boniato in Santiago de Cuba, a map showed me where to find a prison within the prison known as Boniatico—little Boniato—and a special cell block, 4C, where the punishment cells were located.

A visitor who did not know where to look and did not insist on seeing these cells could easily miss them. Though Boniatico is in the middle of Boniato, I saw no corridors leading to it. When I demanded to see it, I was led through the entire prison and out the back and had to circle around to enter. Boniatico had two cell blocks, one above the other, holding more than a hundred prisoners in tiny individual cells with solid iron doors. A four-inch-wide space at the top of each door permitted food to be passed into the cell and allowed in a little light from the corridors. The cells also had natural light in the daytime from a one-foot-square barred window without glass—which let in mosquitoes as well as light and air—but there was no electric light in the cells. In the generally warm climate of Santiago, these cells were often stiflingly hot, and when the weather was cool, as during my visit in February, they were probably very cold at night. To relieve their boredom, some prisoners carved chess sets from soap, drew a board on a piece of cloth, and played by calling out moves to one another.

I selected at random a number of the prisoners in Boniatico to interview and found they were confined for common crimes and had been put in this wing for disciplinary infractions. Their conditions in Boniatico helped to explain the almost perfect order and discipline elsewhere in the prison. They had been in those tiny cells for many months and got out only an hour a week to take the sun; at those times, they were led to large iron cages where they could walk no more than two or three steps. New clothes had been issued a few days before I arrived. My visit was also responsible for a few days of better food, for fresh bedding, and for the distribution of reading material—some of it incongruous, such as a chemistry manual. (Another prison had a fresh coat of paint for my visit, as I discovered when I leaned against a wall and found paint all over my sleeve.)

Although I saw no prisoners held for political offenses in Boniatico, at least one political prisoner, Amado Rodríguez Fernández, then forty-five, was ordinarily held there. He had spent half his life in prison. A "historic *plantado*"—that is, a defiant prisoner who refused to accept reeducation and one of a group known as "historic" to distinguish them from new plantados—Rodríguez had been released in 1979 after eighteen years behind bars, but was reimprisoned in 1984 for another fifteen years. Rodríguez was one of the prisoners I had asked to see in advance, but he was transferred to the prison infirmary a few days before my arrival so I would not be able to see him in Boniatico. I did see him, however. I interviewed him outdoors in a courtyard, where he told me he identified with the political views of Jorge Valls; that he was the only historic plantado at Boniato; and that his main concern was to be transferred to Combinado del Este, the large men's prison near Havana, where he could be with the other historic plantados—some sixty-eight of them at the time—remaining in prison. Through Colonel Guzmán, I was able to arrange for his transfer. He was subsequently released before completing his sentence and now lives in Miami, where he maintains occasional contact with me through Gisela Hidalgo's group, Human Rights in Cuba, in which he is active.

As bad as the cells were in Boniatico, they were worse in the punishment section of Boniato, 4C. In this cell block, as in cell blocks at two other prisons I saw, prisoners had only bare cement slabs to sleep on. There was no bedding. At Kilo 7 prison in Camaguey, the prison commandant, a general in the Ministry of the Interior, attempted to block me from entering the punishment block. I told him if I were not allowed to see it, I would terminate my visit to the Cuban prisons and announce publicly that the Cuban government reneged on its agreement to allow me to inspect them. After an angry standoff in the corridor leading to the punishment block, the general backed down. The sixteen punishment cells I saw there were as wretched as any I have seen anywhere. They measured five feet by seven feet and held three prisoners each on three slabs, with a few half-dollar-sized holes in an iron door to admit air and a tiny amount of electric light from the corridor. There was no natural light. The toilet was a hole in the ground. A spigot over this provided cold water to flush, to bathe in, and to drink. The meals consisted of a sparse breakfast and one other meal a day. Prisoners told me they had been confined naked in such cells.

The most severe punishment cells were used for twenty-one-day periods to punish infractions of prison discipline, such as not showing respect for guards. But some prisoners were held for years in only slightly less harsh circumstances in a ninety-nine-cell punishment building at Combinado del Este. This building was known by the prisoners as "Rectangulo de Muerte" (rectangle of death) or as the "pizzeria," for the oven-like conditions in hot weather. One prisoner I talked to there had been locked up in such conditions for six years; another had been there for seven years.

With more than 3,000 inmates, Combinado del Este was the largest prison in Cuba; because it served the Havana area, it also held most of the prisoners in Cuba charged with politically motivated offenses. At Combinado and at Boniato, though not at the other prisons I visited, I heard complaints of beatings by the guards—with rubber hoses (*mangueras*), sticks, fists, and kicks. The beatings were not systematic. Guards beat prisoners whom they considered disrespectful or defiant. None of the prisoners with whom I spoke complained of outright torture, and I did not hear of any disappearances or extrajudicial executions, as alleged by Ambassador Walters. A number of prisoners at Combinado del Este told me that a prisoner there had been kicked to death by guards the previous year, and at least one of the guards involved had been demoted for this incident.

Why should the humane conditions enjoyed by the great majority of prisoners—employment under decent conditions, clean facilities, educational programs, good health care, and attractive conjugal visiting facilities—exist side by side with the horrible conditions in the punishment blocks and those prisons within the prisons where defiant prisoners were confined? The answer, I believe, lies in the Castro regime's ideological commitment to reeducation. Prisoners who resist or disrupt the state's efforts to reeducate them are subversive of the entire enterprise. The zeal with which reeducation is pursued elicits a comparable determination to resist, especially against programs that glorify the revolution that some of the prisoners staunchly oppose. In reprisal, the regime demonstrates its determination to punish resistance unsparingly.

Though the Cuban prisons were once the subject of much attention in discussions of human rights internationally, they have faded from view in the past decade. Several factors are responsible. After the wars in Central America and Cuban and U.S. involvement in them ended, the U.S. government lost interest in demonizing Cuba's human rights practices. Another factor was that the historic plantados, the focus of much of the international concern with the Cuban prisons, finally completed their sentences. Prisoners in Cuba not executed in the early 1960s—when Castro was consolidating his control of the country and when thousands of secret executions of opponents took place—received maximum sentences of thirty years. By the early 1990s, these sentences had expired and the last surviving long-term political prisoners were released. Finally, its experience with me probably helped persuade the Cuban government to discontinue such free-ranging visits.

In one respect the Cuban government achieved its purpose in allowing my visit. Human Rights Watch's reporting on Cuba and articles I published in such periodicals as *The New York Review of Books* refuted the U.S. claim that there were 15,000 or more political prisoners. I made clear that I found no evidence to justify the allegation by the Reagan administration that the Cuban government then practiced extrajudicial executions and disappearances, though our reports and my articles did note the thousands of executions that had taken place a quarter of a century earlier. The upshot was that a delegation from the UN Commission on Human Rights visited Cuba in September 1988 and published a lengthy report on February 21, 1989, that never even referred to the claims by Ambassador Walters about 15,000 political prisoners, even though those claims had inspired the UN commission's concern with Cuba. Its only reference to the number of political prisoners was to cite a Cuban government assertion that, "in recent months, the number of counter-revolutionary prisoners had dropped from 458 to 145"; and that following the visit of its delegation, the Cuban government had reported a further decrease in the number to 121. The commission provided no support for the claims of disappearances and extrajudicial executions. By the time that report was issued, even the United States had retreated, and the George H.W. Bush administration joined Cuba at the United Nations in voting in favor of a resolution that thanked Cuba for its cooperation with the UN Human Rights Commission. The resolution welcomed "the reaffirmation of the Cuban authorities to continue cooperation in the human rights sphere" and its "willingness . . . [to] take into account the objective assessment formulated in the course of the debate." It contained not one word of criticism of Cuba.

The Cuban government did not appreciate my reporting about the punishment facilities at the prisons. Moreover, the authorities in Havana were incensed that I used my trip to Cuba to meet with critics of the government as well as to visit the prisons. Some months after my visit, Cuban television broadcast a program attacking one of the country's best known dissenters that included a scene, filmed without my knowledge, that showed me meeting him at the church where he was known to worship. While I was in Cuba, another dissenter, who visited me at my Havana hotel before dawn, was able to give me a form used by neighborhood surveillance groups to inform on their neighbors' views. These groups are known as the Committees for the Defense of the Revolution. A copy of the form was reproduced with one of my articles in *The New York Review of Books*.[5] On one side, it provides a space to record an opinion that a person is supposed to have expressed on a political subject. On the other side, it provides boxes to check off to indicate the person's approximate age; his or her profession; where the opinion was expressed; whether the person is

CHAPTER FOURTEEN

Suffering Defeat over China

I n Spring 2000, the United States adopted legislation granting China permanent normal trade relations status—or PNTR. It was one of the most hotly debated foreign policy decisions of recent years. Adoption of PNTR was a triumph for President Clinton and was hailed as an historic achievement by proponents of free trade and globalization. On the cover of an issue of *The Economist* depicting a red-sailed Chinese junk in the reflecting pond in front of the Washington Monument, it was called "A Vote for China's Freedom."[1] The opposition to PNTR was led by the AFL-CIO, whose members were concerned about the export of jobs to China. Missing from the voluminous press coverage I saw was any mention of a factor that had launched the dispute over U.S. trade relations with China in the first place: exploitation of an accident of timing by advocates of human rights.

PNTR ended the annual debate that had become a ritual of U.S. politics during the previous decade over whether China should be granted "most-favored-nation" trading status, or MFN (the substitution of "normal" for "most-favored" no doubt played a part in the success of the PNTR legislation). MFN was an issue because of a law adopted in 1974—known as the Jackson-Vanik Amendment for its Senate and House sponsors—that bars a country with a non-market economy from most favored, or normal, trade relations with the United States if it denies its citizens the right to emigrate. Jackson-Vanik was aimed at the Soviet Union and a few other East European countries, such as Romania, that blocked Jews from leaving or required them to pay large sums to go.

Application of the law to China was problematic as the right to emigrate was never an issue. Legend has it the matter was once raised by a visiting American with Deng Xiaoping, who responded: "How many do you want? Ten million? A hundred million?" Yet as a non-market economy when Jackson-Vanik was adopted, and to a lesser extent in recent years, China was subject to its terms. The law permits the president to issue a waiver in certain circumstances. The waiver allows normal trade to proceed, though Congress may override it. The possibility of an override set the stage for a politically contentious process.

MFN for China was a hard-fought issue throughout the 1990s because of the massacre in Beijing in connection with the ouster of student demonstrators from Tiananmen Square in 1989. The accident of timing was that the massacre took place the night of June 3–4. In the case of China, the presidential waiver of Jackson-Vanik was required each year by June 3 for MFN to continue. That meant the president marked the anniversary of the massacre each year by issuing a waiver in favor of China.

In May 1989, as word circulated that the Chinese government was massing military forces to crack down on the demonstrators, Human Rights Watch called on the George H.W. Bush administration to apply pressure to the Beijing regime by threatening to interrupt trade relations. As an organization founded to deal with the countries that were the intended targets of Jackson-Vanik, we cited the law not by focusing on its concern with emigration but by emphasizing its preamble, which states that its purpose is "to assure the continued dedication of the United States to fundamental human rights." It was a slender thread, but it was all we had. As the first anniversary of the massacre approached the following year, we tried to persuade the Bush administration not to mark the occasion by issuing another waiver. That effort set in motion a debate that lasted a decade.

A few months prior to the events in Tiananmen Square, in October 1988, I traveled to China. My visit was sponsored by the Fund for the Reform and Opening of China, a foundation established there by George Soros two years earlier. It was only the second of the foundations he created outside the United States (the first was in Hungary). In setting it up, he signified his belief that the time was ripe for promoting the principles and institutions of an open society in China. It was a view I shared. I had assisted George in establishing the Fund by introducing him to the young émigré from China, Liang Heng, whom he hired to organize it, and by assembling a group of China specialists who met with George periodically to advise on his dealings with Beijing. If anyone had asked me at the time about the prospects for change in the Soviet bloc countries of Eastern Europe and in China, I would have responded unhesitatingly that these were better in the latter. I anticipated neither the speed with which the Communist systems in Eastern Europe crumbled in the face of an outpouring of dissent in 1989 nor the inflexibility and resilience of the Chinese authorities when confronted with similar manifestations at about the same time.

Though I had high hopes for China more than a decade after the nightmare years of the Cultural Revolution and at a time when Deng Xiaoping was gradually opening the country to the West, I had no success in achieving the main purpose of my visit: to persuade some Chinese intellectuals to form an open human rights group. The scholars, writers, lawyers, and others I met all told me they had never known a time when the climate for human rights in China was better than in 1988. They listened politely to my arguments for forming an organization that might begin cautiously by promoting Chinese ratification of international human rights agreements and by conducting educational programs on the meaning of those agreements. Yet none of them expressed readiness to take up such an effort.

One place I went to try to provoke interest in forming a human rights group was Beijing University. My hosts arranged for me to give a talk on the worldwide human rights movement to the graduate students in international relations. It was, I was told, the first time anyone associated with efforts to promote human rights had ever spoken on such a topic at the university. About eighty students turned up. As they seemed to know little on the subject, I had to speak on an elementary level. Yet the students kept me answering questions for four hours and I was able to cover a lot of territory. Most of the time, I talked of the rest of the world, focusing on the Soviet Union, Poland, and other Communist countries with which I thought they might identify, rarely mentioning China. The revolutions of 1989 had not yet taken place, but it was a time of ferment, and change was in the air in Eastern Europe. At one point, however, I commented on the Democracy Wall movement in China of the late 1970s and mentioned the internationally known Chinese political prisoner, Wei Jingsheng, then still serving the fifteen-year prison sentence he had begun in 1979. As the students did not react to the mention of his name, I wondered whether I had mispronounced it or if they had not heard of him. I asked for a show of hands by those who could identify Wei. Only three raised their hands. I asked one whether I had said the name comprehensibly. I had. Whether others also recognized his name but considered it prudent to feign ignorance, I have no way of knowing.

Soon after returning to the United States, I was approached by a group of Chinese graduate students and scientific researchers who asked for my help in forming an organization we named Human Rights in China (HRIC). Our first public event was a forum at which I spoke at Columbia University on March 29, 1989, to mark the tenth anniversary of the imprisonment of Wei Jingsheng. At about the same time, Chinese intellectuals in China were also taking up Wei's case. There, the effort was initiated by the noted astrophysicist Fang Lizhi, who sent an open letter to Deng Xiaoping in January 1989 calling for Wei's release. Soon after, the poet Bei Dao enlisted thirty-three intellectuals in an appeal for Wei to the People's Congress and the Central Committee of the Communist Party. By about the time we were meeting in New York on the tenth anniversary of Wei's imprisonment, thousands of intellectuals in China were signing petitions for his release. Though only a few months had elapsed since I could find no one to take the lead in forming a human rights group, and had seen little sign of recognition of Wei's name among graduate students at the country's leading university who attended a talk on human rights, suddenly a large group of intellectuals was engaged in a full-fledged campaign for his release. It made me guess that the reluctance I encountered to identify with the human rights cause reflected prudence in dealing with a stranger.

The campaign for Wei's release played a major part in precipitating the events that unfolded in Tiananmen Square that spring. It was the first time in a decade that intellectuals had been so outspoken in any cause. Also, the campaign was linked to the episode that brought students to the square: the death of Hu Yaobang.

Hu was a former general secretary of the Communist Party. Long a close associate of Deng Xiaoping's and, like Deng, a victim of persecution during the Cultural Revolution, Hu was considered a reformer in Communist Party circles. From time to time he opposed bureaucratic rigidity, and he was a steadfast antagonist of corruption, maintaining a far simpler lifestyle than other party leaders. By 1989, Hu had been removed from his principal party posts and was considered to have lost all power. He was also ill. He suffered a heart attack in 1988 and had a bad case of the flu in the winter of 1988–1989. Though enfeebled physically and politically, Hu still attended Politburo meetings. Not fully recovered, he attended the meeting on April 8, 1989, when the campaign for the release of Wei Jing-sheng was on the agenda. Reportedly, he became upset during the discussion, collapsed, and was rushed to a hospital, where he died a week later, on April 15.[2]

Within hours of the announcement of Hu's death, hundreds of students rushed to Tiananmen Square, Beijing's traditional gathering place at the time of great events. By April 17, two days after he died, the number who converged on the square to lionize Hu as a proponent of democracy and human rights (an exaggeration) and as an opponent of corruption (more accurate) reached into the thousands. Some did not leave the square until the fateful night of June 3–4 a month and a half later, when the square was cleared by tanks. Hundreds of Beijing residents trying to block streets leading to the square were killed by advancing tanks and thousands more were arrested. Additional killings and arrests took place in subsequent days in many Chinese cities.

One of the casualties of Tiananmen Square was a fifty-seven-year-old aide to Premier Zhao Ziyang, Bao Tong. Like Hu, Zhao was considered a reformer. Bao, a member of the Central Committee of the party, also headed an important think tank known as the Research Institute for the Reform of the Political Structure. On behalf of Premier Zhao, Bao had negotiated with George Soros for the establishment of the Fund for the Reform and Opening of China. Bao was the highest level government official imprisoned for what happened in Tiananmen Square.

Initially, one of the allegations against Bao concerned his arrangement with George for establishment of the Fund. The Chinese authorities suspected George was a front for the CIA. Apparently, it was difficult for them to imagine that a wealthy American would spend his own money on scholarships, fellowships, publishing projects, and the other activities conducted by the Fund for the Reform and Opening of China. George Soros was denounced by Chen Xitong, mayor of Beijing (subsequently imprisoned for corruption), as one of those who fomented the student demonstrations. As there was no truth to this, George asked me to draft a letter for him to Deng Xiaoping denying any connection. The letter was published in an official journal, and charges against Bao Tong for his connection to George were not pressed at his trial. Yet Bao was sentenced to seven years in prison. His main crime, according to the Chinese authorities, was that he gave the demonstrators in Tiananmen Square advance notice of the intent to impose martial law. Bao served his sentence until the last day and, after his release from prison in 1996, spent another year under house arrest. Today, though he is still under close surveillance and receives periodic warnings from the authorities, Bao remains an outspoken advocate of reform.

The connection to George did not figure in the sentencing of Bao Tong. Yet some in the Beijing leadership maintained their suspicion that the Fund for the Reform and Opening of China was a front for the CIA. To prove this, the Public Security Bureau (the Chinese counterpart of the KGB)—we subsequently learned on good authority—sent two agents to the United States to gather information on George Soros. The purpose may have been to use whatever they found in an intra-party struggle for power to discredit Zhao Ziyang, who was forced to resign as premier for the manner in which he had dealt with the students in Tiananmen Square. Bao was probably a victim of the power struggle against Zhao. Any link that could be established between George and the CIA was ammunition to use in this struggle.

What happened to Bao Tong was one cause of George's decision to close the Fund for the Reform and Opening of China. At about this time, George also obtained reliable information that the Fund had been thoroughly infiltrated by the Public Security Bureau. "It became clear to me in retrospect that I made a mistake in setting up the Foundation in China," he wrote subsequently. "The foundation could not become an institution of civil society because civil society did not really exist."[3] Burned by the episode, and concerned he might have inadvertently contributed to the long prison sentence served by Bao Tong, George has made no effort to start again in China, and the Open Society Institute has generally steered clear of China in its funding.

The George H.W. Bush administration announced on June 6, 1989, just days after the massacre, that it would impose sanctions on China. These included a suspension of high-level diplomatic exchanges, military exchanges, technology and arms transfers, and support for loans to China by the international financial institutions. Some of those sanctions were already mandated by law. The United States is forbidden by legislation adopted in the mid-1970s to provide military assistance or support for loans by the World Bank and other international financial institutions to governments that practice gross violations of internationally recognized human rights.

President Bush circumvented or directly disregarded these same sanctions, however, soon after he imposed them. In July, the administration agreed to sell three Boeing jetliners to China, and a fourth in August, even though the planes could be used for military purposes. In October, forty-two Chinese military officers who had been removed in June from a U.S.-sponsored project to upgrade Chinese fighter aircraft were permitted to resume their work. And in December, President Bush waived a congressional ban (sponsored by Senator Albert Gore) on the export of three communications satellites to China. By 1990, the United States was again supporting many loans for China at the World Bank.

As to high-level diplomatic exchanges, this prohibition was violated notoriously on December 9, 1989, just six months after the crackdown. National Security Adviser Brent Scowcroft and Deputy Secretary of State Lawrence Eagleburger led an unannounced delegation to China that is remembered for a televised image of General Scowcroft raising a glass of champagne to his hosts and saying: "We extend our hand in friendship and hope you will do the same." He added, gratuitously, "In both our societies there are voices of those who seek to redirect or frustrate our cooperation. We both must take bold measures to overcome these negative forces." Subsequently, it was discovered that Scowcroft and Eagleburger also had made a secret trip to Beijing in July, some four weeks after President Bush had announced a ban on high-level exchanges, and even though Secretary of State James Baker had told Congress the December visit was the first after Tiananmen Square. Bush's proclamation of sanctions was a fraud.

Even if the sanctions announced by Bush had been applied in good faith, they would not have had as much of an impact as trade sanctions. None of the items mentioned by Bush mattered as much to China as MFN. That country's trade with the United States, then and now, produced a huge surplus in favor of China: over $12 billion a year then, several times as much now. As trade between the two countries was vital to China and of relatively minor significance to the United States, Washington could have used MFN to exercise great influence. We never did.

From the moment the MFN issue was raised, the Bush administration argued against such restrictions on the grounds that friendly trade relations and the resulting contacts between U.S. entrepreneurs and their Chinese counterparts would open Chinese society. The Chinese would learn about democracy and human rights by doing business with Americans. As the administration did nothing else to promote human rights in China, and the other sanctions it announced were never implemented, or stayed in place for the blink of an eye, it was difficult to regard this assertion as more than a public relations ploy to justify doing business as usual. Yet it became a mantra of trade proponents. Over time, the argument grew a bit more sophisticated. Trade, advocates of MFN/PNTR argued, would produce a middle class and a legal system to deal with trade disputes. The middle class would not be satisfied with material well-being and would demand the expansion of rights, and the judiciary would extend its reach beyond commercial disputes and establish the rule of law. "You can't have W.T.O.-style foreign investment without moving toward an independent judiciary that is free of arbitrary party meddling," gushed *New York Times* columnist Tom Friedman when Congress supported PNTR.[4]

It was on such grounds that *The Economist* hailed the congressional action as "A Vote for China's Freedom." The Clinton administration, which promoted "engagement" with China, progressed to talking about a "strategic partnership." Not only would trade lead to human rights and democracy, but these, in turn, would provide the basis for peaceful relations. The theory, which has gained widespread public acceptance, was articulated by Clinton's deputy secretary of state, Strobe Talbott, who wrote, "Democracies are demonstrably more likely to maintain their international commitments, less likely to engage in terrorism or wreak environmental damage, and less likely to make war on each other. That proposition is the essence of the national security rationale for vigorously supporting, promoting, and when necessary, defending democracy in other countries."[5] Or, as Clinton himself put it, his China policy would produce "peace through trade, investment, and commerce."

Henry Kissinger (echoing George Kennan) has labeled this view, disparagingly, as "Wilsonianism."[6] But most Republican leaders seem to agree with the Clinton administration. Secretary of State Colin Powell has argued, "Trade with China is not only good economic policy; it is good human rights policy." Representative Dick Armey, the retiring majority leader of the House of Representatives, claimed that, "Freedom to trade is the great subversive and liberating force in human history." And President George W. Bush has said, "Trade freely with China, and time is on our side."[7]

The main difficulty with these arguments is that there is little evidence to support the claimed causal connection between commerce and human rights. Two centuries ago, slavery and the slave trade flourished in mercantile economies. In the past century, the industrial and commercial strength of Germany and Japan did not slow the rise of Nazism and fascism and made it possible for those states to embark on their calamitous paths of conquest. Commerce is linked to the end of apartheid in South Africa only because it made the country vulnerable to economic sanctions. Elsewhere in Africa, it is states with vast natural resources, and therefore extensive commerce—such as Angola and the Democratic Republic of Congo (formerly Zaire)—that have suffered particularly from conflict and despotic government. Today, states such as Singapore, Malaysia, Kuwait, and Saudi Arabia are thriving commercially without any noticeable gains for civil liberties. Ideology that links free trade in material goods with free trade in ideas has taken precedence over what is plain for all to see.

China has enjoyed normal trade relations with the United States for close to a quarter of a century, and the volume of trade has steadily increased over that period (along with the balance in favor of China). It now amounts to about $100 billion a year, but there is no sign of any mitigation in abuses of human rights. To the contrary, according to the annual human rights reports of the U.S. State Department, the situation has deteriorated, as manifest recently by mass imprisonment of adherents of the Falun Gong sect for the mildest expressions of nonconformity. As to contributing to peace, tensions over Taiwan have increased in recent years. Heightened nationalism has seemed to be a concomitant of China's commercial success.

The potential that MFN had to influence Chinese behavior on human rights was demonstrated in the weeks prior to June 3, 1990, the first time a waiver was required after Tiananmen Square. In late April, Beijing announced that martial law was being lifted in Lhasa, where it had been imposed in March 1989 after violent clashes there between demonstrators for Tibetan independence and security forces. Previously, China's security chief, Qiao Shi, had announced a policy of "merciless repression" in Tibet, and after MFN was renewed, on July 29, 1990, Party General Secretary Jiang Zemin ordered "a tough new crackdown on the independence movement in Tibet." But in the weeks that MFN was being questioned, repression was at least nominally relaxed. And, on May 10, 1990, Beijing reported the release of 211 political prisoners. Two weeks later, on May

24, when President George H.W. Bush announced his decision to renew MFN, he cited the release of these 211, as well as the end to martial law in Tibet, in addition to economic factors, as justification.

From the standpoint of Human Rights Watch, the annual debates over MFN had value in periodically shining the spotlight of international attention on Chinese abuses of human rights. Also, as each June 3 rolled around, and whenever China had some other important international concern, such as its unsuccessful bid in 1993 for the 2000 Olympics to be held in Beijing, a few of the more prominent political prisoners were released.[8] In addition, the Chinese announced their commencement of negotiations with the International Committee of the Red Cross for access to security prisoners. With human rights pressure all but abandoned by 2001, no releases were needed to help China win the 2008 Olympics. Nor were there any other human rights concessions.

As the time approached for a decision on MFN in 1991, we introduced a new issue to the debate: the export of goods to the United States made by prison labor. We were able to do this because of the work of our principal China researcher, Robin Munro. A Scotsman who had followed events in China closely since the 1970s and translated into English the writings of some of the Democracy Wall reformers, Robin had served for a time as a consultant for Amnesty International. In the spring of 1989, he went to China to write a travel guide to the Yangtze River. When the student occupation of Tiananmen Square began, Robin abandoned his travel-writing assignment and went to Beijing to see what was going on. He was one of the last foreigners—or perhaps the very last—to remain in Tiananmen Square the night the tanks came in, and he has provided an invaluable record of the period leading up to June 3 and of events during that night.[9] Robin donated his unique collection of posters, leaflets, and other artifacts from the square to the New York Public Library.

Robin Munro joined Human Rights Watch's staff immediately following the events in Tiananmen Square. Initially, he was based in New York, where his odd working habits did not fit in well. He rarely showed up in the office before mid-afternoon, but then generally worked through the night and often did not leave until other members of the staff showed up in the morning. We were much happier with him after he relocated to Hong Kong to open an office for us there, because we could readily get him on the phone at the office during work hours in New York. In Hong Kong, he was able to make better use of his extensive network of contacts in China. He regularly obtained secret Chinese government documents (*neibu*) that we published to demonstrate that human rights abuses were being committed to carry out policies determined at the highest levels of government.

In April 1991, we released a report entitled "Prison Labor in China" based on secret documents Robin obtained. These demonstrated that the Chinese authorities as a matter of policy promoted export to the United States of products made by a million prisoners doing forced labor. Many of those prisoners had been sent to labor camps without judicial hearings. Some were required to remain in the camps after their prison sentences expired. The prisoners included political dissenters, among them thousands arrested for "counterrevolution" after Tiananmen Square. Working conditions were terrible and often dangerous.

Our report caused a stir. Since enactment of the Smoot-Hawley Act of 1930, U.S. law has forbidden the import of prison-made goods. Other exposés followed quickly. One was a sensational broadcast on CBS's *60 Minutes,* with which we cooperated, that included footage of prisoners working in appalling conditions.[10] It also showed a transaction in which a hidden camera filmed Ed Bradley, pretending to be an American businessman, arranging for the purchase of prison-made goods from Chinese merchants. Asked how quality control could be assured, one of the merchants responded on camera, "We beat them." A member of Congress, Representative Frank Wolf of Virginia, contributed a pair of socks that also figured in the debate. During a visit to a prison in Beijing, where he saw prisoners producing the socks, Wolf noticed they were labeled to be sold in the United States. He took along a pair to exhibit back home.

Our revelations about the export of prison-made goods gave us a chance to secure a congressional vote to override that year's waiver of Jackson-Vanik. President Bush beat back this challenge, however, with a July 19, 1991, letter to the Senate saying his administration would negotiate an agreement with China permitting the United States to investigate allegations that imports were produced by prison labor and that the U.S. Customs Service would bar products "when there is a reasonable indication" they were made by prisoners. Little came of the president's pledges. The Customs Service did engage in a handful of well-publicized raids on companies that imported prison-made goods, but no systematic effort was undertaken to ensure these were excluded from Chinese exports to the United States.

After failing to block MFN by raising the prison labor issue, it was apparent we had no realistic chance to prevail in this fight. The economic interests arrayed on the other side were too powerful. The United States also had major political interests at stake. To cite one example, it was crucial to President Bush that China not use its veto power in the Security Council to block United Nations sponsorship of the Gulf War to liberate Kuwait from Iraqi occupation. Accordingly, I looked for a way to impose a lesser trade sanction on China for its abuses of human rights. That would still draw attention to abuses, and we would have a chance to prevail.

Along with my Washington, D.C., colleague, Holly Burkhalter, I met with Representative Nancy Pelosi of California to propose a new approach. Pelosi, whose district included a large Chinese American constituency in San Francisco, had emerged as the foremost congressional critic of Chinese abuses of human rights and the leading advocate of economic sanctions. Holly and I suggested to her that we might do better if, instead of ending MFN, we proposed that tariffs be selectively imposed and adjusted according to the way the human rights situation evolved. Government-owned industries should be the targets for penalties to counter the argument that denial of MFN would harm an emerging entrepreneurial class that would liberalize China. My espousal of this approach was based on the success of the Reagan administration's calibration of the sanctions against Poland after the imposition of martial law.

Pelosi introduced legislation embodying this approach and Holly rounded up support. It was adopted by both houses of Congress, but President Bush vetoed it on September 28, 1992. The House voted to override, but the Senate vote of 59 to 40 fell short of the two-thirds majority required to enact the law. Had we succeeded, we would have avoided the ill-fated all-or-nothing approach of trying to deny MFN to China and staved off a severe setback for the human rights cause.

Running for the presidency in 1992, candidate Bill Clinton accused President Bush of coddling tyrants "from Belgrade to Beijing." The reference to Beijing was a swipe at Bush's annual renewal of MFN and his vetoes of measures such as the Pelosi bill. As president, however, Clinton was the target of extensive lobbying by the business community and by a bipartisan array of foreign policy heavyweights—from Henry Kissinger to Cyrus Vance—to maintain MFN. (Kissinger does not delude himself about the consequences of trade but endorses it for his own "Hamiltonian" reasons.) To no one's surprise, a few months after taking office Clinton did what he had denounced George H.W. Bush for doing and waived Jackson-Vanik.

The following year, 1994, Clinton went further. He announced that in renewing MFN, he was severing the link with human rights. From then on, he would not even consider human rights in making determinations about trade. The Chinese responded predictably. Where previously they had released prominent political prisoners as the annual debate over MFN approached, in 1994 they celebrated delinkage by reimprisoning two of those previously released, Wei Jingsheng and Chen Ziming (the latter had been accused of being one of the "black hands" behind the demonstrations in Tiananmen Square). They also cut off negotiations with the International Committee for the Red Cross over access to security prisoners. Pretenses of respect for human rights were no longer needed. And although there was no evidence that delinkage was to blame, there also seemed to be an increase in the sort of abuses that are endemic in China: mass executions of those convicted of ordinary crimes after trials wholly lacking in due process; arbitrary detention of suspected dissidents; crackdowns on minorities in Tibet, Inner Mongolia, and other regions; the persecution of religious believers; and cruelties to prisoners.

A striking consequence of delinkage was China's discovery that it could turn the tables on its critics. Freed from the possibility that the United States would use its economic muscle to promote human rights, China seized the opportunity to employ its own potential as a vast market for Western goods to silence those who speak out about human rights abuses. When the Bundestag adopted a resolution criticizing China's actions in Tibet, Beijing canceled a visit by Foreign Minister Klaus Kinkel. China exploited competition between Airbus and Boeing to quiet potential critics in both Europe and the United States. This became Beijing's modus operandi.

To appease congressional critics of its China policy, including some particularly exercised over persecution of the country's Christian churches, the Clinton administration did sponsor a number of resolutions critical of China at meetings of the United Nations Human Rights Commission. These had little effect. It was clear in advance that such resolutions would not be adopted as several governments that can be counted on to support condemnations of similar practices elsewhere were unwilling to provoke Beijing's wrath. As the Clinton administration forswore the use of economic pressure—which it could apply unilaterally—its sponsorship of doomed resolutions that could only be adopted with multilateral support were readily dismissed by China's leaders.

Delinkage symbolized what I labeled in an article in *Foreign Policy* as "the new double standard."[11] In the 1970s and 1980s, geopolitical considerations generally made the United States condemn violations of human rights by the Soviet Union and its client states far more harshly than it criticized those by governments aligned with the United States. With the end of the Cold War, that double standard no longer applied. A new double standard emerged in its place. The United States forcefully condemns and takes measures against unimportant countries for their abuses that it will not apply against large, significant countries. Burma and Cuba are subject to economic sanctions, but China is rewarded with PNTR. Yugoslavia is bombed for its indiscriminate attacks on Kosovar civilians, while the United States, Britain, and other Western governments make certain there is no interruption in International Monetary Fund loans to Russia as it razes to the ground Grozny and other Chechen towns. We have courted the leaders, Presidents Boris Yeltsin and Vladimir Putin, responsible for the carnage. With no apparent embarrassment, President George W. Bush proclaims his special rapport with Putin.

Challenging the double standard of the Cold War era was a formidable task. In doing so, the human rights movement established its credentials and its public significance. Because the movement became important, it was able to help bring an end to the Cold War. The double standard of the 1990s proved to be a tougher nut, and the human rights movement did not succeed in cracking it. Matters have become far more difficult in the first decade of the twenty-first century as the global struggle against terrorism has come to dominate international public policy. It is clear from the debacle that we suffered in attempting to deny China MFN in the 1990s that taking on trade, except with countries where the economic stakes are paltry, is beyond the capacity of the human rights movement. What is less clear is how else to have an impact on a country so large and so significant as China.

The organization that has thought most systematically about how to have an impact when placing conditions on trade is not an option is the group I assisted in forming in 1989, Human Rights in China. Over time, the young Chinese organizers of this group, many of them scientists affiliated with American universities and other research institutions, have become increasingly sophisticated in their grasp of human rights. Their organization is now recognized as an important part of the U.S.-based international human rights movement. HRIC's institutional development has been aided by Robert L. Bernstein's commitment to it and his leading role in raising funds for it and in applying his gifts as a publicist to its cause.

As Bob periodically reminds me when he solicits support from the Open Society Institute for HRIC, I bear some responsibility for his dedication to the promotion of human rights in China. Previously, he devoted himself particularly to winning freedom for prisoners of conscience in the Soviet Union. As it happens, the collapse of the Soviet Union and the release of its remaining political prisoners more or less coincided with the end of Bob's tenure as CEO of Random House. He had more time for human rights work at the very moment that what he was doing in the field was no longer needed. I suggested to him that he would be most effective if he focused his energies on one country. The obvious choice was China because of its size and significance and because, as in the old Soviet Union, the imprisonment of dissenters is a central feature of the repressive system. It is essential for someone to do for prisoners of conscience in China what Bob did for their Soviet counterparts in identifying with them and, by his emotional engagement, making others aware of them as individuals. The cause needed someone with Bob's contacts and talents.

Human Rights in China's scheme for promoting its cause involves trade only to the extent of using trade relations and China's admission to the World Trade Organization to promote workers rights, a volatile issue because of widespread discontent over unsanitary and unsafe conditions, denial of the right to organize free trade unions, and frequent failure to pay wages, pensions, or other required benefits either on a timely basis or at all. Another sensitive issue involves discrimination against peasants, including a system of residence registration that prevents them from obtaining jobs in the cities. One consequence of this system is the widening gap between the affluence of China's urbanized coastal regions and the poverty of the rural interior.

Another HRIC focus is China's system of extrajudicial punishment. Though it is difficult to obtain numbers, it appears that many more Chinese are detained administratively in camps for "reeducation through labor," detention centers for "custody and repatriation," and psychiatric hospitals than are held in prisons and jails for sentenced criminals and those awaiting trial. Other projects include efforts to familiarize Chinese with the concept of accountability for human rights abuses; to provide international support for those Chinese lawyers defending victims of political and religious persecution; to assist the development of independent human rights monitoring from Hong Kong; to promote awareness of human rights in the large Chinese diaspora; to develop ties between Asian nongovernmental organizations and their counterparts in China; and, underlying all these, to develop a "culture of human rights" in China.

A principal means of creating awareness of human rights, and for supplying rights-based analyses of China's many difficulties, is through Internet communications. China currently attempts to block such communications to the roughly 46 million Internet users in the country. But the number of users will grow, and it may be that the technology for dissemination will develop more rapidly than the technology for obstruction.

China is one of the human rights movement's failures. The failure is so great that many of the organizations in the field devote less attention than they should to China because they see so little prospect of making headway. As a consequence, except for efforts by Christian groups concerned with religious persecution, a disproportionate share of the burden falls on a small organization such as Human Rights in China. It is often difficult to discern the tangible results of its efforts. But when a movement for human rights again emerges in China itself, as it did in 1989—and that could be a long way off—I believe that the effort today to build an understanding of human rights among Chinese scholars at American universities, in the larger Chinese diaspora, and within China will turn out to be an investment of extraordinary value.

III

The Soros Years:
1993–

I met George Soros in 1979. After leaving the American Civil Liberties Union, in addition to teaching at New York University Law School, I was directing the university's New York Institute for the Humanities, where I organized a series of "conversations" with prominent writers—many of them political exiles—on writing and politics. In those conversations, I and others interviewed the writers before a small invited audience of friends and fellows of the institute about the way political developments had shaped their literary work. Among the writers who took part were Joseph Brodsky, Pavel Kohout, Czeslaw Milosz, Alberto Moravia, and Vladimir Voinovich. An associate of Soros's, Svetlana Stone, attended some of these conversations, and she suggested that I meet him. At the time, I had not heard of Soros. He was not known as an investor outside of financial circles, and, as his philanthropy was just beginning, I did not yet know of him as a potential donor to causes in which I was involved. Svetlana gave me an article about him from a periodical for investors that said he had by then made about $100 million. She told me he was interested in supporting projects at the institute. Accordingly, I readily accepted an invitation to dinner at George Soros's Central Park West apartment.

George agreed to underwrite a project I was eager to launch. It enabled the Humanities Institute to bring a number of scholars and writers from countries in Eastern Europe, principally Hungary and Poland, to New York as visiting fellows. I identified some of the recipients of the fellowships through the contacts established by the newly formed Helsinki Watch, and more through Annette Laborey. Today my colleague in the Soros Foundations, Annette directed a Paris-based organization that arranged visits to the West and appointments at West European universities for independent scholars and intellectuals from East European countries.

She had a remarkable ability to identify the bravest and most talented people in the region and in many cases provided them with their first opportunities to spend time in the West. Over a period of fifteen years starting in 1974, close to 3,000 East Europeans participated.

On some of Annette's travels about the region to seek candidates, she was accompanied by whichever of her babies she was nursing at the time. Many leading East European intellectuals still cherish fond memories of their first encounters with Annette and of excellent dinners they subsequently enjoyed in her rambling apartment in an unfashionable district of Paris on a rooftop that one reached after climbing several flights of stairs (I enriched her English vocabulary by describing it to her as "funky"). All the while, she maintained a low profile, taking care to avoid identification of her program as focusing solely on dissenters by occasionally arranging appointments for party hacks.

Annette's organization was called the Fondation Pour Une Entr'Aide Intellectuelle Européenne (the Foundation for European Intellectual Mutual Aid). In its later years, George Soros became its principal supporter, but before that it was primarily underwritten by the Ford Foundation. Its board included some of the leading intellectual luminaries of the era, including, at various times, Raymond Aron, Heinrich Böll, Peter Calvocoresi, Nicola Chiaramonte, Herbert Luethy, Lionel Trilling, and Morton White. The chairman was Pierre Emmanuel, a French writer I got to know when we were establishing the International Helsinki Federation. We enlisted him to form a French affiliate that never amounted to much. Emmanuel, a veteran of the Resistance during World War II, was a member of the French Academy but had resigned when someone he considered a collaborator was elected to that august body. Thereafter, he always took care to cross out references in various documents to his Academy membership. He was, it was said, "a former immortal."

Annette's style in directing the foundation was captured in a report prepared for the Ford Foundation, which pointed out that "home intermingled with office life." The author of the report described a typical day:

Morning in Annette and Jean-Francois Laborey's apartment at the Rue St. Maur. Three grantees, a German, a Hungarian and a Romanian, are still sleeping. One story below, at the Voskoveces, Czech friends, former Foundation grantees and now emigrants, two other Czechs and one Pole, also grantees, are staying. They all met through Annette Laborey and spent in her kitchen a good part of the night. Before nine, Annette Laborey leaves for the office accompanied by her dog Hektor of unknown provenance (the cleverest dog I ever met; in Poland it managed to get into a dive where even guests were not admitted). She works with either Anna, a Hungarian, or Maryna, a Pole—her secretaries who alternate in that position. At noon a group of Polish acquaintances show up, and a couple of Czechs come to collect their grant. They start a conversation and it's a shame to stop it so they all go to a *dejeuner.* It is still a shame to stop the conversation, so the *dejeuner* lasts until four. The Polish woman is worried that Annette Laborey might be sacked. Annette Laborey goes back to the office, the rest of the company deciding to continue the conversation in the apartment at Rue St. Maur. When Annette Laborey returns home in the evening, she finds there ten East Europeans and her calm, though by now almost resigned husband, as well as three children of her own and four from the neighborhood. After the children are fed, the whole party sets off to Rue de Prague. On Thursday evenings, all "friends and relatives" meet in an Arab bistro there. Grantees, friends, friends' children, friends of the friends, emigrants and native Parisians, university professors and the unemployed come there; one never knows who will come and what will happen. In the bistro life becomes animated, there is more talk, more wine, and Arab and Moravian dances. At about two o'clock in the morning, Thursday is over, Annette Laborey returns home accompanied by eight persons, and they sit in the kitchen to finish the as yet unexhausted threads of their conversation.

That's how it was during the entire period of the Foundation's existence.[1]

Annette was eager to place some of the independent intellectuals she identified at universities in the United States and was glad to make a connection with the Humanities Institute. George agreed to support her Paris-based program as well as what I wanted to do at NYU. (In August 1990, after not seeing Annette for a while, I met her again at George Soros's sixtieth birthday celebration at his Long Island summer home and asked what she would do after the revolutions of the previous year. She told me she was thinking of opening her own bar in Paris that might be visited by the East Europeans she had brought to the West. The conversations could continue there. Instead, she became the director of the Open Society Institute's Paris office.) Among westerners I know, I believe Annette did more than anyone else to bring about the transformations in Eastern Europe. George Soros was, of course, another of those in the West who had a part in the fall of communism. I place his support for Annette's efforts high on the list of his contributions.

In 1981, when I left NYU to direct Helsinki Watch and the newly established Americas Watch, I asked George to join the board and to contribute financially. He agreed. In addition to becoming one of our main supporters, he took an active part in the weekly Wednesday morning meetings where we formulated our policies and discussed how to deal with human rights issues in the countries on which we focused. For all the participants, those meetings in the early 1980s were exciting, and George still speaks of them warmly because of the part they played in the evolution of his own thinking on how to be influential in promoting open societies. I think they played a part in persuading him that a private individual could have a significant impact on totalitarian societies that public policy savants such as Jeane Kirkpatrick claimed were impervious to change.

George became an important supporter of many of the initiatives I took at Human Rights Watch, and also a friend. He was unlike anyone I had met previously. I was struck by his capacity to compartmentalize his thinking. From time to time my lunches with him or my meetings with him in his office were interrupted by his financial transactions. From snatches of conversations I overheard, I realized that these sometimes involved sizable amounts of money. Yet he instantly returned to his discussions with me, giving no impression he had been distracted. Occasionally, I would read in the newspaper the next day about a major business deal in which he was involved and then realize why our conversation had been interrupted. But I didn't hear it from him. His talks with me were about public policy, philanthropy, or some other matter where I had something to contribute. They were never about business; it would have been a waste of time to talk to me about his financial transactions. George's engagement with his business never seemed to diminish his focus on the matters we discussed.

I enjoyed George's company because of his intellect, his boldness, and his wry humor. I watched him with growing admiration establish his network of foundations and sometimes I lent a hand. He rejected my offer to obtain public attention for the foundation he established in Hungary in 1984, the first in his network overseas, as he was then accustomed to maintaining a low profile. Though he has become a media celebrity in recent years and now exploits his capacity to attract press coverage to promote his views on many issues, at the time his instinct was that he could get more done if he avoided notice. I was able to be helpful a couple of years later when he expressed interest in China by introducing him to scholars who could advise him about establishing a foundation in Beijing (unfortunately, their counsel did not help him to avert the difficulties he encountered there). When the advent of Gorbachev, and the Soviet leader's decision to allow Andrei Sakharov to return to Moscow from his isolation in Gorky, persuaded George there was a possibility of establishing a foundation in Russia, I found someone to go to Moscow with him as his translator and guide. And at various times I sought and obtained his financial support for causes that seemed to me to comport with his desire to assist those promoting open societies. Though he was becoming known for his interest in opening countries subject to Communist rule, his interests were wider. In the 1980s, I helped him quietly disburse grants to organizations in such countries as Chile, South Africa, Guatemala, and the Philippines.

In 1992, after about a dozen years directing Human Rights Watch, I felt a need for a change. The organization had grown large and I was no longer able to spend as much time as I wanted undertaking missions to conduct investigations, organizing campaigns against abuses, and directly engaging in struggles with governments over critical issues. Most of my time was devoted to the mundane business of managing the organization and to raising the ever larger sums needed to pay for its operations. As happened at the ACLU, I had built up the organization rapidly and paid a penalty by having to dedicate an increasing amount of time to what I liked least. Also, I was greatly irritated at that moment by an internal dispute that arose when I proposed to the staff that we stop using the names of the regional Watch Committees when we issued reports or public statements. To build our institutional identity, I decided that they should all be issued in the name of Human Rights Watch. This idea was strenuously resisted by some members of the staff—particularly the two women who directed what had been Helsinki Watch and Asia Watch—because it appeared to mean a loss of status for them. Instead of seeming to be the directors of their own organizations, they would become known as directors of divisions of Human Rights Watch, as had been the case all along. They were aided and abetted in their objections by a few board members who were loyal to them.

Though I readily prevailed in this matter, helping to gain for Human Rights Watch the recognition it enjoys today, the episode left a bad taste in my mouth—in part, because I had allowed it to bother me so much—hastening my decision to move on. Human Rights Watch was doing well both in its work and its finances. I had an outstanding deputy in Ken Roth, who had been seasoned by several years on the staff and was ready to step into my shoes. It was a good moment to leave an organization that I had built but that had clearly outgrown the point where it depended on me. Though I had been somewhat apprehensive a decade and a half earlier about leaving the ACLU, that change had worked out very well for me and had enabled me to approach a new set of duties with greatly renewed energy. It had led to what I thought of as a period of particular creativity. This made the prospect of another such change very appealing. Accordingly, I spoke to George about joining his network of foundations where I would be relieved of the need to raise funds and could devote myself to a new set of challenges.

Another factor that made me turn to George Soros was the war in Bosnia. Though I cared deeply about all the issues I dealt with at Human Rights Watch, nothing had affected me more than the reemergence of Nazi-like crimes in Europe. George had reacted in much the same way. In fall 1992, he called to tell me he was establishing a $50 million fund to deal with the humanitarian consequences of the Bosnian War. He asked me to serve on a five-member committee to guide its expenditures. This experience had provided me an opportunity to respond to the crimes committed in Bosnia in ways not otherwise possible. It helped me to grasp what I could do if I could regularly influence the expenditure of his funds.

My timing turned out to be right. George had been directing his foundations network by himself, involving himself in a myriad of details. Its operations in the field vastly exceeded the capacity of its then understaffed New York headquarters to manage it effectively. He had reached the point where he finally realized he could no longer carry the burden alone. Also, he wanted to increase significantly the amount of money he was spending and needed assistance in developing new programs and expanding operations to other regions. This prospect enhanced the excitement of the opportunity. It was already evident that George's efforts in the countries of the former Soviet bloc were having a transformative impact. The possibility of becoming engaged not only in that region but in other parts of the world as well with the backing of his resources and the manner in which he was ready to use them was immensely attractive. We readily reached an agreement over the course of the dinner at which I made the proposal. About six months later, after nailing down a few major grants from other foundations to Human Rights Watch that I thought might be jeopardized if they came up for decision at a moment of transition and uncertainty, I announced my acceptance of the new post as president of the Soros Foundations and of the Open Society Institute (OSI). The latter is the body through which the foundations are governed and that also makes grants directly and operates a large range of programs.

Though I had known George Soros for nearly a decade and a half before joining his foundations network, had talked to him frequently during that period about what he was doing, and had been involved in a modest way in helping him to establish a few of his foundations, I realized soon after assuming my new post that I had only a faint inkling of the range of activities in which they were engaged. More dismaying was that I had a hard time finding out. With program and funding decisions made by boards and staff of foundations George had rapidly established in many countries, the network was highly decentralized. Decisions for the network were generally made by George himself. Paper trails either did not exist or were so scant as to be meaningless. George took pride in operating the network in its early years without a budget, reflecting the fact that—in that era—the only limit on spending was his ability to identify worthwhile projects. By the time I arrived, the network was just beginning to develop a spending plan, but George insisted on referring to it as a "soft budget," signifying his readiness to spend more when the opportunity arose. As he was already expending close to $300 million a year—a large multiple of the sums I had previously managed—I found this a bit frightening. The looseness of the finances added to my difficulty in getting a picture of what was being done. Some of the national foundations published annual reports, but there was then no such report for the network as a whole. (The first person I hired right after joining the network was Ari Korpivaara, who had worked for me at the ACLU. I brought him on to produce our annual reports.)

George's disdain for budgets and reports in that era reflected his view that he needed to operate in a revolutionary manner to take advantage of a revolutionary moment created by the collapse of the Soviet Union. It was an historic opportunity and he was intent on making the most of it. His career as an investor had been characterized by speed and dexterity, and he approached philanthropy in the same way he approached investing. There was no need for reports and budgets because he was not answerable to anyone else and was not trying to impress others; he was spending his own money and not interested in getting credit for what he was accomplishing. He felt no need to establish an enduring institution; the foundations network would only last, he assumed at the outset, so long as circumstances made it possible for him to influence the transformation of what had been closed societies. Fortunately for me, my arrival in 1993 more or less coincided with a shift in which he began to think in long-range terms. If not, I probably would have encountered stronger resistance than I did to changes that introduced more standard institutional practices.

Soon after my arrival, I realized that, although the members of the foundations network headquarters staff in New York were familiar with the programs they managed, only George himself had an overview of the activities of the whole network. During my first year in my new post, hardly a day passed in which I did not learn of some significant activity of the foundations that I had not known about previously. Thereafter, the surprises were fewer and further between, but they did not end. At times, they were embarrassing. One such occasion arose about two years after I had joined the foundations network when I attended a lunch at the Council on Foreign Relations for the president of Albania. As is customary at the council, those asking questions of the speaker state their name and their affiliation. One questioner gave his name, which I did not recognize, and then said "Soros Foundations." The president, who was seated next to me, leaned over to ask, "Who is he?" I had to confess that I had no idea (it turned out that he was an officer of the East-West Management Institute, a loosely affiliated subsidiary that was in the process of becoming independent).

Up to that point, the Soros Foundations had only operated outside the United States. With my arrival, we also launched domestic programs, starting with an effort to promote alternatives to law enforcement to reduce the harm done by drugs and drug policies and a program to aid the dying in obtaining comfort, dignity, and relief from pain. A couple of years later, we supplemented those programs with several others dealing with a broad array of domestic issues in the United States, such as campaign finances, education for the disadvantaged, criminal justice, the devolution of responsibility for welfare to the states, reproductive rights, fair treatment for immigrants, legal services for the poor, and professionalism in law and medicine.

Some of these were issues with which I was familiar because I had dealt with them years earlier at the ACLU. I was glad of an opportunity to get involved in them again with much larger resources than I had ever been able to tap previously. An example was the drug issue, which George wished to deal with in part because he thought it illustrated his concerns—derived from Karl Popper's classic work on *The Open Society and Its Enemies*—about fallibility and unintended consequences. The unintended consequence of a policy intended to control the harm done by drugs was far greater harm. As he often stated, he had no solution to the drug problem. He was attracted to the concept of "harm reduction" by its modesty and its skepticism about ultimate solutions. I was glad to reengage with the issue. Starting in the 1960s I had promoted decriminalization of marijuana, methadone maintenance for heroin addicts, the availability of treatment as an alternative to prison, and a number of other policies that remained at the forefront of public debate three decades later.

Other initiatives, such as our program on death, were new to me. George focused on the issue because his recent experience with the death of his mother had affected him profoundly. Though I had never dealt with dying as a policy issue previously and had not thought about it a lot, I found it particularly satisfying to establish a program on death, both because of the significance and complexity of the questions I had to confront—among them, the ethical issues involved in physician-assisted suicides—and because it proved to be an area where we have made a real difference for large numbers of people who are mistreated at the end of life.

In 1996, when we made the commitment to undertake a wide-ranging series of programs in the United States, I enlisted Gara LaMarche, who had previously worked with me at both the ACLU and Human Rights Watch, to establish and direct our domestic activities. Gara, who began his association with the ACLU at the age of eighteen by becoming a student member of our Academic Freedom Committee while a Columbia University freshman, turned out to be the ideal choice for my purposes because he made it possible for me to involve myself deeply in the policy issues we confront in our U.S. programs without having to be concerned with managerial issues. Working with Gara and the talented staff he assembled, and enjoying the backing of George Soros, has permitted me to have an effect on many matters that were the focus of my efforts more than two decades ago.

I have found it particularly gratifying to be able to launch programs to deal with what I regard as the most urgent civil liberties issues in the United States at the beginning of the twenty-first century: the poor quality of legal representation provided to indigent defendants in criminal cases, the incarceration of 2 million Americans at a time and of tens of millions over the course of a lifetime, and the racial factors that are both causes and consequences. It remains to be seen, of course, to what extent our programs will have a significant long-term impact, but I think we are making headway. Reports have indicated that the steep growth in imprisonment has finally been halted and, in a few places, reversed. In the wake of September 11, with another former ACLU colleague, Morton Halperin, at the helm of our Washington office, our programs in the United States have enabled me to play a part in opposing the Bush-Ashcroft use of the war on terrorism as a rationale—and sometimes as a pretext—for resurrecting many of the intrusions on civil liberties that we fought more than a quarter of a century ago.

George has also given me the opportunity to launch programs in parts of the world beyond the former Soviet empire, where he first developed his network of foundations. Initially, we chose Burma, Guatemala, Haiti, and Southern Africa as places where we might assist in promoting transitions from repression to open societies. Subsequently, we broadened our horizons to deal with other parts of Africa, Southeast Asia (especially Indonesia), Latin America, Turkey, and the Middle East. Today, we are a global institution.

My post in the Soros Foundations has also permitted me to pursue some causes with which I was particularly identified at Human Rights Watch. Starting in the mid-1980s, I became concerned about the indiscriminate deaths and injuries attributable to landmines. My interest resulted from Americas Watch's monitoring of the conflicts in El Salvador and Nicaragua and Helsinki Watch's monitoring of Afghanistan. In 1986, I commissioned and helped write the first human rights report focusing on landmines, and, thereafter, I saw to it that Human Rights Watch became the first significant organization to call for an outright prohibition on them. In 1992, I was a founder of the International Campaign to Ban Landmines (which subsequently won a Nobel Peace Prize), delivering the opening remarks at the meeting in London where the campaign was established. At the Open Society Institute, we established a landmines fund that promoted the campaign to prohibit their use and, once the treaty against landmines was adopted, to seek compliance.

Another cause in which I was deeply involved at Human Rights Watch was the effort to hold accountable officials responsible for such grave abuses as war crimes, crimes against humanity, and genocide. At OSI, we supported projects that assisted the work of the ad hoc international criminal tribunals for ex-Yugoslavia and Rwanda, the effort to create a special tribunal for Sierra Leone, and the campaign to establish a permanent International Criminal Court. In addition, in a number of countries, among them Guatemala, South Africa, Ghana, Indonesia, and Serbia, we helped those locally promoting domestic efforts to confront the crimes of the past. There were a number of other such opportunities that benefited from George Soros's willingness to use his own growing celebrity and his wide-ranging contacts with presidents, prime ministers, foreign ministers, and officials of intergovernmental bodies, as well as his financial resources, on behalf of such efforts, and his readiness to allow me to put together a staff with the capacity to promote causes that matter to both of us.

George's biographer, Michael Kaufman, has written that he is, arguably, "the most broadly and deeply engaged private citizen in the entire world."[2] Noting the comment that George has his own foreign policy, Kaufman has likened my role to that of secretary of state. In that capacity, the range of issues in which I have been involved is astonishing. I have had the chance to promote attempts to secure fair elections in Peru, the Ivory Coast, and Zimbabwe; criminal justice reform in South Africa and Russia; democratic change in Burma and other countries of Southeast Asia; programs to combat corruption worldwide; humanitarian assistance in Bosnia and Chechnya; the use of increased development assistance to impoverished countries as an incentive for democratic reforms; efforts to bring about international intervention that would end ethnic cleansing in ex-Yugoslavia; and heightened American engagement in multilateral institutions. My participation in such matters is made possible by my capacity to influence the deployment of George's resources and also by the convening power that derives from the activities of the Soros Foundations and from the networks of individuals and institutions with which the foundations are associated in the many countries where we operate. It is difficult for me to think of any other nongovernmental institution that would enable me to play a meaningful part in such an array of public policy matters in so many parts of the world.

The opportunity to bring a rights perspective to the full range of our programs has been one of the most satisfying aspects of my work for the Soros Foundations. An example is our programs in public health. I have been able to ensure that these include a focus on the health needs of outcast sectors such as prisoners, the mentally disabled, and drug addicts. As it happens, ensuring the availability of services for them is among the best means for protecting the health of the general population. In the case of intravenous drug users, for example, providing clean needles and informing them about the dangers of HIV/AIDS is probably the most effective way to curb the spread of that disease in the countries of the former Soviet bloc. In Russia, Ukraine, and the countries of Central Asia that are close to Afghanistan, the world's leading supplier of heroin in recent years, HIV/AIDS is now spreading even more rapidly than in Africa. The extensive harm reduction programs of the Soros Foundations in that region, which have attracted support from a number of other donors, are leading the effort to stem the tide. Similarly, our program to treat tuberculosis and its more frightening offshoot, multidrug-resistant tuberculosis (MDRTB), in the Russian prisons is probably the most effective way that can be devised to prevent those diseases from also becoming epidemic in the general population. From a human rights standpoint, it is unconscionable that the consequence of imprisonment should be the likelihood of contracting TB or, worse, MDRTB; from a public health standpoint, it is equally appalling that everyone should be exposed to those diseases because 300,000 Russian prisoners are released each year. With George Soros's strong support, I have had the chance to serve both interests simultaneously.

When I went to work for George, many predicted our association would be short-lived. He was known as strong-willed, and I had a similar reputation. Inevitably, we would clash, it was suggested, both by those who knew us and those who didn't. My own view was different. I knew we would have disagreements, and some were likely to arouse strong feelings in us both. As it was his money and his foundation, though, ultimately he could prevail in any dispute. Having come to know him well for nearly a decade and a half before I went to work for him, I thought our core commitments were similar and believed he was sincere in accepting the fallibility he recognized as a matter of philosophical principle. When we had strong disagreements, I knew I would have a reasonable opportunity to persuade him to change his position. He does not insist that those who work for him should defer to his views. Far from it. Most of those for

whom he has high regard argue with him. Also, I respect George sufficiently to realize that when we disagree, he might be right and I might be
wrong. Accordingly, I thought that either we would work out our disagreements or, where that proved impossible, it need not disrupt our ability to
work together.

Our most serious quarrel took place during my first year working for
George. In 1994, we learned of financial wrongdoing in the foundation he
had established in Russia. We organized an investigation, and I went to
Moscow to deal with the matter. On the basis of a report I got from
forensic auditors we had engaged, I fired two top officials of the foundation. Two others, including the executive director, resigned. In addition,
we reorganized the board of the foundation.

On the way back from Moscow, I met George in London and told him
what I had done. He was very unhappy. On the one hand, he agreed that
the situation had called for action; on the other hand, he was concerned
that I had overreacted. He was particularly upset that my actions had
forced out the executive director, as he considered her fundamentally honest, though he acknowledged she had made errors of judgment in a deeply
corrupt environment and that there had been serious consequences. My
own view was that, if anything, I did not go far enough. As corruption is
endemic in Russia, it seemed to me all the more important to demonstrate
it would not be tolerated.

Our sharp argument over this matter sufficiently upset George so that
he canceled his attendance at a dinner that evening at the home of a prominent British writer where he was the guest of honor. I went to the dinner,
which was attended by several other well-known writers, and found our
host livid at the cancellation. George's feelings about the episode in
Moscow were reflected in an unflattering profile of him in *The New Yorker*
by Connie Bruck in which she quoted him as saying, sarcastically, I imagine, "Aryeh is very pure." Yet we easily got past this episode, though it had
the effect of making me circumscribe my own involvement with our Russia Foundation for a period to avoid a repetition of that conflict. It had no
effect on our ability to work together closely on other matters or on our
trust in each other.

Inevitably, we have had additional disagreements. Some reflect our dif-
fering life experiences. George has succeeded as an investor by sizing up
situations quickly and acting decisively. He is known for his readiness to
make big bets, reflecting trust in his own judgment. The manner in which

he invests also requires him to shift course on a moment's notice to adapt to changing conditions and always to be ready to cut his losses. In contrast, my experience in directing large nongovernmental organizations that could succeed only through prolonged effort has made me value steadiness of course and reliability. In the world I came from, I had a reputation for boldness, but in comparison to George I am a cautious person. Before I worked with George, I thought that I was quick to size up those whom I encountered, but next to George I am a slouch. He isn't always right in his rapid-fire judgments, but he is right often enough so that I think the benefits more than compensate for the occasional mistake. George is skeptical of institutions, as he believes they lose their sense of mission over time and become preoccupied with their own survival or aggrandizement. I have been a man of institutions, believing that bodies such as the ACLU, Human Rights Watch, and, indeed, the Open Society Institute play crucial roles in making possible a just, democratic, and open society.

Rather than causing difficulty, however, I believe that the adjustments each of us has had to make to accommodate the other's approach and to see the other's point of view has had a beneficial impact on our work together. Because we have recognized this, things have worked out much more as I expected than in accordance with the predictions of those who confidently asserted there would be an early parting of the ways. Over time, our disagreements have been fewer and further between. When they take place, they are amicable. It has been a very satisfying period because George has allowed me to deal with both the domestic issues that were my foremost civil liberties concerns, the international issues on which I focused at Human Rights Watch, and a range of matters that are new to me—many of them reflecting his interests—that have expanded my horizons. There are no geographical limits; nothing is foreclosed because it is too controversial; I am not required to raise funds; and George has provided not only his ideas and his resources but also his considerable personal clout to back the work I most want to do. His engagement often makes it easier to enlist others also to contribute. As I consider myself fortunate to devote my career to protecting rights, I believe I am doubly blessed to arrive at a point where I can maintain and build upon my lifelong commitments from such a favored setting.

CHAPTER FIFTEEN

Sarajevo, Chechnya, and the Loss of Fred Cuny

I t was minus sixteen degrees Celsius when I arrived in Sarajevo a few days after New Year's Day of 1993. Virtually every building I saw there was damaged by shelling or pockmarked with bullets from the eight-months-old siege that lasted nearly another three years. Hardly a pane of glass was intact; there was no electricity, no heat, no running water. I felt colder indoors than outside and was barely able to speak at a press conference because I couldn't stop my teeth from chattering. Trees in the city streets, except for those that obscured the view for the snipers in the surrounding hills, were being cut down for firewood. UN food deliveries were providing the 300,000 or so remaining residents of the city with about 600 calories a day, a third of what they needed in that climate. By then, many Sarajevans were running out of any supplies they had had on hand to supplement this meager diet. To get water, people trundled children's sleds behind them through the snow with plastic jugs, which they filled at a well at the city's old brewery. Getting water was a particular hardship for the elderly, the sick, and the wounded. Some had to carry the water up many flights of stairs to high-rise apartments no longer reachable by elevator because the electricity was cut off. Cold and hunger seemed as life threatening as the firepower of the besieging Serbs.

I went to Sarajevo to see whether it was possible to use private funds to make a difference in the lives of the city's residents. George Soros had called me at Human Rights Watch a few weeks earlier to say he was donating $50 million for humanitarian assistance in Bosnia. He asked me to serve on a five-member advisory committee to guide expenditure of the funds. My colleagues on that committee were Morton Abramowitz, a crusty, seasoned U.S. diplomat, then president of the Carnegie Endowment for International Peace; Kurt Bolliger, the retired commander of the Swiss Air Force, then vice chairman of the International Federation of Red Cross and Red Crescent Societies; Mark Malloch Brown, an international political consultant of British origin who had played key roles in Corazon Aquino's defeat of Ferdinand Marcos in the 1986 Philippine presidential election and in General Augusto Pinochet's repudiation in the 1988 plebiscite in Chile, and who was later appointed in 1999 to head the United Nations Development Program; and Prince Sadruddin Aga Khan, former United Nations High Commissioner for Refugees.

George had an ulterior motive in establishing this fund. In addition to relieving misery, he hoped to strengthen the will of Western governments to stop the ethnic cleansing that was both the means and the end of the war in Bosnia. By distributing funds to international humanitarian organizations, he would bring their personnel to Bosnia to witness the crimes committed there. In speaking out, they might influence their governments. All of us on the advisory committee passionately supported decisive international intervention to stop the war.

At Human Rights Watch, we had closely monitored the events leading to the 1991 war in Croatia and the crimes committed in that conflict, and we were on the scene in Bosnia when the war began there in April 1992. Three months later, we published a book-length report I entitled "War Crimes in Bosnia-Herzegovina." Much of the report was based on the field investigations of a young researcher, Ivana Nizich, who subsequently joined the staff of the International Criminal Tribunal for the former Yugoslavia. When Jeri Laber recommended we hire her, I hesitated because of her youth. A decade earlier, several very young women had been instrumental to the success of Americas Watch, but that was before it was possible to find a significant number of experienced human rights researchers to work for us. By the beginning of the 1990s, the field was well established and tested investigators were not in short supply. My doubts were overcome by a strong recommendation from Warren Zimmermann, the last U.S. ambassador to a united Yugoslavia. He said Ivana had held an internship at the State Department when the desk officer for Yugoslavia got sick. Knowing the language, she was pressed into service. She performed splendidly. Though several more experienced researchers accompanied her on missions to Yugoslavia during the period the country was disintegrating and the wars were beginning, she did the lion's share of our fact-finding. The report on "War Crimes" was a landmark in our history. I wrote the Introduction, where we asserted:

A policy of "ethnic cleansing" has resulted in the summary execution, disappearance, arbitrary detention, deportation and forcible displacement of hundreds of thousands of people on the basis of their religion or nationality. In sum, the extent of the violence and the fact that it is targeted along ethnic/religious lines raises the question of whether genocide is taking place.

Human Rights Watch calls on the Security Council of the United Nations to exercise its authority under the 1951 Convention on the Prevention and Punishment of the Crime of Genocide to intervene in Bosnia-Herzegovina to prevent and suppress genocide. Human Rights Watch also calls upon the United Nations Security Council to enforce the prohibition of "grave breaches" of the Geneva Conventions by establishing an international tribunal at the highest level to investigate, prosecute, adjudicate and punish those on all sides who have been responsible for war crimes on the territory of the former Yugoslavia.[1]

This report set a number of precedents. Though we had published hundreds of reports, it was the first time Human Rights Watch invoked the Genocide Convention; the first time we called for international intervention; and the first time we called for establishment of a war crimes tribunal.

This last matter turned out to be our most significant contribution. It was the first serious call to establish such a tribunal. Because of an accident of timing, our call resonated publicly, which gave it a great boost. Six months after we issued our call, the Security Council unanimously adopted a resolution authorizing a tribunal; three months after that, the council unanimously adopted another resolution approving a specific plan for its operation.

The accident of timing was that our report was issued just as *Newsday* reporter Roy Gutman began publishing revelations about Omarska and other camps where Bosnian Serbs were torturing, starving, and murdering Bosnian Muslims. Gutman's articles caused a sensation. Our call for the first international criminal tribunal since Nuremberg and Tokyo seemed the right response to crimes eerily reminiscent of those of the Nazis a half century earlier.

Though I was pleased our call for an international criminal tribunal was taken seriously, watching developments in Bosnia and the pathetic response in Western capitals and at the United Nations made me angrier and more frustrated about public policy than I'd ever been before. There had never been a moment in my lifetime when I thought the opportunity to promote respect for human rights globally was better than in the immediate post–Cold War period. The revolutions of 1989 in Eastern Europe had transformed virtually overnight a vast region that suffered from institutionalized repression. Throughout the previous decade, military dictatorships had given way to democratic governments in South America. The murderous wars in Central America had come to an end as the Cold War sponsors of the opposing forces lost interest. Nelson Mandela was freed from prison in South Africa, and negotiations were under way to end apartheid. Democracy was advancing in South Korea, the Philippines, and Taiwan; and though the Chinese Communist Party and the People's Army had crushed the democracy movement in Tiananmen Square to prevent the spread of "the Polish disease," I thought that if the West remained resolute in condemning Beijing and in supporting human rights, change in China could not be postponed indefinitely. Yet at that moment, when none of the complex calculations that inhibited efforts to safeguard rights during the Cold War era were at play, the European powers, the United States, and the United Nations had small-minded leaders such as Bush, Major, Mitterrand, Kohl, and Boutros-Ghali who were preoccupied with their own political fortunes. They could not muster the resolve to stop even the ghastliest crimes in the center of Europe. I believed then that Western inaction in Bosnia in 1992 and 1993 would have disastrous consequences worldwide. Events of the ensuing decade have confirmed that judgment.

I was glad to accept George's invitation to help manage his fund for Bosnia. The largest gift ever by a private individual to meet a humanitarian emergency manifested his belief in the need to respond in a way commensurate with the magnitude of the crisis. It also gave me an opportunity to go beyond reporting on human rights abuses and proposing legal remedies. Human Rights Watch had gone to the limit of its self-defined mandate in calling on the Security Council to intervene to prevent and punish genocide. Association with George's fund would give me a chance to get involved in a broader range of public policy debates over Bosnia.

The first task was to spend the $50 million well. Two other members of the advisory committee, Mort Abramowitz and Mark Malloch Brown, joined me on that New Year's visit to Sarajevo for a quick on-the-scene survey and to talk to officials of the Bosnian government about their needs. Lionel Rosenblatt, formerly a State Department official who worked for Mort when he was Ambassador to Thailand in the 1970s, accompanied us. He had made refugees his life's work, having discovered the interest when he was assigned to deal with Cambodian refugees from the Khmer Rouge at the Thai border. It was the first of several trips to the besieged city that I made with Lionel. I tried to make sure I traveled with him, as I enjoyed his company and because he always knew how to deal with the many hassles that arose. A veteran of war zones all over the world, Lionel seemed able to cope with any bureaucratic or logistical difficulty we encountered.

Much the most impressive Bosnian official we met was Hakija Turajlić, the deputy prime minister. Bundled up in our coats, we had lunch with him in his freezing office, delighted that he managed to serve us hot soup. Four days later, I was horrified to hear that he was murdered on his way to the airport. The UN armored personnel carrier in which he was riding was stopped at a Serb checkpoint. The Serbs demanded that the APC be opened so they could check the contents. A British officer on the scene refused. A higher ranking French officer, a Colonel Sartre, came by, countermanded this, and had the doors to the APC opened. Peering into the APC, a Serb soldier saw Turajlić and shot him point blank. On a subsequent visit to Sarajevo, I visited his grave, marked by a typical Bosnian Muslim tombstone, a post with a carving on top that resembled a turban, to pay my respects. I also silently cursed Colonel Sartre, whose government recognized his distinguished service in Bosnia by awarding him the Légion d'Honneur.

In an effort to ensure that George Soros's money was used effectively, Mort Abramowitz enlisted a disaster relief specialist, Fred Cuny, to go to Sarajevo to undertake projects we could support. In 1991, working with Mort, who was then U.S. ambassador to Turkey, Fred had been the architect of the successful repatriation of several hundred thousand Kurds who fled into Turkey from northern Iraq after Saddam Hussein's forces turned on them in the aftermath of the Gulf War. The "security zone" Fred proposed has protected the Kurds to this day. I knew of Fred but had never worked with him previously. Over the next twenty-seven months, until he disappeared in Chechnya in April 1995, Fred became my close collaborator and my friend.

A large, good-humored Texan, Fred had some attributes of a "good ol' boy." He was fond of telling stories (including tall tales), was a near fanatic devotee of the Dallas Cowboys, and loved piloting his own plane. (At a point when we were having difficulty getting certain supplies into Sarajevo, Fred recommended to me that we lease a Russian Antonov jet for a month. As I was mulling this over, he added, "There's just one more thing." "What's that?" "I get to fly it," he said.) There was another side of Fred as well: Growing up in Texas in the 1960s, he had been caught up in the civil rights struggle. Though it is hard to know what motivates someone to take risks like those Fred took throughout his life, it is possible that the passions aroused in him by the campaign for racial equality in the United States had prompted him to take on his first humanitarian relief assignment. Not long after attending college, he became a pilot in the Red Cross airlift in Biafra in 1969. In the quarter of a century between Biafra and Chechnya, Fred provided help to the victims of more than a score of the disasters—man-made and natural—of the era. He assisted victims of earthquakes in Guatemala and Armenia; of civil wars in Cambodia, Lebanon, Sri Lanka, and Sudan; and of the famine in Ethiopia. At Mort Abramowitz's initiative, he went to Somalia before President Bush sent in U.S. troops and proposed a plan to assist the victims of the conflict there. Fred urged that military intervention should focus on protection of food distribution in the countryside so that starving Somalis would not be drawn into the cities. He warned U.S. officials against involvement in what he labeled "the concrete snakepit" of Mogadishu. If his plan had been adopted, it probably would have averted the painful incidents that severely tarnished the concept of humanitarian intervention.

The best known of Fred's many projects for us was his effort to provide Sarajevo with running water after the regular supply was cut off by besieging Serb forces. The system Fred created, with the help of a Bosnian engineer, Farouk Shllaku, whose father was a Kosovar Albanian, was a marvel. As it had to be protected against Serb shelling, Fred installed the main purification plant in an old road tunnel that ran under a hill and connected the system he installed there to long, unused, nineteenth-century culverts that he rediscovered by consulting local historians and examining old maps. These delivered the water by gravity to a majority of the city's residents. He also built a smaller plant at a higher elevation to reach residents who lived on Sarajevo's hillsides. The water for the main plant came from the Miljacka River, which flowed through the city. It had to be pumped from the river to the purification plant. Fred arranged that the plant should be built in Texas in long, narrow segments that could be rolled onto UN C-130 relief planes flying to Sarajevo, then rolled off at the city's airport, attached to trucks, and finally assembled in what was eventually a 200-meter-long system in the tunnel.

As Fred showed this to me on one of my trips to Sarajevo, it all seemed quite fantastic. I recall, on that occasion, that he was particularly excited about the speed with which the segments of the purification plant were being unloaded at the Sarajevo airport. He had it down to seconds. Speed was essential as the equipment was vulnerable to shelling and because the relief planes only flew during daylight hours. They had to make several trips a day to bring in other supplies needed by the besieged population. The water system became operational in November 1993, though city officials delayed its use because Fred refused to pay the customary bribes. When it began operating, it often provided the city its only source of running water.

Fred focused on the water project because he noticed that many of the Sarajevans who had been killed and wounded by sniper fire were struck while getting water. To get to the brewery, they had to traverse areas where buildings or makeshift corrugated metal barricades did not shield them. As they moved slowly, carrying or dragging large plastic jugs filled with water, they were easy targets. The project was first and foremost about saving lives. Improving the quality of life mattered a lot, but it was secondary.

Another project Fred undertook at the same time connected a large number of Sarajevo's homes to natural gas to keep the city's residents warm in winter. Before the war, only about 10 percent of Sarajevan residences were connected to gas. The gas came by pipeline from Russia through Ukraine and Hungary and passed through Serbia and parts of Bosnia controlled by Serbs before getting to the city. Fred established that the same pipeline also brought gas to Belgrade. Whenever the Serbs turned off the gas to Sarajevo, as happened a number of times, Fred called me. My assignment was to call U.S. officials to get them to put pressure on the Hungarians, either directly or through the UN Sanctions Committee, to threaten the Serbs with a shutdown. This way, we kept the gas flowing most of the time.

To connect Sarajevans to gas, Fred brought plastic gas pipes in on relief planes and enlisted some 15,000 of the city's residents to dig trenches through the streets for pipes that eventually reached another 60 percent of the homes in the city. He also designed a small gas heater that could be manufactured for about $15 and could keep a single room warm. Turned on its side, the heater was used by Sarajevans for cooking. Fred also added variety and nourishment to the diet of besieged Sarajevans by bringing in large quantities of seeds. Many of the city's high-rise apartments had terraces, he noted. Old buckets and coffee cans could be used to grow vegetables. In summer, as a consequence, virtually every terrace was covered with tomato and pepper plants.

One of the projects we could not disclose during the war boosted the supply of electricity in the city. I visited Sarajevo several times during 1993; much of the time, it seemed the only electricity was provided by a generator that served the city's main hospital and by a few rudimentary homemade generators that some handy Sarajevans had built at hillside streams. Later, however, some electricity was restored to the city. Fred explored a number of ways of adding to the supply and, in 1994, told me he had come up with a plan. He had located two large, unused transformers in Croatia. They could be trucked to a point some distance from Sarajevo and installed on land controlled by the Bosnian government. There was no way to get them into the city, as they were too big for relief planes. Nor could they pass through a secret tunnel that led to the city from territory controlled by government forces. The tunnel was too low for an adult to pass through upright. A connecting cable would have to go through the tunnel. At other points, it would go underground. Secrecy was required so Serb marksmen would not pick off the men laying the cable. The transformers would be nestled in the hills at a relatively safe spot, but if the Serbs knew about them, they might destroy them by shelling.

I went to see Bosnian President Alija Izetbegović to inform him of the project and to get his support. He was delighted to hear of it. I then discussed it with the U.S. Office of Foreign Disaster Assistance, which agreed to contribute $300,000, half the cost. Its effect was to increase the electricity supply to Sarajevo by about 30 percent. On a few occasions when all other sources of power failed, Fred's transformers supplied enough electricity to maintain emergency services.

As Fred did such splendid work in Sarajevo, I enlisted him to undertake other projects for the Open Society Institute, where I started work in September 1993. In 1994, George Soros launched a program to reform primary and secondary education in Albania. It included a plan to rebuild a large number of schools. They were shoddily constructed by the old Communist regime, and many had been vandalized and looted during the upheaval that accompanied that regime's fall. At a number of schools I visited, window frames had been cut out of the walls and roofs had been pulled down. Many were in such poor condition that it was impossible to conduct classes in them. Fred brought along to Albania the Bosnian engineer, Farouk Shllaku, who worked with him on the water project in Sarajevo. Farouk's Kosovar provenance came in handy; he spoke Albanian, understood the culture, and was particularly effective in protecting our construction projects against the country's endemic corruption. Some of Fred's Texas associates also went to Albania. As in the case of the Sarajevo gas project, Farouk and Terrice Bassler, a World Bank official we borrowed to direct the project, enlisted local residents as volunteers to assist in the rebuilding. Involving the locals turned out to be crucial. When Albania went through another period of turmoil in 1996 after several pyramid schemes collapsed and large numbers of people lost their life savings, many public buildings were again looted. The schools we repaired were unscathed, however. Having contributed their labor, villagers and townspeople refused to let them be vandalized. In some places, they guarded the schools at night to ensure their safety.

In January 1995, I went to Russia with George Soros to see how we might provide humanitarian assistance to victims of the war in Chechnya. The crisis had begun in earnest the previous month when Russian troops had entered the breakaway territory. From Moscow, I called Fred and asked him to go to Chechnya to advise us on projects we might support. Fred went in February and arranged for us to establish a hospital in nearby Nazran, Ingushetia—the neighboring province—to provide emergency care for victims of the conflict. He also thought he saw an opportunity to use another of the projects he proposed as a basis for a cease-fire.

Almost all the noncombatants who could get out of the capital, Grozny, had fled the city. Among those remaining were about 30,000 elderly persons. Most were ethnic Russians. The city's Chechen residents had relatives in nearby provincial communities and the surrounding countryside with whom they took refuge. The elderly Russians had no such options. Their situation was critical. As Fred wrote in a report he submitted to me:

> In Grozny, no one lives above ground. Most of the remaining civilians are living in the basements of large apartment complexes, partially destroyed factories, or in old civil defense shelters built during the Cold War. There is no light, heat, water, or sanitary facilities in any of these refuges. People

are afraid to cook in their shelters because they are poorly ventilated and they're fearful that the smoke will attract shelling. The only time they can cook is when there are lulls in the fighting during daylight hours and when it is foggy and overcast. Then the men go out and cook behind walls so that if they are attacked, only a few will be exposed.

The only warmth in the shelters is provided by blankets. The civil defense shelters are fairly deep so there is some natural insulation from the earth, but even so temperatures at night are below 10 degrees celsius. In the factories and apartment building basements, the temperatures are only slightly warmer than outside.

Fred proposed that we charter a fleet of 100 buses to evacuate the city's old people. It would take about ten days to get them out, and it could only be done if a cease-fire were declared. He hoped the ethnicity of most of those involved would persuade the Russian government to go along with the scheme. Sergei Kovalev, a biologist who was a leading Soviet-era dissident and then a member of the Russian Parliament and the country's national human rights commissioner, and who had risked his own life to protest the Chechen war by moving into an apartment in Grozny when the Russian bombing began, presented Fred's plan to President Boris Yeltsin. Nothing came of it as Yeltsin rejected the plan. The Russian military was more intent on destroying the Chechen enemy than on saving the lives of thousands of elderly Russians.

When Fred returned to the United States, he conducted briefings on Chechnya for government officials, such as Deputy Secretary of State Strobe Talbott, the principal architect of U.S. policy toward Russia during the Clinton years, and others concerned with foreign policy. One of those who attended a briefing I organized at our offices was Robert Silvers, editor of *The New York Review of Books*. The result was an article for that publication by Fred that was highly critical of the Russian government and also of the Chechen leadership.

In March, Fred called me and proposed that he return to Chechnya because the situation had changed and he thought he should revise his proposals for humanitarian assistance to take account of the developments. Chechen fighters had withdrawn from Grozny, the bombardment of the city had stopped, and some civilians were resettling the city. Fred wanted to see what could be done for them. As Chechnya had become one of the most dangerous places in the world, some of my colleagues were reluctant to have Fred take this risk. They also worried that his article in *The New York Review of Books,* which was about to appear in April, would antagonize the Russian government. Our educational programs and the other activities of the Soros Foundation in Russia depended on the government's cooperation. I shared some of those concerns and consulted George Soros. We agreed that Fred should go again on a carefully circumscribed mission.

On his way to Russia from Texas on March 22, Fred stopped by my office in New York and, as on previous occasions, we drew up a brief consulting agreement. This time, however, when I gave it to Fred to sign, he pointed out that I had failed to include a statement that we would not be responsible if he came to any harm, as he carried his own insurance. I thought that was his way of responding to the concerns about the danger in Chechnya. Though I had not included such a provision in any previous consulting agreement, I added the statement he suggested. Later, I wondered whether he had a premonition of disaster. This was his way to declare that he was responsible for his own safety.

Fred called me from Chechnya on April 1. He had just visited Grozny and was on his way back to Nazran, where the hospital we had established was located. He would go from there to Moscow and then return to the United States to keep a speaking engagement in California. On the phone, he briefly proposed three projects. He wanted us to establish a small radio station in Chechnya to broadcast information on missing persons to help reunite families separated by the war; to bring small tool kits to Grozny so residents returning to shattered homes could make basic repairs; and to establish a small epidemiological laboratory in Grozny because he feared an outbreak of cholera.

I do not know exactly where Fred was when he called me or what kind of phone he used, and he did not give me a clear indication of when he would reach Ingushetia. All he said was that he might be delayed a bit as he would take a detour to avoid an area of combat. I did not press him for details; I thought the Russian authorities were probably monitoring calls and I saw no reason to keep them informed of Fred's movements. They were not enthusiastic about humanitarian assistance to Chechens. As far as I know, that was Fred's last contact with anyone outside Chechnya.

A few days later, I was traveling in Europe when I got a call from Elizabeth Socolow, a young American who had worked with me at Human Rights Watch before joining the Soros Foundations. Elizabeth was overseeing support for Fred's relief projects in Chechnya from our office in Moscow. She was worried because she had not heard from Fred. I mentioned his detour to avoid combat, and we agreed to wait a couple of days longer before sounding an alarm. When those days passed with no word from Fred, however, we started calling his family and friends. I went to Moscow to launch a search for Fred and for three Russians who had accompanied him to Grozny: Galina Oleinik, Fred's translator, and Andrey Sereda and Sergei Makarov, two doctors associated with the Russian Red Cross who worked at the hospital we had established.

One of those I called to report that Fred was missing was Lionel Rosenblatt, who had worked closely with us in Bosnia. Lionel dropped everything and went to Moscow right away, where we met to launch the search. Fred's brother Chris and his son Craig joined us in Moscow and then went with Lionel to Ingushetia to pursue the search in Chechnya. Lionel spent several weeks there with the Cunys. Over time, several other friends, relatives, and associates of Fred's also took part. Among them was Bill Stuebner, a former military man who took a leave from his post as an investigator for the International Criminal Tribunal for the former Yugoslavia. Bill called me to volunteer. Though I knew he knew Fred, I had not thought they were close. Why did he want to do this? He said if he were missing, he was sure Fred would try to find him. He felt an obligation to do the same for Fred. Knowing something of Bill's work in other difficult and dangerous circumstances, I welcomed him to the search.

In the military, from which he had retired after twenty years of service in 1992, Bill had served in Central America. Assigned to the Pentagon subsequently, he collaborated with the late Representative Joe Moakley of Massachusetts and Moakley's aide, Jim McGovern, now also a member of Congress, in solving the November 1989 murder in El Salvador of six Jesuit priests along with their housekeeper and her daughter. They established that the murder had been planned by the Salvadoran military high command. When I asked Bill about his role in this matter, he pointed out that he had carried out Secretary of Defense Dick Cheney's directive never to lie to Congress. Though the U.S. ambassador in El Salvador at the time, William Walker, had stated publicly that he thought the murders had been committed by the guerrillas in an attempt to discredit the armed forces, Bill was not satisfied with that explanation. Drawing on his contacts in the Salvadoran military, he helped Moakley and McGovern establish that the murders had been directly ordered by Colonel Rene Emilio

Ponce, chief of staff of the armed forces, in the presence of four other top officers of the General Staff. This finding was later confirmed by the United Nations Truth Commission for El Salvador. Ponce and the others were ousted from their posts, though never prosecuted. President Alfredo Cristiani pushed an amnesty law through the Salvadoran Congress to protect them.

In January 1993, a day or two after New Year's, on the way to Sarajevo, I encountered Bill in the lobby of the Esplanade Hotel in Zagreb. Lionel Rosenblatt, who had spent New Year's eve in Sarajevo sharing one of the rooms not destroyed by a mortar shell at the Holiday Inn with Richard Holbrooke (Holbrooke got the bed while Lionel slept on the floor), and was about to go back into the besieged city with me, joined me in talking to Bill about the extraordinary mission he had just completed. On behalf of the U.S. Government's Office of Foreign Disaster Assistance, he had conducted a needs assessment in Goražde, another Bosnian government-controlled town surrounded by Serb forces. Lionel and I could fly into Sarajevo on a military transport plane because its airport was controlled by UN forces. There was no airport in Goražde. It had been cut off from the rest of the country for several months. How did Bill get in?

Bill told us he went to Goražde on foot. He had walked 35 kilometers through the snow and through Serb lines to get there, spent three weeks in the town to do his survey, and then left the same way he had come. Bill gave us a graphic picture of the dire needs in Goražde; he also told us that some of the men of the besieged town were bringing in a few supplies by nighttime forays on sturdy ponies to territory where they made contact with Bosnian government forces. He tried to persuade us that his visit to Goražde—the only one by an outsider until much later in the war, I believe—was not as dangerous as it sounded. The Bosnian Serbs had too few troops to patrol effectively at night. The main danger was landmines. I was not reassured.

The search for Fred was filled with false leads and harrowing episodes that the searchers themselves barely escaped with their lives. Even men as accustomed to hardship and danger as Lionel Rosenblatt, Bill Stuebner, Fred's humanitarian assistance colleagues, and his brother Chris and his son Craig, who had both joined Fred on a number of perilous assignments, had never experienced anything like it. Fred had told me that Chechnya was the scariest place he had ever been. Over time, various participants in the search said the same to me. Yet I never heard a complaint from any of them, even after so much time passed that all the searchers must have despaired of finding Fred alive.

The search extended far beyond Chechnya. We pursued any lead that seemed plausible. An example was a call I got that a couple of Fred's associates had seen a brief report on Euronews of the capture of Samashki, a town that achieved brief notoriety as the site of a massacre of a portion of its civilian population by Russian troops. The report on Euronews included a film clip that lasted a few seconds showing a column of prisoners from behind. One of the prisoners, seen for an instant, was very large. Fred's associates thought it might be him.

We arranged for Euronews, based in Lyons, France, to send all its footage on Chechnya to Paris, where it could be screened by my colleague there, Annette Laborey. As Annette did not know Fred, she was joined by Yvette Pierpaoli, a French colleague of Lionel Rosenblatt's in Refugees International. Yvette knew Fred well as their paths had crossed in many places. Like Lionel, her involvement in humanitarian assistance began in the 1970s with the Cambodian refugees from the Khmer Rouge. It continued until she died on a mission on behalf of Kosovar refugees in Northern Albania in 1999, when her car slid off a muddy mountain road. A woman of great charm as well as passion for the causes to which she devoted herself, she became the real-life model for Tessa, the heroine of her friend John Le Carre's novel *The Constant Gardener.*

Unfortunately, the Euronews footage proved of no help. The same was true of contacts with individuals with Chechen connections from Brooklyn to Canada to Jordan and of efforts we made through the leaders of Ingushetia and through Russian government officials. None of our leads went anywhere.

Chris and Craig Cuny continued their search in Chechnya. Four months passed before they announced that they had established that Fred and his companions had been killed by Chechen rebels. They had been set up by Russian agents who had conveyed the disinformation that they were Russian spies. I did not find this account entirely convincing. All the evidence indicated that Fred and his Russian colleagues had been killed by Chechens. Which Chechens, and why, were less clear. There were many possibilities. They could have been taken for spies regardless of whether the Russians set them up. They could have been the innocent victims of a factional dispute between rival Chechen leaders. It might have been a robbery or a kidnapping for ransom that went sour. Yet another possible scenario is the one favored by journalist Scott Anderson in his book about Fred, *The Man Who Tried to Save the World*.[2]

Anderson makes much of the fact that the town in Chechnya where Fred and his companions were last seen, Bamut, is the site of an old Russian nuclear missile base. It was deactivated in 1987, but Anderson wrote that the Chechen "president," Dzhokar Dudayev, a former Russian Air Force general later killed by a Russian missile that honed in on his satellite phone, had persuaded the Russians that he might have gotten hold of nuclear warheads that he stored in the unused missile silos at Bamut. Suspicious that Fred had traveled to Bamut to find out what was in the silos, Dudayev had Fred and his companions executed on April 14, 1995.[3]

Another theory that surfaces from time to time is that Fred was intent on arranging an exclusive interview with Dzhokar Dudayev that he would provide to one of the television networks. Dudayev, according to the proponents of this theory, was furious that Fred had tracked him down because he believed this would tip off the Russians to his whereabouts—and had Fred executed. This story seems highly unlikely. Fred would have known that Dudayev's location was a very sensitive matter. It would not be worth finding him merely to get an interview. Moreover, as far as I know, Fred did not have a video camera with him. A slightly more plausible version is that Fred tried to find Dudayev because he had an idea for a ceasefire that could lead to a peace settlement. Fred would have found such an idea attractive; it is similar to his earlier proposal to suspend the fighting so that Grozny's elderly Russian residents could be bused to safety, and he might have taken a risk to pursue it. But I am sure he would have sought permission to see Dudayev before setting out in search of him. The difficulty with this theory, like all the others, is that I know of no evidence to support it.

Yet another theory is that it was not Fred who was the target but the Russian doctors and Fred's translator, Galina Oleinik. When I went to Moscow to announce that Fred was missing, I learned for the first time of an episode in which they had been involved ten days before they had joined Fred on the visit to Grozny. They had been arrested by Russian troops at a checkpoint near Assinovskaya on suspicion of carrying supplies to Chechen guerrillas. After a lengthy interrogation in which they were threatened with execution, the doctors were put on board an army helicopter and taken away to be questioned further. Somehow, Galina Oleinik was left unguarded, ran away, and made her way back to Nazran, the Ingush capital. There, she persuaded officials to intercede with the Russian authorities to secure the release of the doctors.

After this episode, the Russian Red Cross, the employer of the doctors, forbade them to travel to Chechnya. They were violating this rule when they set out with Fred. Perhaps the Russian troops made good on their earlier threats against the doctors. Or, maybe there was something fishy about the story that Galina Oleinik had escaped and secured their release.

In Moscow, I went to see the head of the Russian Red Cross. He seemed not very interested in the disappearance of the doctors. No one had even bothered to notify their families. When I held a press conference the next morning to announce that Fred was missing, and to solicit information from anyone who might have seen him or knew what happened to him, I could not even mention the names of the doctors because I did not want their families to get the news that way.

When Scott Anderson interviewed me for his book, I told him I thought his theory was neither more nor less credible than any other I had heard. Reading his book did not convince me. Anderson makes a good adventure story out of his effort to retrace Fred's footsteps, but his account of why Fred was killed rests on speculation. I still do not know why Fred was killed and do not believe any of those who have publicly propounded their theories have made a convincing case. One of the theories may be right, but I can't tell which one.

Losing Fred weighs more heavily on me than anything else that has happened in the four decades of my career. I asked him to go to Chechnya, and he went there for the visit that cost him his life under the terms of a contract I signed. Though little fuss has been made of them in Russia or elsewhere, I am also painfully aware of the loss of his three Russian companions. They devoted themselves to providing humanitarian assistance under the most dangerous circumstances to people hated and despised by the overwhelming majority of their fellow citizens. Though I can't be sure, I assume they perished solely because they were with Fred.

Thanks largely to Fred Cuny, George Soros's $50 million contribution for humanitarian assistance in Bosnia did much to relieve misery. It did not do much to further George's other purpose, however, as he is the first to acknowledge. There is no indication that the expenditure of the funds affected the course of the war. When Western governments eventually summoned the resolve to end the conflict, it was because of a number of events in 1995, including the slaughter of up to 8,000 Muslim men and boys at Srebrenica and the designation of Richard Holbrooke as principal negotiator for the United States. The International Criminal Tribunal for the former Yugoslavia also made a contribution. In July 1995, it handed down criminal indictments against the Bosnian Serb leaders Radovan Karadzić and General Ratko Mladić; later in the year, it indicted them again for Srebrenica.

That prevented them from participating in the November 1995 peace negotiations at Dayton, Ohio. Western leaders could not negotiate with indicted war criminals, and Karadzić and Mladić did not dare leave Serb-controlled territory for fear they would be apprehended. That meant the Bosnian Serbs had to rely on Serbian President Slobodan Milošević, who had not yet been indicted, to represent their interests. By 1995, Milošević's own interests diverged from those of the Bosnian Serbs, facilitating a settlement. Some Western officials, such as those in the government of Prime Minister John Major in Britain, feared the indictments would stand in the way of a settlement. The reverse turned out to be the case. The Tribunal's indictments also prevented Karadzić and Mladić from holding office in Bosnia after the settlement, improving prospects for long-term peace.

B y every measure, the war in Bosnia was a catastrophe. Some 200,000 people were killed. Many more were seriously injured. Thousands of women were raped and sexually enslaved. About 2 million Bosnians were forced to flee their homes and communities; the majority have not returned. Much of Bosnia's rich architectural heritage, from the sixteenth-century mosques of Banja Luka to the beautiful old bridge at Mostar, was destroyed. Sarajevo, which maintained a cosmopolitan character during the darkest days of the siege in 1992 and 1993, has lost much of the diversity that gave it its special flavor. Many of those who survived the war have gone elsewhere, and their place has been taken by rural Bosnians driven out of their communities. It is now dominated by venal politicians.

Though the main architects of the Bosnian disaster are those publicly indicted by the International Criminal Tribunal and some of their colleagues who may have been secretly indicted or who may yet be indicted, my visits there during the war made me feel that some international officials share the blame. From time to time, I clashed with some of those officials. Among those I single out for the way their actions contributed to the suffering in Bosnia are General Sir Michael Rose, who commanded UN forces there in 1994, and Yasushi Akashi, who served at about the same time as UN civilian administrator.

I met General Rose for the first time in Sarajevo in January 1994 when he took up his duties. Fred Cuny and Lionel Rosenblatt joined me in visiting him in his office. It was, I believe, Rose's second day on the job, but he had wasted no time in forming opinions: The opposing sides were equally culpable; the Serb forces attacking Sarajevo—that is, sniping at civilians and lobbing shells into apartment houses, schools, and markets—were engaged in appropriate military action; and Sarajevo was not under siege (asked by a journalist what term he would use in place of siege, one of General Rose's subordinates suggested "strategically advanced encirclement"). Sergio Vieira de Mello, the UN's civilian administrator and, now, the UN high commissioner for human rights, accompanied Rose to the meeting but did not intervene at any point to demur from his colleague's outlandish assertions, though he certainly knew better.

Rose also told us the Bosnians had committed the 1992 "bread line massacre"—in which about twenty people were killed and many more were maimed—against their own people to arouse international sympathy. I asked if he had visited the site. He had not. When this episode took place, Serb propagandists claimed the Bosnians exploded a landmine there. Yet as anyone who visited the spot could see, the pavement bore the unmistakable flower-like pattern made by a mortal shell. These were all over Sarajevo.

Though I gave Rose a hard time—as he recounts in his memoir of his service in Bosnia—I had no impact on his performance. A few days after we met, a mortar shell landed in a market in Sarajevo, killing sixty-eight people. This induced NATO to issue its toughest threats up to that point that it would take reprisals. Rose counteracted this response by spreading the word that the Bosnians had shelled themselves. Rose was not named, but it was easy to identify him as the source several weeks later for a *New York Times* story about the plight of Goražde, one of the "safe areas" supposedly protected by the United Nations. It had come under intense attack by Serb forces the year before their notorious attack on another safe area, Srebrenica:

The senior United Nations official, who insisted on not being identified, said that damage to the Goražde Hospital and other buildings was not as great as had been suggested and that reports of 700 dead and up to 2000 wounded were inflated with a view to stirring up international outrage.

"Reports on Goražde were deliberately exaggerated in order to shame the world into doing something," said the officer who had been to Goražde. . . . The senior United Nations military officer suggested that military observers were of a low standard, that the relief workers were overly emotional in their accounts, and that the ham radio operators [that is, all the sources for accounts on Goražde, to which journalists had no access] were not trustworthy.[4]

As the Bosnian Serbs knew they could count on the top UN military officer to play down their attacks on safe areas—even to the extent of disparaging his own observers who risked their lives in a town under intense bombardment—it may not be surprising that they thought they could get away with the slaughter at Srebrenica.

I first met Yasushi Akashi in Phnom Penh, Cambodia, in 1991 when he headed the United Nations Transitional Authority there. His performance in Cambodia was creditable, I thought, so I expected he would do well in Bosnia. Like General Rose, however, he seemed to think his main responsibility was to head off armed intervention to halt the war. One of our encounters took place over lunch at a restaurant in Zagreb. The writer William Shawcross was also present. Akashi and I got into an argument over a UN practice I found reprehensible. One of the ways some residents of Sarajevo fled during the siege was to cross the airport at night to Bosnian government territory. The airport itself was controlled by United Nations forces. French troops running the airport trained spotlights on those trying to escape this way. That made them easy targets for Serb snipers in the nearby hills. Akashi defended the practice on the grounds that the UN's control of the airport was at the sufferance of the Serbs. It could not allow the airport to be used in ways that fell outside of its agreement with them. Akashi was not swayed when I said this did not justify collaboration in war crimes.

My disagreements with Rose and Akashi made me sympathize somewhat with the critique of "humanitarianism" expressed scathingly by my former Human Rights Watch colleague Alex de Waal, a specialist on the Horn of Africa, and more moderately by journalist David Rieff, among others.[5] They have argued that humanitarian assistance is sometimes a substitute for more decisive measures and can become a rationale for not addressing crises in meaningful ways. This was certainly true of the policy towards Bosnia of the British government under Prime Minister John Major, of the French government under President François Mitterrand and Foreign Minister Alain Juppé, and of the United Nations Secretariat under Secretary General Boutros Boutros-Ghali. General Sir Michael Rose arrived in Sarajevo claiming the Bosnian Serbs and the Bosnian Muslims were equally culpable. This view was analogous to arguing that the Allies, who firebombed Berlin, Hamburg, and Dresden, were equally culpable to the Nazis during World War II. (Fred Cuny used to joke bitterly that if the UN were around when World War II began, we'd all be speaking German.)

Rose took this stand because it furthered the Major government's policy against intervention. Yasushi Akashi and his boss, the secretary general, also opposed intervention to halt the slaughter. They saw the UN's main role as delivering humanitarian assistance. This was made possible principally by Britain and France, which provided the lion's share of the troops to guard the delivery of supplies, though their forces did little or nothing to protect the recipients. In consequence, the UN's humanitarian agenda became the public rationale for supporting the policies espoused by London and Paris. (The United States sidelined itself by neither contributing troops nor paying its bills.) By construing an agreement with the Bosnian Serbs in a manner that made the UN complicit in murder, Akashi and Boutros-Ghali promoted the interests of the governments on which the world body depended.

As Fred demonstrated, there is another way to provide humanitarian assistance. The water project in Sarajevo was designed to save the lives of Sarajevans as well as to allow them to drink, cook, and bathe. The security zone for the Kurds in northern Iraq protected them against Saddam Hussein's forces and averted a humanitarian catastrophe. The proposal to evacuate Grozny's elderly residents was conceived both as a way to save their lives and as a means to get a cease-fire that might lead to a broader settlement. Fred was not neutral in such conflicts. He made moral and political judgments about them and used his formidable skills to promote causes he believed in at the same time as he alleviated suffering. I am proud to have known him, still mourn his loss, and every day rue my part in it.

CHAPTER SIXTEEN

Confronting the Past in South Africa

My work with the Open Society Institute requires me to travel frequently to South Africa to deal with our many programs there involving such matters as community radio broadcasting, education of black children in math and science, crime and criminal justice, and a large-scale effort to finance housing for the poor. Like most of our programs in South Africa, this last one addresses a legacy of apartheid, which made it a matter of policy not to make permanent residences available to blacks in parts of the country reserved for whites. Most of those moving into the small, well-constructed, well-equipped houses that we help to build previously lived in what South Africans sometimes refer to as "informal settlements"—squatter camps and shantytowns.

The programs we support are attempts to construct the future. Yet, as in other parts of the world that have suffered repression, it is not possible to think seriously about the future without addressing the past. Accordingly, my work in South Africa has also focused on the formal mechanism the country has relied upon to confront the past: the South African Truth and Reconciliation Commission.

I learned about the apartheid era in a couple of visits to South Africa that long preceded the 1994 transition. Entering for the first time in 1979, I unwittingly committed two crimes. I brought with me a book by my host, Witwatersrand law professor John Dugard, published by Princeton University Press. Its jacket carried a blurb from another South African lawyer who, as a banned person, could not be quoted. My other offense was that, when I stopped off in London en route, I had bought a copy of Nadine Gordimer's just-published novel, *Burger's Daughter*. It was banned in South Africa a day or two before I arrived on grounds of obscenity, blasphemy, bringing a section of the population into ridicule or contempt, damaging race relations, and prejudicing the safety of the state—quite a lot for one novel. Fortunately, my transgressions went undetected. If I had been found out, I assume the consequences would not have been severe. The books would have been confiscated, but probably nothing else would have happened. My U.S. citizenship and my skin color would have protected me.

My visit coincided with a campaign by the South African government to persuade the West that the country had turned a corner and was abandoning apartheid. Shortly before I started my trip, Dr. Piet Koornhof, South Africa's minister of cooperation and development (a title he chose because it sounded better than the previous name for the same post, minister of Bantu areas development), had told the National Press Club in Washington: "I and my government are seeking to create a happy and meaningful life, therefore, a new blueprint, for all in South Africa. We are entering a period of complete reformation. We are presently in a new era. We have reached a turning point in our history. Apartheid, as you came to know it in the United States, is dying and dead. We are in a period of reform." His speech was greeted by a standing ovation, and a *Washington Post* editorial called South Africa "the most lively and ambitious social laboratory in the world."[1]

What I saw in South Africa bore no resemblance to the picture painted in Washington by Koornhof. The statutes that incriminated me for bringing two books by South African authors into the country were representative of an intricate web of laws, decrees, and regulations intended to ensure that apartheid would last forever.

I saw the way those laws were enforced against South African blacks one afternoon in the Johannesburg pass courts, where I spent several hours observing the procedures. Five courtrooms operated simultaneously. The basic routine was simple; if efficiency is the test of a court, these rated high. A defendant was led into court; there were no defense lawyers present. A judge, the only white in the courtroom other than me, asked: "Guilty or not guilty?" A multilingual African interpreter translated into Zulu, Khosa, Sotho, or Tswana but, as the African lawyer who accompanied me pointed out, what the translator said was not exactly the question posed by the judge. Instead, the translator asked: "Were you in Johannesburg?" Defendant: "Yes." The translator then turned to the judge and said in English: "Guilty, your honor." A prosecutor said: "Move to accept the plea." The judge asked the defendant why he or she had been in Johannesburg. One woman's answer was typical: "I came to find my husband and ask him for money." The judge sentenced the defendant to 30 days. If the defendant had a record of previous violations, the sentence was 60 or 90 days. The defendant was then led off. Keeping count, I found that cases lasted an average of 95 seconds. No case I watched that afternoon took much longer than three minutes.

Typically, about 1,000 black Africans a day were convicted of pass law violations. In the year preceding my visit, there were 272,887 cases. Largely as a consequence, South Africa then had the highest incarceration rate in the world. Today, of course, that dubious distinction is shared by Russia and the United States.

Though Dr. Koornhof said in Washington that he disliked the pass laws, at the time he spoke penalties were increasing. The pass laws enforced the system he was promoting to replace apartheid "as you came to know it in the United States." In referring to a system that was dying or dead, he was talking about "petty apartheid": requirements that nonwhites, or *nieblankes,* must use separate toilets and water fountains, ride separate buses, purchase tickets for trains at separate counters, ride in separate rail cars, use separate entrances to shops, live in separate communities, and on and on. All these were strictly enforced except in a few places exempted by law because they were frequented by international travelers. Five-star hotels and the restaurants in them—which few South African blacks could afford—served blacks and whites together. There were no signs requiring separation of the races in the international sections of the Johannesburg and Cape Town airports, only in the areas for domestic flights. (Another feature of those airports I found striking were the booths where passengers could check their guns before boarding planes.)

What Koornhof was selling as the replacement for the apartheid known in the United States—which Americans imagined was the equivalent of Jim Crow—was "grand apartheid": the denationalization of all South African blacks by making them citizens of the "homelands," or Bantustans. By 1979, two homelands, Transkei and Bophuthatswana, had been granted independence by South Africa, though their sovereignty was recognized by no one else. Ciskei, Lebowa, Venda, Gazankulu, Qwaqua, and KwaZulu were considered self-governing and on their way to independence. In all, 13 percent of the land of South Africa, most of it the poorest soil, was set aside for these statelets. The pass laws were used to prosecute those designated as their nationals by reason of ethnicity or language, though most had never visited their purported homelands and had no connection to them. As they were stripped of their South African nationality, they committed crimes by being without permission in Johannesburg or other parts of the 87 percent of the territory reserved for whites. Most of those I saw sentenced to jail were women. Their husbands' jobs, many as miners, who accounted for much of the country's wealth, allowed the men to reside in the vast townships near the cities (not in the cities themselves under the Group Areas Act) as long as they were employed. Many lived in "hostels." The pass laws did not permit wives to join their husbands unless they, too, had jobs that included permission to live in the townships.

The contrast between the way South Africa advertised itself to westerners and its actual practices made me an advocate of sanctions. They would be effective, I thought, not so much because economic pressure would end apartheid as because it mattered greatly to white South Africans to be accepted as part of the West. Geographically remote from others with whom they identified, South African whites were eager to compete against fellow whites in sports, do business with them, and enjoy recognition as an important outpost of Western (white) civilization. Sanctions made clear that the penalty for stripping most of South Africa's people of their nationality and systematically tearing apart families on grounds of race was the one thing the country's whites feared most: isolation.

I had difficulty gaining entry to South Africa for that first visit and, for a few years thereafter, was denied the right to return. Three months before my first trip, I applied for a visa. I did not get it because of my background with the ACLU, I suppose, and because I said I was going to serve as an adviser to the country's first public-interest law group, recently established by Professor Dugard. Eventually, after pulling a few strings, I obtained my visa five hours before my flight was to leave and startled Yvette by calling her from the airport to say I was going for a month; she had by then dismissed the possibility that I would get a visa and had all but forgotten I might go. In later publishing several articles about the pass courts and other things I saw, I knew, of course, that I doomed my chances of returning.[2] Nevertheless, the visit began a period of deep engagement with South Africa that has persisted to this day. It is a country to which I feel a strong commitment. I have despaired for it and I have been inspired by it—often at the same time.

When I got permission to go again in 1983, I was somewhat mystified by the fact that my application for a visa had been granted. The reason became clear during a meeting with a government official, Louis LeGrange, minister of law and order (a separate post from minister of justice).

I went to see LeGrange to talk about freedom of the press. My visit was on behalf of the Committee to Protect Journalists, a group I had helped establish three years earlier. Most of our conversation focused on several black African journalists imprisoned without charges. It was not even known where some of them were being detained. Before seeing LeGrange, I went to the homes of these journalists in Soweto and other townships and talked to their wives. One woman told me that when her husband was seized, she was never informed. Though she made inquiries, she was unable to learn where he was being held or the reasons. When a white journalist asked the authorities, he was told "administrative reasons." His wife located him by traveling around South Africa from jail to jail, standing outside and calling out his name. After four months, she got an answer from a jail in eastern Transvaal, several hundred kilometers from her home, that he was in that jail. By circling the institution, she reached a point where she could exchange a few shouted words with him. They were allowed neither visits nor correspondence. When I saw her, she did not know whether he was still in the jail where she had found him or had been moved elsewhere.

LeGrange seemed to see nothing wrong with the detention of journalists without charge or judicial proceeding. I asked exasperatedly how he could say detentions under such circumstances were reasonable. He looked up in surprise and said, "Why, I approve them all myself." I had no response.

As our meeting was concluding, LeGrange held up the letter from the Committee to Protect Journalists requesting our meeting and observed that it bore the signature of the committee's honorary chairman, Walter Cronkite. "I met him once," LeGrange said. I asked if he would like me to convey his regards to Cronkite. "Oh no," LeGrange said. "He wouldn't remember me. But I did meet him." That seemed to solve the mystery of the visa. LeGrange was all powerful in determining to imprison a black

South African journalist, but servile when confronted with the star power of an American media celebrity. The letter informing the South African Foreign Ministry of my mission and requesting cooperation also bore Cronkite's name.

My visits to South Africa in 1979 and 1983 made me unable to envision how a transition might take place. It was evident the apartheid regime could not last, but I imagined its end would be accompanied by a blood-bath. I recall telling friends after those visits that I thought a million lives would be lost in the struggle and, as in most cases when a change in the form of government comes about through violent upheaval, the succes-sor regime would leave much to be desired. Many South Africans thought the same; an apocalyptic vision of the transition appears in *July's People,* a novel by Nadine Gordimer, with whom I became friendly in my early vis-its to South Africa.[3] I did not anticipate that events in a distant part of the globe—the advent of Mikhail Gorbachev, the fall of communism, and the end of the Cold War—would have profound consequences in South Africa that would help avert the bloodletting I and many others feared.

A key to the determination by South Africa's white leaders to maintain apartheid in the face of economic sanctions and an international sports boycott, I believe, was their confidence that their system would ultimately be tolerated, if not embraced, by the West because of South Africa's sig-nificance in the global struggle against world communism. The end to that struggle shattered their illusions. Even with the Cold War in full swing, South Africa became a pariah state. Such sympathizers as Ronald Reagan and Margaret Thatcher were not able to prevent its isolation. The unex-pected end to the bipolar struggle for world dominion ended Pretoria's hope that a white-ruled South Africa could regain Western favor.

In his fine book on South Africa's negotiated revolution, *Tomorrow Is Another Country,* journalist Allister Sparks wrote that the February 2, 1990, speech by President F. W. de Klerk legalizing the African National Con-gress and other banned organizations, announcing the release of Nelson Mandela, and declaring readiness to negotiate a new constitution "was to race relations everywhere what the collapse of the Berlin Wall was to com-munism."[4] I go further. I believe the fall of the Berlin Wall on November 9, 1989, and the events leading up to it played a crucial role in making pos-sible President de Klerk's speech three months later and the circumstances that surrounded it. That is not intended to detract from the efforts of black and white South Africans in bringing about a peaceful transition; it is simply that I believe the political climate in which they acted was changed by distant events that diminished or eliminated South Africa's Cold War significance.

Although I could not travel to South Africa while its negotiated revolution was under way, I had opportunities to be involved from afar. George Soros began his philanthropy in South Africa in 1979, funding scholarships for black students to attend the University of Cape Town, and he had sought my help in identifying other projects he could support, such as computer training at black secondary schools, medical education for South African blacks, fellowships to train black journalists, and support for Black Sash, an anti-apartheid white women's group whose work advising blacks on pass-law issues impressed me greatly during my visits. It seemed to me that leaders of Black Sash, such as Sheena Duncan, Ethel Walt, Audrey Coleman, and Mary Burton, did as much as anyone to alleviate the misery caused by the cruelties of the apartheid regime. Ultimately, I believe their efforts also helped make possible a peaceful transition. Thereby, they helped save the lives and the fortunes of their fellow whites who reviled them as "kaffir-lovers" during the long years of struggle.

George Soros's support for the medical education project typified his philanthropic style in the era before the Open Society Institute and the network of Soros Foundations became a large bureaucratic enterprise. I had a call one day at Human Rights Watch from Herb and Joy Kaiser, an American couple who had recently created an organization called Medical Education for South African Blacks (MESAB). Herb had been an official in the U.S. embassy in South Africa when he became gravely ill. The excellent medical care he received there restored his health. It also made the Kaisers think about the fact that if he were a South African black, the care he received as a white foreigner in their country would not have been available to him. When he retired from the Foreign Service, they launched MESAB.

The Kaisers told me that a Dr. Nthato Motlana was visiting New York, and they wondered if I could arrange for the three of them to see George. I had not met Motlana but knew of him as South Africa's most prominent black physician and as the unofficial leader of Soweto. His daughter, then a law student, had accompanied me a decade earlier on my visit to the Johannesburg pass courts. I called George and he suggested they come by that afternoon. I joined them.

George began the conversation by telling Dr. Motlana, "You don't remember me, do you?" Motlana was puzzled. George explained that he had visited him in his Soweto home several years earlier. "You didn't know then I was Mr. Moneybags," George said. He went on to recount what Motlana had said at the time. Motlana expressed surprise both at George's detailed recall and that his own thinking about the prospects about a transition from apartheid had evolved by then to the point reported by George. We went on to talk for a while about plans for MESAB until the Kaisers and Motlana had to leave for a flight to Boston in time for an evening reception in Cambridge. Soon after I returned to my office, I got a call from George telling me he wanted to give them $250,000. Would I tell them? Later that day, I tracked them down in Cambridge at the reception and got Motlana on the phone. He was literally speechless. It was MESAB's first sizable contribution. MESAB flourished and, in subsequent years, George's support increased. That first contribution probably meant more than any of those that followed as it gave MESAB an opportunity to show what it could do, enhancing its ability to obtain support from other donors.

In 1987, George called me about a project on which he was approached by Frederik van Zyl Slabbert, who had resigned his seat in Parliament the previous year. There, he had been leader of the opposition Progressive Federal Party. Slabbert, a burly former rugby star, and Alex Boraine, a tall, white-haired former clergyman, who had followed Slabbert in short order in resigning from Parliament, thought they could do more against apartheid outside the government than from within. They established the Institute for a Democratic Alternative for South Africa (IDASA), with Slabbert as chairman and Boraine as executive director. The project on which Slabbert approached Soros was a plan to bring fifty prominent white South Africans together with fifty leaders of the banned African National Congress outside South Africa.

George called to ask my advice on whether to provide funds for the meeting. It was clear he had already made up his mind to do so. I confirmed his judgment, so he asked me to work out some details with Boraine for the transfer of funds. I did so, and the meeting was held in Dakar, Senegal, that July under the auspices of Danielle Mitterrand's foundation, France Libertés (I served on the U.S. Advisory Board of the foundation). Madame Mitterrand's participation was secured by the Afrikaans poet, Breyten Breytenbach, a friend of Slabbert's who had served a long prison sentence for his activities against the apartheid state and was living in exile in Paris after getting out of prison. It turned out to be an event of some significance, helping to persuade both sides there were individuals on the other side to whom they could talk, one of the many building blocks for South Africa's negotiated revolution.

By the time I returned to South Africa again in February 1994, I was working for George Soros. My purpose was to take part in a meeting organized by Alex Boraine to deal with an important aspect of the peaceful transition, which would culminate two months later in the first elections in which South Africans of all races participated. Several months earlier, I had met Alex for breakfast in Budapest to talk about the role he wished to play in the new South Africa. With transition under way, Alex thought it was time he step aside to make way for appointment of a black executive director for IDASA. He wanted to devote himself to the task of confronting the crimes of the past. How best to do this was the very issue that also was being hotly debated in Eastern Europe in the early 1990s. Alex told me he thought it would be useful to bring some of those involved in the controversies in Eastern Europe to South Africa. I agreed but also suggested that experiences in other parts of the world, especially in Latin America during the previous decade, might be even more relevant to South Africa. The upshot of our conversation was the establishment in 1994 in South Africa of a Project on Justice in Transition, with Alex Boraine as its director, funded by the Open Society Institute. The meeting that brought me to South Africa was the launching pad for the project.

In 1994, South Africa was governed under an Interim Constitution negotiated the previous year. National Party officials had made it clear they would allow a peaceful transition only if it were accompanied by an amnesty for political crimes. Their demand had been met by the "postamble" of the Interim Constitution, which stated: "In order to advance such reconciliation and reconstruction, amnesty shall be granted in respect of acts, omissions and offences associated with political objectives and committed in the course of the conflicts of the past. To this end, Parliament under this Constitution shall adopt a law ... providing for the mechanisms, criteria and procedures, including tribunals, if any, through which such amnesty shall be dealt with at any time after the law has been passed." South Africa's confrontation of the past would be governed by the postamble's requirement of amnesty.

I spoke at the opening session of Alex Boraine's meeting along with José Zalaquett of Chile and Adam Michnik of Poland. Michnik, like Zalaquett, attaches much greater significance than I to the restorative value of forgiveness and reconciliation in reconstructing a moral order following a period of state criminality. I emphasize the importance that those who supported or tolerated criminality should accept political responsibility for the past. Doing justice—that is, prosecuting and punishing those who committed the most heinous crimes—is crucial, I believe, in promoting acceptance of responsibility.

In my talk, I emphasized acknowledgment: "It is not enough that the truth should be known, because in many places it is in fact widely known who was responsible. Even if there have been efforts to engage in secretive and deceptive ways of killing people and to provide deniability, everybody in a sense knows who was responsible for these disappearances. What is required beyond truth, therefore, is acknowledgment. ... Acknowledgment is also a way of providing an assurance to the victims that at least those perpetrators have recognized their own guilt and, in that fashion, have suggested that their wrongdoing is of a form that will not be repeated."[5]

I had learned the significance of acknowledgment in Latin America. Although disappearances were carried out in countries such as Argentina and Chile in a manner intended to allow the state to deny responsibility, the families of the victims were in no doubt as to who committed those crimes. They knew it was the armed forces. Even so, it was important to them that the state officially acknowledge what they had known all along in a published report that named their child. The process in Chile, which was deficient in not naming the military officers who had ordered and carried out the disappearances, nevertheless became meaningful when President Patricio Aylwin sent copies of the three-volume report of the country's Truth and Reconciliation Commission to the families of victims. The reports were accompanied by letters from the president pointing out the pages where their child's case was reported and offering his apologies on behalf of the Chilean nation. As philosopher Thomas Nagel has pointed out, acknowledgment is "what happens and can only happen to knowledge when it becomes officially sanctioned, when it is made part of the public cognitive scene."[6]

The acknowledgment I urged in South Africa went beyond recognition by the state of official culpability. I advocated individual acknowledgment by the perpetrators of their crimes. There was no precedent. Yet, in the South African context, where amnesty was required by the postamble to the Interim Constitution, it seemed the best way to hold accountable the authors of great crimes. I did not imagine how to bring pressure on the perpetrators to acknowledge their crimes but was pleased that the South African authors of the legislation establishing the Truth and Reconciliation Commission later devised a way to make this concept central to their country's confrontation with the past.

Following the meeting, Alex Boraine wrote to Nelson Mandela to propose the Commission on Truth and Reconciliation. A few days prior to the election in which Mandela was chosen as the country's first post-apartheid president, he met with Alex to discuss this proposal. Mandela passed the proposal to Dullah Omar, whom he appointed minister of justice. On May 27, 1994, Omar announced to the newly elected Parliament the government's intent to establish a commission. From the start, Omar emphasized acknowledgment, telling Parliament: "We cannot forgive on behalf of victims, nor do we have the moral right to do so. It is the victims themselves who must speak. Their voices need to be heard. The fundamental issue for all South Africans is therefore to come to terms with our past on the only moral basis possible, namely that the truth be told and that the truth be acknowledged."[7] Dullah Omar went on to signal the distinctive way in which the commission would operate. Instead of interpreting the amnesty required by the postamble as collective—the practice in Latin America where military governments across the continent copied the example of General Augusto Pinochet, who decreed an amnesty in 1978 for his own regime's crimes—individual applications were required. This point proved crucial. It led to the requirement in the legislation that amnesty would only be granted to those who individually acknowledged and fully disclosed their crimes. Those who did not acknowledge remained subject to criminal penalties and civil suits for damages.

While the legislation was being prepared, South Africa had a Government of National Unity. Former President F. W. de Klerk and other National Party representatives were members of the Cabinet. In this Cabinet, it was decided that the hearings where perpetrators would disclose their crimes in exchange for amnesty would be held behind closed doors. South African human rights groups challenged this decision and Parliament acceded, providing that these hearings, as well as those at which victims testified, would be public. In the Roman Catholic tradition, confessions must be oral because the shame is heightened; requiring that they should be public makes the humiliation still greater. This way of proceeding departed from the Latin American model; all deliberations of the commissions in Argentina, Chile, and El Salvador took place behind closed doors.

In combination with the requirement that amnesty only be granted to those who acknowledged and fully disclosed their crimes, this innovation gave the South African process its extraordinary impact. It meant that officials who previously had wielded unchecked power over the bodies and lives of others appeared before the entire country to tell in detail about their crimes as petitioners for amnesty. The law establishing the commission was signed by President Mandela on July 19, 1995, fourteen months after he took office.

At the urging of Alex Boraine, Mandela took another step that helped engage the country in the work of the commission. Instead of just naming its members, the president appointed a committee to assist in identifying those who should serve and invited nominations; 299 names were submitted. The committee held public hearings and selected 25 to forward to Mandela. He chose 17 from this list, appointing Archbishop Desmond Tutu as chairman and Alex Boraine as deputy chairman. Among the members was Mary Burton of Black Sash.

The commission began its public hearings in East London in April 1996 by listening to a woman whose husband had been killed in police custody in nearby Port Elizabeth twenty years earlier. At the time, a policeman came to her door to say her twenty-five-year-old husband had hanged himself with a pair of jeans in his cell at a police station. She was followed to the stand by a parade of widows with similar stories. More dramatic than these accounts by victims were the testimonies of police torturers and murderers seeking amnesty. They came forward to tell of the techniques they had used—and sometimes to demonstrate those techniques—and of the bombs they had planted.

Along the way, the commission faced many challenges. Former President P. W. Botha, who created much of South Africa's security apparatus and presided over it at the height of its criminal activity, defied the commission's authority, forcing that body to take him to court for contempt. Former President F. W. de Klerk, who shared a Nobel Peace Prize with Nelson Mandela for their efforts in bringing about a peaceful transition, testified evasively. Archbishop Tutu, their fellow Nobelist, had to drag out of an unrepentant Winnie Mandela a grudging admission that "things went horribly wrong" when young Stompie Seipei had been murdered by her "Mandela United Football Club." The most formidable opposition to the commission occurred when the African National Congress claimed its members need not apply for amnesty because their crimes had been committed in a just war against apartheid. This stand was articulated for the ANC in August 1996 by Thabo Mbeki, the country's deputy president and, subsequently, Nelson Mandela's successor as president of South Africa. He said that the ANC accepted "collective responsibility" for its acts and that its members would not make "any representation about those activities in its conduct of the struggle for liberation which constitute legitimate actions carried out during a just and irregular war for national liberation."

Alex Boraine called me in New York when Mbeki announced this stand to tell me it had so infuriated Archbishop Tutu that he had threatened to resign. We agreed I would prepare a memo for Alex to give Tutu discussing the equal application of the laws of war to both sides in an armed conflict. The 1977 Protocols to the Geneva Conventions, which prohibit the crimes Mbeki attempted to justify, apply explicitly to wars "against racist regimes." The struggle in South Africa had been very much on the minds of the authors. There was no moral, philosophical, or legal basis for Mbeki's argument that a just war warranted unjust methods of warfare, such as urban bombings, "necklacings" (where a tire is placed over the victim's head and set on fire), and the torture and murder of their own combatants suspected of disloyalty. These are never "legitimate actions."

Archbishop Tutu firmly rejected the ANC stand, but his position was undercut by the commission's own Amnesty Committee, a three-judge body that operated autonomously. In 1997, the committee granted amnesty collectively to thirty-seven ANC officials, including Mbeki, though they did not individually acknowledge and disclose fully their crimes. The Truth and Reconciliation Commission was forced to go to court to set aside the action of its own Amnesty Committee.

The firm stand by Archbishop Tutu and his fellow commissioners paid off when Thabo Mbeki returned to the witness stand with a 137-page memorandum providing detailed information on the conduct of the ANC's armed wing, Umkhonto we Sizwe. Under sharp questioning by the commission, to which he responded testily, Mbeki conceded additional crimes. He also cautioned the commission that its focus on criminality "could convey the impression that the struggle for liberation was itself a gross violation of human rights."

The Truth and Reconciliation Commission scheduled presentation of its five-volume, 2,738-page report to President Mandela, and publication the same day, for October 29, 1998. On October 28, the ANC went to court to block its publication. Deputy President Thabo Mbeki—who resurrected the discredited just war argument—in his capacity as president of the ANC, had made the decision to sue. Archbishop Tutu responded angrily, telling a hastily called press conference: "I didn't struggle in order to remove one set of those who thought they were tin gods and replace them with others who think they are." Tutu's stand was quickly backed by the South African High Court, which dismissed the ANC case the day it was filed. That enabled Tutu to go forward. He presented the report to President Mandela as scheduled.

Mandela adopted a conciliatory approach, saying: "I accept this report as it is, with all its imperfections." In subsequent interviews, he agreed with Mbeki that the ANC had fought a just war, but added, "No one can deny that some people died in our camps and that is what the TRC said." Specifically addressing Mbeki's conflict with Tutu, Mandela said: "It is not easy for me to be questioned about whether there is a difference between me and Deputy President Mbeki on the publishing of the report. There is no doubt that Thabo Mbeki had good intentions. . . . I am convinced my approach was correct and on the basis that he may not have seen the report he responded on the information he had."

I oppose amnesties for severe abuses of human rights. The amnesty decrees in Latin America that inspired the amnesty provision in the postamble of the Interim Constitution in South Africa turn upside down the historic purpose of amnesty. Traditionally, amnesty was the prerogative of the sovereign, who could forgive those who took up arms against him. As the victim or intended victim of their crimes, the sovereign exercised discretion to forgive and forget. Contemporary amnesties, in contrast, protect the officials who issue them. In the South African case, the efforts of Alex Boraine, Dullah Omar, and Archbishop Desmond Tutu made the best of an amnesty by applying it individually rather than collectively; requiring acknowledgment and disclosure in exchange; engaging South Africans broadly in the work of the commission; and endowing the commission's work with moral integrity by insisting that all parties to the struggle to end apartheid, regardless of which side they were on, should be called to account. I was glad of the opportunity to support their efforts.

Yet I do not want to overstate the achievements of the Truth and Reconciliation Commission. It addressed the crimes committed in the war over apartheid, but not the crime of apartheid itself. It could not deal with the forced removals of millions of blacks from their lands, the disruption of their communities, and the destruction of family life that were the consequences of the enforcement of grand apartheid. The women I saw sentenced to jail in the Johannesburg pass courts did not have recourse to the Truth and Reconciliation Commission, which had all it could do to cope with the torture, disappearances, and murders that had sustained the apartheid system.

This is not a criticism of the commission. Rather, it is a comment on the limits of such bodies. Hearings at which victims and perpetrators testify are not an adequate way to come to grips with the social consequences of complex systems of repression. This may be why truth commissions have not caught on in the former Communist countries, where, after the party consolidated control, violent crimes were generally not essential to its maintenance of absolute power.

T he South Africa that I visit today is a land of contradictions. As I have said before, my visits leave me both despairing and inspired. I despair because of the poverty, the crime, and the AIDS pandemic—all, in varying degrees, consequences of the social disruption that is the legacy of apartheid. Though I recognize the lasting effects of the crimes of the past, I also despair because of the readiness of President Mbeki and some of his associates to attribute all the country's many afflictions to white racism. This tendency readily translates into justification for irresponsibility. The most striking example was the president's stand on AIDS, from which he has now partially retreated. In commenting on the link between HIV and AIDS, he shifted the blame to other factors. His policies continue to prevent South Africans from modifying their behavior in ways that might protect them and, for an extended period until a court decision forced a change, from investing in low-cost pharmaceuticals that would at least limit the transmission of the disease from mothers to their children. And yet, I am inspired by the peacefulness of the transition, the maintenance of the rule of law at a time of upheaval, and the extraordinary efforts by some South Africans of all races to address the country's immense problems. The Truth and Reconciliation Commission was not capable of addressing all the matters that cause despair, but it was a factor in South Africa's continuing capacity to inspire.

CHAPTER SEVENTEEN

Intervening in Kosovo

One of the first things I noticed in Pristina, the Kosovar capital, was the fresh fruit, including quantities of imported clementines, on display in the windows of several grocery stores. I had just left Belgrade, where the food shops were empty or had only a few cans on the shelves that December 1993. It had been two and a half years since Serbian President Slobodan Milošević had begun wars against Slovenia and Croatia, and a year and a half since he had started the calamitous war in Bosnia and Herzegovina. The latter still had another two years to run, but the Federal Republic of Yugoslavia was already suffering from international economic sanctions and, more severely, from hyperinflation caused by its own economic policies (I still have a 500 billion dinar note I acquired in that period). In Belgrade, not only were the grocery stores empty, but, because of a gas shortage, the only cars on the street were police vehicles and luxury cars said to belong to Milošević cronies who were getting rich smuggling goods subject to the sanctions. The restaurants in the Yugoslav capital were deserted, except for a table here and there at the more expensive places, where eight or ten men, officials, and politically connected gangsters (the categories were blurred) dined on copious portions of steak, scotch, cognac, *slivovica,* and cigarette smoke.

What made the contrast remarkable between the well-stocked groceries of Pristina and the bare shops in Belgrade is that Kosovo was much the poorest part of Yugoslavia. In 1990, the year before the breakup began, per capita income in Kosovo (according to the World Bank) was $662, a figure comparable to many countries in Africa. The figure for Serbia was four times higher, and in Slovenia, the wealthiest republic of Yugoslavia, it was nearly ten times greater than in Kosovo. The sanctions blamed by Milošević for the shortages in Serbia applied equally to Kosovo, whose autonomy he canceled in 1990 after placing the territory under martial law the previous year.

It was not that the economy of Kosovo had improved under Milošević. On the contrary, it got worse as a result of political repression. Virtually every Albanian university professor, teacher, doctor, nurse, orderly, court official, janitor, or other public employee had been dismissed from public service or had resigned in protest against dismissals of their fellow Albanians by the end of 1991. This group included some 73,000 Albanians. Many thousands more had been fired or had quit their jobs in commercial enterprises. Albanian students no longer attended Pristina University; Albanian children stopped going to state schools; and, for the most part, Kosovar Albanians avoided the hospitals. Instead, the Albanians, who made up roughly 90 percent of Kosovo's population of about 2 million, had established their own unrecognized university; had organized schools in their living rooms and basements for more than 300,000 children; and turned to clinics they had organized in private homes for most medical care. Virtually overnight, in the poorest part of Europe, the Albanians had created a parallel society.

In elections deemed illegal by the Serb authorities, they had chosen a multiparty Parliament that had nowhere to meet and a president who made his office in a small building adjacent to a muddy lot that bore a sign identifying it as the home of the Writers Union of Kosovo. The president, Ibrahim Rugova, a neurasthenic literary critic who wore a wool sweater under his jacket and a silk scarf around his neck in the hottest weather, advocated nonviolent resistance against the Serb authorities, who had deployed tens of thousands of heavily armed police and soldiers to patrol Kosovo. When I visited in 1993, and for some time thereafter, it appeared that Rugova's strategy of nonviolence enjoyed near universal support among Kosovar Albanians despite severe harassment by the Serb troops in Kosovo and the hardships resulting from exclusion of the Kosovar Albanians from government employment and services. The parallel institutions they created were supported by generous remittances from scores of thousands of Kosovar workers in Germany, Switzerland, and other Western countries. Remittances provided the hard currency that made it possible for the Kosovars to avoid the effects of hyperinflation in Serbia and to stock their shops with imported fresh fruits.

All the Albanians I spoke to in Kosovo—political party leaders, journalists, doctors, relief workers, former faculty members of the University of Pristina then teaching at the alternative university, and human rights workers—told me they were seeking independence for Kosovo. Though I repeatedly asked whether restoring the autonomy granted by Yugoslavia's

1974 constitution that had been abolished by Milošević might be the solution, no one wanted to discuss this even as a temporary measure. The breakup of the Yugoslav federation in 1991 and 1992, I was told, made autonomy irrelevant. It was one thing to enjoy autonomy in a multiethnic Yugoslavia made up of Serbs, Croats, Slovenes, Macedonians, Muslims, Bosnians, Kosovar Albanians, and many other nationalities; it was quite another in a state defined as the Serbian homeland, even if that homeland still had a diverse population within its borders. Independence, the Kosovars said, was their only option.

How was independence to be achieved? Most Kosovars I spoke to in 1993 seemed confident they would ultimately prevail by nonviolent means. I was not so sure, as this endeavor would require international support I had difficulty envisioning. At the time, the horrible things taking place in Bosnia were well known worldwide. The siege of Sarajevo was shown daily on television everywhere. The cruelties of the Bosnian Serbs in camps such as Omarska and Keratem had been exposed and extensively documented. Everyone knew about the rapes of Bosnian Muslim women. "Ethnic cleansing" had entered the language. Yet there was little indication that the international community was prepared to do anything about the ghastly crimes in Bosnia other than to send humanitarian assistance to the victims. How was it possible the world would become sufficiently aroused over the plight of the Albanians in Kosovo to intervene in a manner that would secure their independence? Few journalists ever visited, and most well-informed people were ignorant about Kosovo.

Following my visit, I published an article about Kosovo in *The New York Review of Books*.[1] It was the first on the territory to appear in that journal and one of only a handful published up to that point in any American periodical of general circulation. Though expressing hope that a way might be found "to fulfill the aspirations of the Kosovars without a bloodbath," I was not optimistic. I noted the danger that widespread brutality by the Serb police would "set off a violent response, or that Albanians eager for a confrontation will resort to terrorism." At the time, the Kosovo Liberation Army did not exist. Yet it was easy to imagine that some Albanians would tire of nonviolence. Rugova's rhetoric was morally admirable, but unlike Gandhi or Martin Luther King, he lacked a political strategy. If nonviolence failed to yield results, as seemed likely, a handful of Kosovars could readily take matters into their own hands.

My article in *The New York Review*, and a few additional ones that I published elsewhere, apparently displeased the Yugoslav authorities. For more than three years thereafter, they repeatedly turned down my requests for visas. Others who sought to go had similar difficulties. On one occasion, I helped to arrange a visit to Kosovo by a delegation representing humanitarian aid agencies. As such groups generally refrain from criticizing even the most repressive governments, because they require permission from the authorities to deliver relief assistance, there was little prospect that anyone in that delegation would speak out on Kosovo. Nonetheless, at the last moment, the Federal Republic of Yugoslavia created difficulties over visas, and the visit had to be scrapped. In combination, Rugova's political ineptitude and the exclusionary policies of the Belgrade authorities ensured that the international community remained ignorant of the nonviolent struggle in Kosovo. Inevitably, some Albanians came to believe their only hope lay in violence.

Though I could not travel to Kosovo, I did my best to follow developments there and maintained close contact with some I met in Pristina, notably a young journalist, Veton Surroi. The Soros Foundations assisted him in establishing a weekly magazine in Kosovo, *Koha* (Time), which later became a newspaper, *Koha Ditore* (Time Daily), when we helped finance his acquisition of a printing press. The son of a Yugoslav ambassador during Tito's time when it was government policy to appoint members of different nationalities to important posts, Veton spoke fluent, barely accented English (as well as French, Spanish, Serbo-Croatian, and Albanian) and became an articulate and persuasive spokesman for the Kosovar cause internationally. Other than Rugova and Adem Demaci—who styled himself as the Kosovar Mandela because he had spent twenty-eight years in Yugoslav prisons for espousing Albanian nationalism—Veton was the only Kosovar to acquire a substantial international reputation before the 1998–1999 war. Like Rugova, he was a firm proponent of nonviolence. At the same time, he was critical of Rugova.

The Kosovar "president," according to Veton and other critics, seemed too easily satisfied with token acknowledgment of his position by the Milošević regime while failing to address effectively such urgent issues as the quality of education Albanian children obtained in the alternative schools. Under the influence of Veton and other Kosovar Albanian intellectuals such as Shkelzen Maliqi, another advocate of nonviolence, our foundation in Yugoslavia focused its work in Kosovo on efforts to improve the alternative schools through training programs for teachers and by providing Albanian-language teaching materials. We attempted to get other donors also to invest in Kosovo, though with only minor success. It was a territory that attracted little notice, and because of the Milošević regime's restrictions on access, it was difficult to work there.

In June 1997, after an absence of three and a half years, I had a chance to visit Kosovo again. George Soros applied for a visa to travel to Yugoslavia, and I submitted an application to accompany him. Though George's views were no more congenial to the Belgrade authorities than mine, a visit by a high-profile international investor was not something to pass up for a country suffering economic isolation. He got a visa and, since I was traveling with him, so did I.

In Belgrade, one of our stops was a call on the foreign minister, Milan Milutinović. Asked by a journalist why we were seeing Milutinović, George responded that we wanted to thank him for the visas. We had nothing more in mind and imagined our visit would last just a few minutes. It did not turn out that way. Milutinović began the conversation by asking George his impression of Yugoslavia. George responded that he had last visited in 1990. He also had gone to Poland at about the same time. Yugoslavia was then far ahead of Poland economically. As George had met several Yugoslav officials who were sophisticated in their thinking about economic issues, he said he had expected their country would be still further ahead several years later. Instead, George pointed out, Poland had made great strides and was doing very well while Yugoslavia had regressed economically. The country seemed in a sad state.

It was all because of the sanctions, Milutinović responded, contending they had been maintained despite Yugoslav compliance with the conditions negotiated at Dayton in 1995 for their removal. I demurred, pointing out that one of the conditions was cooperation with the International Criminal Tribunal for the former Yugoslavia in The Hague. Those indicted included three regular officers of the Yugoslav Army accused of murdering 261 hospital patients in the Croatian city of Vukovar in 1991. Belgrade had refused to turn them over to the Tribunal for trial.

This comment precipitated a lengthy argument between Milutinović and me. George and the director of our foundation in Yugoslavia, Sonja Licht, who had accompanied us, sat back and enjoyed it. Milutinović got angrier and angrier as the argument went on, annoyed that I kept contradicting his version of the facts of the case. It was a matter I knew well; at Human Rights Watch one of our researchers had helped to uncover the massacre. I was then completing the book on *War Crimes* that I published the following year in which the case figures prominently.[2] Sure of myself, I was not about to let the foreign minister get away with gross misstatements. A couple of times, George interjected laughingly to tell Milutinović he had picked the wrong subject for a debate. The minister persisted for most of an hour, finally saying exasperatedly, "You may know a lot about this matter, but we have experts who know a lot more than you do."

Two years later, when Yugoslav President Slobodan Milošević was indicted by The Hague Tribunal for war crimes in Kosovo, four other officials of his government were indicted with him. The first named after Milošević was Milutinović, by then president of Serbia (the post previously held by Milošević, who had shifted to the federal presidency). When Milutinović was indicted for atrocities in Kosovo, and again when Milošević was sent to The Hague in June 2001, I wondered whether he recalled our argument and what I had said to him: There is no statute of limitations on war crimes. Even if the Tribunal in The Hague were abolished, under principles of universal jurisdiction, any competent court anywhere in the world may prosecute accused war criminals. For those indicted by the Tribunal who expect to live another twenty, thirty, or forty years, the chances they will be brought to trial some day, in their own country or in another, are great. I was glad I had an opportunity to inform Milutinović of his prospects.

After Belgrade, we went on to Kosovo. Superficially, little had changed since I was last there. The separation between Serbs and Albanians remained greater than between blacks and whites under apartheid in South Africa when I had first gone there two decades earlier. Even in the 1970s, a handful of blacks attended South African universities together with whites, whereas in Kosovo in the 1990s, the ethnic divide between students at all levels of education was absolute. There had been an important change in the political climate since my earlier visit, however. The strategy of nonviolence no longer commanded the near universal support that prevailed when I visited Kosovo in 1993. In South Africa, the prospect that change would take place peacefully improved over time; in Kosovo, thanks largely to Slobodan Milošević, it declined.

Following my visit, I again wrote for *The New York Review of Books*.[3] By then, articles about Kosovo were appearing more frequently, and developments there were beginning to be taken seriously in Washington, London, and other capitals. The territory attracted attention because, as I wrote,

"In the past year, there has been more violence there than in Northern Ireland. Young men who are presumed to be members of an Albanian underground movement calling itself the Kosovo Liberation Army are attacking, and in some cases killing Serbian police." It was obvious the violence could readily escalate. I pointed out that in neighboring Albania, where the collapse of several pyramid schemes had provoked violence that led to the ouster of the government of President Sali Berisha:

> One of the consequences of the turmoil . . . is that most Albanian men have seized weapons belonging to the armed forces and the country is bristling with guns. Though the border between Albania and Kosovo is guarded by Yugoslav forces, much smuggling takes place, and one can readily imagine that Kosovars bent on violence will find a way to bring weapons across it. The edginess of Serb forces over this prospect was evident at the beginning of August when they opened fire, reportedly without warning, on a group of young men in their own village on the border. Two brothers were killed and a third young man was wounded. Three days later, several young men with an automatic weapon attacked a police car, severely wounding two Serb police officers and also injuring a third. Two other such attacks took place the same day. If such violence continues to grow, and if the political leaders who are committed to nonviolence lose more ground, the darkest predictions about war in Kosovo could come true.

Those predictions came true within six months. In late February 1998, Yugoslav forces began an all-out war to wipe out the Kosovo Liberation Army (KLA). As is characteristic in such conflicts, they found it difficult to engage the KLA in direct combat, so they attacked villages suspected of providing the guerrillas with recruits or logistical support. Over the next thirteen months, more than 100 villages were destroyed and 200,000 to 300,000 Kosovar Albanians were driven from their homes into the woods and the hills. In several villages from which attacks on Serb police or soldiers were thought to emanate, retaliation took the form of massacres of their residents.

As soon as Milošević launched his campaign of forcible displacement in Kosovo, I telephoned Louise Arbour, the Canadian jurist who then served as chief prosecutor of the International Criminal Tribunal for the former Yugoslavia—having succeeded Richard Goldstone more than a year earlier—to remind her that the ICTY's jurisdiction, which included crimes committed in the whole territory of ex-Yugoslavia since 1991 in international or internal armed conflict, applied to developments in Kosovo. I called on her to send investigators there right away to look into the destruction of villages. I made similar calls to officials at the U.S. State Department and also urged journalists covering the events to point out that the Tribunal had jurisdiction. One of those I spoke to was Bronislaw Geremek, foreign minister of Poland and chairman of the fifty-five nation Organization for Security and Cooperation in Europe. Geremek raised the issue at a meeting of the "Contact Group" of foreign ministers, which issued its own call for an investigation by the Tribunal. A few weeks later, the Tribunal's jurisdiction to deal with Kosovo was reaffirmed in a UN Security Council resolution. Its adoption coincided with a conference in Washington, where one of my duties was to introduce Judge Arbour as keynote speaker. I used the occasion to cite the Security Council resolution and to suggest to the participants in the conference—who included many of the leading scholars and practitioners concerned with war crimes issues internationally—that events in Kosovo gave heightened significance to her office.

As Veton Surroi was in Washington at the same time, I organized a lunch for him with Judge Arbour to discuss what the Tribunal could do in Kosovo. Louise Arbour's reluctance to proceed caught me by surprise. Despite the Security Council resolution, she told Veton and me that she had grave doubts about whether she had jurisdiction to bring a prosecution in Kosovo. She said she was not convinced the struggle there constituted an internal armed conflict within the meaning of the Geneva Conventions. Her doubts were based on her view that the Kosovo Liberation Army, the guerrilla force Milošević was intent on wiping out, did not have an organized command structure. That meant it would be difficult or impossible for her to prosecute KLA leaders for war crimes by their forces. A fundamental principle of the laws of war is that they apply equally to both sides. Arbour said she could not exercise jurisdiction unless she could hold both sides accountable.

I disagreed. Judge Arbour's reading of the Geneva Conventions echoed Milošević's claim that he was engaged in a struggle against terrorists and that this permitted his forces free rein to commit gross abuses against the Kosovar civilian population without being held to account. The Geneva Conventions are not so rigid in their requirements for determining when combat warrants recognition as an internal armed conflict. There are two standards under the Geneva Conventions. The lower standard involves the application of Common Article 3 (so named because the identical language appears in each of the four Geneva Conventions of 1949). Common Article 3 prohibits the murder or cruel or degrading treatment of noncombatants and the taking of hostages and requires that noncombatants must be treated humanely regardless of race, color, religion, faith, sex, birth, wealth, or other similar criteria. The forced displacement of ethnic Albanians on grounds of their race, nationality, or birth plainly violated Common Article 3.

There is no reference in Common Article 3 to command structure. The authoritative "Commentary" to the Geneva Conventions by the International Committee of the Red Cross cites a number of "convenient criteria" for determining when Article 3 applies. One criterion is that the guerrillas have an "organized military force, an authority responsible for its acts." The Commentary goes on to point out that these criteria are not prerequisites. Rather, they are "useful as a means of distinguishing a genuine armed conflict from a mere act of banditry or an unorganized and short-lived insurrection." Plainly, the scale and duration of the struggle in Kosovo showed this was a genuine armed conflict. Another criterion cited in the Commentary, and the most important for Kosovo, is that "the legal Government is obliged to have recourse to the regular military forces against insurgents." Milošević deployed massive military force in an attempt to crush the KLA, thereby demonstrating that Kosovo was a Common Article 3 internal armed conflict.

Protocol II of 1977 sets forth additional, more detailed rules that apply to certain internal armed conflicts but also sets a higher standard for determining when such rules apply. In Article I, the Protocol states that it applies only when there is a conflict between regular armed forces "and dissident armed forces or other organized armed groups which, under responsible command, exercise such control over a part of its territory as to enable them to carry out sustained and concerted military operations and to implement this Protocol." Indeed, there was some uncertainty whether KLA activity in Kosovo had crossed this higher threshold. A respectable argument that it did meet this standard could be made, however. The fact that Yugoslav armed forces were attacking and destroying villages suggested that the Milošević regime believed the KLA exercised control. Application of Protocol II was in doubt primarily because of the provision that required the KLA to be capable of carrying out "sustained and concerted military operations." Most KLA activity then consisted of ambushes of Yugoslav police and military vehicles. Even if Arbour deemed Protocol II not applicable, I argued, she had ample basis for bringing prosecutions under Common Article 3.

I did not persuade Arbour on that occasion nor in contacts with her over the next several months. One of those with whom I shared my frustration was my longtime ACLU colleague John Shattuck, then assistant secretary of state for human rights. John also attempted to persuade Arbour to initiate prosecutions for war crimes in Kosovo in 1998. Nothing doing.

That October, I made another attempt. I went to The Hague with Mabel Wisse Smit, director of OSI's Brussels office, to meet with Arbour and, separately, with the president of the Tribunal, Judge Gabrielle Kirk McDonald. Judge McDonald, whom I saw first, was sympathetic, but she pointed out—as, of course, I knew full well—that she could not tell the chief prosecutor what to do and that it would be inappropriate for her to address the issue. McDonald did agree, however, to attend a conference on war crimes to be held in Belgrade in December under the auspices of the Humanitarian Law Center, a human rights organization for which the Soros Foundations had provided the main support since its establishment six years previously. Under the leadership of Nataša Kandić, the center had documented violations of the laws of war by all sides in the conflicts in ex-Yugoslavia, including Kosovo. A redoubtable woman, Nataša Kandić had emerged as the most effective and reliable human rights monitor in the region. A Serb, she had established an office in Pristina staffed by both Serbs and Albanians—one of the few institutions where individuals of the two ethnic groups worked alongside each other—that provided detailed reports on the abuses I thought should be the focus of prosecutions by the Tribunal. During the NATO bombing in 1999, Nataša traveled back and forth to Kosovo to escort her Albanian staff to safety and to document war crimes as they took place. For her efforts, she was reviled by many of her fellow Serbs but—though a policeman slammed a car door on her legs on one of her visits to Kosovo—was undeterred in her efforts. In the immediate aftermath of the war, when Kosovars avenged themselves against Serbs residing in the territory, she was the only Serb I knew who traveled about Kosovo freely, speaking Serbian. Her work there included reporting on Kosovar crimes against the remaining Serb minority and the Roma in the territory.

In my meeting in The Hague over lunch with Arbour, I was pleased to discover that she had made headway. She told me she had identified the leadership of the KLA. That satisfied her that it was an organized armed force and that events in Kosovo—where, by this time, the number of Albanians who had been forcibly displaced numbered in the hundreds of thousands—constituted an internal armed conflict within the meaning of the Geneva Conventions. We discussed what kind of prosecution might be brought. Several massacres of groups of ten or twenty Kosovar Albanian civilians at a time had taken place. I urged that these should not be the main focus of prosecutions, as I doubted the Tribunal could demonstrate culpability by Milošević and his principal lieutenants except in failing in their duty to take action against those responsible. I thought these had probably been committed under the direction of local commanders in revenge for ambushes of police or military vehicles.

I suggested focusing instead on the practice of bombarding villages, forcing the residents to flee, and then burning down the houses, which was so widespread that the Tribunal could demonstrate it was a policy determined at the highest level. Expulsion of people from their homes and communities in this manner had not been the focus of prosecutions in the indictments brought for crimes committed in Bosnia and Croatia. Instead, prosecutions in those cases had been based on large-scale massacres, mass rapes, detention camps, the murder of prisoners, and the prolonged bombardment of besieged cities. Those crimes had been largely avoided by Milošević's troops in Kosovo. This suggested to me that fear of prosecutions had shaped the conduct of Serbian forces. It was important to demonstrate that forcible displacement is a war crime in its own right. Again, however, Louise Arbour reacted in what I thought an excessively conservative manner. She said that to bring such an indictment she would insist on being able to prove that no firefight had taken place in any of the villages that were the subject of the indictment. As proving such a negative is virtually impossible, it was evident this approach would not yield an indictment.

I also urged Arbour to visit Kosovo. Previously, she had expressed reluctance to do so. This time, however, she agreed; she would accept Nataša Kandić's invitation to the December conference in Belgrade sponsored by the Humanitarian Law Center. Arbour asked whether I thought it would be appropriate for her to visit Kosovo under the center's auspices. Eager to get her to Kosovo, and aware that the center adhered to the highest standards of international human rights reporting, I agreed this would be a good way to go. When Arbour applied for a visa, however, the Yugoslav authorities informed her they would permit her to go only to Belgrade. She was barred from Kosovo. Arbour declined to go under such a restriction. In solidarity, Judge McDonald also canceled her visit to Belgrade (I went, however). Subsequently, Arbour made an attempt to enter Kosovo from Macedonia, but she was turned back at the border.

Though pleased that Arbour had demonstrated an interest in Kosovo by attempting to go, I remained deeply disappointed by her failure to bring timely indictments. Another half year elapsed before Milošević, Milutinović, and three others were finally indicted. As I expected from my conversations with Arbour, the indictments did not deal with forced displacement. The focus was solely on killings. The crime that represented the essence of Milošević's policy in Kosovo was ignored. By then, in May 1999, NATO's bombing had been under way for two months. Judge Arbour was a candidate for a post on Canada's Supreme Court, and her appointment was announced the following month. Questions about whether the conflict in Kosovo met the standards of Common Article 3 or Protocol II no longer mattered; the war had become international and the comprehensive rules that apply in such circumstances could be invoked. All but one of the episodes described in the indictment had taken place following NATO's intervention (the exception was the January 1999 massacre at Racak, one of the events that had precipitated NATO's involvement). By waiting so long, Arbour gave credence to those who charged that the indictments were politically motivated both by a desire to assist NATO in demonizing Milošević and to cap her own service with the Tribunal before leaving for Ottawa. On August 30, 2001, Carla del Ponte, the seasoned Swiss prosecutor who succeeded Louise Arbour in The Hague when the latter left for Ottawa, told the Tribunal she would bring expanded charges against Milošević for the crimes he committed in Kosovo and that the indictment against him would also charge genocide in Bosnia.

At this writing, the trial of Milošević is under way. Declining the assistance of counsel in the courtroom, he is defending himself. Journalists covering it have focused on the defendant's skilled and knowledgeable questioning of many of the Kosovar Albanian witnesses against him. Missing from any of the accounts I have read is any recognition of the ease with which he is able to inform himself of the details of what transpired in the villages of Kosovo even now as he occupies a jail cell in The

Hague; it is a performance that demonstrates how readily he could obtain such information while he held power. From a legal standpoint, he is assisting the prosecution in establishing his own command responsibility for the war crimes and crimes against humanity that were committed in Kosovo. That is the basis for the charges against him.

A t peace negotiations to try to end the war in Kosovo at Rambouillet near Paris in early 1999, Veton Surroi played a crucial role. He persuaded the KLA to accept terms proposed by international negotiators even though they did not guarantee achievement of the goal for which they had fought: independence. Milošević, however, rejected terms that would permit NATO troops to enter Kosovo to protect forcibly displaced Albanians in returning to their villages and rebuilding. The result was the nightmare seventy-eight-day war during which Serbian soldiers, police, and paramilitaries slaughtered thousands, systematically looted and burned homes, and expelled more than three-quarters of a million Kosovar Albanians from the territory. In turn, NATO destroyed much of Serbia's military and civilian infrastructure before Milošević agreed to a settlement much like the one his negotiators had rejected at Rambouillet.

While the war was under way, I found myself in an unusual position. Having written and spoken extensively about Kosovo and about war crimes, I received many invitations to speak on the conflict and many calls from journalists who wanted to interview me about it. Though I was eager to comment, I could not. My statements might endanger the staff of the Soros Foundation in Yugoslavia. For several years, the foundation there had been regarded as a hostile presence by the Milošević regime, which orchestrated denunciations of it in the government-controlled media and for a time closed it down. By mounting an international campaign in support of the foundation, we had succeeded in reopening it. Foreign Minister Milan Milutinović had called the foundation president, Sonja Licht, immediately after she held a publicized meeting with Vice President Al Gore, and issued a statement on the foundation to tell her the regime had previously decided to allow it to reopen. Its position remained precarious, however. When NATO began to bomb Serbia on March 24, 1999, the foundation and Sonja Licht became the targets of vicious threats.

If I had been able to speak out, I would have said I believed NATO was waging a just war *(jus ad bellum)* but was not conducting it in a just way *(jus in bello)*. The war was just, I thought, because its purpose was to allow forcibly displaced Kosovar Albanians to return to their destroyed villages and to rebuild. Extensive diplomatic efforts to achieve this result prior to the commencement of bombing had been blocked by Milošević. He had conducted wars since 1991 against Slovenia, Croatia, and Bosnia. Political and economic sanctions had been imposed to try to alter Milošević's policies, but they were ineffectual. As most sanctions were still in place when he began the war in Kosovo, there was little more that could be done along those lines to get him to accept terms. Force was the only recourse.

The war was not conducted in a just way because the United States and its NATO allies gave priority to avoiding casualties among their own combatants. They were astonishingly successful. Not a single member of NATO's forces was killed in combat. Yet, the sad consequence of the security NATO sought for its own troops was that it offered no protection to Kosovar Albanians, who were forcibly displaced in far greater numbers than previously with a lot more rapes, murders, and destruction of property than during the previous thirteen months. The vast damage to civilian objects in Serbia was another byproduct of NATO's preoccupation with the safety of its own forces. Unable to locate camouflaged tanks and artillery from the high altitudes from which its bombs were dropped, NATO found it easier to destroy factories, bridges, and electric power plants. Another consequence was that hundreds of Serb and Kosovar civilians were injured and killed in bombing accidents and mistakes. A few, such as the Serbs who died when the building housing the government broadcasting network was bombed, were killed in a manner that seemed to me to violate the Geneva Conventions. (It was not until much later that I learned that NATO gave advance notice of this attack to Milošević. Senior officials of the network were apparently warned and were not in the building when the bomb struck. The warning was not passed on to lower ranking staff, however, and eighteen technicians were killed. After they found out about the warning, the families of the technicians who died filed suit against Milošević and top officials of the network. More recently, the Serb authorities have launched criminal charges against the director of the network.)

To conduct the war justly, NATO should have used low flying planes and sent in ground troops. Inevitably, that would mean NATO casualties.

As I would not have shared the danger, I am acutely aware I have little moral standing to criticize the refusal to put NATO troops in harm's way. Yet it is probably the only way NATO could have protected the Kosovar Albanians and avoided much of the "collateral damage." Conducting a war justly means that, to the extent possible, its risks are borne by combatants, not civilians. Leaders of NATO governments, such as President Clinton, were not ready to face the domestic political consequences of casualties among their troops, however. They chose a course that turned upside down the principles that underlie the laws of war: They waged a war in which the risks were borne by civilians, not combatants. The question that necessarily arises is, Should a readiness to fight a war in a just manner be a prerequisite for conducting a just war? I think so.

I recognize, of course, that my argument that this was a just war is subject to criticism by those—such as Noam Chomsky, who debated the question with me in the pages of *Dissent*[4]—who claim that its purpose had more to do with establishing NATO hegemony than with protecting Kosovars against Milošević's depredations. Those holding this view will find confirmation in the memoir of the war by NATO's commander, General Wesley Clark. He reported a conversation in London with Secretary of State Madeleine Albright on March 6, 1999, a little more than two weeks before the commencement of NATO's bombing campaign:

> I told her what was happening on the ground. "The continuing build-up and deployment of the Serb forces," I said, was occurring "in larger numbers than we anticipated. And, we've given them full warning of the possibility of air strikes, so we've probably lost the element of surprise."
>
> If we commence the strikes, will the Serbs attack the population?
>
> "Almost certainly they will attack the civilian population. This is what they are promising to do."
>
> So what should we do? How can we prevent their striking the civilians?
>
> "We can't. Despite our best efforts the civilians are going to be targeted by the Serbs. It will just be a race, our air strikes and the damage we cause them against what they can do on the ground. But in the short term, they can win the race."
>
> So, what should we do? She was seeking my personal opinion.
>
> "We will have to reinforce our capabilities. Ultimately, we can bring more to bear against them—we can overmatch anything they have—but it's not going to be pleasant." The Secretary did not seem surprised by my bleak assessment, even though it wasn't what she wanted to hear.

But you think we should go ahead?

"Yes, we have to." I had crossed the divide from forecasting to recommending. I was now responsible for the outcome, in a way I hadn't been before. I could feel the weight bear down on me as I continued. "We put NATO's credibility on the line. We have to follow through and make it work. There's no real alternative now."

Yes, I think so too, she said.[5]

Clark's rationale for going to war deprives it of justness, the more so because he was aware of the reprisals that would be suffered by civilians and of the likelihood that he would be denied authorization to use ground troops that might be more effective than air strikes in protecting civilians. Had I known these things during the war, I would have had more doubts about its justness. On the one hand, it shouldn't matter that the military commander has a different rationale for going to war than the one that was persuasive to me. On the other hand, the priority he gives to NATO's credibility over the protection of the civilian population indicates a readiness to accept the conduct of the war in an unjust way. That undermines my basis for believing that going to war was just. As Michael Walzer has pointed out, "The dualism of *jus ad bellum* and *jus in bello* is at the heart of all that is most problematic in the moral reality of war."[6] So it was in Kosovo.

The justness of the war and the way it was conducted were closely intertwined in a debate that erupted between civil society opponents of Milošević in Belgrade and their longtime allies in the international human rights movement.

On April 6, 1999, two weeks after the commencement of NATO's bombing campaign, seventeen Belgrade-based nongovernmental organizations issued an appeal to international groups. They denounced the bombing, asserting, "The most powerful military, political and economic powers of the world are for two weeks incessantly killing people and destroying not only military but also civilian objects, blowing up bridges, rail tracks, factories, heating plants, warehouses and basins. At the same time, in fear of the bombing campaign and military actions by the regime and KLA, hundreds of thousands of Kosovo Albanians, in an unprecedented exodus, are forced to leave their devastated homes and look for salvation in the tragedy and uncertainty of fleeing."

The groups included a trade union federation, the Serbian Helsinki Committee for Human Rights, the Yugoslav Lawyers Committee for

Human Rights, the Belgrade Circle, and Women in Black. They said that they had "always raised our voices against the repression against Kosovo Albanians," but that "NATO military intervention has undermined all results we have achieved and endangered the very survival of the civil sector in Serbia."

This letter, particularly its contention that the Kosovar Albanian exodus was based on fear of NATO's bombing and of the KLA, drew a sharp response from the International Helsinki Federation for Human Rights (IHF), the group of which I had been a founder some seventeen years earlier. The IHF statement was signed by leaders of national Helsinki committees in Russia, Germany, Norway, the United States, Denmark, Bulgaria, Poland, and Serbia. Sonja Biserko, the Serbian signatory, had by this time left the country and broken with her colleagues who denounced NATO's bombing. She joined in issuing the IHF statement.

The IHF said the April 6 letter and subsequent letters and appeals by Belgrade intellectuals

> reflect a view of the Kosovo crisis to which we cannot subscribe. . . . The Kosovo Albanians who have arrived in Albania, Macedonia and Montenegro have been extensively interviewed by members of various Helsinki committees as well as by news media. Their stories confirm beyond any reasonable doubt that they were driven from their houses by Serbian police and paramilitary forces; that seemingly thousands have been systematically killed, maimed, raped and robbed. This is ethnic cleansing on a horrific scale. Neither the NATO bombing nor military actions by the Kosovo Liberation Army are responsible for the unprecedented exodus which you describe. Based on the extensive information we have collected about the catastrophe in Kosovo, we consider it intellectually and morally unsound to equate these campaigns.

Expressing respect for "your lonely and courageous struggle for democratization in the Federal Republic of Yugoslavia, a struggle we have supported for years," the IHF went on to argue: "When you say that NATO military intervention has undermined all results we have achieved, one must ask if these results were of such a scope and significance to bring hope that the plight of Kosovo could be relieved by peaceful means. . . . It is our view that your appeal should properly be addressed to the FRY and Serbian authorities which bear the responsibility for systematic and grave crimes of war and crimes against humanity in Kosovo, and for the dangers you, as members of the civil sector in Serbia, are currently facing."

Other groups joined the debate. Leading Bulgarian and Greek human rights activists took the side of the Serbian nongovernmental groups and criticized the International Helsinki Federation and its officers, calling them "arrogant and insulting" and accusing them of being apologists for NATO. In turn, leaders of the Romanian Helsinki Committee sided with the IHF, describing the Bulgarian and Greek letters as "conjectural," "incorrect," and "unjust."

The debate went deeper than a conflict between those who regarded the Serbs as their Slavic and Orthodox kin and those who blamed them as the prime instigators of the Balkan troubles of the entire decade. It also exposed a deep fault line in the international human rights movement. On one side stood many with strong connections to antiwar movements that had opposed the U.S. military intervention in Vietnam and, in more recent times, the Gulf War and the periodic bombing of Iraq to coerce Saddam Hussein's compliance with the terms concluding that conflict. On the other side stood those—some also veterans of antiwar movements of an earlier era—who believed that Western governments shared the blame for the slaughter in Bosnia by failing to intervene forcefully to halt it until it had been under way for more than three years, and who consider France, the United States, and other international powers complicit in the genocide in Rwanda for their role in withdrawing UN troops as it was under way.

The latter espouse intervention, up to and including military intervention, to combat gross violations of human rights. The former, with comparable credentials as proponents of human rights, condemn resorting to military force in virtually all circumstances. That the bombing campaign was launched by NATO on its own authority rather than with the backing of the United Nations Security Council provided the Serbian nongovernmental groups and their allies in some sectors of the international human rights movement with perhaps their strongest argument. NATO bypassed the Security Council to evade vetoes from Russia and China. In the process, it seemed to say that its military might gave it the right to intervene.

Though I was troubled by the failure to obtain the consent of the Security Council, it did not alter my view that military intervention was justified. The need to stop Milošević's crimes against the Kosovar Albanians took precedence over whether Russia, which saw parallels to Chechnya, and China, which worried about Tibet, could exercise their UN Charter–authorized vetoes. From the standpoint of international law, the obligation to prevent genocide stands on the same level as the requirement to defer to the Security Council to authorize the use of force; and from the standpoint of morality, nothing seems to me to be more urgent than the former. Given Milošević's record in Bosnia and what had already taken place in Kosovo, I thought apprehensions that genocide could take place were well warranted. My main concern as a supporter of military intervention was over the way the war was conducted, which seemed to me to negate much of its moral basis. I was pleased that Human Rights Watch denounced NATO's use of cluster bombs and its attacks on civilian objects, and that it documented the civilian deaths attributable to NATO. I favor an even broader critique. A just war must be fought in a just way. Readiness to condemn forcefully methods that are unjust seems to me a responsibility of human rights advocates. If anything, that obligation is even greater in circumstances when we back military intervention and the forces we support are at fault.

I did not visit Kosovo again until nearly three months after Milošević yielded to NATO's demands to withdraw his forces and the war ended. By then, virtually all the Kosovar refugees had returned from Macedonia and Albania. Unfortunately, a new exodus was taking place: This time, the territory's Serbs and Roma were fleeing. More than 40,000 NATO troops patrolled the territory, which was ostensibly governed by my longtime friend Bernard Kouchner, who was appointed to head the United Nations Mission in Kosovo (UNMIK).

As an outgrowth of his experience as a young French doctor who volunteered to do humanitarian work in the Biafran war of the late 1960s, Bernard was the charismatic founder of Médecins sans Frontières (MSF); a decade or so later—after a conflict with some of his colleagues in MSF over his insistence on chartering a ship to pick up Vietnamese boat people in the South China Sea—he was the principal organizer of another group with a similar mission and operating style, Médecins du Monde (MDM). That is when I got to know him. Bernard sought my assistance in establishing an American branch of MDM. Though I was skeptical that American doctors would find it possible to take leaves from their practices in the same way as French and other European doctors did in volunteering for MSF and MDM, I agreed to help. Eventually, I was able to assist in launching the U.S. affiliate of MDM, Doctors of the World, and I persuaded another charismatic physician, the late Jonathan Mann, known for his leadership in the struggle against the AIDS pandemic, to chair it. In the 1980s, Bernard Kouchner pioneered in proclaiming "the duty of humanitarian intervention" in places like Kosovo (I have often seen this referred to as a "right" to intervene; Bernard, however, used *le devoir,* "the duty"). He enlisted my participation in an international conference on the subject in 1986 and asked me to contribute to a book on the issue that he edited.[7] Most recently, he has served as health minister of France. I was delighted when he was chosen to head UNMIK. He would bring to the assignment the flair, the energy, the understanding of humanitarian crises, and the passionate engagement that he brought to everything he did.

When I saw Bernard in Pristina, I felt sorry for him. NATO's large military presence had created the illusion that he had the power to stop the violence that was causing the Serbs and the Roma to flee. In fact, however, heavily armed troops riding around in tanks could do little to stop clandestine attacks on the homes of ethnic minorities, and they had scant capacity to conduct investigations that might result in arrests and prosecutions of those responsible for violence.

The night I arrived in Pristina for that first visit after the war, I went to dinner with Bernard, who brought along the UN police commissioner, Sven Frederiksen. (Richard Holbrooke, who arrived in town the same day, also joined us and had us go with him after dinner to visit a bar called "Tricky Dick's," named not for the president who earned that sobriquet but for the Dick who loomed so large in the Balkans.) When I asked Frederiksen how many police he had, he said 891. At a minimum, five times that number would have been required to do what was needed. Even if the numbers had been adequate, the task would have been Herculean. The police did not know the territory; they came from many countries and therefore did not know each other; they did not know the local languages; and they had none of the databases or knowledge of the local population that are essential for effective police work. The NATO governments were able to deploy vast resources to conduct the war and were maintaining a large, well-equipped military force in Kosovo to deter Milošević from starting a new war. But they sent only a handful of police. Most of those available to Frederiksen and Kouchner came from non-NATO countries. They were unable to stop Kosovars from doing unto others what had been done to them.

In the two decades I had known Bernard, no matter what the difficulty of the many humanitarian causes he took on, he had always exhibited great self-confidence and élan. In Pristina just a few weeks after he took up his duties, he seemed defeated by his inability to halt the new version of ethnic cleansing. In mid-August, two weeks prior to my visit, Veton Surroi had vehemently denounced the attacks on the Serbs and the Roma in his newspaper, *Koha Ditore*. As a result, elements of the KLA had issued threats against Veton and the paper's editor, Baton Haxhiu. Previously, they had faced danger from the territory's Serb rulers, who targeted the moderate intellectual leaders among the Kosovar Albanians. Now, they were in danger from their fellow Kosovar Albanians for speaking out in defense of Serbs. When I visited Kosovo again a few months later, my lunch with Bernard was cut short by a report that a landmine planted on a road traveled by Serbs had blown up and killed two people. Bernard left the restaurant to go to the scene. The look on his face as he departed seemed to sum up his experience in Kosovo.

Another casualty of NATO's and UNMIK's failure to stop the violence against the Serbs of Kosovo was that it made it far more difficult to persuade Serbs in Serbia to revise their thinking about what had happened in the territory. I argued to Serb colleagues that Serbs should accept collective political responsibility for the crimes committed in Kosovo, Bosnia, and Croatia. Facing up to the past, and recognizing the part played by various statements, such as the one by opposition groups claiming that the exodus of the Kosovar Albanians had been caused by NATO's bombing, seems to me an essential part of an effort to build a democratic society in Serbia. I persuaded colleagues in Serbia to bring to Belgrade the architects of the South African and Chilean Truth and Reconciliation Commissions, Alex Boraine and José Zalaquett, and the director of the UN Truth Commission for El Salvador, Patricia Valdez, to launch discussions that might lead to the establishment of a Serbian counterpart, and I assisted them in publishing translations in Serbia of such works as Karl Jaspers's post–World War II book *The Question of German Guilt* and Hannah Arendt's *Eichmann in Jerusalem*. The prospect that these efforts would succeed were greatly diminished, however, by the continuing violence in Kosovo.

Vojislav Koštunica, Yugoslavia's president, repeatedly denounced the Tribunal as illegitimate during his successful campaign that ousted Slobodan Milošević in September 2000 and pledged that he would not send his predecessor there to stand trial. Unfortunately, I believe that the issuance of the indictment against Milošević while the NATO bombing was under way instead of earlier led Koštunica and others in Serbia to view the Tribunal as a tool of U.S. foreign policy. When Milošević was dispatched to The Hague on June 28, 2001—as it happens, the anniversary of the Serb defeat at the battle of Kosovo in 1389 and of Milošević's infamous speech in Kosovo twelve years earlier marking the 600th anniversary of that defeat—it was on the eve of a meeting where the United States and other international donors were to decide what they would contribute to rebuild Serbia's ruined economy.

This timing made it clear that the action was a consequence of international pressure. It was not a sign that there was sufficient sentiment in Serbia to bring about a critical examination by Serbs of what Serbs had done to their neighbors during the 1990s. Some Serbs are likely to see Milošević's presence in The Hague, I fear, as putting paid to whatever responsibility they bear for all the crimes of that horrible decade. The sense of victimization that contributed so powerfully to Serb nationalism has been reinforced by the expulsion of most of the Serbs of Kosovo. Koštunica did establish a truth commission and asked Alex Boraine to serve as an adviser, but even before it began operating, three of its members resigned. They complained that it lacked a mandate to engage in the kind of investigation they thought necessary.

On the Kosovo side, because those dedicated to nonviolent resistance failed to make headway in throwing off Serb oppression, the Kosovo Liberation Army still enjoys legitimacy. Fortunately, the KLA did not fare well in the municipal elections of late 2000, and in 2001, it fared badly in the national elections won by Ibrahim Rugova's party. But it retained its capacity for mischief, as was manifest from its involvement in a new armed conflict in Macedonia in 2001. At this writing, Kosovo itself is peaceful; attacks against Serbs and Roma have subsided; and a few of the former and more of the latter have returned to the territory. Its legal status remains unresolved, however, and that could be a source of difficulty in the future. As time passes, however, the prospects for a peaceful solution are improving.

Internationally, Kosovo should have led to a great debate about intervention in response to human rights or humanitarian disasters: not only whether or when it should take place but also how. Can the manner of intervention protect those who are its intended beneficiaries? How can collateral damage be minimized? Are the will and the means available to cope with the postwar consequences of military intervention? Instead of facing up to such issues, leaders of the NATO alliance congratulated themselves on their famous victory. Some of the same issues have arisen following the post–September 11 war in Afghanistan. There, too, the issues of collateral damage and responsibility for rebuilding the country after the war have raised important questions. At this writing, the debate about when to intervene is still waiting to happen and the many other questions arising from the wars in Kosovo and Afghanistan have not been answered adequately.

Summing Up

Looking back on four decades, I see that the greatest gains for liberties with which I was associated were made under adverse circumstances. The vast political surveillance system that developed in the United States during the twentieth century, accumulating derogatory dossiers on many millions of citizens, was dismantled during and immediately following the presidency of Richard Nixon. Popular disgust with the excesses of his administration made it possible for the ACLU to succeed despite a major setback in the U.S. Supreme Court. We prevailed in a litigation and public information campaign that brought an end to practices that mirrored those of America's totalitarian foes. In the more than thirty years since Nixon's Justice Department lost the Pentagon Papers case in the Supreme Court, there has been no comparable threat to freedom of the press.

Personal privacy is endangered today by the ease with which data is collected and disseminated, by the increasing prevalence of drug testing, and by the lack of adequate safeguards to prevent the circulation of health and criminal justice records. Perhaps the greatest danger is that, in the wake of September 11, Attorney General John Ashcroft and his associates in the Department of Justice will attempt to construct a new system of political surveillance to meet the terrorist threat. Unfortunately, if past experience is a guide, the collection of data and the uses to which the information is put will bear little relationship to the actual protection of public safety. Yet the situation would be far worse if it were not for legal protections such as the Privacy Act, the Fair Credit Reporting Act, the Family Educational Rights and Privacy Act, and the 1974 amendments to the Freedom of Information Act that were all adopted during the first half of the 1970s, the era in which we were able to capitalize on public alarm over Nixon's assaults on civil liberties. Moreover, remembered revulsion against those practices remains a powerful factor three decades after Watergate.

The human rights cause became a force in international affairs during the Reagan era. His administration entered office in 1981 intent on repudiating Carter's concern with human rights. Reagan and company routinely served as apologists for brutal dictatorships in all parts of the world aligned with the United States and directly sponsored military campaigns by armed forces, both governmental and guerrilla, that grossly violated the laws of war. Yet by the time Reagan left office eight years later, a commitment to promote human rights internationally was firmly entrenched in U.S. thinking about foreign policy, even if our government's practices often fell short. It was, by then, becoming accepted worldwide to assess the conduct of military forces in accordance with their adherence to the rules of international humanitarian law, as Americas Watch had done in Central America since the beginning of Reagan's presidency. The Reaganites attacked Carter for helping to bring down Somoza and the Shah of Iran, but by the fortieth president's second term, they themselves were playing leading if grudging roles in ousting Duvalier, Marcos, and Pinochet. It was during the Reagan years that Human Rights Watch, along with more specialized human rights groups representing lawyers, physicians, and journalists, evolved into a significant institutional presence in American public life. In the same period, law schools and graduate programs in international affairs began to incorporate the study of human rights in the curriculum, reflecting their recognition that engagement in this cause was emerging as a professional choice for some of their students.

The advances for the international human rights cause during the Reagan years were even more remarkable than the gains for civil liberties at home during the Nixon era. That is because Reagan was not discredited. It was not a case in which we made progress by exploiting antagonism to a president who went too far. We did not prevail by defeating Reagan—except, of course, in the crucial early battle over Lefever. Rather, we made headway by persuading his administration to embrace a cause it disdained when it took office. At first, the Reaganites only joined us in espousing human rights rhetorically. Over time, however, they found they had to bring the administration's practices more into line with its pretenses. When Reagan left office, we were still at odds over many matters, but the argument over whether promoting human rights should be a component of U.S. foreign policy was over. We won.

In measuring progress in human rights, a standard that is often used is the number of countries that have undergone transitions from dictatorship to democracy, with regular, contested elections that are more or less free and fair. By that criterion, great headway was made during the 1980s and 1990s. Looked at from another standpoint, however—that is, the number of persons worldwide suffering severe deprivation, physical abuse, or loss of life as a consequence of human rights abuses—it is more difficult to discern advances.

I am sometimes asked whether the evident difficulty that human rights groups encounter in stopping people from inflicting misery on each other makes me despair. Why struggle for human rights in the face of what seems to be an unending series of horrors? Isn't there something quixotic about organized efforts to mitigate terrible abuses—torture, disappearances, war crimes, crimes against humanity, genocide—that are manifestations of human nature?

My response to such questions is that I am not starry-eyed and I hold out no great hope of transforming people to make them less brutal. And yet, I do think that there are ways to influence behavior through the establishment of norms and through institutional mechanisms that promote adherence to those norms. The principles of human rights are such norms, and among the mechanisms that promote compliance are those that hold public officials accountable for gross violations.

Augusto Pinochet and Slobodan Milošević are symbols of the cruelty and barbarity of the last third of the twentieth century, but they also inspired the most significant advances in international accountability for the authors of great crimes. Up to now, neither man has been convicted criminally, and age and infirmity have enabled Pinochet to escape his just deserts. Yet the fact that these two former heads of state were arrested on charges based on their conduct in power demonstrates the advance of international justice. Reactions to their deeds have revolutionized international criminal law, leading to widespread acceptance of universal jurisdiction; judicial affirmation that a head of state does not enjoy immunity against prosecutions for torture and murder; the establishment of the first international criminal tribunals since Nuremberg and Tokyo; extension of culpability for war crimes to acts committed in internal armed conflicts; and the creation in 2002 of a permanent international criminal court. Zhou Enlai famously responded to a question about the impact of the French Revolution that, "It's too soon to tell." The same might be said about the much younger movement to do justice internationally. But it is a cause for hope.

I do not mean to suggest there is anything inevitable about the way adversity brings about advances for liberty. Much of the time, violations of rights lead to more of the same; those to whom evil is done do it in return. The only lasting safeguards for rights that are a direct legacy of the Red scares in the United States that followed both World Wars are the eloquent and elegant Supreme Court opinions of Justices Brandeis and Holmes after World War I, some of them in dissent; the establishment of the American Civil Liberties Union in 1920; and the antagonism against certain investigative practices symbolized by the use of the term "McCarthyism" as a slur. What was different about the period in which I had the good fortune to devote my career to "taking liberties" is that, though it was an era of great suffering due to violations of rights, it was also a time of greater awareness of rights than ever before. That made it possible to rally supporters of rights around measures to counter abuses.

Will that be possible again in the new era that began on September 11, 2001? One among a multitude of signs of the difficulties that lie ahead was an episode that took place about three months after the terrorist attacks in New York City and Washington. The publisher of the *Sacramento Bee* delivered a commencement address at California State University in Sacramento but was unable to complete her talk about the need to protect civil liberties even as the government wages war on terrorism. As the *New York Times* reported: "When Ms. Heaphy urged that citizens safeguard their rights to free speech, against unlawful detainment and for a fair trial she was loudly booed. When she wondered what would happen if racial profiling became routine, the audience cheered. The speech was halted as Dr. Gerth [the university president] urged the crowd to be civil. Ms. Heaphy tried to finish. But just as she argued that "the Constitution makes it our right to challenge government policies," a clapping chant and further heckling forced her off the stage."[1] Another sign was that only one member of the U.S. Senate, Russell Feingold of Wisconsin, voted against the USA PATRIOT Act, adopted a few weeks after September 11, which contained a host of violations of civil liberties.

Plainly, the struggle to turn around the mood of the country and to seek advances for civil liberties in such circumstances will be arduous. The effort that is required seems as daunting as any I faced in the four decades covered in this memoir. Whether it will succeed, I cannot say. What worries me most about the current situation is not the ultimate outcome of such a struggle but whether the institutional forces that are required to lead it are ready to do so. From my current vantage point as an officer of a foundation with substantial resources, and with a donor and colleagues who share my commitments, I can assist those individuals and organizations that undertake a head-on challenge to restrictions on liberties, but I am not in a position to play the role that I assumed in earlier struggles. Others, among them those now responsible for the work of the organizations I previously directed, must lead if the period in which rights are taken seriously is not to end.

The era of rights began in the United States in 1954 with the Supreme Court's decision in *Brown v. Board of Education*[2] outlawing segregation in the schools. Its consequences for race relations in the United States were important, but just as important was what the decision meant for thinking about rights. It signified that a rights approach could cut the Gordian knot that had thereto prevented the country from addressing its most profound and intractable social problem. The Court's decision helped give birth to the contemporary civil rights movement, which manifested itself several months after the ruling in *Brown* with the Montgomery bus boycott. That movement, in turn, inspired a host of rights movements in the United States that, like their model, achieved many of their most significant victories in the courts.

Globally, the era of rights is of more recent origin. The international human rights movement has developed as a movement only during the past quarter of a century. Yet it has already acquired enormous influence and is only matched by the environmental movement in the extent of its reach globally and its organized development.

With its long tradition of going to court, the American Civil Liberties Union was an ideal vehicle for me to take advantage of the possibilities provided by a judiciary emboldened by *Brown* in the 1960s and 1970s to promote rights in the United States. My entry into the international human rights field coincided with the emergence of opportunities to have an impact on the protection of liberties across borders. There was no ready-made institution to take full advantage of those opportunities, and so Human Rights Watch filled the gap. As we could not use the methods that were effective domestically, we invented a modus operandi appropriate to the cause and to the political climate of the times.

It is unclear whether the era of rights has ended, and if so, to what extent. Before and after September 11, 2001, the international human rights movement seemed to be faring better than its domestic counterpart. At home, even before the terrorist attacks the rights movement was required to devote much of its energy to defending gains made more than twenty years ago. Thankfully, even now the freedoms protected by the First Amendment are in no serious danger. These days, mainstream institutions such as the news media and universities can generally be counted on to oppose new threats to these freedoms, such as restrictions based on concerns about national security or fears of terrorism. Since Skokie, there has been no serious attempt by state institutions to curb speech solely on the basis of the views expressed. It is difficult to imagine a new wave of anti-subversive measures like those of the first two-thirds of the twentieth century or those of the Nixon years, when there was widespread misuse of federal agencies for political harassment purposes against dissenters. Nevertheless, it has been necessary for civil liberties advocates to fight an unending series of rearguard battles to defend the rights protected by the Fourth Amendment (against unwarranted search and seizure); the Fifth Amendment (for due process of law and against coerced self incrimination); the Sixth Amendment (for the right to counsel) and the Fourteenth Amendment (for equal protection of the laws).

Many constitutional protections have fallen victim to the drug war and to efforts by political leaders and law-enforcement agencies to demonstrate they are tough on crime. The institutions that confine millions of Americans for deviancy or delinquency are not as closed as they were when I enlisted in the civil liberties cause, but prisons and jails have expanded and multiplied and recognition that their inmates retain certain rights has declined during the past decade. Legislation, judicial decisions, and actions by executive agencies have undermined or invalidated many measures to promote racial equality. The harassment continues of women exercising reproductive choice and of the medical personnel who care for them. Racial profiling and restrictions on the rights of aliens have gained new legitimacy in the wake of September 11, 2001. Recognizing that advocates of civil liberties place their main trust in the courts, opponents have made a systematic effort to capture control not only of the U.S. Supreme Court but also of the lower federal courts and the state judiciary. To a significant extent, they have succeeded. Justices Rehnquist, Scalia, and Thomas are judicial activists on behalf of a right-wing political agenda and are often able to prevail by enlisting the support of Justices

O'Connor and Kennedy. In some parts of the country, judicial independence and integrity have been seriously compromised by the manner in which campaigns for elected judgeships are financed and the political criteria for appointments. It appears that ideological criteria are a more important factor in President Bush's nominees to the federal bench than they were for any other administration. Today in the United States, momentum lies with the antagonists of liberties, not with proponents.

The picture is not entirely bleak. In the area where there have been many of the greatest setbacks for civil liberties, due process of law in criminal cases, issues that aroused scant attention a few years ago are being widely debated, in part because of efforts supported by the Open Society Institute. The three most prominent of these are capital punishment, racial profiling against African Americans, and the drug war.

Capital punishment has become an issue again after two decades of little controversy, primarily because serious doubts have been raised about the guilt of some of those sentenced to die, and to a much lesser extent because the United States is reviled by Europe for our extensive use of the death penalty.[3] A number of murder convictions have been reversed on grounds of innocence. In some cases, DNA evidence has shown that convictions were wrong; in others, teams of journalism students have uncovered crucial evidence not brought to light by police, prosecutors, or defense attorneys. Such discoveries have turned a spotlight on police and prosecutorial misconduct and, more important, on the inadequacy of the legal representation provided to defendants. A Texas Supreme Court decision—ultimately reversed in the federal courts—upholding a death sentence in a case where defense counsel slept during the trial has become a notorious symbol. In some parts of the United States, representation of those who cannot afford counsel in criminal cases is auctioned off to the lowest bidder, making a mockery of the U.S. Supreme Court's landmark 1963 decision in *Gideon v. Wainwright*.[4] A supposedly enlightened state, New York, ranks near the bottom in expenditures on defense for those accused of crime. These practices are now attracting a second look by the state legislatures that put them in place.

In an earlier period when capital punishment was seriously questioned in the United States, the mid-1960s, doubts about guilt were also at the forefront. In that era, DNA testing was not available, of course, but some Americans became suspicious of the principal evidence often used to secure death sentences: confessions. A succession of cases in which detailed confessions obtained by police turned out to be false undermined confidence in the guilt of those sentenced to die. An example was the false confession of George Whitmore in New York (see Chapter 1). As a consequence, Oregon ended the death penalty by a 60–40 vote in a popular referendum in 1964; the following year, the New York, Iowa, Vermont, and West Virginia legislatures abolished or virtually abolished executions. Doubts about the reliability of confessions also helped persuade the U.S. Supreme Court to rule as it did in *Miranda*,[5] making it more difficult for police to obtain confessions, and further turned the American public against executions. It is not yet clear whether the present-day controversy over poor legal representation in death cases will provoke a more general examination of the adequacy of counsel provided to criminal defendants, and a much needed overhaul of the system, but it provides an opening to deal with the issue.

Racial profiling against African Americans became a controversial public issue relatively recently because of well-publicized cases where skin color seemed a decisive factor in police shootings, such as in the killings of Amadou Diallo and Patrick Dorismond in New York City. The widespread experience of black motorists and pedestrians, who regularly find themselves subject to racially motivated stops and searches, has also figured prominently in the debate. The term "driving while black" (DWB) has entered popular usage. Though some police agencies—and apologists, such as columnist George Will—have defended racial profiling, it does not readily bear scrutiny. Ironically, many Americans now endorse racial profiling when it comes to those from Middle Eastern countries but are less supportive of targeting African Americans. The latter are more readily considered victims rather than perpetrators of terrorism and as participants in the patriotic reaction to the events of September 11.

What is not often mentioned is that most arrests of African Americans that result from racial profiling are for drug offenses. The use of marijuana by blacks and whites is roughly comparable, but the vast majority of those arrested and jailed for possession are black. Such arrests contribute to the grossly disproportionate number of blacks in prisons and jails. Racial profiling has been around for a long time, but the practice has increased greatly because of the drug war. It is difficult to say which is cause and which is effect. Probably all that can be said is that each provides a rationale for the other. The drug war subjects large numbers of blacks to police power, jail, and control by the criminal justice system. In turn, racial profiling provides the payoff for the drug war in arrests, prosecutions, and convictions. They are mutually reinforcing evils.

But Americans are having doubts about the drug war. Indications of this can be detected in the results of numerous state referenda held in recent years on drug issues. Almost all of these have been lost by the drug warriors. By far the most important was a lopsided decision by California voters in November 2000 to enact a requirement that those arrested for drug possession should be offered treatment instead of prison. This measure could result in a reduction in the state's prison and jail population of 20 percent or more. I am glad to say that funds provided by George Soros played a helpful role in this and other state referenda on drug issues.

In certain respects, the ACLU is as well placed as ever to lead the struggle for civil liberties. Its membership is at or near its peak, its finances are sound, and it has taken steps to ensure that its state affiliates are capable of addressing issues that arise in their own communities. This last point is particularly important because many abuses of civil liberties, including those resulting from concerns about terrorism, are committed by local officials. Only an organization with the nationwide reach of the ACLU is in a position to respond effectively. Unfortunately, the care taken by my successor, Ira Glasser, to ensure that the organizational structure is strong, for which he deserves credit, was not matched by national leadership in addressing such critical issues as the four-fold increase in incarceration in the past twenty years and the poor quality of legal representation provided to millions of poor defendants. Also, the organization's refusal to address the campaign finance problem has alienated many advocates of civil liberties. The billions of dollars expended by private interests to influence elections damages democratic governance. Most important, under Glasser the ACLU never organized a significant national campaign that could serve as a model for what is required in the current circumstances of new threats to civil liberties. My hope is that the current executive director, Anthony Romero, will reinvigorate the institution, diversify its methods, focus its attention on the urgent civil liberties issues that should now be at the forefront of its agenda, and provide the national leadership that is so urgently required. As noted, the early signs are very promising.

The international human rights movement is flourishing both in the United States and worldwide. This is true even though it has suffered a severe setback. The executive branch of the U.S. government has effectively withdrawn from the effort to promote its goals in countries supporting the struggle against terrorism, and the Bush administration has shown extreme hostility to the International Criminal Court. At home, the movement was principally associated with Democrats in the 1980s, during the Reagan and George H.W. Bush presidencies. No longer. Today, it enjoys bipartisan support. Many Republicans in Congress are as active as Democrats in demanding that the United States condition its relations with other governments on their human rights practices.

As a consequence, before September 11, the Bush administration made no effort to scuttle concern with the human rights issue as President Reagan had done two decades ago when he first took office. A few of those holding key positions dealing with rights issues in the Bush administration are credible choices; they see to it that the United States is still a factor in attempting to limit abuses in countries such as Burma and Sierra Leone that are not of primary concern to those managing the war against terrorism. Encouragingly, the Bush administration has also taken a strong stand on the persecution of democracy activists in Egypt, a country of greater significance than ever after September 11.

Beyond our borders, the human rights movement has spread globally and has taken root everywhere except in a diminishing number of the most repressive countries on earth. To some extent, Europe has supplanted the United States in promoting human rights globally. An example is the European Union's leadership in securing ratification of the treaty for the International Criminal Court much faster than anyone had predicted. Human Rights Watch, which is evolving into a global institution, enjoys outstanding leadership from Ken Roth and his colleagues and is the most dynamic part of the worldwide movement. I admire greatly the work of many of those Ken has added to the staff since my departure. Several other international groups with more narrowly defined missions are also thriving. Along with national bodies in many countries, they make the rights cause a force to be reckoned with in much of the world.

Though of recent origin, the international human rights movement has already achieved much. It was a factor in political transformations in the past two decades in several regions: Latin America, the former Soviet bloc, several countries of East and Southeast Asia, and a few countries of sub-Saharan Africa. In greatly varying degree, violations of rights continue, though often of a different character, wherever such transformations have taken place. Yet the progress is nevertheless remarkable, and in many places rights organizations have broadened their mandates to deal with the abuses that persist in democratic societies. Even taking into account China's vast size, most people worldwide now live in countries where they may express themselves more or less freely. This gives them at least the opportunity to speak out against continuing abuses and to seek remedies.

As yet, the human rights movement has had, at best, a modest impact on the carnage in the internal armed conflicts that continue in many countries. It was a factor in international intervention in Bosnia, Kosovo, East Timor, and even Afghanistan. In each case, however, the timing or the manner of intervention left much to be desired. For example, in Afghanistan, as in Kosovo, much of the war was waged from heights that made it difficult to avoid a substantial number of civilian casualties. What has been achieved by the human rights movement is that combatants are increasingly aware that their conduct will be judged according to the norms of international humanitarian law. The risk that they will ultimately be called to account before a domestic or international criminal tribunal is increasing. That understanding is only beginning to be reflected in their practices, however. It is part of the conventional wisdom in ordinary criminal cases that the prospect of punishment is effective as a deterrent in proportion to its swiftness and certainty. We are a long way from the point that those committing war crimes need fear that they will be promptly apprehended, and retribution is anything but sure. Barring a turn of events that seems unimaginable at this writing, for example, Vladimir Putin will not be called to account for the crimes committed by Russian forces under his direction in Chechnya. But we have reached the point where accountability is at least a cloud on the horizon for the leaders of lesser powers responsible for crimes against humanity. When Slobodan Milošević was arrested and subsequently sent to The Hague for trial before the International Criminal Tribunal for the former Yugoslavia, the significance was not lost on warlords worldwide.

The greatest challenge the human rights movement faces in the period ahead is how to have an impact on despotic regimes that have thus far seemed immune to pressure. The most notable case, of course, is China. Its size and its current and future economic importance have enabled Beijing to hold itself apart from the rights revolution. There is little mystery about what should be done about this. Its economic advances make China increasingly dependent on the rest of the world. To advance liberty in China, the human rights movement must find ways to exploit China's international economic engagement to create awareness and understanding of rights within China and to bring pressure to bear on those who do business with China on issues such as labor rights. Currently, foreign businesses compete for favor by kowtowing to Chinese demands not to raise concerns about rights. Proponents of rights must also find a way to hold accountable those who are complicit in Chinese oppression. This is easier said than done, of course. As yet, those engaged in commerce with China are holding fast to their self-serving but unsupported claim that free trade by itself produces free people. President George W. Bush, like President Clinton before him, is sticking to this mantra, and, of course, he appreciates Beijing's help against terrorism. China's Communist Party leaders evidently believe that trade and repression can go hand in hand. Perhaps even some of those doing business with China are privately skeptical of their own claims. It is up to the human rights movement to win acknowledgment of what should be plain for all to see: that trade with China without effort to promote human rights simply reinforces tyranny.

As is obvious to readers who have gotten this far, I have said little about my life apart from the struggles for rights that have been my career. Every so often, however, I find myself unable to keep them separate. An example was an incident in November 1985. Yvette and I and David, who had graduated from law school the previous year, went to France to celebrate the seventieth birthday of Yvette's mother. Though her home is in Brittany, in those days she spent the cooler months in Nice. On her birthday, we took her to lunch nearby at one of the three-star restaurants of France, the Moulin de Mougins. A few moments after we sat down, several men, who were evidently security guards, black and white, came into the restaurant and began examining the table next to ours. After they assured themselves that all was well, four of them took another table, and one man entered and sat alone at the table that had undergone such careful scrutiny. It was Mobutu. Whispering to each other, I consulted Yvette on the proper etiquette for a human rights activist seated next to a despot. Yvette suggested I should simply say to him, "Lumumba!" That had a certain appeal, but in the end I did nothing. As we left the restaurant, however, I realized I had no idea what I had eaten. The cuisine at a temple of gastronomy was wasted on me. I was too preoccupied with Mobutu to notice my food.

Most of the time, I am glad to say, I have been committed to my work without being obsessed by it. In the midst of the most intense battles, I have always taken time to live a life that has other satisfactions and passions. During such periods as the campaign to impeach Nixon, or the battles over Skokie and Lefever, I managed not to miss any of the Knick games, which I attended with David, or the performances of the New York City Ballet, for which Yvette and I maintained double subscriptions during the Balanchine years. These days, I try to time my travels in late February and early March so that I will not miss the annual season of Paul Taylor's dance company at New York's City Center. Wherever I travel, I try to find time to visit an art exhibit or a site of architectural interest. I have never canceled a Nantucket summer vacation, and only infrequently interrupted one, for a day or two at a time, to attend to business in New York or Washington. Even in the most difficult circumstances, I have enjoyed struggling for rights, because I believe that what I do makes a difference. That many of those who are my fellow combatants in those struggles are people whose company I enjoy adds considerably to the pleasure. Not as often as I would like, I have seen results that reinforce my belief that my work matters. Even where I have been defeated, I think the effort is worthwhile. Maintaining the battle for rights in the face of losses seems to me valuable in its own right. It also enhances the prospect of future victories.

Acknowledgments

In my effort to reconstruct the struggles for rights in which I engaged over four decades, I was aided by a number of sources. They include many articles I published in newspapers and magazines that gave accounts of those struggles as I saw them at the time. I was also able to consult calendars that I have preserved since 1965 that refreshed my recollection of the sequence of events, and books and articles by others who were directly involved or who published their own studies of matters that engaged me. In the endnotes, I have made an effort to include references to works on which I relied except where I was myself the author.

Inevitably, of course, I have drawn on memory to provide the connecting tissue and, in some cases, for descriptions of events. I am, of course, mindful that memory can deceive. Where I have had doubts whether I recalled matters accurately, I have sought sources that allow me to check myself. If errors have nevertheless slipped through, I can only express embarrassment and regret.

As is obvious, I was not alone in the struggles recounted here. My efforts to take liberties were made in the service of institutions, principally the American Civil Liberties Union, Human Rights Watch, and the Open Society Institute. It would be impossible to list here all those who took part in the various battles for rights that I had an opportunity to take on. Many, but by no means all who had significant roles, are identified in the text. To them, and to the many others not mentioned, I wish to make explicit what I believe is at least implicit in the pages that follow: that I am deeply grateful to my colleagues not only for guiding me and sharing with me the burdens and joys of struggle, but also for making it possible for me to derive immense satisfaction from a career devoted to the advancement of rights.

Peter Osnos, Publisher and CEO of PublicAffairs, and Robert Kimzey, my editor, pressed me in a number of long conversations both to deepen my analysis and to add anecdotal flavor. I believe the result is a better book and I express my appreciation to them. Their own substantial background in dealing with rights contributed greatly to the process. A painstaking copy editor, Katherine Streckfus, spared readers a number of infelicities. I take full responsibility for those that remain. And, as before, I owe special thanks to my agent, Patricia van der Leun.

The largest part of the extensive work on the manuscript, including more revisions than I can count, was born unstintingly and ever cheerfully by Maria Ribar. My deepest thanks to her and to Claudia Hernández who was always ready to pitch in. And, as has been the case for even longer than the four decades that are my focus in this book, my greatest debt of all is to Yvette, my life's companion.

NOTES

INTRODUCTION

1. See Martin Gilbert, *The Boys* (New York: Henry Holt and Company, 1997), for an account of these survivors of the death camps.
2. Todd Gitlin, *The Sixties: Years of Hope, Days of Rage* (New York: Bantam, 1987), p. 76.
3. Peggy Lamson, *Roger Baldwin* (Boston: Houghton Mifflin, 1976), pp. 266–267.
4. Ford Foundation, *Law: Ford Foundation Grantees and the Pursuit of Justice* (New York: Ford Foundation, 2000), p. 14.
5. Mary Ann Glendon, *A World Made New: Eleanor Roosevelt and the Universal Declaration of Human Rights* (New York: Random House, 2001), pp. xviii–xx.
6. "The Politics of Human Rights," *The Economist* August 18–24, 2001.
7. "Two Concepts of Liberty," reprinted in Isaiah Berlin, *Four Essays on Liberty* (New York: Oxford University Press, 1969).
8. Amartya Sen, *Poverty and Famines: An Essay on Entitlement and Deprivation* (Oxford: Clarendon Press, 1981).
9. See Leon Friedman and Burt Neuborne, *Unquestioning Obedience to the President: The ACLU Case Against the Legality of the War in Vietnam* (New York: W. W. Norton, 1972), for those arguments.
10. The first to describe Soros that way was Morton Abramowitz, a longtime high official of the U.S. State Department.

PART I: THE ACLU YEARS: 1963–1978

1. *Engel v. Vitale,* 370 U.S. 421 (1962).
2. Iver Peterson, "New Jersey Court Orders Parole for Man Who Killed Two Officers in 1963," *New York Times,* January 19, 2001.
3. Ira Glasser succeeded me as executive director of NYCLU in 1970 and as executive director of the ACLU in 1978.
4. Francis Biddle, *In Brief Authority* (Garden City, N.Y.: Doubleday, 1962), pp. 205–226.
5. Peter Irons, *Justice at War* (New York: Oxford University Press, 1983), pp. 260–268.
6. "The Expanding Reach of Civil Rights," *New York Times,* December 24, 1999.

CHAPTER 1: CONFRONTING POLICE ABUSE

1. See Selwyn Raab, *Justice in the Back Room* (Cleveland: World Publishing, 1967).
2. *Miranda v. Arizona,* 384 U.S. 436 (1966).

3. The Walker Report to the National Commission on the Causes and Prevention of Violence, *Rights in Conflict* (New York: Bantam Books, 1968). The Government Printing Office declined to publish the report because it contained many four-letter words. It had to be published commercially.

Chapter 2: Defending Draft Opponents

1. A. J. Liebling, "Do You Belong in Journalism?" *The New Yorker,* May 14, 1960.
2. *United States v. McGee,* 426 F.2d 691 (2d Cir.1970).
3. See Dwight MacDonald, *Discriminations: Essays & Afterthoughts, 1938–1974* (New York: Viking, 1974), p. 373.
4. Dwight MacDonald, "Why Do Men Have to Die?" in Ibid., p. 417.
5. *United States v. O'Brien,* 391 U.S. 367 (1968).
6. Soon after I began work for the ACLU in 1963, a longtime board member, B. W. Huebsch, publisher of Viking Books—who contributed the word *blurb* to the English language many years earlier by producing a special edition of one of his books with a dust jacket adorned by a picture of a pulchritudinous Miss Blinda Blurb, to whom comments about the book were attributed—took me aside and asked if I knew why the board met so frequently. I said I did not know. With a twinkle in his eye, he told me the practice developed because the board felt it had to keep a close watch on Baldwin. "We never knew what Roger was going to do next," he said.
7. John Rawls, *A Theory of Justice* (Cambridge: Harvard University Press, 1971), p. 366.
8. Jessica Mitford, *The Trial of Dr. Spock, the Rev. William Sloane Coffin, Jr., Michael Ferber, Mitchell Goodman, and Marcus Raskin* (New York: Knopf, 1969), p. 139.
9. *United States v. Spock,* 416 F.2d 165, 2SSLR 3090 (1st Cir. 1969).
10. *Oestereich v. Selective Service Board,* 393 U.S. 233 (1968).
11. *Gutknecht v. United States,* 396 U.S. 295 (1970).
12. Zechariah Chafee, Jr., *Free Speech in the United States* (Cambridge: Harvard University Press, 1941), pp. 100–101.

Chapter 3: Opening Asylums

1. *Stroud v. Swope,* 187 F.2d 850 (9th Cir.), cert. denied, 342 U.S. 829 (1951).
2. *Monroe v. Pape,* 363 U.S. 167 (1961).
3. See *Attica: The Official Report of the New York State Special Commission on Attica* (New York: Bantam Books, 1972).
4. *Lollis v. New York State Department of Social Services,* 322 F.Supp. 473 (S.D.N.Y. 1970).
5. *O'Connor v. Donaldson,* 422 U.S. 563 (1975).
6. *Wyatt v. Stickney,* 325 F.Supp. 781 (M.D. Ala. 1971).
7. Bruce Ennis, *Prisoners of Psychiatry* (New York: Harcourt, Brace, Jovanovich, 1972), p. 106.
8. *New York State Association for Retarded Children, Inc., v. Rockefeller,* 357 F.Supp. 752 (1973).
9. David J. Rothman and Sheila Rothman, *The Willowbrook Wars: A Decade of Struggle for Social Justice* (New York: Harper & Row, 1984), p. 253.

10. Norval White and Elliot Willensky, *AIA Guide to New York City* (New York: Macmillan, 1978), p. 351.

11. *Pugh v. Locke,* 406 F.Supp. 318 (M.D. Ala. 1976).

12. Many years later, Wallace—who repented of his inflammatory championship of racial segregation in the years after a would-be assassin's bullet left him crippled—said he would like to get Judge Johnson's forgiveness. Johnson, who died in July 1999, some ten months after his longtime antagonist, responded that Wallace would have to obtain forgiveness from a higher authority.

13. *Palmigiano v. Garrahy,* 448 F.Supp. 956 (D.R.I. 1977).

14. Daniel Ellsberg, "Laos: What Nixon's Up To," *The New York Review of Books,* March 11, 1971.

15. "Mass Move Adds Inmates to Alabama's Crowded State Prisons," *New York Times,* May 9, 2001.

16. See, for example, Aryeh Neier, *Crime and Punishment: A Radical Solution* (New York: Stein & Day, 1976), Chapter 15, "Eliminate Parole and God-Playing," pp. 187–200.

17. See David Rudenstine, *Prison Without Walls: Report on New York Parole* (New York: Praeger, 1975).

CHAPTER 4: LEGALIZING ABORTION

1. In 1950, Dorothy was the first person accused by name by Senator Joseph McCarthy of being a Communist. The accusation was false. After she appeared before his investigative committee, a newspaper cartoon was published showing McCarthy cowering in the Senate cloakroom asking, "Is she gone yet?"

2. *Poe v. Ullman,* 367 U.S. 497 (1961).

3. *Griswold v. Connecticut,* 381 U.S. 479 (1965).

4. Howard Moody was a well-known figure in New York. Under his leadership, Judson Church was an important venue for avant garde theater and dance. As it is located on the south side of Washington Square Park, Howard did public battle with the police over their arrests of musicians in the park. We provided legal representation to some of those arrested, though, to my chagrin, I never got to deliver the line of one of my ACLU colleagues in San Francisco. He began a defense argument for a park musician by saying: "My client is charged with committing Mozart in public."

5. Edward Fiske, "Clergymen Offer Abortion Advice: 21 Ministers and Rabbis Form New Group—Will Propose Alternatives," *New York Times,* May 22, 1967.

6. Arlene Carmen and Howard Moody, *Abortion Counseling and Social Change* (Valley Forge, Pa.: Judson Press, 1973), p. 58.

7. *Roe v. Wade,* 410 U.S. 113 (1973).

8. David Garrow, *Liberty and Sexuality: The Right to Privacy and the Making of Roe. v. Wade* (Berkeley: University of California Press, 1998).

9. Henry Friendly, "Some Equal Protection Problems of the 1970s," address delivered at NYU School of Law, 1970.

10. *Doe v. Bolton,* 410 U.S. 179 (1973), and *Roe v. Wade* 410 U.S. 113 (1973).

11. John Hart Ely, "The Wages of Crying Wolf," 82 *Yale Law Journal* 920 (1973).

12. Archibald Cox, *The Role of the Supreme Court in American Life* (Cambridge: Harvard University Press, 1976), p. 1133.
13. *Beal v. Doe*, 432 U.S. 438 (1977).
14. *Maher v. Doe*, 432 U.S. 464 (1977).
15. *Poelker v. Doe*, 432 U.S. 519 (1977).
16. See Ruth Bader Ginsburg, "Speaking in a Judicial Voice," 67 *New York University Law Review* 1185 (1992); and "Some Thoughts on Autonomy and Equality in Relation to *Roe v. Wade*," 63 *North Carolina Law Review* 375 (1985).
17. *Planned Parenthood of Southeastern Pennsylvania v. Casey*, 505 U.S. 833 (1992).

CHAPTER 5: FORGING RESTRAINTS ON STIGMA

1. *Menard v. Saxbe*, 498 F.2d 1017 (DC Cir. 1974).
2. See, for example, Aryeh Neier, "Marked for Life: Have You Ever Been Arrested?" *The New York Times Magazine*, April 15, 1973.
3. Op. cit.
4. *Paul v. Davis*, 424 U.S. 693 (1976).
5. *Laird v. Tatum*, 408 U.S. 1 (1972).
6. Christopher Pyle, "CONUS Intelligence: The Army Watches Civilian Politics," *The Washington Monthly*, January 1970.
7. George Lardner, Jr., "Nixon on Appointing Rehnquist," *Washington Post*, October 30, 2000.
8. *Paton v. LaPrade*, 524 F.2d 862 (3d Cir. 1975).
9. Jeffrey Rosen, *Unwanted Gaze: The Destruction of Privacy in America* (New York: Vintage Books, 2001).
10. Ibid., p. 225.

CHAPTER 6: IMPEACHING NIXON

1. *New York Times*, September 17, 1963.
2. *United States v. United States District Court*, 407 U.S. 297 (1972).
3. A year or so after we began the lawsuit for Mort, I asked him to direct a Project on National Security and Civil Liberties for the ACLU. In 1984, some years after I left the ACLU, Ira Glasser appointed him Washington director. Subsequently, he returned to government, serving again in the Defense Department and the National Security Council and then as director of policy planning at the Department of State. At this writing, as noted, we are working together again as Mort is directing the Washington office of the Open Society Institute.

CHAPTER 7: DEFENDING FREE SPEECH IN SKOKIE, ILLINOIS

1. *Rockwell v. Morris*, 10 N.Y. 2d 721, 166 N.E.id 48 (1961).
2. *Terminiello v. City of Chicago*, 337 U.S. 1 (1949).

3. *Brandenburg v. Ohio*, 305 U.S. 444 (1969).

4. Donald A. Downs, *Nazis in Skokie* (Notre Dame, Ind.: University of Notre Dame Press, 1985), p. 107.

5. *Chicago Sun-Times*, February 27, 1978.

6. Astonishingly, more than two decades later, the man who said he made the object got in touch with the ACLU to ask about its whereabouts. He seemed to think it was an historic artifact. I advised the ACLU to inform him that I had discarded it. He was welcome to search for the remains in the landfill.

7. *Carroll v. President and Commissioners of Princess Anne*, 393 U.S. 175 (1968).

8. "Some People Derive Their Energy from Struggle: A Conversation with Eleanor Holmes Norton," *The Civil Liberties Review,* Winter 1975, p. 95.

9. *Smith v. Collin,* cert. den., 439 U.S. 916 (1978).

10. As I write, the two men who owned and operated Radio Milles Collines, a station that played a leading role in inciting and organizing the Rwanda genocide of 1994, are being tried by the International Criminal Tribunal for Rwanda in Arusha, Tanzania.

Chapter 8: Exposing Betrayal: The ACLU and the FBI

1. A useful account of these events appears in Jerold S. Auerbach, "The Depression Decade," in Alan Reitman, *The Pulse of Freedom* (New York: W. W. Norton, 1975), pp. 86–104.

2. Juvenile Justice Standards Project, *Standards for Juvenile Justice* (Cambridge, Mass.: Ballinger, 1977).

3. The only other person who ever made a similar comment to me was a partner of Judge Rifkind's, Morris Abram, a one-time candidate for the U.S. Senate and, in later years, the Reagan administration's ambassador to the UN in Geneva. Abram tried to get me to withdraw a lawsuit we filed against one of his private clients, a New York restaurant popular in the 1970s called Maxwell's Plum. It was one of a group of prominent restaurants we sued for refusing to hire women as waiters. He insisted on getting me out of a meeting I was attending in Philadelphia to threaten me with the loss of support from one of our most steadfast foundation donors, whose board chair he had recently become. I responded to Abram in the same way I'd responded to Rifkind. Both foundations maintained their support for the ACLU.

4. The Smith Act, also known as the Alien Registration Act, adopted by Congress in 1940, made it a crime to *advocate* overthrow of the government by force or violence, or to organize or become a member of such a group knowing its purpose. It was the law under which the "11 top Communists" were convicted in 1949. In that case, *Dennis v. United States,* the Smith Act's constitutionality was upheld by the U.S. Supreme Court in 1951, 341 U.S. 494 (1951). Subsequent High Court decisions in 1957, such as *Yates v. United States,* 354 U.S. 298 (1957), and *Jencks v. United States,* 353 U.S. 657 (1957), chipped away at the act, making it unenforceable.

5. *Colyer v. Skeffington,* 265 F. 17 (D. Mass. 1920).

6. Max Lowenthal, *The Federal Bureau of Investigation* (New York: William Sloan, 1950).

7. Athan G. Theoharis and John Stuart Cox, *The Boss: J. Edgar Hoover and the Great American Inquisition* (Philadelphia: Temple University Press, 1988), pp. 275–278.

8. Samuel Walker, *In Defense of American Liberties: A History of the ACLU* (New York: Oxford University Press, 1990), p. 192.
9. Cited in Lowenthal, *The Federal Bureau of Investigation,* p. 449.
10. See Frank Donner, "Political Informers," in Pat Watters and Stephen Gillers, eds. *Investigating the FBI* (Garden City, N.Y.: Doubleday, 1973), pp. 350–351.
11. *The New York Review of Books,* March 11, 1971.

PART II: THE HUMAN RIGHTS WATCH YEARS: 1978–1993

1. Aryeh Neier, *Only Judgment* (Middletown, Conn.: Wesleyan University Press, 1982).
2. See *New York Times,* June 19, 1978.
3. Today, Gerald still heads the Swedish Helsinki Committee and we continue to work together. As the Swedish government relies on the committee to distribute its assistance to civil society and independent media in ex-Yugoslavia, it does so in close collaboration with the Soros Foundations.
4. Robert Gates, *From the Shadows* (New York: Simon & Schuster, 1996), p. 89.
5. Middle East Watch, *Human Rights in Iraq* (New Haven, Conn.: Yale University Press, 1990).
6. Susan Meiselas, *Kurdistan: In the Shadow of History* (New York: Random House, 1997).
7. William Korey, *NGOs and the Universal Declaration of Human Rights* (New York: St. Martin's Press, 1998), p. 346.
8. T. S. Eliot, *Murder in the Cathedral* (London: Faber and Faber, 1935).
9. Korey, *NGOs,* p. 344.
10. Human Rights Watch, *Leave None to Tell the Story: Genocide in Rwanda* (New York: Human Rights Watch, 1999).

CHAPTER 9: DEFEATING REAGAN

1. *New York Times,* January 24, 1981.
2. Sections 116 and 502B of the Foreign Assistance Act of 1961.
3. Section 624 (f) of the Foreign Assistance Act of 1961.
4. Jacobo Timerman, *Prisoner Without a Name, Cell Without a Number* (New York: Alfred A. Knopf, 1981), pp. 9–10.
5. Richard Kennedy, undersecretary of state for management, confidential "Memorandum for the Secretary," October 27, 1981.

CHAPTER 10: AMERICAS WATCH: A TESTING BY FIRE

1. FMLN stands for Frente Farabundo Martí para la Liberación Nacional, or Farabundo Martí National Liberation Front.
2. It was subsequently republished in book form as *Report on Human Rights in El Salvador* (New York: Vintage, 1982), in an edition of 25,000 copies. Few human rights reports achieve that circulation.

3. Years later, I obtained a copy of a confidential internal document circulated within the State Department that described the backgrounds of all those who had contributed to the report in unflattering and misleading terms. I do not know how widely this document was distributed or how it was compiled.
4. Jean-Marie Simon, *Eternal Spring, Eternal Tyranny* (New York: W. W. Norton, 1987).
5. Press conference, November 8, 1983.
6. Public address, November 25, 1983.
7. Public address, December 11, 1983.
8. *Velásquez Rodríguez Case,* Judgment of July 29, 1988, Inter-American Court of Human Rights, Ser.C, No. 49 Hum.Rts L.J. 212 (1988).
9. *Nightline,* ABC Television, February 13, 1985.
10. Jeane Kirkpatrick, "Guatemala's Revolution-Democracy," *Washington Post,* December 2, 1998.
11. The acronym stands for Grupo de Apoyo Mutuo.
12. Beatriz Manz, "A Guatemalan Dies, and What It Means," *New York Times,* May 14, 1986.

CHAPTER 11: PROMOTING ACCOUNTABILITY

1. Americas Watch, "The Argentine Military Junta's 'Final Document': A Call for Condemnation," May 20, 1983.
2. See Scott Anderson and Jon Lee Anderson, *Inside the League* (New York: Dodd, Mead, 1986).
3. *Forti v. Suárez-Mason,* U.S. District Court, Northern District California, 1987, 672 F.Supp. 1531.
4. Lawrence Weschler, *A Miracle, A Universe: Settling Accounts with Torturers* (New York: Pantheon, 1990), pp. 243–245.
5. The acronyms stand for Dirección de Inteligencia Nacional and Central Nacional de Informaciones.
6. Istvan Deak, "Misjudgment at Nuremberg," *The New York Review of Books,* October 7, 1993.
7. Aryeh Neier and Istvan Deak, "The Nuremberg Precedent," *The New York Review of Books,* November 4, 1993.
8. Ariel Dorfman, "Who Thought We'd Get This Close to Justice?" *Washington Post,* August 6, 2000.
9. Henry Kissinger, "The Pitfalls of Universal Jurisdiction," *Foreign Affairs,* July/August 2001, pp. 86–96. The essay is adapted from Kissinger's book, *Does America Need a Foreign Policy?* (New York: Simon & Schuster, 2001).

CHAPTER 12: CONTACTING THE UNDERGROUND IN POLAND

1. Aryeh Neier, "The Other Poland," *New York Times,* May 18, 1984.
2. Czeslaw Milosz, *A Treatise on Poetry* (New York: Ecco Press, 2001), p. 102.
3. Richard N. Haass, ed., *Economic Sanctions and American Diplomacy* (New York: Council on Foreign Relations Press, 1998).

4. Henry Kissinger, *Does America Need a Foreign Policy?* (New York: Simon & Schuster, 2001), p. 271.
5. Timothy Garton Ash, "Helena's Kitchen," *The New Yorker,* February 15, 1999.

Chapter 13: Visiting Prisons in Cuba

1. Armando Valladares, *Against All Hope,* translated by Andrew Hurley (New York: Knopf, 1986).
2. The others were Peter Bell, then the president of the Edna McConnell Clark Foundation, the main private supporter of prison reform efforts in the United States, and today the president of CARE; Howard Hiatt, professor of medicine at Harvard and the former dean of Harvard's School of Public Health; and Herman Schwartz, professor of law at American University and my longtime colleague, both at the ACLU and at Human Rights Watch, in prison reform efforts.
3. A young Cuban-American researcher, Mary Jane Camejo, was particularly helpful in preparing me for the visit.
4. My translator, Julia E. Sweig, subsequently developed as a leading Cuba scholar. She is the author of *Inside the Cuban Revolution* (Cambridge: Harvard University Press, 2002).
5. *The New York Review of Books,* June 30, 1988.

Chapter 14: Suffering Defeat over China

1. *The Economist,* May 20–26, 2000.
2. See George Black and Robin Munro, *Black Hands of Beijing: Lives of Defiance in China's Democracy Movement* (New York: John Wiley & Sons, 1993).
3. George Soros, *Opening the Soviet System* (London: Weidenfeld and Nicolson, 1990).
4. *New York Times,* June 6, 2000.
5. Strobe Talbott, "Democracy and the National Interest," *Foreign Affairs,* November/ December 1996, pp. 48–49.
6. Henry Kissinger, *Does America Need a Foreign Policy?* (New York: Simon & Schuster, 2001), pp. 240–256.
7. Powell, Armey, and President Bush are quoted in Lawrence F. Kaplan, "Trade Barrier: Why Trade Won't Bring Democracy to China," *The New Republic,* July 9 and 16, 2001.
8. Wei Jingsheng was released shortly before the International Olympic Committee voted on September 23, 1993, to hold the games in Sidney, Australia.
9. The students evacuated the square in an orderly way after taking a vote on whether to leave. Contrary to popular belief, few students were killed. Most of those massacred were ordinary workers attempting to halt the military occupation. They were killed in the streets near the square and in other parts of Beijing. See Black and Munro, *Black Hands of Beijing.*
10. This footage was made with a hidden camera by Harry Wu, a former political prisoner. He visited China clandestinely and got into a prison to take the film. We assisted Wu by getting *Newsweek* to publish his memoir of his imprisonment in China (September 23, 1991), but subsequently I distanced Human Rights Watch from him. Though I thought

him brave, I was uncomfortable with his claims about the number of political prisoners in China, which I thought were exaggerated.

11. Aryeh Neier, "The New Double Standard," *Foreign Policy,* Winter 1996–1997.

PART III: THE SOROS YEARS: 1993–

1. Marek Beylin, "Fondation Pour Une Entr'Aide Intellectuelle Européenne" (unpublished and undated), pp. 91–92.
2. Michael T. Kaufman, *Soros: The Life and Times of a Messianic Billionaire* (New York: Knopf, 2002), p. 163.

CHAPTER 15: SARAJEVO, CHECHNYA, AND THE LOSS OF FRED CUNY

1. Human Rights Watch, "War Crimes in Bosnia-Herzegovina," August 1992, p. 1.
2. Scott Anderson, *The Man Who Tried to Save the World: The Dangerous Life and Mysterious Disappearance of Fred Cuny* (New York: Doubleday, 1999).
3. Ibid., pp. 340–345.
4. Roger Cohen, "UN Military Aide Says Plight of Goražde is Exaggerated," *New York Times,* April 30, 1994.
5. See David Rieff, *A Bed for the Night* (New York: Simon & Schuster, 2002).

CHAPTER 16: CONFRONTING THE PAST IN SOUTH AFRICA

1. *Washington Post,* July 17, 1979.
2. See, for example, Aryeh Neier, "The Hated Pass Laws Are Alive and Well—And So Is Apartheid," *Los Angeles Times,* August 21, 1979, and "Censorship: South Africa's Legalistic Tie That Binds," *Los Angeles Times,* September 23, 1979.
3. Nadine Gordimer, *July's People* (New York: Viking, 1981).
4. Allister Sparks, *Tomorrow Is Another Country* (South Africa: Struik, Sandton, 1994), p. 10.
5. Quoted in Alex Boraine, Janet Levy, and Ronel Scheffered, eds., *Dealing with the Past: Truth and Reconciliation in South Africa* (Cape Town: IDASA, 1994), p. 6.
6. Quoted in Lawrence Weschler, *A Miracle, A Universe* (New York: Penguin, 1990), p. 4.
7. Quoted in Alex Boraine, *A Country Unmasked: Inside South Africa's Truth and Reconciliation Commission* (Cape Town: Oxford University Press Southern Africa, 2000), p. 41.

CHAPTER 17: INTERVENING IN KOSOVO

1. Aryeh Neier, "Kosovo Survives," February 3, 1994.
2. Aryeh Neier, *War Crimes: Brutality, Genocide, Terror and the Struggle for Justice* (New York: Times Books, 1998).
3. Aryeh Neier, "Impasse in Kosovo," September 25, 1997.

4. Aryeh Neier, "Inconvenient Facts," *Dissent,* Spring 2000, and Noam Chomsky and Aryeh Neier, "Letters," *Dissent,* Summer 2000.

5. General Wesley K. Clark, *Waging Modern War* (New York: PublicAffairs, 2001), pp. 170–171.

6. Michael Walzer, *Just and Unjust Wars* (New York: Basic Books, 1977), p. 21.

7. Mario Bettati and Bernard Kouchner, *Le Devoir d'ingérence* (Paris: Denoël, 1987).

SUMMING UP

1. Timothy Egan, "In Sacramento, a Publisher's Questions Draw the Wrath of the Crowd," *New York Times,* December 21, 2001.

2. *Brown v. Board of Education,* 347 U.S. 483 (1954).

3. In early 2001, when the United States was voted off the UN Human Rights Commission, many attributed this to a desire to remove the most consistent critic of abuses in countries such as China, Cuba, and Sudan. Probably a more important factor was the European belief that we are ourselves a leading abuser of human rights, principally because of executions and secondarily because of our staggeringly high rates of imprisonment.

4. *Gideon v. Wainwright,* 372 U.S. 335 (1963).

5. *Miranda v. Arizona,* 384 U.S. 436 (1966).

INDEX

PUBLICAFFAIRS is a publishing house founded in 1997. It is a tribute to the standards, values, and flair of three persons who have served as mentors to countless reporters, writers, editors, and book people of all kinds, including me.

I. F. STONE, proprietor of *I. F. Stone's Weekly,* combined a commitment to the First Amendment with entrepreneurial zeal and reporting skill and became one of the great independent journalists in American history. At the age of eighty, Izzy published *The Trial of Socrates,* which was a national bestseller. He wrote the book after he taught himself ancient Greek.

BENJAMIN C. BRADLEE was for nearly thirty years the charismatic editorial leader of *The Washington Post.* It was Ben who gave the *Post* the range and courage to pursue such historic issues as Watergate. He supported his reporters with a tenacity that made them fearless, and it is no accident that so many became authors of influential, best-selling books.

ROBERT L. BERNSTEIN, the chief executive of Random House for more than a quarter century, guided one of the nation's premier publishing houses. Bob was personally responsible for many books of political dissent and argument that challenged tyranny around the globe. He is also the founder and was the longtime chair of Human Rights Watch, one of the most respected human rights organizations in the world.

.   .   .

For fifty years, the banner of Public Affairs Press was carried by its owner Morris B. Schnapper, who published Gandhi, Nasser, Toynbee, Truman, and about 1,500 other authors. In 1983 Schnapper was described by *The Washington Post* as "a redoubtable gadfly." His legacy will endure in the books to come.

Peter Osnos, *Publisher*